DATE DUE

MAY 1 7 2001			
GAYLORD			PRINTED IN U.S.A.

SHARING
THE EARTH

Local Identity
in Global Culture

THE
ROBERT GORDON UNIVERSITY
HERITAGE LIBRARY

Arbor Seaculorum or Tree of Life by Patrick Geddes. See Introduction, page xiii.
Reproduced by kind permission of the Patrick Geddes Centre for Planning Studies,
Edinburgh University.

SHARING
THE EARTH

Local Identity
in Global Culture

Edited by
J. M. FLADMARK

Papers presented at
The Robert Gordon University
Heritage Convention 1995

DONHEAD

34087548

11/19/96

© The Robert Gordon University, Aberdeen, 1995
Individual chapters are the copyright
of their authors.

First published in the United Kingdom
in 1995 by
Donhead Publishing Ltd
28 Southdean Gardens
Wimbledon
London SW19 6NU
Tel. 0181-789 0138

ISBN 1 873394 19 5

A CIP catalogue record for this book is available
from the British Library.

Printed in Great Britain by
Bell & Bain Ltd, Glasgow

In order to produce this book quickly for the conference
delegates, the publishers have used camera ready copy
provided by the editors and contributors

CONTENTS

FOREWORD

This book is the third in a series of annual volumes of contributions from conferences hosted by the Robert Gordon University Heritage Unit, conceived and edited by its indefatigable director, Professor J Magnus Fladmark. This volume may usefully be considered in conjunction with its predecessors, for all bear on the protean topic of heritage in its myriad manifestations.

The first focused on how heritage is identified, enhanced, and protected against threats of neglect, despoliation, and development; its purview was largely that of the heritage steward, charged by law and by love to manage and maintain a resource of benefit to all. The second, on cultural tourism, dealt with issues of heritage popularity and populism, access and marketing, and the impact and containment of ever-expanding clienteles; its purview was largely that of the consumer, for whom heritage is packaged and presented.

This volume concentrates on a particularly stressful arena – that of heritage ownership and control. Heritage as a global resource, shared by all the world's inhabitants, is an ideal increasingly proclaimed by international agencies and conceded by national states. That the legacies of nature, from earth and water and air to ecosystems, are global resources requiring global management, has become patently obvious. Fresh water and fossil fuels, rain forests and gene pools are common to all mankind and need all our care. Cultural as well as natural legacies are seen to form part of a universal human heritage. The legacies of the great ancient civilizations of China and Egypt and Greece, along with the irreplaceable diversities of a thousand tribal traditions, animate and enrich life the world over.

That the shared heritage of mankind takes precedence over any national heritage is reiterated whenever folly threatens – this very year has seen international outcry against a Portuguese dam that would flood the Coa Valley's primordial rock art, and against industrial pollution at Agra that might doom the Taj Mahal. The designation of over 400 World Heritage Sites enhances their fame, enables their care, and promotes the feeling that all the world shares them with their national stewards.

Yet sharing is neither simple nor easy. Most heritage remains the property of a particular national or local community, and indeed must do so, for possession above all endears our legacy to us. Heritage celebrates what makes a people innately themselves, as distinct from others. We zealously cherish it as personal to ourselves, rooted in our domestic being, unsuited to outsiders. Though heritage more and more addresses similar goals with similar strategies, narrow possessive passions largely fuel these goals and direct these strategies; heritage is normally cherished not as common but as exclusive property. Self-esteem enjoins us to view our inheritance as unique; lauding our own legacy, we dismiss or discredit others.

The stress between these two equally valid and essential views of heritage, the one as a universal good, the other as a defining mark of some particular community, everywhere engenders bellicose conflict. That stress lies at the heart of the issues discussed in the first two volumes of this series. Efforts to alleviate such strife by bridging global and local concerns are, in my view, the most significant insights that emerge from the multifaceted issues explored in the following essays.

David Lowenthal
Emeritus Professor of Geography
University College London

Harrow on the Hill
Middlesex
July 1995

ACKNOWLEDGEMENTS

Our mission is to study interactions
across the spectrum of our natural & cultural assets.
It covers the arts, science & technology
and embraces the ethos of both conservation & enterprise.
The core of our philosophy is the cultural continuity
of yesterday, today & tomorrow.

Fladmark, 1993

The Heritage Unit was established to enhance our capability at the interface between cultural and environmental subjects. The above mission statement, still standing as a talismanic message of intent, was penned by the editor of this volume at the time when the Unit was formally launched in 1993 by the mounting of a major heritage convention in Aberdeen.

Like the University itself, the Unit's success is founded on a strong commitment to partnership in the community, where the relevance of our academic endeavours can be tested against the real world. Indeed, we are committed to working together with government, industry and voluntary bodies whenever possible, and we are always grateful when our initiatives meet with a positive response.

The second convention in Elgin last year, was born from a partnership with the regional and district councils, the local enterprise company, The Scottish Office, and several other government agencies. The event upon which this volume is based was the outcome of a partnership forged at the request of Highland Regional Council. It was made possible with their support and sponsorship, together with that of Inverness District Council, Inverness & Nairn Enterprise, the Scottish Tourist Board, Inverness Loch Ness and Nairn Tourist Board, Comunn na Gàidhlig and Scottish Natural Heritage, as well as the European Commission and the Council of Europe. We are particularly indebted for the enthusiastic support of Iain Robertson, Derek Reid, Gordon Adams, William McDermott, Gordon Fyfe, Fiona Larg, Allan Campbell, Caroline Munro and Jane Grant and her colleagues at Eden Court.

The content bears witness to the enormous range of talents that we were able to call upon for contributions, and we are indeed most grateful to each author for finding time to write the papers so that they could be published in time for delegates arriving in Inverness. Active encouragement by several members of the Unit's Advisory Board has been a source of strength, and we are particularly grateful to Lord Balfour of Burleigh and John Foster for their insistence on the pursuit of excellence at all times. The keen eyes of the refereeing panel are also clearly reflected in the high standard of papers to have found their way into this volume.

The Unit's Director, Professor Magnus Fladmark, had to cope with several other major initiatives at the same time, and we are grateful for his willingness to put in the extra hours required to meet the high standards associated with the work of his team. In his task as editor, he has been ably supported, well beyond the call of duty, by the deputy-editor and convention organiser, Brian Hill, as well as by Stephen Emerson. Other colleagues who have contributed in one way or another and deserve special thanks are Professor Seaton Baxter, David Silbergh, Anne Simpson and Irene Van Kuyk in the Faculty of Design, as well as Gordon Craig, Leonard Forman, Katherine Pacitti, Mitchell Milmore and Martin Parker in External Affairs.

On behalf of the University, we extend special thanks to two people. First to Tom Band for wise counsel in planning of the Convention, and for serving as Chairman of the Steering Group which kept a diverse team of helpers in order. The success of the arrangements was in great part due to his firm hand on the tiller. Second, we are grateful to Professor David Lowenthal for writing the Foreword. His contribution to our first Convention in 1993 was greatly appreciated and much valued, and his continued interest in the Unit's work is a source of pride and inspiration for its staff.

We are indebted to Jill Pearce and Bronwen Silcox at Donhead and Robert Chaundy of Bookstyle for a high quality product, as well as for an EU presence in the person of Jacques Blanc, President of the Committee of the Regions who kindly agreed to travel from France to address delegates. The proceedings were greatly enhanced by the distinguished array of personalities who kindly agreed to chair sessions at Eden Court, i.e. Iain Anderson, Lady Balfour of Burleigh, Lester Borley, Allan Campbell, Norman Cordiner, Provost William Fraser, Fiona Larg, Nicol Manson, William McDermott, Duncan McPherson and Derek Reid.

David Kennedy   Professor Eric Spiller
Principal & Vice-Chancellor   Assistant Principal & Dean

The Robert Gordon University
Aberdeen

INTRODUCTION

The tree has its roots amid the fires of life, and is perpetually renewed from them. But the spirals of smoke which curl among its branches bind the thinkers and workers of each successive age to the thought and work of their precursors. Two sphinxes guard the tree and gaze upward in eternal questioning, their lion-bodies recalling man's origin in the animal world, their human faces the ascent of man. The branches symbolize the past and passing developments of society, while the bud at the tree-top suggests the hope of the opening future. Issuing from the smoke-wreaths at the top you can also see the phoenix of man's ever-renewed body and the butterfly or Psyke of the deathless soul of humanity.

Patrick Geddes, c 1904

The Tree of Life, described above, was Patrick Geddes' idea for a stained glass window in the Outlook Tower, his Edinburgh laboratory for the study of man's relationship to the natural environment. The window never saw the light of day, but the design for it thankfully survived (see page ii). Through this, he sought to express some the fundamental tenets of his philosophy which have a striking relevance to many chapters of this book.

First, there is the notion of 'cultural continuity and sustainability,' based on his belief that each generation builds on the achievements of its predecessors. Then, there is reference to man's origin in the animal world, which touches on a central theme in his teaching. Geddes pioneered what we now call ecology and holistic thinking, which laid the foundations for the vogue concept of environmental sustainability. The 'ascent of man' is his way of alluding to the awesome responsibility falling on us as the only species capable of both the destruction and the sustainable use of Planet Earth. Yet, in this age of uncertainty, we can seek inspiration from his spirit of optimism and faith in the soul of humanity. In essence, the Geddesian message is simple. While we may be destructive, the conscience and soul of humanity, like the two sphinxes, will prevail and stand guard against cataclysmic action to ensure our survival.

Who was Professor Sir Patrick Geddes? He was born in Ballater in 1854, and his first discipline was biology. His fertile mind and polymath tendencies were ignited by the ideas of Charles Darwin and Thomas Huxley, and his appetite for multidisciplinary learning was stimulated in dialogue with John Ruskin. He took the theory of evolution and, more than anyone else, was responsible for translating it into modern environmental ecology. But by the time he died in 1932, he had embraced the subjects of philosophy, sociology, economics, the arts and town planning. This multidisciplinary approach led him into laying the foundations for what might be called cultural ecology, where human identity has a central place. His analytical construct of 'place, work and folk' sought to define and explain that identity.

We are very proud of Geddes in Scotland. He was an iconoclastic Scot who ranks among our intellectual giants. His achievement was to forge a new synthesis of the early 19th century Zeitgeist and the *Genius Loci* of Scotland, thereby helping us to break away from the conventional thinking of compartmentalised disciplines and to understand our own place and national identity in the modern world. Indeed, his greatest gift was perhaps to leave us with a legacy of cross-cultural understanding. Geddes applied the Global Village concept to his own life through visits to North America and by working in France, Israel, Egypt and India. This enabled him to see Scotland in a new light, through the eyes of others, and he acquired a fresh interest in the evolution of urban cultures. He also acquired an international following. For example, the American historian and urban philosopher, Lewis Mumford, acknowledged the profound influence of Geddesian thinking on his own writings.

Why dedicate this volume to the memory of Patrick Geddes? The decision was made on discovering that the author of the first chapter, Nicholas Luard, invokes Lewis Mumford, and thereby establishes a direct Geddesian link back to Charles Darwin and Thomas Huxley (the latter had Geddes staying as a resident apprentice). Such linkages can also be found in other chapters which show that many of us are still serving our apprenticeship under their collective tutelage. In terms of Geddes' symbolism in the Tree of Life, we are actively inhaling 'the spirals of smoke which curl among its branches bind(ing) the thinker and workers of each successive age to the thought and work of their precursors.'

The theme of Luard's opening paper is more directly inspired by John Muir than by Patrick Geddes, but his storyline is very much about the Geddesian recall of ' man's origin in the animal world' and 'the ascent of man.' He argues that whether we are aware of it or not, or indeed willing to admit it, our identity is still deeply rooted in the natural world of which we were once an integral part. Before reading the daily headlines over breakfast, we first consult the horoscope page in the same way that an aboriginal bushman or Stonehenge Man would have read the signs of the celestial bodies in the sky before starting his daily tasks.

At the end of the evolutionary road, we turned ourselves into urban creatures with a fear of wilderness, and built city walls to protect us from it. We came to regard the land as something apart from ourselves, to be exploited, rather than something of which we are part and dependent upon. Luard finds the concept of wilderness a nonsense, even counterproductive. Very little of this planet remains untouched by human interference, and he contends that the global dilemma is really about the kind of strategies we need to adopt for dismantling the wall between ourselves and what we perceive of as 'wilderness.'

The idea for the conference behind this book arose from discussions about whether national and regional identity is threatened by globalisation of the media and the corporate culture of multinational companies. Magnus Linklater leads a suite of papers examining issues relevant to this question. As a former editor of several newspapers, he is able to draw on experience at first hand on how the new 'media barons' think and operate. The recent spectacle of Tony Blair pleading at the court of Rupert Murdoch in Australia on behalf of a national political party from the other side of the globe confirms the dangers alluded to by Linklater. The threats are real, here and now, and he reckons that only those with the political will to protect their cultural identity will survive. As an example, he cites Murdoch's experience of failure in China and South East Asia when attempting to introduce Americanised media coverage. Only after adopting the languages of the area and using local production talent did he find a ready market for his product.

The role of multinational companies, specifically the Disney Corporation in this case, is examined by William Tramposch. He concludes that there is more scope to learn than to fear from Disney as he leaves his footprint outside the US. The likelihood of host cultures being corrupted is minimal, and Tramposch argues convincingly that Disney has much to teach heritage professionals, particularly in the public sector, about how to reach the customer through imaginative thinking, a clear vision, effective promotion and quality of service delivery. There is too much preoccupation with story lines and love of one's own voice. Far better to spend time listening to what the visitor has to say.

Lynne Williamson, another US contributor, ably demonstrates how much we in Europe can learn from colleagues across the Atlantic. Her paper is about a series of initiatives, mostly arts and crafts related, which have been the outcome of responding to the voice of different ethnic cultures. In many cases, these have stemmed from group dissatisfaction with the way their own cultural heritage has been interpreted and presented by others. Active participation by those belonging to individual groups, supported by public funding programmes, has engendered a new sense of pride in heritage assets now seen as worthy of investment. However, the most compelling part of her story is about the New York Memorial Wall Artists who make a living from painting memorials to those killed by inner city crime. Here, she raises an issue for the 21st century. Can we contribute to lasting solutions by studying the culture of urban deprivation and crime?

In the next suite of four papers, Lord Gowrie brings us back to the UK. The text is based on his presentation to the 1994 Convention, and he deals with the contribution of the arts to both cultural identity and economic prosperity. As Chairman of the Arts Council, he naturally extols its role as a key benefactor of the arts and, perhaps vainly, expresses optimism about the distinction between high and low culture being a thing of the past. Robert Hewison challenges this, and readers are treated to a vigorous exchange of views between the two authors. Hewison contends that low culture is still very much alive, but neglected by public agencies, and he argues that the Arts Council should be abolished in the interest of a more democratic definition of culture. This plea for a more democratic approach to culture is by implication endorsed by Professor Terry Stevens who argues that the sports sector has been neglected as a cultural asset and deserves a more prominent position in national heritage policy.

The heritage of national identity has been a subject of fascination for potentates, politicians and scholars throughout history, but it has now become the stamping ground of tourism marketeers and heritage managers. Angela Morris et al report on a study of attitudes among life members of the National Trust for Scotland, which shows that national identity is important to people and that they are proud of belonging to its associated cultural heritage. They distinguish between 'history' and 'heritage,' the latter being part of their daily lives today, but their pride in being Scottish seems to have little to do with political affiliations. Alongside this Scottish profile, sits three interesting papers discussing issues associated with national iconography and heritage management in The Netherlands, Norway and Malta.

The next set of papers introduces the concept of 'supra-national' identity, or the continuum between national cultures and a civilisation in the sense that Scottish culture is part of European civilisation. Michel Thomas-Penette describes the Cultural Routes Programme initiated by the Council of Europe in 1987, and a case study of the Silk and Textile Routes is provided by Moira Stevenson. The aim of the programme is to establish a network of scholars and heritage managers for each route theme across national boundaries to underpin both education and tourism at local level. The potential value of the Council's initiative is borne out by Ross Noble's fascinating account of chasing his own tail in a search for the roots of vernacular furniture in the Highlands and Islands of Scotland, as well as by John Purser's search for the origins of the Scottish triple pipes. The processes through which cultural identity is formed are complex. And, in his paper on the North Sea as a cultural highway, Professor Martin Carver suggests that a proper understanding may require a new look at history, as well as study against time horizons further back than modern civilisation.

The sharing of heritage assets with visitors raises many difficult questions for the host community. The relevant papers in this volume focus on access policy, and Gordon Adams describes the approach of the Scottish Tourist Board. Their objective is to match the range of tourism products with the markets, and to ensure that the necessary infrastructure of promotional information, accommodation , transportation and attractions is in place to meet demand. Their promotional ethos and inter-agency collaboration has in recent years given high priority to the natural environment and the arts. The first paper by Roger Crofts is based on the text of his contribution to the 1994 Convention. It offers an excellent summary of the access policy being pursued by Scottish Natural Heritage, where improved access to the countryside within sustainable limits and partnership are the key elements. Robert Gordon Reid undertakes a penetrating analysis of attitudes, policies and lack of legislation concerned with free access to the countryside as in many other European countries. He concludes that the present system is inadequate to cope with future demand, and recommends that 'freedom to roam' legislation be introduced as a matter of urgency.

In his second paper, Crofts describes work on a new system of 'biogeographic zones' being developed for determining environmental quality and carrying capacity in the application of national and international protective designations. He argues for simplification in the system of such designations, and strongly favours less difference being made between areas designated for protection and the wider countryside. To this end, his agency has proposed a new system of 'natural heritage zones' which will make more use of partnership and the voluntary principle in environmental protection.

A new system of unitary local authorities in Scotland come into operation in April 1996. Peter Peacock, in his capacity as Convener Designate of the Highland Council, outlines his ideas for the new agenda in regard to both protecting the area's heritage assets and how they might best be shared with others who come as tourists. In a region on the very fringe of Europe, where environmental and cultural assets are fragile and economic prosperity is low, community involvement is of vital importance. Graham Watson provides an illuminating case study on how Ross and Cromarty District Council has pioneered a series of independent museums to be responsible for this type of service delivery, drawing on a combination of public funding and a cadre of local volunteers.

A potent force in the cultural identity of Scotland, particularly in the Highlands and the Islands, was the diaspora of native population to the New World as a consequence of poverty and enforced land 'clearances' by estate owners in the 18th and 19th centuries. However, expatriate Scots throughout the world, as John Alec MacPherson eloquently describes from a Canadian perspective, have nurtured their native identity to the extent that it is now a source of inspiration and encouragement to those at home who are seeking to promote greater pride in things Scottish.

In a powerful essay, Jim Hunter looks beyond the sorrow of the diaspora, and explores the deep affinity between people and the natural world in Gaelic culture as expressed through literature, poetry and song. The Gaelic language has benefited greatly from generous government funding in recent years. It has enjoyed a considerable revival, and Roy Pedersen reports on an ambitious Gaelic tourism strategy which builds on this revival. Unfortunately, the Scots language, Scotland's third language reviewed by Billy Kay, has not enjoyed the same level of government funding. In the last paper of the section, this author argues that a full-blooded Scottish identity can only flourish when Scotland declares itself a trilingual nation.

The book concludes with five papers discussing cultural identity in relation to the iconography of the built environment. Professor Frank Walker speculates on where Scottish architecture has been and where it is going 'at the edge of Europe and at the edge of the millennium,' seeking the answer through applying the concepts of the zeitgeist and genius loci much in the same way that Patrick Geddes did almost a century earlier. Likewise, Graeme Munro also picks up a Geddesian theme by looking at historic buildings as cultural icons. Through a case study from Southside Edinburgh, he illustrates how old buildings of the modest variety give a sense of place to the local streetscape, arguing that 'buildings of different periods contribute to an evolving townscape and provide a window on local history.' They are not simply bits of history worthy of conservation, but an essential part of a living urban fabric that shapes our cultural identity.

Professor Richard England of Malta is possibly the greatest living exponent of architecture as a manifestation of place rather than a celebration of creativity through modern technology, and the purpose of inviting a paper from him was to stimulate renewed interest in his work and ideas. His belief is that, if architecture is to have real meaning, it must be part of the environment and culture out of which it springs. This is in contrast to 'the international style,' and he once observed that the modern movement in architecture 'tried to find the universal solution to what was never a universal problem.' Universal ideas have been and still are influential in building design, but Richard England contends that the best architecture comes from listening to the voice of the site and local culture.

In true Geddesian fashion, Brian Evans draws similar conclusions in respect of urban design and town planning. He describes a design competition for the next development phase for Randstad Holland, and can see parallels with the situation in the Central Belt of Scotland where two expanding cities are located. He suggests that we should design at a scale greater than the city to ensure that what is built respects the identity of our environmental heritage and will thereby not compromise the cultural landscapes which provide the setting for our urban lives.

This introduction opened with a tribute to the legacy of Patrick Geddes, and so it concludes. The last chapter of the book is by Christopher Andrew who followed in his footsteps to the sub-continent of India, not to work there as Geddes did, but to study the stewardship of historic buildings as a travelling scholar with a Churchill Fellowship. Like Geddes and other fellow travellers, Christopher Andrew is struck by the enormous richness of the architectural heritage of India, but dismayed by the lack of resources available for its conservation, interpretation and presentation to both local people and tourists. He signs off by invoking the title of this book in a strong plea for more sharing. As tourists from more prosperous countries, we expect Indians to share their cultural heritage with us. In return, we should show more readiness to share with them the technical expertise and resources at our disposal in the field of heritage management.

Professor Magnus Fladmark
Heritage Unit
The Robert Gordon University

1

SURVIVAL AND WILDERNESS
A Global Dilemma

Nicholas Luard

The title is not mine. It was devised by the editor of this volume. When he first suggested it to me as the controlling theme for this address, I was wary. The twin topics are so vast they almost defy definition on their own, let alone in a linked relationship. And then as I considered it, I found his choice both challenging and in a sense inspired. Professor Fladmark barely knows me but, instinctively, he had reached for two of my life's central concerns.

I have loved wilderness, and I will come to what it means for me, from my early childhood when I used to accompany my father, an oil explorer, on dawn gazelle hunting expeditions in the Persian deserts. Later, still as a child, I was exposed to the mountains and plains of Africa. Under the guidance of the legendary white hunter Eric Sherbroke Walker, an ardent suitor (successful or not I will never know) of my beautiful young mother, I started to learn at first hand not just about Africa's animals – we had wonderful adventures as we watched lions and leopards and tracked marauding rogue elephants – but about the whole landscape of the dark continent, its rivers and savannahs and forests. To this day, I warm myself in winter with memories of sleeping out under the Aberdare stars or swimming in river pools which, I was certain, no one had ever plunged into before.

I was not aware of survival then. There were tall strong men like Walker with their high velocity rifles and their knowledge of the bush to look after me. I felt free, secure and unthreatened. I behaved like the 'mischievous monkey' my urban-bred London nanny fretfully called me. I swung on the ropes of the banyan tree, I searched the early dew-laden scrub for the caterpillars the young Masai morans had taught me I could eat. I followed as honey-guides led me to wild bee hives, although I never had quite enough courage to break into them. And then I returned to Britain and I grew up.

The first real rite of passage into adulthood was when I became a soldier. I was a linguist, an athlete, and a Bisley marksman. I had also been marked down a by the army as 'difficult'. The obvious move for the military authorities was to second me to the 'special forces'. I was assigned to lead covert long-range patrols. The time was the late fifties, and the preoccupation that haunted everyone, the shadow over all our lives, was the possibility of nuclear war between West and East. If war broke out, patrols like mine were to be dropped deep inside what was code-named 'Redland'.

Whenever we found a concentration of Soviet forces, we were to radio back the location. We were then given five hours to escape before a battlefield nuclear weapon attacked the target.

Many skills were required of us, and each patrol member specialised in one or sometimes two. But there was one overriding need in common to us all. We were extremely expensive to train and equip. To be cost-effective to the army and its paymasters, the nation, we had to survive. We were like VW's or Ford pickups in the hands of canny farmers. They had paid good money for their cattle trucks and they wanted to keep them on the road. We needed to be kept on the road too. We would be operating mainly at night, under rain, wind, and snow, in a hostile landscape of marsh, hill, rock and plain – forty or so years ago Central Europe was much less tidily manicured and managed than it is today. We had to survive in wilderness. That was where the central thrust of our training was directed, and I am eternally grateful it was. For me a cover of adult learning was added to insights gained in childhood, 'survival' and 'wilderness' were brought together.

Yet what do we really mean by these words? They both seem to be reasonably short and certainly clear, two of the simpler expressions in the world's richest and most precise language. They surely do not need analysis and explication. I wonder. Let us start with wilderness. To many, the first association, so heavy still is the weight of our cultural past, is with the Bible. Wilderness is where Jesus Christ spent his forty days and nights, the loneliest, most desolate period of his life until the journey on the Calvary Road and the hours after the hammer-blows on the cross. It was too, where he came face to face with the Devil. The experience of the Jewish Palestinian carpenter, filtered through the majestic language of the Jamesian Bible, defined the word for generations. Wilderness was planet earth's equivalent of hell – and just to confirm it Satan resided there.

Subtle and sophisticated as we believe we have come to be, we tend to mock that great legacy of our past, our tribal beliefs, the hopes and fears and convictions of our ancestors. Few of my readers, I hazard a guess, actively believe in a Christian God, fewer still in the Devil. Most of us are much too grown-up for that. We travel. We drive Volvo's. We have mobile telephones. We tap into the Internet. We have Sainsburys and Ikea to shop in. We admire or deride Lady Thatcher or Tony Blair or whoever is the current political icon. In spite of a few private uncertainties, we are proud to live in a caring secular age. Largely, we live our lives boldly with intellectual confidence.

And yet I find that when my friends come to stay – old and young, feminists and new men, many with honours degrees – the first thing they notice is that I buy the *Sun*, and the second is that, after jovial patronising chuckles at seeing the paper on the hall table, they seize and read it. They read their horoscopes. As we reach the end of the twentieth century, the best and brightest of my generation and the one that follows want to know what the stars foretell.

Like the stars for hope – even when the planets are in the worst possible conjunction horoscope writers always prophesy good cheer – the ancient view of wilderness as a symbol for the dark and threatening aspect of the human experience remains with us. Stars for our encouragement, wilderness to frighten us. It was not always so of course. For perhaps the first two million years of human existence, man made no distinction between what lay within or without the wall. To the hunter-gatherer clans, the whole planet was an indivisible garden, granary, and hunting ground. Even as recently as thirty years ago, when I made my first expedition into southern Africa's Kalahari desert, a few groups of the San, the so-called bushmen, still lived as their ancestors did hundreds of generations before Troy's foundation stones were laid.

When it came, the change in our attitude to wilderness spread swiftly. Ten or twenty thousand years ago someone somewhere, probably in the Jordan or the Bekaa Valley where Gaston Hochar now grows his vines, learnt how to plant and harvest wheat. about the same time we discovered animals could be herded and tamed. The first stockades went up to enclose and protect the grain and the herds, and overnight, in human evolutionary terms, the world was divided in two. Suddenly, what lay inside those primitive walls was safe, what lay beyond was menacing. All that was now needed for our species to switch from a nomadic strategy for survival to a settled one, was permanent shelter. We found out how to build houses, and civilisation. The culture emerged, first of trading-posts and then of cities.

It was, I think, the American writer and philosopher, Lewis Mumford, who defined civilisation as plumbing, and cities as lines of stone tents pitched on top of sewers. His characteristically robust and perceptive observations carry an implicit message that every householder and certainly every plumber will recognise. Piped systems of water supply and waste disposal are notoriously fragile. Frost and drought are annual hazards. Apart from them it only needs a relatively mild earth tremor, a ripple from some small tectonic plate movement, for a complex of conduits and water courses that has functioned effectively since Roman times to be obliterated in a matter of seconds. From Peru to Zimbabwe, to Arabia's fertile crescent, the archaeological record shows almost countless cities and civilisations that have vanished utterly. In most cases we cannot be sure of the reasons. All we know beyond doubt is that when the stone tents collapse and the sewers choke, the green tide of the wild reasserts itself. It advances inexorably Wilderness, for all we have done to shut it out, remains perilously close to our walls.

Perhaps in belated recognition of the power of the natural world, of the dynamic of the wild, the past few centuries of human colonisation of the planet – I use the term 'colonisation' in its imperial sense of conquest, imposition, and exploitation – have seen adaptations in our attitude to wilderness. Soon after the first Dutch landings in South Africa, Jan van Riebeeck, who reached the Cape in 1652, was forced to impose hunting restrictions on his fellow settlers. He realised that not even the apparently inexhaustible cornucopia of wildlife the Cape supported, could withstand the toll of the slaughter levelled against it by the advancing wave of ranchers. A century earlier, and for much the same reasons, the good burghers and farmers of Switzerland had created at Karpf, in the canton of Glarus, what was in effect the world's first conservation area.

The motives of van Riebeeck and the Swiss, seem to have been largely utilitarian. Jan van Riebeeck was advancing into new uninhabited territory, Magistrate Baldi and his fellow town fathers were protecting an old settled landscape. They were defending a resource of use to man. There may well have been other, more altruistic reasons for their actions, but however it came about, between them they have a fair claim to be considered the parents of the modern world's conservation movement – at least their hands rocked its cradle. A hundred and fifty or so years after van Riebeeck, the movement was given fresh impetus and a new dimension by the romantic revolution. To Wordsworth and his peers, swept forward by French currents of thought – French philosophers inevitably crop up wherever ideas (the worst as well as the best) are born – wild landscapes had a majesty and a beauty, an ability to foster spiritual regeneration and dreams of higher matters than anything urban life could stimulate. For the first time in tens of thousands of years wilderness was fashionable. It had always, of course been fashionable to hunter-gatherers.

Wordsworth – and I use the Lakeland poet simply as a symbol of all the waves of thought that were rippling round the European consciousness of the time – brought the idea of the wild back to us not as a threat, but almost as a sacrament. Like the daffodils it nurtured on the ground, like the sculptural tumult of the clouds and storms that passed above, it could invigorate and inspire. Yet wilderness was still something to look out upon from the city's battlements, to be viewed on quick carefully-planned visits, a place where you could go to if you were daring but from where it was essential you return. Men, proper civilised humanity, lived in urban communities. Wilderness lay beyond the walls. It was still perilous.

As the nineteenth century progressed other thinkers and writers began to examine more deeply what we meant by the wild. Building on what Wordsworth and his contemporaries had begun to frame and express, people like Henry David Thoreau advanced the idea of an integral relationship between modern American man – which by definition centrally included European man – and wilderness; a relationship that was partly mystical, partly pragmatic, and in the end wholly symbiotic. Neither could exist without the other. In his remarkable book *Walden, or Life in the Woods*, Thoreau reaches the conclusion that: 'In wilderness is the preservation of the world'.

Among Thoreau's American contemporaries was someone even more influential in redefining our attitude to the wild, the Dunbar-born visionary, John Muir. If there was ever an exemplar of the prophet without honour in his homeland, then it must surely be Muir. In the United States he has the recognition and status of a legend. Every schoolchild knows of his achievements; mountains, lakes, forests, and rivers, have been named after him; the Sierra Club, which he founded, now has 600,000 members and annual revenues of $100m. It is probably the most influential conservation body in the world. Yet in his native Scotland he remains virtually unknown. It may be helpful briefly to recollect who John Muir was and what he did.

Emigrating to the USA with his family in 1843 as a child of eleven, Muir rapidly proved an inventor of genius. Like Baird or Carnegie, ideas cascaded from him in catherine wheels of brilliance. Set John Muir a problem requiring a technological solution – whether it be improving a domestic appliance or devising a machine to simplify some agricultural activity – and he would instantly come up with the answer. Muir's inventions made him rich. Wealth for him was not enough. Always restless in spirit, a temporary devastating spell of blindness, caused by an accident, prompted him to turn his protean energies elsewhere. He looked at the landscape of his adopted home and he found his mission – although he claimed later that the seeds of what he had to do had been planted during his childhood rambles along the shores of the Dunbar coastline.

Muir saw America, his adopted country, being plundered and degraded. The ancient forests were being scythed down, rivers were being dammed, diverted, and bled to death, ill-planned roads were scarring the land, the intricate communities of birds and animals were in retreat, toxins were billowing out everywhere. On all sides the mantle of life was being ripped away. Muir set out to halt the destruction. Such was the force of his personality, the powers of his persuasion, the vigour and sanity of his writings, that over the years which followed he achieved much. He became a friend and counsellor to Presidents, notably Theodore Roosevelt; he was the driving force behind the proclamation of Yellowstone and Yosemite as National Parks; he created a new awareness among his fellow citizens – that the wild was not something to be ransacked for short-term gratification, but rather a treasure-chest of life to be guarded and nurtured for generations to come. 'Do something for wildness', was Muir's injunction, 'and make the mountains glad'.

Muir died in 1914 but, long before his death, his message had begun to take wings. Today it flies more strongly than ever. In Britain we tend to pride ourselves as conservators. Indeed, I often suspect we believe we are the world's leaders in the field. In my experience the truth is very different. Were John Muir alive today he would find himself at home in a small rambling building outside Pietermaritzburg in the South African province of Natal. The building houses the headquarters of Natal's Parks, Game and Fisheries Board (NPGFB), the most effective and experienced of its kind anywhere. The parks and reserves the Board administers with such care and skill should be models for everyone involved in conservation. In managing our Scottish landscapes, we really only have to deal with one wild creature: the red deer, one recently imported one, the rabbit, and one domestic animal, the sheep. The NPGFB, in contrast, is constantly engaged in balancing some forty major mammals, ranging from lion and rhino down to shy bush-dwelling antelope, all of them part of the delicate equilibrium of the wild. They describe their work as 'management by intervention' and they do it superbly.

Muir, I know, would have raised his worn rain-sodden hat to today's Natal. And although he would have found much in modern America to make him despair, much to make him believe his worst fears had been realised, he would also see pointers of encouragement. Apart from his own Sierra Club, he would see the growing power of the equally vast Audubon Society, dedicated initially to birds but now embracing every facet of landscape conservation. He would look with warm approval on that extraordinary body, the US Nature Conservancy, which administers lands close in size to the whole area of mainland Britain. Unquestionably, he would hail the thousands of other state and national organisations, which multiply every year, devoted to the protection of the environment. Muir was a capitalist operating in the world's most unfettered free market. That market has produced the world's most powerful conservation movement. The Sierra Club alone – and this surprises many – has more registered lobbyists in Washington than the fearsome National Rifle Association, America's strident mouthpiece for the gun. Trees and rivers, indeed, may prove to be more popular than rifles. Perhaps in leaving it to the people to choose, Lady Thatcher did not get it altogether wrong after all.

Where does all of that leave us here in Scotland? Where does it leave wilderness, survival, and the dilemma posed, if there is one, by the conjunction of the two? Book-learning is a splendid tool and the spoken words of the wise can be immensely illuminating, but we reach our soundest conclusions, I believe, when we anchor them in our own observations and experiences. I remember watching the great biologist, Dr Miriam Rothschild, sitting for hours in a meadow looking at butterflies. Scientists had long since asserted and recorded in those tablets of stone, their scientific journals and monographs, that some particular aspect of butterfly behaviour had been decoded and explained beyond any possible doubt. Dr Rothschild was not convinced. She was right and her peers were wrong. The shrewd patient eyes of one old lady turned scientific certainty on its head, and her fellow-scientists were forced to tear up their papers and return to the drawing-board. Perhaps in a much more modest way my own observations of a lifetime of travelling the world's distant places may have an echo here.

I said at the start that I would try to define what wilderness means to me. I will do so now. Wilderness means absolutely nothing to me. I do not believe in it. Neither as a mosaic of lonely landscapes with precise geographical locations, nor as a philosophical concept, nor even as a religious metaphor for the dark night of the soul. And since I have written this paper for a conference in Scotland, I have to say I do not believe in the so-called wilderness of the Cairngorms, or our northern coastline round Cape Wrath, or even in the Hebrides which include those talismanic island jewels, Mull and Iona, where I grew up. I do not believe in the Himalayas and the austere mountain landscape of the Tibetan border through whose snows I climbed with my son and daughter; I do not believe in Spain's bare Castilian plain, across which I have recently been walking on pilgrimage to Santiago de Compostela, or the marshes of the Guadalquivir river, the Coto Doñana sanctuary south of Seville; I do not even believe in my favourite place on Earth, the great stone plateau of the Kalahari desert with the golden Okavango delta at its north-western limits.

They are all of course magical places. I am fortunate to have travelled them and, in most cases, to have known them for years. Their beauty will haunt me for ever: by turns lush and exuberant, or, in the look they give the voyager, stark and challenging as the cold agate eye of a hunting lioness. But they are not wilderness. There is no wilderness. There is only the roaming tumbling sphere of this planet earth. The Hebrides, the Kalahari, the Himalayan approaches, the fecund Coto Doñana, are inextricably linked together in patterns as formal as a Gay Gordons reel. If one partner drops out of line or misses the rhythm, the entire pattern of the dance is lost.

We, the dancers, can start again. Birds and animals, trees and dolphins, are not so fortunate. What to the guest at the ceilidh, is no more than a step back on the floor, a glance at sparkling eyes above a still-swirling tartan skirt, is to the creatures of the wild, generations of painful recovery. We separate ourselves from other creatures at our peril. We are all fellows in the animal kingdom. That the measure of the dance is slower or faster is merely a matter for the piper.

How have we become so distanced, so out of step with a single and common support system? The reasons are far too complex even to begin to explore here. If I had to reduce them to a single phrase, I would suggest it is this: walls and tools. I have referred to the walls before, the ramparts and parapets we erect to guard our grain and herds against the wild. The tools we use in the process are part and parcel of our transition from hunter-gatherer to city dweller as civilised man. Californian sea-otters and Egyptian vultures use tools, both hammering with stones to gain access to food sources. We are no different. When we access the Internet, detonate a nuclear weapon, or submit our bodies to keyhole surgery, we are doing no more than what the otter or the vulture does. We are using tools. All that distinguishes us is that our tools are more elaborate. If we lose them, we find ourselves in the same position as the otter or the vulture deprived of stone to crack open oysters or break ostrich egg-shells. Without tools, the otter and vulture must use their wits and look elsewhere to eat, to survive – and slip back effortlessly into the mainstream of non-tool-utilising wilderness. Happily for them, the earth's surface is littered with stones – ask any gardener – and they seldom face the problem. We are not so fortunate. Once lost, tools, starting with the plumbing and sewers on which we have erected civilisation, take years, generations maybe, to reconstruct.

The author James Clavell, for several years a prisoner-of-war of the Japanese, was asked not long ago what was the most important lesson he had learned from the experience. By then a millionaire, he replied: 'That all I needed in life, all any man needs, is a bag of seed corn and a hunting knife. With those two I could feed and protect my wife and children. Nothing else matters, and I still want nothing more'. My friend, Sir Laurens van der Post, has said much the same in his inspiring and evocative writings about Africa. Both men stand in an old and proud tradition. Their philosophy runs back to blind Homer; it was passed down to the eleventh century Gawain poet (the epic of the Green Knight says more about wilderness than anything I know). For centuries it was lost; and then recently it has emerged again, as I have suggested, in the writings of people like Wordsworth, Thoreau and John Muir. I could add many to the list, but Muir must remain pre-eminent.

I chair several British conservation bodies. The one in which I take the greatest pride – and which almost daily presents me with the greatest challenges – is the John Muir Trust. We now own four major wild landscapes in Scotland. When three friends and I founded the Trust, we thought our task would be simple: we would acquire and conserve wild land. The reality soon proved rather different. We found that for centuries our wildernesses had been abused and degraded. We also discovered we had to deal with the shattered human communities which lived on the edge of the wild. We learnt, in short, that we were involved in much more than straightforward wilderness conservation: we were involved in regeneration, the active healing of landscapes, and above all with people. We re-set our sails and began to navigate on a new course. Fortune and a fair wind followed us. Today, the John Muir Trust, with its holistic approach to wilderness, is at the cutting edge of British conservation.

What are we trying to do? I have mentioned the restoration work we carry out on our lands. If the concept of wilderness has a meaning, it is to be found in the planet's living mantle at its finest and most intricate. So much of the riches have been lost. We are trying to put some of the treasures back. Who knows, we may yet see beavers on Knoydart and wolves in the Cuillins? I have mentioned people. People are now an integral component of virtually all the world's landscapes however remote. We try to build bridges towards the old traditional settlements, to create understanding of what we are up to, and to take them forward, the crofting townships for instance, in partnership with us. While I greatly dislike jargon phrases, the term 'sustainable use' might at least be appropriate for our aims.

More than that, we are, I think, trying to turn the clock back, and for that I make no apologies at all. We are trying to dismantle the walls between man and the so-called wild, the intellectual barriers entrenched in human thought and the physical stockades thrown up on the ground. We are trying to diminish our dependence on tools, not in a Luddite sense because we cannot unlearn the past, we cannot un-invent inventions. But we are trying to harness our capacities as a tool-making animal with newer, stronger and simpler strategies for survival. We are trying, like Dr Rothschild, to use our eyes.

Some months ago in the *Daily Mail* (June 8), the influential columnist, Paul Johnson, launched a tirade against television's Channel 4 – 'the haven for filth' as he called it. In a major article peppered with angry references to pornography, perverts, and genitalia, Mr Johnson revealed that what he found as offensive as anything, was some footage of people eating 'live worms'. One could feel his shudder of disgust at the notion. It was a sad but vivid illustration of how far our opinion-makers, our gurus, have become distanced from the support system of the natural world. Worms, as every young special forces soldier is taught, and you will certainly not need reminding, are an excellent source of protein. They come from wilderness, they require no tools to gather, they are sweet, nutritious and healthy and they represent survival.

There is no global dilemma about wilderness or survival. The lesson is there for the learning. There is, however, a need for a major reassessment of our attitudes and perceptions, for gentle and quiet education. Gently and quietly I would like to seize Mr Johnson by the scruff of the neck, march him through a hole in the wall – the wall of his own making, the hole of ours – and make him eat those worms. I doubt he will find the experience pornographic. In fact, if I can find some wild chanterelle mushrooms with which to garnish the dish, he may even find the recipe delicious. If he asks for a second helping, we can then move on to fried genitalia – but that is a story which must wait until the next volume in this series.

The Author

Born in London, but raised on the Isle of Mull, Nicholas Luard was taught at Winchester, the Sorbonne University in Paris, Cambridge University, and, on a graduate fellowship, at the University of Pennsylvania, USA. He was educated by himself and the British army. A co-founder of *Private Eye* magazine and The Establishment Theatre Club, he subsequently became a writer, naturalist, and explorer. He has led expeditions across the Kalahari and Namib deserts, and in the Himalayas, and has also travelled widely in many other parts of the world. The author of eighteen books, he is married to the writer Elizabeth Luard, and divides his time between London and his hill farm in Wales. He is chairman of the John Muir Trust, the Wilderness Trust, the Gaia Trust, the Hebridean Whale and Dolphin Trust, and is a Council Member of WWF. He is also advisor to the British Joint Services mountaineering expeditions.

References

Johnson, P., *Time to Sack Britain's Pornographer-in-Chief*, The Daily Mail, 8 June 1995

Luard, E., *European Peasant Cookery*, Bantam Press, 1986

Luard, N., *Andalucia*, Century, 1984

Luard, N., *The Wildlife Parks of Africa*, Michael Joseph, 1985

Muir, J., *The Eight Wilderness Books*, Gifford, T. (ed), London, 1994

Mumford, L., *The Human Prospect*, Beacon Press, 1955

Oelschlaeger, M., *The Idea of Wilderness*, Yale University Press, 1991

Spearing, A. C., *The Gawain Poet: A Critical Study*, Cambridge University Press, 1970

Thoreau, H. D., *Walden, or Life in the Woods*, David Campbell, 1992

van der Post, L., *The Lost World of the Kalahari*, Chatto & Windus, 1951

Wordsworth, W., *Poems*, (Vols I & II), Penguin, 1977

2

GLOBALISATION OF THE MEDIA
The Impact on National Cultures

Magnus Linklater

I would like readers to take themselves westwards, to Los Angeles to be precise, and the headquarters of Twentieth Century Fox Television. Zooming in, as they do in the movies, we find ourselves on the top floor, in a large, luxurious room, with a sprawling desk, and that absence of clutter that suggests real power. Behind it sits a man with thinning grey hair and a deeply lined face. He has big spectacles which barely shield the penetrating gaze behind them. He is the most influential media tycoon in the world.

No discussion about culture today, whether it is the survival of Old Norse, the promotion of New Gaelic, or the popularity of The Simpsons on television, can take place without some assessment of this character. Grandson on one side of a fiercely puritan Free Church minister from the parish of Cruden in Aberdeenshire, and on the other of a charming but feckless half-Irish gambler from Melbourne, Australia, he has inherited some of the qualities of both. The vast empire of the airwaves that belongs to Rupert Murdoch broods over the contents of this volume, whether we like it or not. His sprawling information network, which makes a mockery of national frontiers and which reaches every corner of our globe, is changing the way we communicate, the way we learn, the way we think, the way we speak. Unless we can come to terms with the direction in which that is taking us, my theme of links across the North Sea and reviving a legacy of cultural interaction has as much relevance as last week's shinty report in the Inverness Courier.

It is not just that Mr Murdoch, together with a handful of other barons, wields power in the electronic and print media of a kind and on a scale that would have been unimaginable even five years ago; he also takes control at the other end – over the material which we watch, read and listen to. Joseph Stalin is reputed to have said once: 'If I could control the American film industry, I could control the world.' Marshall McLuhan thought that the invention of the Xerox machine would make 'Everyman' his own publisher. Neither of them could have envisaged the way in which one man was able to influence so thoroughly the means of producing news and entertainment, and the product itself. Through multi-media machines, processing voice, video and data, linked by optical-fibre networks, where one gossamer thread carries more electronic traffic round the world than a thousand copper wires, the Murdoch vision invades our consciousness, and in particular the consciousness of our young people. For they are the true heirs to this revolution. Those of us of the post-war generation, may have grown up worrying about global warfare. Those of 'The Internet Generation' are willing participants in a technological war. The Evil Empire has been defeated, but the Video Empire is marching on.

So what kind of a world are the young inheriting, and what happens to our native cultures as these latter-day Titans expand their vast empires at each others' expense? Can the local village survive when the global village threatens to steamroller it out of existence? Is there a place for traditional culture? And what form will it take if it comes through? I do not wish to alarm you, but even the spider at the centre of this web – Mr Murdoch himself – is alarmed at the implications of his own revolution. He concedes that one result has been the Americanisation of the world. He believes that on the whole this has been of global benefit, a force for peace, he insists.

But he understands the dangers: 'Are we going to homogenise the whole world with satellite and cable, with no room for local culture?' he has asked. 'I think there is a danger. One benefit may be that it is more peaceful. And more prosperous. But there will be fewer differences.' And to illustrate his point, he tells the story (possibly apocryphal) of how the North African tribesmen, the Tuareg, once delayed their traditional annual camel caravan across the Sahara, in order to watch an episode of *Dallas*.

I think I myself first became conscious of this when I visited a small cottage on the island of Papa Westray in Orkney some 20 years ago. The furniture was traditional, the fireplace had not changed much since the last century, the floor was worn stone. But in a corner was a vast television screen, and in front of it sat an old man nursing a cup of tea. He was watching a Las Vegas floor show, with scantily-clad chorus-girls strutting their stuff on a stage 6,000 miles away. He appeared quite impassive in the face of this grotesque invasion of an alien culture. I wondered what he, as a man whose father and grandfather had gone down to the sea from that same cottage, to haul fish in nets onto their square-sterned Orkney boats and had then relaxed by swapping Orkney tales over Orkney beer to a background of Orkney fiddle music, made of the bump and grind of a Las Vegas showgirl. I asked his daughter. She shook her head. 'My, I would'na ken,' she said, 'he just goes to sleep in front of it most nights.'

Of course I would not pretend that we can rely entirely on a one-man straw poll conducted on Papa Westray in 1975. There has been enormous, and understandable, alarm expressed about the threat of global communication to our native cultures. But I argue in this paper that, while no one should underestimate the challenge which such cultural hegemony poses, there is evidence that in some ways it can be turned to the advantage of what we treasure: that the invading forces not only have to recognise the strength of an indigenous civilisation, but need to nurture it in order to survive. We need look no further back than the invasion of the Huns in the first few centuries AD. Where they laid waste the lands and drove the natives from their homesteads, they found their tenure was short-lived and their victories unprofitable. Where they took trouble to encourage those whom they had defeated, they held on longer – particularly when it came to encouraging the local production of gold and jewellery, for which they had 'an insatiable lust'.

Just so did Rupert Murdoch fare when he conquered Asia, and established what is known as his 'footprint' over the vastly profitable media territory of China, India and South East Asia with its three billion inhabitants. Far from finding them receptive to the Americanisation which his satellite invasion offered, he and his fellow media purveyors, discovered that if they were to survive at all, they had to adapt to local requirements. Until their television programmes absorbed and adapted to native cultures they enjoyed only partial success. *Dallas* and *Baywatch* were scorned if they were the only diet available. Only when Murdoch and the others started helping to make programmes in Hindi, in Mandarin, in Urdu or Malaysian, using the talents and instinctive tastes of local producers, did they start having any mass impact. One effect, incidentally, has been to rejuvenate the Indian television industry which now churns out a whole series of sit-coms in native dialects, which have become immensely popular. Both sides, it seems, have learned a lot about each other.

I think, however, that this is only part of the answer. And in any event we need to return closer to home if we are to make judgements about the homogenising effect of the modern mass media on what we most value – Scottish culture, language and literature. I have one small advantage in seeking an answer, in that I have worked with and under Mr Murdoch, and indeed have had the doubtful privilege of being employed by two of the lesser gods, left reeling in his wake – Mr Robert Maxwell and Mr Tiny Rowland. I have also worked in one area which finds itself currently under threat, the Scottish newspaper industry, and in another which has begun erecting some hasty barricades, the Scottish broadcasting industry.

The first point to make is that we must recognise the challenge: it is a real one. None of these latter-day moguls will have any great respect for a local culture that does not defend itself. There is no point in expecting that any of them will arrive in a spirit of earnest enquiry, or will be particularly sympathetic to local sensibilities. They are governed by the law of the market-place and an instinct for territorial gain, and if access is made easy for them, they will simply expand further and faster.

A good example of this faces us currently in Scotland where newspapers from Mr Murdoch's News International organisation, together with those from other groups following his example, have cut their prices in order to raise circulation and put pressure on the opposition. It is hardly surprising that the offer of a lower-priced newspaper which offers good all-round coverage of British and foreign affairs should be a tempting one. In broadcasting too, there has been great pressure on public and commercial radio and television in Scotland from satellite and cable channels which offer an expanding, frequently bewildering choice of viewing and listening. This range of choice, this threat to the established order of things is only just beginning. It would be absurd to pretend that things will ever be the same again.

The second point is that the culture that stands still, or tries to cocoon itself from the changes that rage around it, will probably not survive. A language, for instance, that is not in regular use may become an interesting museum-piece, may even stand as an important icon, but will not be part of a living culture. A newspaper that fails to be aware of the changes taking place within the industry will find itself overtaken by its rivals. A radio or television station that attempts to disregard the standards being set elsewhere, however much it may affect to despise them, will find itself steadily deserted even by its most loyal audience.

The third point is, however, that all these apparent threats can be turned to advantage if the real strengths of a native culture are used as part of its natural defence. The striking evidence of the last decade is not how much we have lost but how much we have retained, and what resilience Scottish language and literature in particular have shown. There are difficult and testing times still ahead, but we can, I think, identify a way forward, and by using the strength of our native inheritance, together with the cultural links established over centuries with our northern European neighbours, we can actually reinforce rather than weaken our local and national identity.

To take these points in order: attack, as they say, is the best form of defence, and I can see many examples of that in Scotland today. Probably the best is the defence of our language. Among the contributors to this volume is Billy Kay, whose battle for the Scots tongue is a legend in his own lifetime, and who can take much credit for its state of rude good health; and Dr James Hunter whose involvement in many of the bodies established to promote the native culture of the Highlands fully qualifies him as an honoured member of the Gaelic Mafia. The brief point that I would make here, is that, while Government intervention and the provision of public money to support Gaelic education and Gaelic broadcasting is an important plank in its defence, it is the enthusiasm and involvement of the people, and their active participation in speaking, learning and teaching the language that is in the end the most vital component. Without them the money is simply poured down a dark hole. The advantage gained in demonstrating such a high-profile commitment to native language is that those who wish to establish their 'footprint' in Scotland, whether through television or radio, have to take that commitment on board, to find means themselves of promoting it, and, in a sense, to 'go native' in doing so. I refer you back to the remarkable experience of satellite broadcasting in India.

Governments do, of course, have a crucial role in protecting local cultures, and I would not seek to downplay it. Perhaps the most important recent example lies in the plans to dilute the enormous powers of cross-media ownership. The latest, from this Government, involve proposals which would allow newspaper groups which control under 20 per cent of the national market to expand and control up to 15 per cent of the total television market. Again, newspapers below the 20 per cent threshold, would be able to apply for control of licenses for national and local radio provided that the company does not, as a result, control more than 30 per cent of the media on a local area. Broadcasters, while still facing limits, would be allowed to expand up to 15 per cent of total TV audience share. Terrestrial broadcasters would be allowed to buy controlling interests in satellite and cable companies, but not beyond a 15 per cent share. There would be limits on the cross-control of regional newspaper and TV groups. All this sounds reasonable, and the fact that it has attracted hostility mainly from the larger giants, suggest that it may be on target – giving smaller groups the capacity to compete with the multi-media moguls, while binding the more ruthlessly acquisitive ambitions of the latter.

But this is only, in a sense, adjusting the dimensions of the battlefield. It does not prevent the mayhem that can still occur on the field itself. The most immediate example of bloodshed lies in my own industry, the print media.

Here the invasion has been every bit as brutal, every bit as rapacious as anything in the television world. The Scottish market was viewed by several large newspaper organisations as 'soft' territory, ripe for plunder. The notion, which began amongst the owners of tabloid newspapers, but spread rapidly to the broadsheets, was that Scottish readers were ready to be wooed and won, that the Scottish newspapers which supplied them with their regular diet were complacent, and that if the invigorating and abrasive climate that pervaded Fleet Street – or rather London's Docklands where most of the empires have their hub these days – were introduced north of the Border, there would be a mass defection of readers.

Various tactics were adopted in this campaign. First, prices were cut, in some cases by more than half, notably by the ubiquitous Mr Murdoch, who decided that his newspapers were over-priced compared to those he owned in America. It cost him huge amounts of money, but for a multi-national communications giant worth many billions of pounds, paying £40 million a year to cut the price of The Times alone, was a flea bite. The flea might become more irritating as the years went on, but for the time being it was enough that his readership grew, his advertisers paid more, and his rivals bit their fingernails in anguish as they decided how much they could afford to match him.

Second, staff were increased to provide more Scottish coverage. This meant sending up seasoned executives from London, some of whom had rarely been north of Watford, to inject a bit of Fleet Street know-how into Scottish coverage, and also to pinch some of the local talent. Scottish journalists found themselves on the receiving end of lucrative offers, frequently at rates well above what they were currently being paid. Not surprisingly, for the most part, they accepted. Staff changes became a way of life as reporters swapped jobs and found themselves working for London-based newspapers that tacked the word 'Scottish' onto their titles, and adopted new insignia, usually incorporating the lion rampant or the saltire.

Finally, English newspapers began 'discovering' Scotland, writing with wide-eyed surprise about places like Harris and Helensburgh, about organisations like Convention of Scottish Local Authorities or An Comunn Gàidhlig, about the Court of Session and Caledonian MacBrayne, about devolution and drams. The 'tartanisation' of the British Press had begun.

So what has been its effect? I am inclined to say minimal, but that I think is tempting fate. The alien forces will not give up easily, indeed they may never give up. But I think we have seen how far they can go, and I doubt if there are many more bridgeheads to be won. Amongst the tabloids, there have been gains of course, but the losses suffered by the natives have been less than expected, while the territory won is modest. Scotland's largest-selling tabloid, the Daily Record, continues to hold onto its huge lead, while in the so-called middle-market, newspapers like the Daily Express and the Daily Mail have failed to put on the big increases in readership which they so confidently expected and which their investment envisaged. They have grown, it is true, but the base from which they work is still very low.

Amongst the so-called quality broadsheets the pattern is similar. Newspapers like The Times and the Telegraph have indeed improved their position, but their native rivals, The Scotsman and The Herald, have begun slowly to regain the readers lost in the initial shock-wave, and can in no sense be said to have lost control of their Scottish heartland. If they face a threat at the moment it comes more from the big increases in the price of newsprint which they, in common with all newspapers, are currently having to contemplate.

What has happened could not have been entirely predicted. However professional the London-based press has been in serving its newly-discovered market, it has only half-convinced its readership that it is serious. They know that despite the plethora of Scottish stories on the front page, or the fluttering saltires on the masthead, that they are not truly Scottish. And while they may appreciate the chance of sampling a good London paper at a reduced price, they are not wholly taken in. They know that only a truly Scottish paper can give them the coverage they want – and, by and large, they want Scottish coverage, not an English version of it. There is nothing chauvinistic in saying this – and as someone who contributes regularly to one of the southern invaders, I think I can safely say that much has been gained on both sides. Scottish papers have improved the performance of their own products in response to the competition. English papers have increased their quota of Scottish stories. The result has been a readjustment of positions rather than a major regrouping. This may be a premature judgement, but I think that at the time of writing it is the correct one.

The Scottish press has survived, not by sticking its collective head in the sand, or even by putting up the barricades, but, in the classic way by which cultures survive, by adapting to circumstance. I would take as my text not just those national newspapers which I have mentioned, but some of the regional papers which are the very bedrock of the Scottish media – the Dundee Courier, the Sunday Post, and the Press and Journal. Look at these long-established, traditional papers, and compare them to the way they appeared less than ten years ago. They are unrecognisable. The way they look, the way they present their news, the way they communicate with their readers, all these have changed radically. And beneath the surface, the way they are financed, the way they are staffed, and the way they are distributed, has been transformed as well. On the other hand, while their readership has changed, it has not done so hugely; they still have a lock-hold on their local markets. Their circulations are somewhat diminished, but not drastically, and if you compared them to the market in general you would give them high marks for performance. Their financial position remains healthy.

They may present a rather different picture of Scotland than they once did, but that is because Scotland itself is rather different. You will find more reports of the outside world, a greater reflection of the cultural world we view on our television screens, and of course, the more fractured picture of a rapidly changing society than we could have predicted a decade ago. It is less provincial, less dominated by the bens and glens, the kailyard or the kirk, but what we read is still a reflection of Scotland today rather than one viewed from Metropolitan London. And we've still got the Broons and Oor Wullie, thank God. Incidentally, they tried putting Dennis the Menace into shellsuits and trainers, but it never really worked.

The same evolution is largely true of radio and television where the pressures have been every bit as great, if of a different nature. The BBC in Scotland, while constantly at loggerheads with its controlling headquarters in London over resources, over control and administration, remains clear that the only way it can hold its market against commercial rivals, is by maintaining the quality of its Scottish programming. To take just one example, *Good Morning Scotland*, its flagship current affairs programme, transmitted every weekday, competes with the famous London-based *Today* programme, attempting to match its quality, while having to accept funding which is less than a fifth of its southern rival. The easy route to take would simply have been to accept the basic London diet of news and interviews, interspersed with some local input, or to have accepted a narrowly parochial outlook. Instead, it took the decision to go onto the offensive – to produce a full current affairs show every day, with its own Scottish coverage, not just of local news, but the world in general. Some of the best interviews on foreign affairs can thus be heard on Scottish radio, and it brings a non-metropolitan perspective to United Kingdom affairs which is an excellent balance to what goes out from London. There has, of course, been too much cutting back on Scottish arts and entertainment coverage, and too much of value to Scottish cultural life has been sacrificed on the altar of London's financial imperatives, but the war has not been lost, and there is sufficient recognition of Scotland's separate locus to give cause for hope.

Commercial television too has had to fight some tough battles. Here it has been a case of selling Scottish programmes furth of Scotland as much as satisfying the home market. There was a need to survive, not just in the popularity charts, but in the London boardrooms where hard bargains are struck on what does or does not get onto the national network. It was recognised early on, however, by companies such as Scottish Television and Grampian, that unless they provided strong Scottish programmes which met local demands, they would not survive. *Dallas* and the *Wheel of Fortune* were not enough. They needed *Taggart* and *Take the High Road* as well. They needed to understand and reflect the development of local cultures, to encourage Gaelic programming, to be sensitive to local interests as well as buying in the best of American soaps. A measure of the success of Scottish Television is that it regularly outperforms BBC Scotland when they meet head on with purely Scottish programmes.

I would not want to propose too rosy a view of the media in Scotland, however. I would not be thanked for it by those executives who are currently staring bleakly at balance sheets which have suffered from the ferocious price wars in the newspaper world, for instance; or by those who see take-over battles looming in the cut-throat world of television or radio. But I believe that if certain courses are charted, then survival at least, and expansion at best, could be the rewards for a remarkably resilient sector of Scotland's local culture.

Two things are important, however: firstly, native culture must not be confused with parochialism. At its best, Scottish life is outward-looking, absorbing the best of international life, rather than contemplating its own backyard. Second, there is much to be said for rediscovering and reviving our ancient links with northern Europe, with Scandinavia, with the Netherlands, with France. For too long we have judged the vigour of our arts, and our media against the benchmark of American culture. But our future lies with Europe. If, as we generally hope, Scotland gains its own Parliament again, and acquires the devolved power that the majority of its people seem to want, so we shall be looking to Europe for our longer term political and economic development. Devolution would give Scotland a voice in Europe, and a role to play. We have much to contribute, but we also have much to receive. We have benefited in the past from alliances, trading relationships, and cultural exchanges with Europe, and there is every reason for us to revive them today. If we are to fight Video Wars rather than real wars in the future, then we will need new treaties, new partners, new strategies to survive. It is time to think again about those with whom we should be exchanging envoys and establishing partnerships. This is going to be a long hard struggle against some ferocious opposition. We are going to need all the friends we can get.

The Author

Magnus Linklater has been a journalist for thirty years with experience in several major UK newspapers. He has worked on *The Daily Express* and *The London Evening Standard*, and joined *The Sunday Times* in 1969 where he edited the colour magazine. He moved to *The Observer* in 1983 as managing editor, then launched and edited *The London Evening News*. He was most recently Editor of *The Scotsman*. He became a freelance in 1994, and currently writes a column for *The Times* and broadcasts a weekly programme for the BBC in Scotland

References

Evans, H., *Good Times, Bad Times*, Weidenfeld & Nicolson, 1983
Jacobs, S., *Systems of Survival: A Dialogue on the Moral Foundations of Commerce and Politics*, Random House, 1993
McRae, H., *The World in 2020 – Power, Culture and Prosperity: A Vision of the Future*, Harper Collins, 1994
Pye, M., *Disney's World Shows the Shape of Culture to Come*, in *The Scotsman*, 2 August 1995

3

MICKEYING WITH THE MUSES
Disney World and Regional Identity

William Tramposch

Nearly twenty years ago a colleague and I surveyed visitors at the exit gate of one of America's largest outdoor history museums. One of our questions, in particular, seemed to catch our guests by surprise: 'Did you come to Old Sturbridge Village for entertainment or educational reasons?' Without exception, dutiful parents would respond, 'education'; while couples or independent groups of children would admit to being attracted to the fun of a visit. What struck us, though, was that hardly any guest felt comfortable saying, 'both.' This fact has haunted me since, and the tension that exists between these two words are a central focus of this essay. Why are we so quick to separate the two concepts of education and entertainment? Is learning compromised when it happens to be fun? Of course not, we say, but often in almost the same breath, we in the heritage professions condemn (or at least undervalue) those factors that assist us in reconciling the two.

My case in point is the very word, 'Disneyland.' Mention it to any professional in the heritage trade and immediately a legion of negative associations descend upon the conversation. And if your site happens to be described as having a somewhat 'Disneylandish approach', well then that is at least tantamount to an outlandish one. Oftentimes, in fact, the accusation is so incisive and so intentionally hurtful that the accused is rendered as speechless as if he had just lost a playground 'double dare.' This paper explores that often uncharted world beyond the aspersion by outlining what I believe to be best about the 'the Disney approach.' In the end, I shall hope to have convinced the reader that there is much for us to learn from the master entertainer.

Why have millions of Americans gotten testy over CEO Michael Eisner's interest in building a history theme park within cannon shot of a major Civil War battlefield? First, the clashing juxtaposition of a funhouse to a slaughter-house was reason enough to be upset; while the magnitude of the project understandably sent shivers up the spines of potential rural neighbors, as well. Then, of course, there is the perennial complaint about accuracy and Disney's institutional propensity to over-romanticize the past. To be sure, all of these are justified anxieties, and they have had a way of galvanizing America's heritage community of late. But, to end the conversation at this level is to leave the long-term possibilities of a marriage of talents unexplored, and it is my contention that it is exactly here that the best part of the conversation begins. Imagine if Disney were to take more of an interest in historical accuracy; while at the same time, imagine if we in the heritage field were to become more skilled at learning more from such successful competitors for the leisure dollar. Imagine.

I suggest that a little wishing 'upon a star' is what is needed here. Mix this with a good deal of listening, learning and compromising, and our public (remember them?) could quite possibly end up having the best of both worlds. In fact, do not look now Mouseketeers, but the best of each is already being mixed together at a number of newer sites. This paper concludes by highlighting a few of them.

Before I continue, however, I am bound (as a card-carrying member of the international museum profession) to tell you that I do not under any circumstances condone Disney's traditional disinterest in accuracy. Integrity in research is at the heart (or at least the head) of the heritage profession, and the education of our public is our key obligation. Now, having said that, suspend those disbeliefs and let us journey on.

Four noteworthy elements characterize the Disney approach, and from them we can learn a great deal. They are:

- a clear and simple vision;
- the aggressive promotion of programs;
- an indefatigable public service ethic; and,
- imagination.

If we were to add these outward-looking elements to our already well-defined ethics for collecting, preserving, researching and interpreting we would greatly enhance our effectiveness.

VISION

In the flower-laden central square of Disneyland stands a statue of founder, Walt, and his creation, Mickey Mouse. Their backs to Fantasyland's famous castle, they face the oncoming waves of visitors with a welcoming smile and a warm and loyal wave. On the statue's base are written Walt's following words: 'I think most of all I want Disneyland to be a happy place where parents and children can have fun together.' Walt's words have served well and long as a succinctly stated corporate ethic, and this deceptively simple aspiration has characterized almost everything that the Disney empire has undertaken since the days when Mickey was young.

The clarity and effectiveness of this vision has been so attractive, in fact, that both its brevity and its influence have received the attention of corporate CEOs and management consultants world-wide. Today, the Disney Corporation, in addition to running theme parks, and producing movies and merchandise, offers a full range of professional management programs for businessmen and women representing enterprises of all kinds. During one such session, for instance, trainers work with students in simplifying corporate mission statements (a program that most of us in the heritage profession sorely need). In this class students write successive drafts of their

Figure 1 Walt and friend. 'I want Disneyland to be a happy place where parents and children can have fun together.'

corporate missions in ways that, dare I say, can be remembered and enthusiastically embraced by all staff. More often than not the participants at first draft lengthy and detailed descriptions of their business purposes only to be told by the Disney facilitator that they need to simplify them. During a recent session, and after several frustrating rewrites, a student finally looked-up and challenged the facilitator, 'OK, you tell me BRIEFLY what Disney provides.' The one word response was 'Happiness', A breathtakingly shortened summary of Walt's bronzed statement. And, with that, the student returned humbly to his work.

Unlike those of us in the heritage field, Disney has never been shy to use affective rather than cognitive terminology when stating its purpose. Words like 'happiness' and 'fun' are used freely for they are at the core of Disney's raison d'être; and, while these are not particularly our sole aims at heritage sites, they are close enough to our purpose as public servants to remind us that we could certainly use more emotive (and much less didactic) language in our mission statements and interpretations, especially since affective learning abounds at heritage sites.

PROMOTION

Not surprisingly, my research for this paper led me to a layover in Los Angeles last March. For, what would a piece on Disney be without at least one site visit to the Magic Kingdom. And, I ask, how can one speak authoritatively about a topic without first probing the psycho historical significance of the haunted Southern mansion, or without initially pondering the impact that the Mississippi riverboat ride has had upon our perceptions of regionalism in America?

So, during this all-important research phase, I registered at the Disneyland Hotel and established there my base of investigation. At the front desk I was informed by the young-and-not-surprisingly-attractive receptionist that they (Disney) would be opening the park at 6:30 a.m. the next day for the benefit of hotel guests who wished to experience the new Indiana Jones ride. I left the desk wondering. Did she say, 'just for the benefit of hotel guests', and, 'just tomorrow'? Whatever the specific wording, the inference was clear: Here was a special opportunity for me, and having now been personally invited, I would surely be taking advantage of it. The woman's simple 'pitch' was the obvious work of some behind-the-scenes 'hidden persuaders', but it nevertheless was very successful with me and indeed many other guests.

By early the next morning, I had seen the new Indiana Jones attraction advertised on not only 'Hotelovision' and The Disney Channel but also on two separate billboards during a morning's run. The park, it seemed, would be open 'especially' for everyone. Now, of course you will say, Disney spends millions on promotion each year, while we cannot afford such campaigns, but regardless of the extent of the marketing, my message is this: If we were to attempt to promote our sites as aggressively as we tend to research and interpret them, we would be much closer to the thoughts of more holidaymakers.

Yet, unfortunately, our field has been characterized by a long-standing distrust of promotion and marketing. The back halls of any historic site are

Figure 2 Kodak Picture Point No 10. Life on the Disneyssippi. Departing again at 1.00pm.

Figure 3 Dockside at Disneyland. Another place for history, myth and imagination to mingle.

testimony to the traditional hesitancy we have felt about hawking our wares. Look anywhere in the basements of most museums and historical societies throughout America and you will find a veritable archaeological dig of failed products: posters, books, mapguides and magazines. We heritage types research and design merchandise with an admirable alacrity, but when it comes time to market them, we are often ineffective and even dismissive in our attempts. One mid-western outdoor history museum actually ejected a promotional camera crew several years ago because the presence of modern equipment was too intrusive for the 'first person' interpretive staff. By contrast, Disney's promotion is so thoroughly aggressive that the park now stays open from 6:30 a.m. until midnight every day of the week. By the way, my research shows that if you wait until 7:00 a.m. to join the line at the Indiana Jones ride, you could easily wait for one hour before you board your jeep. Get there precisely at opening.

SERVICE

Despite our profession's nod to public service, the landscape of our field is littered with institutions held hostage to overly-protective curators who figuratively peer cautiously through curtains at visitors who knock upon our doors. Not long ago a curator at a major outdoor history museum recommended to me that we implant broken glass in the concrete (a la Oxford and Cambridge colleges) along the top of the fence surrounding the graveyard. The problem? People with an interest in the stones were actually getting into the yard and tramping down the grass. The story is reminiscent of the cartoon depicting a college professor looking out his window between terms at the empty campus below. He exclaims, 'This would be such a wonderful place if it weren't for the students.'

Happily, such antisocial behavior is more increasingly the exception to the rule, but our field has had a tradition of aloofness and conservatism from the beginning. Just look at the architecture of some of our great temples to the muses. Is it any wonder that visitors often preface their queries with, 'I know this is a silly/stupid question, but....' So, although we 'talk the talk' of public service, we often do not 'walk the walk'; and, even if we do pledge an allegiance to our public's fate, museums in particular still have an unfortunate legacy of elitism to overcome. One leader in our field said, 'Just mention the word 'museum' and you scatter people as quickly as a firehose.' This perceived (and comparative) lack of enthusiasm for public service is at least partially the cause for five years of declining attendance in the field.

Service, on the other hand, is a hallmark of Disney. At its various theme parks staff receive thorough training at the in-house 'Disney University', and here preparation in hospitality and courtesy features heavily in the curriculum. Public service staff are called 'cast', and at employee entrances to the parks there are mirrors reminding cast of the importance of looking presentable while 'on stage.' Rudeness to the visitor is here grounds for dismissal and is considered as serious an infraction as alcohol use or absenteeism. Consequently, Disney is recognized universally for the courtesy, enthusiasm and efficiency of its staff, a standard which (heritage sites aside) few institutions of any kind can match.

IMAGINATION

Yet, if there is one quality that stands out above all of the others it is Disney's ability to create an evocative setting and to kindle the public imagination, be it in film, on stage or in any one of its theme parks. Since the opening of Disneyland in the mid-fifties, millions of youths have been treated to and nurtured by this magic. Disneyland is replete with wonderfully whimsical (and sometimes quite accurate) recreations of settings from our past. Here a scaled down seaport dock and ship complete with an accurately carved figurehead; there a very fair recreation of a Mississippi riverboat plying its way past a very faithfully recreated and working gristmill; here an impressively recreated (but scaled down) frontier fort; and there a depiction of a bayou setting placed in such a magical half-light that it is impossible to tell whether you are outside in the late evening or actually inside.

In the early days of the Williamsburg restoration, John D. Rockefeller walked the city's streets in the twilight, claiming that it was his favorite time of the day. 'The ghosts are alive then,' he said. Disney has long-mastered the art of half-light and engaging scale in exhibits, and those of us in the museum and heritage fields could learn a lot from the creative zest that they have for evocative settings and scenes.

But, Disney is much more than its theme parks, and imagination kindling has been a characteristic of Disney from the start. For those kids who did not have the opportunity to venture to Disneyland, there was television and Sunday evening. For most of my friends it seemed that late Sunday was a somewhat sacred time when the family would gather together to watch Tinkerbell cast her spell over the weekly opening of Disney's 'Wonderful World of Color.' New stories would unfold before us, and some of them would be about our history and culture: Davey Crockett, Huck Finn, Daniel Boone or perhaps even life on the Oregon Trail (the ones I remember). Saccharin though they must have been, these tales nevertheless awakened an historical imagination in many American youth. And, though most likely filmed on the back lots of Burbank, many young viewers willingly suspended disbelief throughout the productions and consequently were soon left with a 'hankering' to visit the actual historical landscapes that Disney portrayed.

Remember, this was the golden age of American tourism, and if the plots were not encouraging enough, then even the commercials invited us to explore: 'See the USA in your Chevrolet/America is wanting you to call.' Many of us of that generation were soon off with our families to see the true pieces of the American historical cross, places like Williamsburg, Monticello, the Alamo, the Cumberland Gap, and the networks of great western trails. Ironically, like our 19th-century counterparts we, too, were now stimulated by wildly imaginative depictions of the West, only our particular messages were coming over the airwaves and not within the pages of exaggerative immigrant guides.

SEPARATING MYTH FROM REALITY

With our imaginations kindled, many of us ultimately followed our budding interest in history, and soon – through study and travel – we became more skilled at separating the myth from the reality, the romance from the fact. Yale historian, Edmund Morgan, said once that 'the historian's task is to simplify without oversimplifying and to bring to life the men and women who can speak across the ages to their human kin.' Although the stories had been grossly 'oversimplified', at the very least the historical 'introductions' were being made in imaginative ways; and the myriad facts of history we were fed by day were often wasted by evening when Disney began to serve-up some yarns. To my way of retrospective thinking, neither diet was a very healthy one, yet a blending of the two would have been welcomed back then.

History has been called the art of 'exact imagining.' Yet, in centers of formal and informal learning alike, history is most often taught with a much greater emphasis on the 'exact' than upon the imagination. Most historic sites and museums inundate their new interpreters with information about the site and its collections, but hardly a suggestion is ever made about how one might use these facts to weave an interpretation in such an artistic way as to surely ignite the imaginations of the guest.

Consequently, most visitors are themselves bludgeoned with information about highboys, lowboys, dates of buildings and techniques of restoration. A remarkably similar condition exists within the walls of colleges and universities which are supposedly in the business of teaching educators. So incessant is teaching of fact and theory in our academic history programs that the mere notion of intermingling the content with a little technique is frowned upon. It would be like teaching bedside manner in medical school. Besides, the objective is to pass the exams, not to kindle imaginations.

LISTENING TO WHOM?

This condition is further complicated by the fact that far too many of us in the heritage industry tend to listen to ourselves more than to our audiences. And why not? It's safer. Consequently, museum evaluation is more often discussed than it is used effectively. Furthermore, learning objectives for sites tend to be much too ambitious for both our's or our visitor's good, and they overlook the fact that most visitors are simply passing-through on vacation, not staying for a degree. In addition, we continue to teach by curriculum at historic sites and museums while totally overlooking the fact that learning in these settings is much more affective than cognitive in nature. That is, it is based more on moments, senses, sounds, and smells rather than upon fact and chronology.

It is what some call 'landmark' or 'anchor' learning when visitors pick and chose buildings or galleries in no particular order. We know that this is how our guests visit and learn, but we seldom build our teaching upon this observation. We are still more likely to give a talk or, as many call it, 'a spiel.' After a full day of program planning at one site, a colleague leaned over to me in his chair and said, 'Bill, a funny thing happens when you gather museum professionals in a room together for a whole day.' 'What', I asked. 'They start to believe one another', he said. A day of watching our guests is worth several in program planning sessions.

One individual who was an exceptional observer was Dr. Frank Oppenheimer, creator of the Exploratorium in San Francisco. Worried that children today were not asking the same questions about natural phenomena that he asked in his childhood, he endeavored to create a setting in which visitors could explore the concepts behind the natural world and begin to inquire for themselves. Exhibits here are successful only when they are heavily used, and those exhibits that are not engaging visitors are generally taken down and replaced immediately by more provocative ones. 'A museum is a woods of learning', Oppenheimer claimed. 'People come back again and again to such a place as the Exploratorium because their curiosity is awakened.' The exhibits here are continually changing and so are the people they serve. The Exploratorium is a place where the exactitude of science meets happily with the boundless energies of ones imagination.

Curiously, Frank Oppenheimer was not a professionally trained museum worker. In fact, enough such museums exist on the American and English landscapes to cause one to wonder whether or not a museum training course might, for some, be a liability. One other such example exists in Bend, Oregon. The High Desert Museum is the creation of Donald Kerr who simply wanted to create a place where the wonders of desert nature and history could be explored. Indoor exhibits here envelope the visitor in half-lit, imaginative settings depicting various times in Oregon history, while the outdoor exhibits create settings equally as provocative as any Disney has fabricated. The difference at the High Desert Museum is that a very credible research base underlies each exhibit.

In England, the Jorvik Viking Museum in York also presents history in a credible and imaginative way, attracting hundreds of thousands of visitors a year. Visitors sit back in moving chairs and explore an authentically recreated Viking settlement replete with the sounds and smells (some quite disgusting) that one would have encountered in such a setting. The entire recreation is based on thorough archaeological research, and the technique is so engaging that it has succeeded in attracting a remarkably democratic audience. Eager families stand alongside of mildly sceptical university dons, who follow skinheads as well as international guests into the historical ride. Upon entering the site, one is transported through a time tunnel which strives to place the Viking period in an understandable perspective. The entire production is built around the visitor's needs, and has been so hugely popular that various other sites have been established in Oxford and Canterbury where those cities' histories are depicted with similar techniques if not successes.

The techniques employed in the above sites are effective, time-tested and fully respectful of how people learn in a museum setting. They also bear no small resemblance to the successful methods that have long been employed at Disneyland: for example, they attempt to introduce people to people, they envelop the visitor in provocative (and often recreated) settings, and they present history in very imaginative ways fully exploiting the sights, sounds, and smells of the past rather than simply describing past events in a detached and passive manner like so many historical sites and museums do.

These sites, as well, do not attempt to teach a great deal to the visitor, but rather they attempt first to provoke an interest in the subject and assume that soon, with an increased curiosity, the visitor will either return to the site or take it upon himself to continue learning about the topics at other venues. Anatole France once said of teaching: 'Do not try to satisfy your own vanity by teaching a great many things. Awaken peoples curiosity. It is enough to open minds, do not overload them. Put there just a spark and if there is some good inflammable stuff it will catch fire.' The most successful heritage parks take this credo to heart; and, consequently, the most successful sites also have very high repeat visitation rates.

Surveys taken at Colonial Williamsburg in the 1980s have revealed that people who visit its historic area are quite likely to follow-up on this visit with any number of the following actions:

– increased participation in civic affairs;
– more reading of historical novels;
– attendance at historical plays and re-enactments.

In short, v ٢ .tors are stimulated to continue their interests and, in so doing, become more active and contributing citizens. Oppenheimer's aim was very similar. He hoped for future generations to become more curious about the world around them so that they would then be more actively engaged in solving the challenges of the nuclear age. His brother and he (along with thousands of other scientists) you may recall, created the atom bomb.

THE MUSEUM OF THE HOLOCAUST MEMORIAL

The Museum of the Holocaust Memorial in Washington, DC is certainly no Disneyland, but then it is not very much like any other museum, either. Largely the result of the interpretive genius of Elaine Heumann Gurian, its Associate Director upon opening, the Museum has had a very clear vision of its purpose from the start several years ago: To tell the story of the tragedy that was the Holocaust and to help ensure that such a tragedy never happens again. Its interpretations have been constructed firmly upon a thorough knowledge of audience and of history.

Exhibits are provocative and learning here is very affective indeed. It is not unusual to hear crying in the galleries as we are introduced to the people we so easily could have been. In fact, upon entering, visitors are given a card which introduces a victim of the holocaust. In time we learn the fate of that person, but in the meantime we are accompanied by them through the exhibits, through that indescribable history of the holocaust.

Finally, we find ourselves in a room of portraits. It seems almost like a room that Alice might have found herself in while pursuing the white rabbit, except there is not a bit of fantasy here. Face to face we stand staring up at legions of Jews who lost their lives. 'To simplify without oversimplifying, and, to bring to life the men and women who can speak across the ages to their human kin.' The room is the embodiment of this notion.

Figure 4 The Holocaust Memorial Museum. Solemn and haunting introductions to our human kin across the ages.

THE GENE AUTRY WESTERN HERITAGE MUSEUM

The Gene Autry Western Heritage Museum in Griffith Park, Los Angeles, is another fairly new initiative (1988) that also attempts to interpret values in very affective ways. Its Chief Executive Officer and Director, Joanne Hale, was not a trained museum worker when she assumed her position; and, once again, her remarkable success suggests that such preparation may not for some be either necessary or advised.

Had she come from a traditional museum background, perhaps she may not have had the freedom of thought needed to create such an engaging institution. Perhaps she would have known better than to have engaged the talents of Van Romans and the Disney Imagineers when planning the museum and its exhibits. Yet, together, Disney and the museum staff developed programs that realized Gene Autry's clear vision of 'combining scholarship and showmanship' within one institution. The results are very impressive and deserving of the attention of museum professionals everywhere.

Exhibits, based upon solid research, present not only facts about the West but also strive as well to recognize and define a 'spirit' of the West. In each gallery and throughout the entire institution's programs and services, the needs of visitors are clearly put first whether they be in the gift shop, restaurant, education facility or among the engaging interactive exhibitry.

Yet, this success did not come easily. Both Ms Hale and Mr Romans recite fascinating tales of the myriad tensions that mount when one places Disney Imagineers in the same room with museum professionals for extended periods of time, but each person quickly agrees that the results have been well worth the 'creative tension' that inevitably accompanies such combined planning.

Gene Autry, Van Romans, Joanne Hale and the staff at the museum deserve great credit for having 'bucked' the common dismissiveness that comes along with the idea of combining Disney with history. By the way, the museum has just opened an exhibit which explores 'Walt Disney's West', the American West as portrayed by Disney.

THE MUSEUM OF NEW ZEALAND TE PAPA TONGAREWA

Finally, the small island country of New Zealand is currently engaged in a bold and creative experiment that will marry these bests of both worlds. The Museum of New Zealand Te Papa Tongarewa, is an extensive initiative that will open in February of 1998 on the waterfront of Wellington, the country's capital. Now nearly complete, the building will contain vast exhibit spaces and engage the talents of more than 200 staff. A truly bicultural museum in both interpretation and administration, it will interpret the natural history of New Zealand as well as the history and culture of the indigenous Maori and the immigrant Pakeha (or European) population. The Museum will be a 'Waharoa', or gateway, for the discussion of national identity, and the exhibits will be highly imaginative, interactive and engaging.

You see, Van Romans and the Imagineers have been here, as well. Interestingly, the interpretive planning effort is here again facilitated by the

Holocaust Memorial's Elaine Heumann Gurian, and as a consequence learning here will be very affective in nature. Learning objectives commonly contain words of emotion as well as thought, and exhibits will not only inform but incite feelings of 'pride', 'frustration', 'awe', etc. Extensive audience surveying has informed the exhibit and program designers; and every effort of the new museum is intent on being customer focused. Towards this end, promotional efforts are very closely tied to national tourism efforts. A smart alliance, for tourism in New Zealand has increased by 15% in the past year and has more than doubled in the past decade.

CONCLUSIONS

It has been my modest hope that this paper will encourage us in the heritage profession to look beyond the aspersion that is commonly assumed when one mentions that our sites are becoming like Disneylands. I hope, too, that this essay has served as a reminder that there is an awful danger in listening more to ourselves than to our publics or to those agencies which have been more successful than us at attracting the attention of the visitor's discretionary time. A continued protectiveness of our so called professional values (read, snobbery) can ultimately be harmful to our health.

Early in his career, Walt Disney visited Colonial Williamsburg, the restored capital city of Colonial Virginia. It is thought by many that, as he sat in the midst of this extensive restoration of 500 buildings and 170 acres, he first began to develop the notion of creating a theme park which, unlike a circus, would stay in one place and not need to move from town to town. Look what a little observation and listening on his part led to. A little more professional open-mindedness, coupled with a lot of watching and listening can lead us into new and exciting directions, as well. Imagine if we were to mix the vision, the promotion, the public service and the imagination of Disney with the integrity that characterizes the work we do. Imagine how the public could benefit.

The Author

Dr William Tramposch is now Director of Museum Resources at the Museum of New Zealand Te Papa Tongarewa. He was formerly President, New York State Historical Association, Executive Director of the Oregon Historical Society, and a director at The Colonial Williamsburg Foundation in Virginia and Old Sturbridge Village in Massachusetts. He has served as Vice Chair of the US National Committee for the International Council of Museums and held two Fulbright Fellowships to New Zealand. His specific interests are in professional training and the educational role of museums and historical societies.

References

Alexander, E. P., *Museums in Motion: An Introduction to the History and Functions of Museums*, American Association for State and Local History, 1979

Grinder, A. I., and McCoy, E. S., *The Good Guide: A Sourcebook for Interpreters*, Ironwood Press, 1985

Loomis, R. J., *Museum Visitor Evaluation*, American Association for State and Local History, 1987

Tilden, F., *Interpreting Our Heritage*, The University of North Carolina Press, 1957

Figure 5 The Gene Autry Western Heritage Museum. What can happen when Disney and determined museum visionaries meet.

Figure 6 The Museum of New Zealand Te Papa Tongarewa. A state of the art gateway for cultural awareness in Wellington. Is it a museum or a national journey?

4

SUSTAINING CULTURAL IDENTITIES
Community Arts in the United States

Lynne Williamson

There is a growing regard for the conceptual and practical knowledge that continues to emerge from indigenous communities. Although under tremendous pressure, indigenous peoples increasingly represent themselves, their communities, and their cultures in national and international events. In a whole range of expressive arts, native peoples share diverse and profound world views.

Jose Barreiro

Traditional Native Americans see an essential relationship between humans and the objects they create. A pot is not just a pot. In our community, the pots we create are seen as vital, breathing entities that must be respected as all other living beings. Respect of all life elements – rocks, trees, clay – is necessary because we understand our inseparable relationship with every part of our world ...

My understanding of relationships has been hard to reconcile with the non-tribal view. Consider museums. Human remains and cultural items are treated as non-living entities. Unacknowledged are the enduring relationships that traditional Native Americans maintain with their ancestors and their world.

I have come to realize that the staffs of most museums and agencies do not share our basic values and philosophic views. Museums certainly have had a great impact on traditional Native Americans and our perceptions of who we are. But we do not share the assumptions underlying what museums do: collection, preservation, documentation, and exhibition.

Tessie Naranjo

Strongly held beliefs such as these expressed by Santa Clara Pueblo member and cultural preservation program officer Tessie Naranjo have led, after many years of quiet persistence, to important changes in the way cultural programming is done throughout the United States. Native communities as well as many ethnic groups based in America are developing their own projects to present their cultures to public audiences. Tourism and economic development are important components of community projects. However, the key goals are more likely to be public education, authenticity of presentation, and service to the community.

Cultural activities in the States these days tend to happen in two different, sometimes mutually exclusive arenas – institutions and communities. As the demographics of America shift to reflect substantial increases in population numbers of immigrants and people of color, cultural institutions must change their programming to attract these new audiences or risk becoming irrelevant and uninviting to them. The changes are slow to take place in organizations such as museums, concert halls, theatres, and most funding agencies.

This paper deals with a selection of places where new ideas for presenting culture to public audiences are taking shape, providing examples of culturally grounded activities which also include a tourism or economic development component. These examples are intended to illustrate the strengths inherent in a community-based approach to public arts projects, as well as the richer cultural understandings which arise from direct contact with members of communities or ethnic groups who encourage others to experience their cultures through participation and education.

The upsurge in community-driven cultural presentations has been powered by several forces. Members of ethnic groups are eager to bring to public attention activities that have been happening within their communities naturally for a long time. It is important to realize that ethnic traditions in the Americas are not currently in 'revival'; rather, they are continuing to be observed by the communities themselves who have long known and practiced shared expressions of their cultural identity. The term 'revival' suggests that an aspect of cultural identity has died and been resurrected, and this is very often not the case here, even with Native American traditions or languages which may have been underground for a long time. Some art forms have been revived, to be sure, but the traditions themselves have survived (despite the odds), have been passed down rather than revived, and they are now thriving on their own within the communities.

A major reason cited by community groups for producing their own projects is the desire to retain control over the way their cultures are presented. They are not willing to negotiate the methods and models of interpretation to fit expected requirements or existing norms. Another objective important to these groups is to give audiences a real (as opposed to virtual) experience, a chance for the public to meet members of the culture in a more natural, informal, and actual life setting. 'Indian artists are the authentic translators of our cultural experience' (W. Richard West Jr. in *Native Peoples*, Winter 1995, p. 49).

Community arts aim to preserve cultural practices at the same time as encouraging new creative expressions to develop organically out of these traditions. The apparent disjuncture between 'old ways' and innovations can be uncomfortable for those who retain stereotypical images or expectations of a cultural group, and it is true that such dissonances can be challenging to present. Interpretation provides the key here, with the people whose lives are both represented and affected giving the information from their inside perspective. A history of distrust, disappointment, and at the very least common misinformation is why groups are taking charge themselves as they work to foster economic development through sensitive tourism and/or cultural programming.

A few federal and private grantmakers in the US are joining community efforts to improve cultural presentations. The Folk and Traditional Arts Program of the National Endowment for the Arts has sponsored many projects, 'homegrown traditional artistic activities' of practitioners 'learning the repertoire from their seniors and absorbing the style as they live the life that the style and repertoire represent.' (Program Prospectus 1995/96) The Fund For Folk Culture, a branch of the largest private charitable foundation in the US, is an innovative funding initiative with a huge impact on the field as it encourages projects involving careful preservation of authenticity and participation of community members in planning and implementation of projects.

The examples which follow speak volumes about local communities who already understand their heritage very well, who are beginning to 'market' their distinctive cultural qualities carefully and successfully, and who have lessons for those who would like to join them. Given the size of the United States, the number of cultural activities, and the wide range of groups and cultures represented here, I can only provide a few carefully chosen illustrations of new and exciting initiatives coming from the community level. Seven projects will be considered: five have been generated by specific communities, three of them Native American; another comes from a rural setting and the last from the streets of New York City. I conclude with a description of two important Indian organizations which are nationwide in scope.

THE MAINE INDIAN BASKETMAKERS ALLIANCE

This is an intertribal organization recently formed to coordinate information, improve communication through meetings and a newsletter, promote the basketmakers' work through exhibits and marketing, and advocate for better ecological conditions in polluted areas. It is truly a community-driven effort, linking the four native groups in Maine (and Nova Scotia) in an exemplary cultural preservation and economic development initiative.

Ash splint basketmaking is a longstanding native tradition throughout the northeastern woodlands. Archaeological evidence clearly indicates the existence of both twined and plaited fiber basketry dating in the latter case to 2 – 3000 years BC. The useful art of basketmaking has survived well in Maine partly because the tourist market has been especially strong here and Maine has been a magnet for vacationers since the early 19th century. The native groups of the Wabanaki Confederacy – the Penobscot, Passamaquoddy, Malecite, and MicMac of Maine and Nova Scotia – all make baskets in the traditional way. This method begins with the location and cutting of a straight young brown ash tree (*Fraxinus nigra*). After soaking, the tree section is vigorously pounded to separate the tree rings into strips which are then pulled apart, planed to a suitable thinness, then cut into differing widths. The resulting splints are then woven into baskets sometimes formed around wooden molds. In the late 19th century Victorian tastes led Indian basket artists to experiment with different forms and embellishments, such as intricate finger-twisted curls. Many basketmakers thread fragrant braided sweetgrass through the splints, creating objects of both visual and sensual beauty.

The basketmaking tradition, along with stories, songs, and knowledge of trees and grasses associated with it, has been continuously practiced in all Maine Indian groups. However, growing ecological concerns along with the loss of some key elder teachers of the tradition led Penobscot basketmakers, working in collaboration with the traditional art program of the Maine Arts Council, to establish the Maine Indian Basketmakers Alliance with tribal and federal grant support. Membership, currently about 120, includes 80 active native basketmakers. The newsletter, reaching over 250 people, is very valuable for sharing information among the far-flung communities. Recognition of the strength of basketmaking and the artistry of its practitioners has come from, among others, the National Endowment for the Arts which awarded a National Heritage Fellowship to 85-year old basketmaker Mary Gabriel last year.

As well as preserving basketmaking traditions and teaching them to a new generation, the Maine Indian Basketmakers Alliance is involved in two other related initiatives. The Brown Ash Task Force links MIBA with the Maine Forest Service and other native basketmaking projects in the northeast to understand and counter the serious threat to the trees from pollution. One model program conducted by a Mohawk scientist in New York State collects *Fraxinus nigra* seeds, plants them in a controlled nursery environment, then replants and monitors seedlings in the field. As Director of MIBA, Penobscot Tribal Geologist and basketmaker, Theresa Hoffman, can translate the science into cultural and artistic terms.

Marketing has always been part of Maine Indian basketmaking, and the Alliance has developed a successful program to promote the baskets to tourists and collectors. As a result of collaboration with the Maine Office of Tourism and the Maine Arts Commission, a case displaying a variety of baskets has been installed in the lobby of the International Airport in Bangor, Maine, along with the MIBA address card. Buyer interest generated by this exhibit has been so great that MIBA will produce a directory of basketmakers and their products so that tourists and buyers can contact artists directly. Theresa believes that direct contact between purchaser and basketmaker is essential to allow individual artists to speak for themselves and make their own terms. Not all basketmakers want to produce for the market; some can produce only at certain times of year, for instance the MicMac, who spend considerable time in traditional food gathering. Some will want to adjust their prices depending on the buyer. MIBA will soon hire a marketing consultant to explore various options such as developing a mail order business, retail outlets, or a basketmakers' cooperative.

Education and public presentation are also central to the Alliance's activities. Several basketmakers have taught their skills to other tribal members through the Maine Arts Commission's Traditional Arts Apprenticeship Program. Each year one of the Wabanaki Confederacy reservations hosts a Gathering during which MIBA offers workshops on different aspects of the craft. Several collaborative exhibits have been produced in Bar Harbor by the Abbé Museum and MIBA, along with an annual Wabanaki Festival open to the public in this busy tourist town. At the 1994 Festival master basketmakers demonstrated all aspects of the process, while about twenty basketmakers, including Indian visitors from California and New York, set up tables to exhibit and sell their work. This was an enjoyable, informal opportunity for visitors see first hand the quality and variety of Wabanaki basketry, to learn about the traditions and ecology underlying the art, and to talk at length to the basketmakers and tribal members.

NORTHERN PLAINS TRIBAL ARTS

In Sioux Falls South Dakota, is a department of American Indian Services, a native-run non-profit agency providing both economic development and child and family services for members of nine tribal groups in the Plains region of America and Canada. Northern Plains Tribal Arts began in 1986 with a research project conducted by Director Rae Burnette, Rosebud Sioux, to understand what art forms were being produced on local reservations. Discovering that many people were making a number of utilitarian arts and crafts, such as beaded key rings or cigarette lighters to sell or barter for essential goods (food, diapers, fuel), Rae developed Northern Plains Tribal Arts to serve as an economic development tool. Governed by a forty-two member advisory council comprised of respected tribal cultural leaders, artists, art professors, and lay people, NPTA operates two special programs: the annual arts show and market and The Northern Plains Gallery in Sioux Falls. The primary focus of NPTA activities is to generate income for tribal artists through the sale of their art.

What separates NPTA from other markets of native art is its firm commitment to exhibiting and selling high quality work which is authentic – that is, truly made by Plains Indian artists whose creativity expresses the realities of their lives. This commitment, guided by the strong involvement of the advisory council which approves all entries for the market, does two things: artists producing work for the market are encouraged to be creative while honoring quality in production, and public audiences have a chance to see, learn from, and buy art which is free from stereotype and commercialism. W. Richard West Jr., Director of the National Museum of the American Indian, describes a key goal of contemporary native cultural organizations as 'To challenge artists to produce images reflective of Indian culture today' (personal communication, Rae Burnette to the author).

In the same way, Rae Burnette's exhibitions at the Tribal Arts Gallery illustrate important but often unexamined historical and contemporary trends which have had an impact on native lives. Recently she organized a gallery show around the theme of boarding schools, asking artists to address this painful time during the late 19th – early 20th century when many Indian children were taken from their reservation homes and placed in distant schools where they were not allowed to speak their languages or show any evidence of their cultures. An entire generation, today's elders, was deeply affected by the boarding schools and the resulting loss of many traditions. Tackling this difficult subject, expressing it through art, can be both instructive and healing.

Although public audiences are invited to both the Market and the Gallery, NPTA does not target South Dakota's considerable tourist population, at least some of whom will have 'Dances With Wolves-influenced' romantic notions of Plains Indians living in times past. In the same way that concessions are not made in order to have the market meet preconceived or stereotypical ideas of Indian art, NPTA is firm about reaching out primarily to those who are serious in their appreciation of quality art. This approach is clearly successful: to date, NPTA activities have enabled at least 100 artisans to increase their income by 1.2 million dollars.

AK-CHIN HIM-DAK ECOMUSEUM

As a collaboration of the Akimel and Tohono O'odham (formerly called Pima and Papago) people, this museum aims to 'not only connect with the past, present, and future, but also incorporate the social and psychological changes within the community… it is a vehicle and a tool used by the community to inform the general public, non-Indians, and other cultures and nations about the spirit and evolution of our community' (tribal member Charles Carlyle in *Museums and Communities*, p. 344). Although the concept of the ecomuseum has a distinguished history in Europe and at least one example in Canada, it has not been embraced in the US The first ecomuseum here, Ak-Chin Him-Dak was generated by a variety of events and ideas flowing together in the 1980's.

A small (532 members at present) but independent group living at the northern edge of the Sonoran desert in Arizona, the Ak-Chin won a battle to preserve the water rights so necessary for supporting their successful agriculture business. Before irrigation building could proceed, archaeological excavation revealed remarkable evidence of thousands of years of occupation by Ak-Chin ancestors. There was a clear need to establish some kind of museum to house the uncovered artifacts, but a more potent inspiration for community members was the profound awareness of their deep cultural identity. 'For example, the discovery of pieces of shell jewelry seemed to confirm the the Ak-Chin ancestors had taken part in commercial exchanges with distant places. Such findings bolstered tribal oral histories that described long treks to Baja California to get salt' (Nancy Fuller in *Museums and Communities*, p. 346).

The process of deciding how best to conserve and present their heritage, then developing and planning the project, reflected all the difficulties and triumphs imaginable for any group of individuals trying to reach consensus. From 1987 to the opening of the Him-Dak Center in 1991, community members held many open meetings to debate and design the kind of institution which would best serve them. With input from the Smithsonian Institution's Native American Museum Program, the Ak-Chin decided to adopt the ecomuseum model because it directly related to the centrality of ecological issues in their culture. 'Native communities share with ecomuseums the concept of collective memory as the cultural wealth of the community as well as the idea that community members are the conservators of a collection that need not be housed in a museum' (Carla Roberts in *Native American Expressive Cultures*, p. 28).

For many Ak-Chin members the development of the project has brought new skills and knowledge as they learn how to manage an ambitious cultural institution which is completely integrated into other aspects of community life and operates 'in a manner consistent with community lifestyle' (Ak-Chin Him-Dak publicity materials). For instance, a new program organized by museum staff will interview elders to record their language skills and oral histories, using their information and teaching methods to develop Ak-Chin language curricula for both children and adults. Also, community members with knowldege of plant use for tools, medicines, and foods will build and tend a traditional home with adjacent garden. The visitor experience at Ak-Chin Him-Dak includes a tour to the community farm, the Catholic Church, and the pre-school Headstart Program – all essential functions of the community.

This project, still evolving, has been difficult but transformative for the Ak-Chin community, whose members have solved many problems first hand and in the process have become more cohesive and clear about their future goals. 'The ecomuseum concept is a different, modern method that can be used with our traditional way of life, which has been escaping our community slowly... To know that our community as a whole will be responsible for taking care of our museum, for designing and interpreting the meaning of our culture, instills pride within the community' (Elaine Boehm, tribal member, in *Museums and Communities*, p. 341).

VESTERHEIM NORWEGIAN-AMERICAN MUSEUM

In honor of Professor Fladmark and other Norwegians reading this paper, I offer information on Vesterheim, the Norwegian-American Museum located in rural Decorah, Iowa, an American heartland region largely settled by Scandinavians. Established in 1877, Vesterheim represents the oldest museum and most comprehensive collection created by an immigrant group in America. Its founders not only sought to preserve the old country artifacts and traditions brought with them, but also wanted to collect, study, and interpret the materials created in their new home. Their mission, continuing at Vesterheim today, has been to focus on the adaptations and traditions within Norwegian-American culture, and more broadly to serve as a window into the immigrant experience so vital in shaping the character of America.

Vesterheim has public programming, research, preservation, and education components, supported by a membership of over 8,000 – more impressive perhaps than its 22,000 annual visitation and ample evidence of the affection and commitment of this ethnic community. Its buildings include a museum and open-air division with 19th century dwellings, outbuildings, a church, and a mill from Valdres, all of which occupy most of a block in Decorah, with a farmstead and church on their original sites outside the town. Collections include clothing and textiles, tools, farm implements, house furnishings, fine and decorative arts, even ships. Resource materials such as archival photographs, documents, books, oral histories, slides, and audio visual materials are augmented by family records in the Geneological Center and Naeseth Library. Taken altogether, Vesterheim portrays a very full picture of Norwegian-American life, its origins, experiences, and adaptations right up to the present.

In addition to its on-site exhibits, Vesterheim mounts numerous workshops and classes in its 'Handverk Skole', as well as language classes, tours and school programs. Quarterly newsletters are published on geneology, 'rosemaling', and woodworking. There are four major annual events – 'Velkommen', Nordic Fest, Scandinavian Food Fest, and Norwegian

Christmas, which is notable for its continuing celebration of 'Julebukk', a mumming tradition no longer practiced in Norway.

Vesterheim's strengths lie in its ability to keep itself interested in and relevant to contemporary expressions of enduring Norwegian-American cultural traditions. The craft and language classes are always full, the Scandinavian community as well as many others turn out en masse for the Nordic Fest in July, and the museum's traveling exhibits on immigrant experiences are booked all over the US Vesterheim's future plans highlight educational outreach programs and a collaboration with its counterpart in Hamar, Norway on an exhibit of expressions of ethnicity in the home. I have seen first hand how true such 'contemporary traditions' are in real life: Eldrid Arntzen, a master 'rosemaler' and trustee of Vesterheim, lives near me in Connecticut. Her home is full of her beautiful work, much of it in use rather than merely on display, with the sounds of Norwegian language and Eldrid's Hardanger fiddle echoing around the house as well.

TATS CRU AND THE NEW YORK MEMORIAL WALL ARTISTS

TATS Cru and other New York memorial wall artists represent a uniquely urban artistic phenomenon arising out of both shared religious tradition and grim contemporary reality. Using cans of spray paint they create huge murals on the walls of inner city buildings or playgrounds to commemorate men and women, usually young, who have died at that place, often as a result of violence. Artistic and cultural antecedents are clearly Latino, as are most of the artists.

Artists such as TATS Cru (which stands for Top Artistic TalentS; 'crew' is the preferred street term for a gang) are commissioned by relatives of the deceased, who dictate how the person is to be depicted and which symbols express most clearly his or her personality, history, and interests. Usually the walls contain the deceased's portrait carefully rendered from photographs (with occasional revisions from relatives), painted alongside favorite objects such as cars, jewelry, Bud Lite or basketballs; symbols of death (skulls, gravestones, the eight-ball from the game of pool) or life after death (the 'sagrado corazon'); insignia of membership, perhaps the flag of Puerto Rico or in one case a Police Department badge. Lettering, giving the person's name and perhaps a poem or anti-violence message, is a major component of the artform, belying its origins in the urban graffiti movement of the 80's.

Wall painting takes place in public as a community activity, with an appreciative crowd offering suggestions to the artists while they work. The murals become the setting for shrines to the deceased, as relatives and friends set up candles, flowers, or food, and make regular visits to the site. Sometimes celebrations are held there on anniversaries or at the honoree's request. In at least one case musicians composed 'plena', traditional Puerto Rican songs of mourning or memory.

Unfortunately, the creation of public memorials to people dying in the inner cities has become a growth industry. TATS Cru members are professionals, making part of their living with their artistic skills. But they do not see this as morbid, instead they are pleased that they can reach out to their community with public art and at the same time feed their families and pay bills. They have also developed successful design and graphic arts businesses, landing a major deal with Coca Cola to paint walls around the City with images from student art work (and of course Coca Cola's logo). Later this summer they will be featured as part of a CBS television show. I have had the opportunity to hear these young men describe their work and its inspirations in urban realities. I can tell you that they are excellent ambassadors and translators from a world alien to most of us. We need to learn more about their world, involving them in our projects in substantial ways because they know how to reach and teach their communities. Beyond that, we need to become involved in their projects so we can help to change the situations they must deal with every day.

Artists, especially those from less-privileged parts of American society, often need support and technical assistance to give them training and access to gallery and marketing opportunities. In turning now to describe two nationwide initiatives organized by Native Americans to provide resources and reach wide public audiences, I wish to point out that their work spans and links communities throughout the entire United States, using interactive technology in the service of traditional communities.

ATLATL

Atlatl is an arts service network based in Phoenix, Arizona. Its mission is to promote the vitality of contemporary Native American art through information exchanges between artists and arts organizations, by increasing economic development and exhibition opportunities for native artists, and by encouraging new audiences to understand and appreciate indigenous aesthetics and modes of expression (Atlatl Prospectus 1995). It is governed by the predominately native First Circle Board of Directors, with the Second Circle Board of all-Indian artists from around the country acting as information transmitters from their regions.

Atlatl offers down-to-earth referral services, marketing workshops, and exhibition programs with both educational and financial benefit, as well as the growing Native Arts Network computer bulletin board. Atlatl's public resource materials include its quarterly publication *Native Arts Update*, catalogues of its exhibitions, special reports on native art issues, videotape productions and slide libraries of work by Indian artists.

Organizations such as Atlatl affect the dynamics of the established art and culture world by giving voice and tools to indigenous artists and culture bearers often ignored or shut out of the process. One important effect of this process has been to bring forward information and wisdom from these artists as culture bearers long valued in their societies but unknown to others. Everyone benefits in some way from expanding the conversation.

THE NATIONAL MUSEUM OF THE AMERICAN INDIAN

The National Museum of the American Indian, established by an Act of Congress in 1989 as the fifteenth museum of the Smithsonian Institution, is making progress towards its ambitious goal of forming a new type of museum. NMAI will actually be four museums, four very different components in three facilities as well as cyberspace. The planning process for all aspects of NMAI is being done in a unique and inclusive way over several years. Meetings were convened in different areas throughout America, with many native cultural leaders from each region participating in discussions of dreams and possibilities for the new project. Their visions, the needs they expressed on behalf of their communities, the requirements of honoring the incredibly diverse traditions represented in all of Native America, were taken very seriously in developing plans.

The first museum has recently opened in New York with an inaugural exhibitions series in the George Gustav Heye Center. In 1997 Heye's vast collection, now stored in a Bronx warehouse, will be moved to a state-of-the-art cultural resources facility in Suitland, Maryland where storage, conservation, exhibition construction, and public access to collections will be housed.

The NMAI approach to its mission can be seen in this statement from Director Rick West: 'Our very special collection requires not only the protection provided by conservation techniques, but also the deep respect which we show by caring for our treasures in a culturally appropriate manner' (*Native Peoples*, Spring 1994, p. 66). For instance, some sensitive spiritual objects will be off-limits to researchers, while special rooms will be used by tribal leaders to care for these pieces. Most visitors will go to the main museum to be built on the Mall near the Capitol in Washington DC, where exhibits will be installed and public programming presented.

'The Fourth Museum' represents the most radical departure from standard museum concepts. It is an outreach initiative which will link museum resources with individuals and organizations anywhere, potentially, through interactive technology and media. The desire of distant tribal members to participate in NMAI activities, and NMAI's commitment to serve and involve all those who embody native cultural traditions, led to this development. One idea of the fourth museum in practice could be enabling a researcher in the collections to use a satellite video link-up to talk to a tribal elder about traditions relating to that collection, learning first hand from a culture bearer who might be thousands of miles away. 'Restoring and reinvigorating dialogue between Indian and non-Indian people' is one of NMAI's most cherished goals (Rick West in *Native Peoples*, Fall 1994, p. 26).

CONCLUSION

It is hoped that the illustrations offered above will provide some insights on ways to develop community arts projects which both generate income and honor the character of the culture represented. From Vesterheim's ability to maintain a cultural institution able to change and adapt while continuing to serve its Norwegian-American constituents for decades, to the energy of TATS Cru bursting onto the scene to create a focus for community healing through art, the diversity of American society is a positive force for social change and social service.

And from newcomer groups to America's first people, themselves extremely diverse in cultures, the 'products' created and more importantly the processes of collaboration used to create them can inspire others. One characteristic seen in each of these projects is the congruence or synchronicity of tradition and modernity. It is my contention that this is how people really live, not mired in the past, not dressed in ceremonial costumes on ordinary days, not passive receptors of natural forces, but as with the Ak-Chin, actively meeting everyday challenges with new solutions supported by traditional values. The most informative and accurate heritage tourism projects will reflect a group's ability to change over time, and will adopt its careful, sensitive, inclusive processes of dealing with contemporary realities.

Those of us responsible for developing heritage policy can tap into new sources of creativity by working intensively with members of the groups whose cultures we claim to promote. Collaborations between community groups and tourism agencies or organizations such as museums and culture presenters can be powerful forces for mutual benefit if these collaborations take the form of full participation and decision-making by all parties, not just a one-way flow of information (or money), or a top-down approach which merely uses local color to expand the coffers of a tourism promoter.

In describing how collaborative promotion and marketing of cultural tourism can proceed in the best way, my opposite number in Tennessee, Roby Cogswell, urges '... a process that combines research and development with public relations, involving the community in the planning and remaining accountable to it, encouraging local self-discovery and pride, and building in incentives for a broad coalition of local interests. Why is this process so important? Because the heritage or way of life defining the tourism draw is, in a real sense, a community property, and because public consensus, especially in smaller scale or rural contexts, can make or break the entire venture' (in Wells, ed., *Preserving and Promoting Cultural Resources*, pp. 4–5).

The Author

Lynne Williamson, formerly of the Native American Center for the Living Arts, she now directs the Connecticut Cultural Heritage Arts Program at the Institute for Community Research where her work involves museum practice, community-based oral history and arts projects.

References

Akwe:kon Journal, Akwe:kon Press, Cornell University (encompassing *Northeast Indian Quarterly*)

Baron, R. and Spitzer, N., *Public Folklore*, Smithsonian Institution Press, 1992

Cooper, M. and Sciorra, J., *R.I.P.: Memorial Wall Art*, Henry Holt, 1994

Fuller, N., *The museum as a vehicle for community empowerment: the Ak-Chin Indian community ecomuseum project*, in Karp, Kreamer, and Lavine, (eds), *Museums and Communities*, Smithsonian Institution Press, 1993

Native American Expressive Culture, Akwe:kon Press and National Museum of the American Indian, 1995

Wells, P. A., (ed) *Preserving and Promoting Cultural Resources. Tennessee's Business*, Vol 6, No 1, Middle Tennessee State University, 1995

Figure 1 Maine Indian Basketry Exhibit at Bangor, ME International Airport. Courtesy of Maine Indian Basketmakers Alliance.

Figure 2 Beginners at a basketmaking workshop lead by Mary Sanipass (Micmac) on Indian Island, ME.

Figure 3 Work by TATS Cru – the phenomenon of the memorial wall artists arises out of both religious tradition and grim contemporary urban reality. Photo: Martha Cooper

5

WHY THE ARTS MATTER

Lord Gowrie

It seems to be my fate to talk and write about art, whose value is in the end itself – and about money, whose value is only in relation to something else. When I was Chairman of Sotheby's, I used to be asked quite often to address seminars and conferences of investment bankers and fund managers about works of art as things worth buying in terms of monetary value and the ability of that value to grow. Now that I am Chairman of the Arts Council of England, Scottish readers will be glad to know that my remit does not run north of the Border. Scotland is quite safe from my attentions, as I can do nothing whatsoever to ameliorate its cultural condition, not that it needs the slightest improvement.

As Chairman of the Arts Council, I am now quite often asked to talk about money and the arts: the poverty of one in relation to the richness of the other. Although the Arts Council is at arm's length from Government, it is nevertheless an arm of Government. It hands over to arts organisations, overwhelmingly to the performing arts, funds Parliament allocates for their encouragement and support.

In England, the amount allocated in 1994 was £186 million and this sum should be seen in the context of public spending in the United Kingdom as a whole. This stood then at a little over two hundred thousand million, and the Chancellor is quite rightly seeking to reduce it, because borrowing and spending by Government is necessarily at the expense of borrowing and spending by individuals and corporations. The arts slice is small, therefore, both in absolute terms (less than one half of one per cent) and in terms of the contribution made by the arts and entertainment industries to the Chancellor's well-being. They are our third or fourth contributors of foreign exchange; they are labour intensive; and they raise a lot of direct and value added tax.

In order that this seedcorn investment of less than £200 million nourishes a multi-billion pound arts and entertainment industry, it is reasonable for the world of the arts to look to the Arts Council not only to make comprehensible, if not always comfortable decisions about who gets the money, but also to lobby and campaign for more money. That is for sufficient money, at very least, to ensure that arts companies, large and small, whose staff never expect to be rich and who are used to their own careers subsidising the arts through insecure jobs at below professional rates of pay, can survive, can plan, can extend their range and win new audiences. You will not be surprised, therefore, that it is frequently my fate to talk about art and money. However, here I am looking towards wider horizons.

I want to discuss ways in which we might start thinking about the contribution of the arts to the national economy, not least to tourism, as the arts are after all substantial earners of foreign exchange. The word 'economy' comes from the Greek word for a 'household'. It is a more inspiring and more resonant word than 'money'. It suggests a family and a community; it suggests a building and something which you can adorn; it suggests housekeeping and money again, to be sure, but money earned and spent for humane purposes. Put enough households together, indeed, lubricate them with money and you get a city, a nation, or even a civilisation.

As a species we are unique, so far as we know, in being able to predict our own demise as individuals. If you are of a theological bent, you might ascribe to this both our fallen condition and our proclivity for doing great harm; our high expertise; our capacity for achievements; and our sense of striving. Even if you are not so minded, you are likely to recognise that we are also unique in being able to create a network of ideas and artefacts which survives us. That is what civilisation means. When we talk, as we must, about housekeeping any money, about individual needs and aspirations, and how to fulfil and pay for them, we must never forget that building a civilisation is something we are forced and programmed to do. Art is an extension of that imperative and that conditioning.

Travel broadens the mind and lightens the wallet. Tourism is a key component of our economy. It is thought to account for nearly five per cent of our gross domestic product. That translates into a figure of nearly £30 billion annually. There is potential for growth too, and that growth could be more widely dispensed than in any other comparable economic activity. Conservatively, I would estimate it translates into work for about one and a half million people, more than the construction industry or (even) the health service. The Department for National Heritage estimates that in 1992, 16 million overseas visitors came to Britain. They need things to see and do, and they need looking after.

Why do they come? It has to do with our civilisation. Even lovers of nature and the countryside are looking at man-made artefacts. Ours is an old and settled civilisation, yet it has never been inward looking, it was always mercantile and sea-faring. The City of London is the biggest financial centre in the world. Its services travel, electronically nowadays, to every corner of the world. So does our language, and a civilisation is locked and unlocked through its language.

Britain is of Europe, yet it has always stood at an oblique angle to European civilisation. You get the echoes, the imitations even, but whether you are looking at medieval cathedrals, or country towns or what remains of the extraordinary outward signs of the early industrial era, rather too little in my view, you are always aware of the difference. It would be unwise to forget the extraordinary effect that the sixteen miles of channel at nearest point, that hangover of the retreating ice-cap, has had on our history. Neither the Maastricht Treaty, nor the Channel Tunnel, in my view, will make the slightest difference. Culturally, which is what matters, we will always be equidistant from our Continental neighbour and the wider world of the English speaking peoples outside. Both our emigrations, and our immigrations, looked westward to the New World. Long after the colonial era we have a special relationship too, with the hugely populated Indian subcontinent, with Australia and New Zealand, to some degree even with China. This peculiarity is why people come.

Aspects of our culture, of course, have suffered greatly from early industrialisation and a conservative tendency to prop up businesses which are no longer economically viable, on account of the need to satisfy, vainly, certain patterns of social organisation. For instance, as a former Minister of Employment , I know lots of coal miners, steel workers and shipbuilders who resent the passing of these industries. I know few who, when they still seemed viable, wanted their children to make careers in them.

Food has suffered. Britain has lost, as Europe is beginning to lose, a food culture linked to regional and local farming conditions. Thank God for Italy, which is holding on. Food is important to the performing arts, which aim to deliver a good night out, as well as aesthetic or spiritual uplift. There has been considerable improvement in my adult lifetime, very considerable in the last ten years. But, it has to be agreed that standards and expertise are low in this country. Catering is still looked upon as a dead end job. It is just as important as health care and it matters a lot to tourism and to the arts.

How important are the arts in respect of tourism?

The physical heritage of the past, that which we apprehend by going about the place and looking at buildings, artefacts, works of arts and landscapes, make a contribution that is self-evident. Literary shrines, royal palaces, stately homes, museums and art galleries, even the commercial sector of trade in works of art and antiques in which, as a Director of Sotheby's I still spend time, are as much as anything our substitute for the sun.

As for myself, I am mad, perhaps literally, about our climate. I refer to the magic of the dramatic shifts within a temperate and comfortable range, the broken light, the feeling you have won the pools on nice days, the way in which, in the words of the poet Philip Larkin:

> Sun destroys
> The interest of what's happening in the shade.

Of the categories I have mentioned, museums and galleries have suffered through public spending constraints at both national and local level. They will benefit from the distributable proceeds of the National Lottery which is to be administered by the National Heritage Memorial Fund. There are 2,000 of them and they need the improvements in display, conservation, security, accessibility, which only capital spending can provide.

But if the contribution of the physical heritage is self-evident, what of the living arts? I have made the professional lobbyist's predictable complaint about money. A sincere complaint, nonetheless, even if the Arts Council does not need as much as it would like. Its budget was cut, in 1994, for the first time in its history. In cash terms it was cut by £3.2 million and of course you have to add inflation to that. Scotland got an indexed standstill. Wales, whose Secretary of State's vision of public spending makes Mrs Thatcher look like Mother Theresa, received a 7% rise.

The Council needs that cut restored, in real terms. If, which is unlikely to happen, it also received an additional £10 million of grant-in-aid, which would give a total sum of about £200 million in all, it could manage. Tough decisions would still have to be made, because the promised bonanza of the Lottery is to be directed to capital not current account. But we could manage and allow companies to plan on sensible three year cycles. Having said that, let me stress that in spite of all the difficulties the living arts are in fierce and fighting good condition. The problem is keeping them in that condition and preserving that startling contribution, in economic terms, which they make.

Consider a few examples. The Edinburgh Festival and its Fringe was a spectacular success in 1994. It is difficult to imagine the summer economy of Scotland without it. Indeed, a new secondary market, for stand-up comics, has grown up around it. Museum officials in Paris have told me that the Philadelphia-based Barnes Collection of Impressionists, which did not come to Britain, generated £50 million of new money for Paris in its first week there. Britain is short of venues for international exhibitions of the first rank. This is something the Lottery distributors need to address.

Nick Serota, the Director of the Tate Gallery, which now has outposts in St Ives and Liverpool as well as London, is applying for a new state of the art gallery of modern art to be built on the Thames in Southwark, at Bankside. His estimates are for 10,000 new jobs in the short term, settling down to 5–6,000 in the longer term. That project will bring thousands of visitors to London. These visitors will not, incidentally, be mainly motivated by our 'heritage' or 'tradition'.

Indeed, if Sir Richard Rogers' international competition winning design for the integration of the arts venues on the South Bank of the Thames by the Royal Festival Hall also gets the go-ahead, we shall at last start to attract new visitors to the Capital who are more interested in the 20th century than the 18th or 19th. The Globe Theatre, further down the river again, will be a window on Shakespeare's works of the turn of the 17th century.

I have been enormously heartened and encouraged by my experiences in travelling around England on behalf of the Arts Council. As well as visiting our own offices and attending performances or exhibitions by local organisations, I spend a great deal of time with our local authority partners in the provision of tax payers' money for the Arts. Ten years ago, as Minister for the Arts, I used to do the same thing. In those days, local authorities were mainly interested in what has come to be called community arts. These were amateur activities in the main which often gave special attention to the needs of minorities in areas of social deprivation. This was very important then, and remains so now.

Our budgets derive from general taxation: everyone has an interest and a stake. But nowadays, ten years later, I find that local authorities, in the north of England especially, have extended their interest and their commitment. Leeds and Manchester in particular, and to some degree Newcastle and Gateshead, see arts and leisure activities as providing a new focus and purpose for city centres. It would stimulate interest in the meaning of cities; the economy of cities; and in civilisation itself. Indeed, the word 'civilisation' derives from the Latin for 'city'. These cities too are subject to political difficulties and expenditure constraints, but my impression is that the commitment is already being translated into action and therefore into cash. The recent recession has been overwhelmingly a southern, white-collar phenomenon.

Northern towns and cities, which experienced rapid de-industrialisation and a devastating shakeout of labour in the early 1980s, have come to terms with our post-heavy industry world. High added value and high technology industries are essential but they are by definition not labour intensive. Financial services, too, are being pruned through global electronic networking. But tourism, sport and the arts and entertainment: the job-for-bid equation is better here than anywhere. Whoever would have thought, ten years ago, that Gateshead, a Labour council with a thoroughly Andy Capp image, would have commissioned and erected a gigantic Claes Oldenberg sculpture and done so against a local resistance which, they tell me, would be even fiercer now if they tried to dismantle it. Whoever would have thought, ten years ago, that the London Borough of Southwark, a People's Republic if ever there was one, would now be getting into bed with the City of London across the river to build a footbridge of international design to go with the new Bankside Museum of London Art?

At the end of September 1994, I went to a City of Birmingham Symphony Orchestra concert in their state-of-the-art concert hall. Sir Simon Rattle, not yet 40, was conducting Schoenberg and only Schoenberg. Admittedly, it was early Schoenberg, late-Romantic Schoenberg, not the atonal stuff, but it was Schoenberg nonetheless. It was 80% full, that huge auditorium, and Saturday's repeat performance was 90% subscribed.

If the museums are spruced up, and the food is improved and the pubs and bars are lively, there is no reason why music-loving Amsterdammers, for example, should not buy package-tour tickets for a jaunt to Birmingham; Brummagens for a jaunt to Amsterdam and the Concertgebouw, an even greater orchestra (though the way Simon is going, not necessarily for much longer). And the great thing about the arts is that they take place indoors. You don't need the sun. You don't even need the summer. The tourist industry likes winter seasons.

So my experience is that the will and the demand is there, that it is with us now, whatever the attendant difficulties. The way and the means are always problematical. The thing to do is not to whinge but get on with it. Local and national politicians need the guts to explain to their electorates that what may seem like icing on the cake is in fact the cake itself, or the bread and butter of our new economies, and not just the jam. The success of the pop music industry should make it easy for younger voters to understand this. Britain has about a 20% world market share in popular music and that is worth hundreds of millions to the Exchequer alone.

You may feel that referring to the commercial sector in a debate about the subsidised sector is irrelevant. You might be wrong. Take the case of a distinguished member of our Council, Trevor Nunn. Trevor is a child of the subsidised system. He was for many years the Director of the RSC, one of the biggest organisations we fund. Yet he also directed Andrew Lloyd Webber's *Cats* the most successful show in the history of theatre on this planet. As a project, *Cats* would have sounded arty and eccentric. A musical without a story, based on poems by T. S. Eliot, that well-known elitist, (to use a word which is, thank God, beginning to go out of fashion), it was driven by developments in contemporary dance, just the sort of thing the Arts Council might get up to if you do not keep a strict eye on them. Sir Andrew, incidentally, won the award for an outstanding contribution to tourism in 1992.

The examples I have given have been big ones, large projects involving relatively large scale investment. But in the second half of 1994 I visited a small mobile theatre, a marvellous piece of design of the late 1940s, involving three trucks and a canopy at Keswick in the Lake District. The trucks are going to be retired for a museum: a fine new theatre, still modest in size and design, will take their place.

The National Lottery is immensely important for improving the infrastructure of the arts and for all arts projects, large and small. I need hardly point out how important such improvements are. To lure visitors from outside a region or from abroad, to lure people at home away from their TVs and into the box office, you need comfortable, efficient and architecturally attractive venues. The Prime Minister himself had the will to get the Lottery onto the statute book and to win cross-party support for it. Others, including myself ten years ago, tried and failed, and the administration deserves unconditional praise.

But consider two things. Lottery money is challenge money; that local will, those political guts I mentioned, will still need to be demonstrated in material ways. Then again, lottery money is, with a few exceptions, reserved for capital projects. I agree with this, for the reasons I have just given. But we must remember, in the jargon of computers, that where the arts are concerned the software is more important than the hardware. It is no use having shiny new palaces of culture with an increasingly threadbare culture taking place within them.

As a beneficiary of a fifth of the distributable proceeds, perhaps as much as £150 million of new money annually, it may seem odd that I am whinging on about that £3.5 million cut on our base line. But it may be the difference between life or death for significant and excellent organisations. I feel rather like someone watching the bailiffs remove his furniture when the doorbell rings and it turns out to be the man from Vernons. Will the cheque clear before the belongings? I have tried to indicate how much there is at stake. How much it matters for our civilisation, for our national morale, for our economy and for tourism.

The Author

The Right Hon Earl of Gowrie is Chairman, Arts Council, and was until recently Chairman of Sotheby's, where he is still a director. Following ten years as a lecturer at US and UK universities and a spell as a fine arts consultant, he served in several government posts, including being Minister for the Arts 1983-85. His writings include *A Portrait of Don Giovanni* (1972) and *The Genius of British Painting* (1975).

This text is based on a paper delivered by the author at the Robert Gordon University Heritage Convention in Elgin on 6 October 1994.

6

AXE THE ARTS COUNCIL
A Threadbare Fig Leaf

Robert Hewison

Between VE-Day and VJ-Day there is one wartime anniversary that few will have been aware of. Fifty years ago tomorrow, the decision to set up the Arts Council of Great Britain was announced. That so few people will remember this is just one measure of the failure of the institution brought into being on 12 June, 1945. Apart from those hoping to get some money out of it, few are interested in the organisation that was set up in recognition that, to quote the official announcement, there was 'a lasting need after the war for a body to encourage knowledge, understanding and practice of the arts in the broadest sense of that term'. The Arts Council was intended to foster the imagination and creativity of the nation: instead most people are still as indifferent about the health of the arts as they are about the Arts Council. The time has come to think again.

In money terms, by far the biggest patron of the arts since the war has been the BBC, whose £1.6 billion budget towers above the Arts Council of England's current £191m. The real purpose of the Arts Council has been to define what 'the arts' are, and by so doing help to define our cultural identity. It was only when the survival of that identity was in doubt, in January 1940, that it was decided that it was essential to show publicly and unmistakably that the government cared about the cultural life of this country. The Arts Council's predecessor, the Council for the Encouragement of Music and Arts (CEMA), was brought into being, a tiny gesture towards the values being fought for.

Yet during the war, the battle for a more democratic definition of what constituted our culture was lost. At first, CEMA's object was to encourage music-making and artistic activity by the British people themselves. The interests of professional artists and the metropolitan cultural establishment were to be served only incidentally. But when John Maynard Keynes took over as Chairman in 1942, he imposed the values of his Bloomsbury background on the organisation, so that CEMA's post-war successor would have been better described as the 'High Art Council of London', rather than the Arts Council of Great Britain.

The reluctance of politicians to acknowledge the part they play has contributed to the failure to stimulate the national imagination. They have drawn a fig leaf of 'independence' between themselves and cultural policy.

51

The government provides the funds and appoints the people who distribute them, but protects itself by remaining at arm's length from the decisions taken by an unelected quango. The Council, in turn, keeps its distance from artists and audiences alike. It may seek their advice but it is not obliged to act on it. The secrecy and unaccountability of the Council's decisions is compounded by the government's refusal to take responsibility for them in parliament, and by the fiction that ministers do not influence its work.

Protected by such institutional insulation, the Arts Council has always preferred a narrow definition of the arts. From Lord Keynes to Lord Gowrie, it has reflected the patrician values of its Chairmen and the metropolitan bias of its thinking. In the 1950s under Lord Clark, Kenneth Clark of the television series, *Civilisation*, it closed down its regional offices to concentrate resources in London. In the 1960s, under Lord Goodman the avantgarde was indulged with scraps, but it was the Royal Shakespeare Company, the National Theatre, Covent Garden and English National Opera that benefited most from the expansion in funding. The growth of the regional arts associations in this period was a local reaction against the dominance of London. In the 1980s, the liberal traditions of Goodman's regime gave way to the conservatism of Lords Rees-Mogg and Palumbo. The Council's answer to the 'devolution' forced on it by the creation of new regional arts boards has been to devise a system that seeks to keep all significant decision-taking in London.

At the same time the Arts Council has been reluctant to move beyond its original definition of the arts as a professional activity done to, as much as for, an audience, and restricted to conventional forms established in the 19th century. People are still trying to persuade it to put proper resources into jazz, when popular culture is developing a whole range of musical styles that exploit new technological possibilities for self-expression. The Council's current attitude towards experiment in the fields of dance, performance and visual art appears to be more, not less, conservative than it was.

The Arts Council is gripped by institutional inertia. Every attempt to break free of established commitments, be they theatres or orchestras, is met with such an outcry that nothing results. In 50 years, the cultural landscape the Arts Council was created to cultivate has changed out of all recognition. Its attempt officially to define the territory of the arts has failed. The great pyramid of high, middlebrow and popular art forms has crumbled, and people feel free to pick and mix amid its ruins, enjoying opera here, stand-up comedy there. The need for a monolithic institution that controls access to a mausoleum of the arts has disappeared, and the time has come to devise new ways of providing the means by which individuals, groups and communities establish and celebrate their identities.

Britain is a more plural society than it was in 1945, and that pluralism needs to be reflected in its institutions. The Arts Council should be broken up into smaller, discrete and competing units that would be closer both to the artists contributing to the specific art forms they would represent, and to the audiences they would be expected to serve. As a sop to the calls for greater national independence within the United Kingdom, the Arts Council of Great Britain has already been separated out into the councils for England, Scotland and Wales, yet these merely replicate the old monolithic system. The regional arts boards being closer to their communities should remain, but the metropolitan bias represented by the Arts Council in London would disappear.

To flourish, the arts need to be truly independent of government which controls the purse-strings through the Arts Council. An opportunity now exists to cut those strings, in the form of the National Lottery. The rules governing the distribution of funds should be changed to allow for the creation of endowments, some of which would go to institutions devoted to promoting specific art forms, others to specific companies. (The Royal Opera House is already trying to establish its own £100m endowment fund.) As a first step, arts organisations should be invited to give up their present revenue funding for a fixed period, in exchange for a substantial endowment fund. Freed of the capricious tyranny of the annual government expenditure round and the interference of the Arts Council, an institution such as the National Theatre would be able to plan its work properly and manage its own affairs, balancing its box-office receipts with the income from its endowment fund.

A proposal as radical as this may well expose the truth about cultural policy in Britain: that governments of whatever colour, do not wish to surrender control of any aspect of public life, and that especially they do not trust the arts to manage themselves. They prefer the fig leaf of the Arts Council, to enact their policies at arm's length from them, constrained by the financial strings that ministers and civil servants pull. But 50 years on, the fig leaf of the Arts Council is looking increasingly threadbare. It is time it was blown away.

The Author and Acknowledgements

Professor Robert Hewison read history at Oxford University, worked in television and spent a year at art school before returning to Oxford to write a thesis on the work of John Ruskin. He is an independent writer and broadcaster who has published four books on Ruskin, and a number of studies in contemporary cultural history, including a three-volumes history of the arts in Britain since 1939. He wrote *The Heritage Industry: Britain in a Climate of Decline*, (Methuen) in 1987, and Oxford awarded him a D.Litt. for his published work in 1989. In 1993 he became a visiting professor in the Faculty of Arts at De Montfort University and in 1995 Professor of Literary and Cultural Studies at Lancaster University. He has presented arts programmes for Radio Four (*Kaleidoscope*) and Radio Three (*Critics' Forum*), *Third Ear Nightwaves*), and presented and taken part in arts programmes for BBC Television. He is Deputy Drama Critic for *The Sunday Times*, and writes arts features and commentary for that newspaper. His current project is an exhibition for the Ashmolean Museum Oxford, *Ruskin and Oxford: The Art Exhibition*, which opens in May 1996.

This article is reproduced by kind permission of *The Sunday Times*. It appeared in their *Culture Supplement* on 11 June 1995. Hewison's *Culture And Consensus: England, Art And Politics Since 1940*, was published by Methuen during the same month.

7

LEAVE THE ARTS COUNCIL ALONE
A Response to Robert Hewison

Lord Gowrie

Robert Hewison's objections to the Arts Council (or, more properly, the Arts Councils of England, Wales, Scotland and Northern Ireland) boil down to a plea 'to devise new ways of providing the means by which individuals, groups and communities establish and celebrate their identities'. To do this, he asks for much greater devolution regionally and greater independence from central government nationally. He considers the present Council (I assume he is referring to England) too metropolitan and too locked into existing funding commitments. He believes that the arts organisations could be freed 'of the capricious tyranny of the annual expenditure round and the interference of the Arts Council' by a combination of National Lottery funds and direct government endowments, the latter being topped up from time to time by the government itself.

I have run into this case since I arrived at the Arts Council of England a little over a year ago. It has some plausibility; it makes certain assumptions which, as an individual, I happen to share. But when 'radical' proposals are made which involve public money, their implementation becomes very difficult, and lottery revenue is treated as public money. Either a quango like the Arts Council must be accountable for it (as at present), or the Minister must take direct responsibility for its distribution. I very much doubt that Hewison realises how unpalatable to most of the arts would be the political consequences of the ministerial alternative. Since tax revenue is gathered from the public on an annual basis, endowments would be expected to follow suit. There is also no political evidence that either Kenneth Clarke or Gordon Brown would consider a different arrangement.

Devising some partial endowment benefit for companies from the National Lottery, and thereby giving them greater independence, is something the Arts Council is looking at long and hard. I personally am convinced of its merits. Watch the Great Peter Street space. However, any changes will require the blessing of the Secretary of State.

Lottery endowments could not by themselves replace Arts Council funding. Given the sums of money required, it would be too costly. For example, to provide the Royal Opera House with a sufficient endowment, would use up the entire Arts Council of England lottery income for a year. This would surely militate against the very groups that Hewison seeks to champion. The lottery is providing for us very well on the capital side and we are confident that we shall be able to accommodate most viable bids, whether great or small.

The 'too metropolitan' jibe has whiskers on it. It is inevitable that in a small country such as England, major artistic institutions are likely to be situated in the capital. Nevertheless, large lottery awards have already demonstrated the immense regenerative potential of this form of capital funding in the regions. Ask Alan Ayckbourn about the recent lottery grant to his theatre in Scarborough. As for our being locked into existing commitments to the main artistic bodies, it is woolly headed to imagine history can be disposed of at an administrative stroke, even if throwing great organisations overboard were desirable. Is it really being suggested that we should be withdrawing support from major opera companies, symphony orchestras, or our great national theatres?

To put it simply, Brahms's symphonies were written and performed in the context of the economics and cost assumptions of his time, when orchestras were cheaper to run. He is not cheap to put on today, but that does not mean that individuals, groups and communities should be denied hearing live performances of his work, or that musicians should be denied the opportunity and challenge of interpreting it. Reliance on box-office receipts alone has always been restrictive, both qualitatively and quantitatively. High art has always received state subsidy, or subsidy from corporations as large as the state – such as the medieval church. But I agree that we are now a plural society. That is why we at the Council bear the costs of funding many art forms of interest to minorities.

Hewison says that the Arts Council's answer to the devolution 'forced on it by the creation of new regional arts boards' has been 'to devise a system that seeks to keep all significant decision taking in London'. This is not the case. It is the case that the Council is accountable for the spending of the Regional Arts Boards (RABs) as the main source of their funds. In the same way, the Department of National Heritage is accountable for the Council's own spending. All this is unavoidable when public money is involved and one of the reasons why private patronage has its attractions. But the Council's own composition is heavily weighted towards the RABs. They are an essential link between the Council and local government, which spends as much on the arts as the council and the RABs combined. I believe that if Hewison talks more to RAB chairmen he will find that there is a better family atmosphere. I myself am devolutionist. Indeed, I argued as Minister for the Arts for the creation of separate Councils for Scotland and Wales and am delighted that this has happened.

A case that is good in parts, and to which we have been responding, is weakened not only by such inaccuracies but by the poverty of Hewison's alternative visions. A proliferation of small collectives is unlikely to serve the creative men and women who constitute the arts, or expand audiences for their work. The arts are not about the organisations that serve them. They are their own dynamo. We are here to lubricate the dynamo with money. We want to be vigorous but not bossy; tough sherpas, if you like, for the assault on Parnassus. There is no point in following Hewison and whinging about them. Onward and upward is where we mean to go.

The Author and Acknowledgements

The Right Hon Earl of Gowrie is Chairman, Arts Council, and was until recently Chairman of Sotheby's, where he is still a director. Following ten years as a lecturer at US and UK universities and a spell as a fine arts consultant, he served in several government posts, including being Minister for the Arts 1983–85. His writings include *A Portrait of Don Giovanni* (1972) and *The Genius of British Painting* (1975).

This article is reproduced by kind permission of The Sunday Times. It appeared in their *Culture Supplement* on 18 June 1995 in response to Robert Hewison's article in the same newspaper on 11 June 1995 as reproduced in the preceding chapter.

BASEBALL CITY, Fla. -- *Kansas City Royals First Baseman George Brett is one of 25 baseball greats, present and past, pictured on giant Topps cards at Boardwalk and Baseball. Brett and his teammates spring train in 7,000-seat Baseball City Stadium, which is connected by boardwalk to the 135-acre amusement park. The complex also features batting cages, pitching alleys and "A Taste of Cooperstown" memorabilia exhibit. Boardwalk and Baseball is a member of the Sea World family of parks.*
88-123-15

Figure 1 Baseball City in Florida. Kansas City Royal's First Baseman, George Brett, pictured on a giant display.

8

THE CULTURAL POTENCY OF SPORT
A Neglected Heritage Asset

Terry Stevens

The place of sport as part of the heritage of a nation, region, or community has been widely recognised and endorsed. Birley's work (1993) which traces the development of sporting conventions against the context of the evolution of society in Britain provides evidence of the centrality of sport to our heritage. This is affirmed by others, who, whether writing generally or from a specific sporting perspective, acknowledge the importance of sport as heritage, (see for example: Ford, 1977; Holt, 1989; Taylor, 1992; Redhead, 1993; Walvin, 1994; Foot, 1994). A similar theme is taken up in the analysis of sport in other countries (Filger, 1981; Filger and Whitaker, 1991) or the development of sport globally (Murray, 1994).

Of particular concern evident in much of this literature is the assessment of how sport has shaped and influenced national identity. Sugden and Bairner (1993) examines sport and the politics of division in Ireland, whilst Jarvie and Walker's (1994) edited collection of essays, *Scottish Sport in the Making of the Nation* is subtitled 'Ninety Minute Patriots' – clearly predicating the sport as heritage thesis. In Wales, Williams and Smith (1989) discuss the integration of heritage, nationalism and rugby union football.

The recent examples of violence in sport, especially at soccer games, has received considerable attention (Canter et al 1989; Burford, 1991; and Giulianotti et al 1994,). These authors are quick to acknowledge, however, that violence is not a new phenomena but rather, that there may even be an identifiable 'heritage' of anti-social behaviour amongst spectators. Certainly crowd disorders due to drinking and gambling were commonplace at soccer and racing events in Victorian Britain.

Allegiance and support for a team, or membership of a sports club, is part of a heritage which takes many forms. It is exhibited in many ways ranging from collecting the ephemera that demonstrates this support (match programmes, cigarette cards, stamps, postcards, artefacts, and autographs) to the wearing of club scarves or the recent trend of wearing a club's replica kit. 'Fans' can now buy shares in the new soccer 'companies' thus creating a range of 'heritage' activities over and above the sheer scale and volume of sports participation or spectatorship.

The influence of sport on heritage is further witnessed by its impact on other features of, what is generally regarded as, heritage. For example, the inclusion of a 'Festival of Sports' as part of the 1995 UK Year of Literature in Swansea demonstrates this aspect of heritage. Speakers at this event reflected upon the sporting content of Dylan Thomas' *The Boys of Summer*; Paul Galico's *Goodbye to Sport*; J B Priestly's *The Good Companions*; and, more obviously, Nicolas Prince's 1950s thriller, *Cup Final Murder*.

This heritage of sporting prose and poetry is more than matched by the veritable 'growth industry' of autobiographical texts from all echelons of sporting involvement, as well as a library of analysis, commentary and reflection upon 'this sporting life'. Whilst cricket and, to a certain extent golf, has enjoyed a high quality literary heritage other sports have not been so well represented. However, the past ten years have witnessed a remarkably fresh generation of authors reflecting upon the dramatic changes taking place throughout sport. Some notable examples of this new genre of writing include Pete Davies' *All Played Out*; Nick Hornby's *Fever Pitch*; Colin Ward's *Steaming In* and Steve Redhead's *Sing When You're Winning*.

The inextricable link between sport and the mass media, including the press, television, popular music and cinema, is not only further evidence of the status of sport as heritage but, as with literature, also represents discrete forms of heritage in their own right. Cinema, perhaps more than any other media has, in recent years, fully embraced these heritage aspects of sport. *Forest Gump, Field of Dreams, Bull Durham, Major League* and *Chariots of Fire* are obvious examples of the heritage sport axiom in popular culture (Mayne, 1993).

Themed sports bars, sport related theatre, and sports heroes as television pundits and stars of game shows, are emerging examples of the mass mediation of sport and the popularisation of the sporting heritage. A development analysed by Real and Mechikoff (1992) in the context of mythic identification and heritage symbolism. In addition, sport combines with art to create a further dimension of heritage so dramatically illustrated at the Olympic Museum in Switzerland, (Pahud, 1991) (see Warhol photo).

Despite these examples of the integration of sport with heritage, and evidence of sport as heritage, there are surprisingly few developments of specific attractions which explicitly capitalise upon the sporting theme. The fact that sport has immense appeal both as a spectator event and as a participant activity is undeniable. For example, the opening ceremony of the 1992 Olympic Games in Barcelona was watched on Global television broadcasts by over half of the World's population (Real and Mechikoff, 1992) and during a full sporting programme on a Saturday in January in Britain over 800,000 people are in stadia watching sport is illustration of this proposal.

The heritage of sport is overflowing with drama; memorable events; of heroes and Cantanaesque anti-heroes. The places hosting these sporting occasions become the venues of legends. The individual events, the sportsmen and women, and the activity itself have immense inherent appeal. The storylines are strong, their impacts memorable. This is a rich seam, to date relatively unexploited, for the 'new heritage industry'.

Figure 2 Cardiff Arms Park

Figure 3 'Joueur de Hockey sur Glace du Frolunda', Andy Warhol, 1984.

HERITAGE ATTRACTIONS DEDICATED TO SPORT

The limited development of formalised sport-related heritage attractions in Europe and, especially, in Britain cannot be easily explained. Horne (1984) hints that the development of sports museums in post-war Europe could be linked to symbolic expressions of nationalism (Gruffudd, 1995), reflecting sport as a key determinant of national character and sporting achievements, often as metaphors for battle honours. Elsewhere, the development of sports museums in Eastern Europe have been ascribed, at various times, to either national revivals or the importance of the physical training movement especially in communist countries (Grulich, 1991). Given the significance of sport in the context of British society, however, it is remarkable that there is not a 'National Museum of Sport' or on the basis of the foregoing, even more remarkable that sports museums do not exist in Wales or Scotland. Yet Finland has had such an institution for more than 30 years, whilst Pragues' National Museum of Sport was established over a century ago (Grulich, 1991).

In Europe, the development of museums dedicated to sport is limited, (see Table 1). This list is not exhaustive but is likely to represent 75% of the total. There are, of course, additional sports heritage exhibitions incorporated within local and regional museums, such as the 'Sports Hall of Fame' within the Museum of Welsh Life in Cardiff. It should also be recognised that most sporting clubs have collections of memorabilia displayed within club facilities. These have limited access to the general public and are rarely organised as heritage attractions (Stevens, 1995).

Table 1: European Sports Museums

The Olympic Museum	Lausanne, Switzerland
National Sports Museum	Paris, France
National Sports Museum	Helsinki, Finland
Sports Museum	Tartu, Estonia
Swiss Sports Museum	Baste, Switzerland
Flemish Museum of Sport	Louvain, Belgium
Museum of Sport	Prague, Czech Republic
National Ski Museum	Oslo, Norway
National Rowing Museum	Limerick, Ireland
Cricket Museum	London, England
Tennis Museum	Wimbledon, England
Horseracing Museum	Newmarket, England
Rugby Museum	Edinburgh, Scotland
Gaelic Athletics	Thurles, Ireland
Museu de la Pelote	Bayonne, France
Barcelona FC Museum	Barcelona, Spain
Manchester United FC Museum	Manchester, England
Liverpool FC Museum	Liverpool, England
Golf Museum	St Andrews, Scotland
Museum of Physical Culture	Poland
Museum Nacional do Desporto	Lisbon, Portugal
Museum of the Olympic Games	Olympia, Greece
Museum of Olympics	Lisbon, Portugal

Despite the potency of the theme, few of these dedicated sports museums attract more than 50,000 visitors per annum. This is primarily due to the traditional style of museum presentations which fails to capture, or reflect the excitement and spirit of the sporting tradition. Research undertaken in North America into the development of sports visitor attractions, especially the 'Hall of Fame' (Stevens, 1993) gives further analysis of this issue.

HALLS OF FAME IN NORTH AMERICA

The emergence of specialist sports museums and halls of fame in North America underlines the recognition of the cultural status of sport, and the impact of such facilities as visitor attractions. Redmond (1991) argues that part of this recognition is economically stimulated using high profile sport to attract the tourist dollar, either for the benefit of the sport or the host community.

The first hall of fame was the (non-sporting) 'Hall of Fame for Great Americans' established in 1901. Today, halls of fame exist to recognise many aspects of societal contribution, especially sporting achievements. In 1971, Lewis and Redmond identified 50 Halls of Fame of all descriptions in North America, whilst six years later Sonderberg et al (1977) detailed 200 with 'new halls of fame opening at, approximately, one every month.' One year later Thurmond (1978) estimated that to this total, 60% were likely to have a sporting focus. By 1990 some 400 halls of fame existed throughout North America of which 83 (21%) were sports based, (Balliett, et al 1993).

The primary, and traditional, raison d'etre of a sports hall of fame 'is the celebration of sporting heritage in which the noun 'fame' is all-important', (Redmond, 1991). The procedures for admission are based upon the elite; they often include a nomination; and, tend to glorify heroic deeds. A sports museum exhibits artefacts with intrinsic historic, or symbolic, interest. There are institutions which are exclusively halls of fame and others which are exclusively sports museums. There is a trend in the US, evident since the early 1960s, towards establishments which incorporate both functions. As a result, there is increasing acceptance of the interchangeablity in the use of terminology. Today sports museums would be expected to contain a 'hall of fame', whilst a traditional hall of fame would embrace a wider range of exhibits and displays.

These museums and halls of fame may be subdivided into five types dependent upon the focus of their contents. Of this total 61 (74%) represents 34 specific and different types of sport. Horse racing, motorsports and baseball each have five dedicated centres, whilst athletics and American Football have four each. In addition, four other categories exist: (i) 12 (14%) halls of fame which represent all sports for a given geographical area; (ii) three which interpret US sports in general; (iii) four attractions which have ethnic groups as their sporting rationale; and, (iv) two centres which reflect particular minority sports.

The geography of these attractions demonstrates a correlation with the main centres of population such that over 50% (42) of the facilities are located in the heavily populated regions of New England, the Mid Atlantic States and the EN Central States. Whilst this general pattern is not surprising, the micro-geography of the distribution of centres reflects a number of locational idiosyncrasies which do not correspond with optimum potential visitor demand. The determinants of location rarely appear to be the maximisation of market potential, instead one or more of the following variable influence decision making:

- individual entrepreneurial, or society/association interest;
- community interest and commitment;
- heritage or historical sporting connections;
- location of stadium or arena or event.

These influences may well explain the poor performances in attendance figures revealed from a survey of halls of fame discussed below. Clearly, opportunities exist to establish attractions in locations more accessible to core markets. Most existing sports halls of fame have located outside of the main metropolitan areas. Indeed, only 28% (23) establishments are located within the top 37 most populated metropolitan areas in the USA.

When this figure is compared to the geography of major league franchises, and hence major stadium developments, the extent of the missed opportunity to physically link a sports stadium with a sports visitor attraction is revealed. Detailed micro-locational issues affecting the potential of each stadia needs to be considered, but nonetheless it is clear that considerable potential to develop the stadium-based visitor attractions exists.

The sports halls of fame concept is a relatively recent phenomenon despite the early developments in the 1920s and 1930s. The 1960s witnessed increased activity in North America which coincided with the general increase in demand for leisure day trip facilities. The pace of development was maintained in the 1970s, consolidating the inter-relationship between sport and the growth in day visitor markets. The sustained boom in developments throughout the 1980s (average two halls of fame being established each year) corresponds with a general popularisation of sport through television coverage; increased participation rates and numbers of spectators; together with the revitalisation and marketing of sports through team franchise and stadium relocation.

The variables which stimulated demand and development for new halls of fame in the 1970s, 1980s and 1990s prompted many of those halls established prior to 1969 to relocate and, in the process, modernise. Indeed, of the 28 halls founded between 1920 and 1969, 15 (54%) have been redesigned and relocated. Consequently, some 55% of all sports halls of fame have opened in the past 13 years. Over three quarters (79%) of the sports halls of fame surveyed less than 75,000 visitors per annum with almost half (46%) attracting less than 25,000. Just 7 (13%) of the sample have visitor attendance figures in excess of 150,000 per annum. Significantly, five of the large scale attractions are recording a recent increase in visitor numbers of 16% over their average annual attendance for the previous five years. It should be noted that the sports represented in these larger attractions embrace the four main US National sports (Baseball, Pro-football, Basketball and Swimming) and are the designated 'national' halls of fame for these sports.

Of the sports halls of fame studied 31 (58.5%) administer an admission charge, whilst 22 (41.5%) allow free entry with the attraction either being associated with the administrative HQ of the Sport, or being a promotional activity which has charitable status. The adult entry charge ranges from $1 to $9, whilst the average charge levied is $4.5 for adults and $2.5 for children (range $1 to $5).

Opportunities to develop secondary spending by visitors at other revenue generating centres within the attraction of fame, features primarily merchandise and food/beverage outlets. In line with the conclusions about charging policies, which revealed that income generation is not an objective for over 40% of halls, it is clear that a significant proportion have not developed secondary spend opportunities through the provision of a merchandise shop (19%) or food/beverage outlet (70%).

A key aspect of this study was to explore the relationship between the sports hall of fame attraction and the use of a stadium as the host venue. Approximately 30% (19) of the Halls in the sample are located within, or adjacent, to a stadium (or arena) within which the sport takes place. Horseracing and motorsports are the sports most commonly using an arena or trackway as the location for the hall of fame. Only the Busch Stadium in St Louis (home of the St Louis Cardinals) and Oriole Park (home of the Baltimore Orioles) provide examples of major league stadia which have exploited the direct link between their sporting rationale and the inherent visitor interest in the heritage of that sport (as represented by the hall of fame).

Table 2: US Halls of Fame

Sport	Stadium	State	Visitors
General	College Campus	Alabama	25,000
Sport Car	Knoxville Raceway	Idaho	25,000
Baseball	Cardinal Stadium	Missouri	40,000
Horseracing	Churchill Downs	Kentucky	200,000
Football	Lambean Fields	Wisconsin	60,000
Trapshot	Ohio State Shoot	Ohio	2,000
Horseracing	Kentucky Horse Park	Kentucky	42,000
Swimming	Ft Lauderdale Complex	Florida	250,000
Lacrosse	Homewood Field	MD	10,000
Trotting	Goshen Track	New York	15,000
Tennis	Newport Casino	RI	50,000
Horse Showing	Kentucky Horse Park	KYentucky	36,000
Baseball	Campden Yards	MD	61,000
Golf	Sheraton Hills	California	30,000
Softball	Fame Stadium	Oklahoma	28,000
Motor Racing	Talladega Speedway	Alabama	98,000
Motor Racing	Indy 500	Indiana	120,000
Track & Field	Hoosier Dome	Indiana	10,000
General	Hoosier Dome	Indiana	10,000

THE SLEEPING GIANT OF TOURISM

The recent, unparalleled scale of investment in sports stadia and arenas world wide provides a very real opportunity to create a new generation of sports visitor attractions as integrated facilities in these new 'cathedrals of sport'. The attraction provides an opportunity to establish year round use of the facility and to generate new sources of income, (Stevens and Wootton, 1995). Sports stadia and arenas are increasingly being recognised as a fundamental features of urban or regional regeneration, offering significant leisure and income potential. The realisation of these venues as community assets is primarily founded upon the economic impact generated by regular sporting occasions and, more recently by the hosting of mega events, such as the Olympic Games or Superbowl (Weiller and Hall, 1992; Hall, 1992). However, Stevens (1992) has already proposed the concept of the Stadium as 'The Sleeping Giant of Tourism' – a giant capable of realising its inherent potential through the development of an integrated sporting visitor attraction, a more sophisticated version of the traditional Sports Hall of Fame as described above.

The importance of the stadium's contribution to enhancing a city's image to attract tourists and corporate business investment has been examined in detail by Petersen (1990) and Lipsitz (1984). More recently, Kitchen (1994) analysed the potential contribution that the new Olympic Stadium would make in reshaping Manchester's tourism prospects advancing the traditional economic perspective discussed by Hall (1992) and Bale (1989).

The classically inspired, often multipurpose venues, of continental Europe has produced inspiring landmarks and civic centre-pieces. British stadia have, on the other hand, tended to have single uses and are rather monolithic assemblages of architectural add-ons. In North America, there is a much stronger tradition of stadia and arenas performing wider leisure functions. Inglis (1993) speculates that this lack of appreciation of the 'Stadium' in Britain, may stem from the fact that sport in Britain evolved using facilities based upon existing sports grounds. There is no 'tradition' (or heritage) of stadium development. Inglis says, 'The Romans did not bequeath to these islands a significant amphitheatre, circus or hippodrome. Britain had no stadium as at Olympia or Delphi, no Colosseum as in Rome, no arena as in Arles, Nimes or Verona'. Inglis goes on to point out that under Napoleon's instructions a 30,000 capacity arena was designed for Milan by Luigi Canonica. Significantly, and ironically, these historic stadia are today vital components of the heritage tourist industry (Luciani, 1990; Watt, 1995).

EVOLUTION OF THE STADIUM

It is possible to identify five phases in the evolution of the modern sports stadium and arena via a number of key sources, particularly the documentation produced by Panstadia, for example Lowry (1992), Twydell (1993), Inglis (1987, 1990), and Neilsen (1986). For the purposes of this paper examples of each era are drawn from North America. However, it should be noted that these developments have clear parallels in the evolution of stadia in Britain and Europe, (John and Sheard, 1995). The five phases of evolution are:

1. *The Classic Ballpark*: Neighbourhood focus, dedicated single sporting activity, basic and limited range of amenities for

spectators, groundsmanship key management task, eg Forbes Field (1909), Griffith Stadium (1911), Tiger Stadium (1912) and Wrigley Field (1914).

2. *The Modernist Super Stadium:* Greenfield, or out of town locations, dramatic visual presentation of design, accommodating a range of events and sports, commercial/funding demands reflected in sponsors boxes, increased attention to spectator safety and comfort, tendency to be soulless places for the spectator and the sportsman, eg Candlestick Park (1960), RKF (1962), The Astrodome (1965), Busch Stadium (1966) and the Riverfront Stadium (1970).

3. *The Neo-Classical Ball Park:* Post-modernist recognition of the strengths of the classic stadium, an attempt to combine the quality and amenity requirements of the late 1980s with the features of the early parks, eg Comiskey Park, Oride Park, and the Arlington Stadium.

4. *The Regenerated Stadium:* Generally phase 2 parks which are receiving a secondary phase of investment to upgrade thereby accommodating new sports (such as soccer for World Cup USA '94) or multiple events to enhance viability (such as exhibitions, fairs or concerts), eg Citrus Bowl in Orlando, Rosebowl in Los Angeles, Meadowlands in New Jersey.

5. *The Millenium Stadia:* Multipurpose venues based upon innovative design and sophisticated management in which every traditional assumption about stadia is challenged (see below), embraces the qualities and strengths inherent in the three previous phases and produces an environment that is managed for high quality leisure experiences, eg Skydome in Toronto, the Olympic Stadium and Georgia Dome in Atlanta, and the American West Arena in Phoenix.

The innovative characteristics of each phase were provoked by a complex interaction of external factors including market, political, technical and socio-economic variables: many of which transcend the entire spectrum of leisure provision. These factors include: personal mobility; disposable income; sports participation; trends and fashions; quality of experience and safety and comfort. They also reflect (i) the geography of franchise sale and purchase arrangements, (ii) the politics of stadium ownership, (iii) city aspirations to be recognised as a vibrant, significant place, (iv) the felicitations of broadcast media, and (v) the exceptional demands of the growing number of global mega-events (such as Superbowl, the Olympic Games, and World Cup Soccer and Rugby).

An essential feature of a city's ability to host a major league sports teams, or, indeed, a primary sporting event or festival, is the provision of modern, high capacity stadia and arenas. The economic rewards inherent in major sporting activities (Bale, 1989; Getz, 1992) have stimulated considerable development in facilities throughout the US over the past 20 years. The public sector has recognised the added value of investment in stadia and accept that they can rarely be expected to make a profit (Herbert, 1992) and that the political risk involved is outweighed by wider economic gains for their community.

There is increasing recognition amongst municipal and state governments around the World, that facility development is essential in attracting a major sports events. Interest in facility development is, therefore, considerable. Stadia and arena are being used as a catalyst for regeneration and economic development. These 'new' facilities are potent visual images and architectural features contributing to positive destination imagery, considered so essential in tourism destination planning and marketing (Gunn, 1988). The Olympic Cities of Barcelona (1992), Atlanta (1996) and Sydney (2000) are fully exploiting these linkages. Indianapolis is, on a more modest scale, also trading on this potential (Indianapolis Chamber of Commerce, 1992).

The growth in the number of teams, major sporting events and attendance levels has spurred interest in developing modern facilities which have to address the comfort, amenity and safety requirements of the spectators as well as the demands of multiple use. These give rise to a wide range of opportunities for utilising a diversity of new technologies within each facility and providing a wide range of ancillary services and attractions (John and Sheard, 1995).

It is estimated that 86 major stadiums for professional sports teams exist in the USA (excluding venues used for professional motor racing, horseracing, amateur track and field or swimming). This represents 4% of the total of 2,223 multi-use facilities used by professional teams, college sides, and minor league teams. At this moment in time, Herbert (1993) estimates there to be 25 to 35 US cities actively involved in building, or refinancing, a major facility, representing a financing market of $15 billion. Of the 86 facilities, 65% are public sector projects.

This impetus has created a range of funding models to produce capital monies. Significantly, a key feature of sporting finance is the ability to produce (a) contractual sources of finance, and (b) a growing realisation that there are other sources of income to create a revenue stream associated with and independent of the actual use of the facility. The concept of a visitor attraction as an inherent feature of a stadium, clearly holds potential to contribute to this independent revenue stream as well as adding a facility adding appeal to other 'sales' and marketing opportunities using the facilities. The economic survival imperative requires facility designers and operators to understand user demands and to optimise and create new revenue opportunities. Owners cannot tolerate new facilities that are loss leaders in an already complex funding equation (Herbert, 1993).

THE CHALLENGE FOR BRITAIN

In Europe, there has been a recent (past 10 years) and urgent need to re-examine the role and place of the stadium in both a spatial and societal context. Although a number of the casual factors requiring this re-evaluation are similar to those occurring in the USA over the past 100 years, such as innovative design and the needs of mega events, several have been provoked by dramatic, often tragic, events. The dramatic development of, often beautiful, stadia structures provided the backcloth against which a series of tragedies were being enacted in other stadia across Europe. Tragedies which highlighted the aged and decrepit state of repair of many facilities, especially in Britain. The tragedies fatally, demonstrated the failures to appropriately manage, to provide even basic amenities, and the scant regard for spectator comfort and safety (Lischer, 1992).

The publication of the Taylor Report in 1990 was, undoubtedly, the single most influential advocacy for a serious review of stadium design and management in Britain. The Report's demand for all-seater stadia has prompted unprecedented activity in Britain, but its recommendations have reverberated around the World calling attention to the issues of customer amenity, safety and comfort.

The UK Government's insistence that clubs invest in their facilities has prompted the 130 soccer league clubs in Britain to evaluate their facilities. The Football Trust has, since its inception in 1990, made available £125m of grant aid as a contribution to over £450m investment in soccer stadia over the past 3 years. Similar upgrading involving major investment is taking place elsewhere. For example, the Scottish Rugby Union has a £40m programme for Murrayfield; the English RFU an £80m investment in Twickenham; whilst Bradford's Odsall Stadium has a £100m scheme proposed. Stadia and arena represents the largest single area of investment in leisure in the UK. Similar levels of activity and investment are evident elsewhere – especially in South Africa (Rugby Union World Cup 1995); France (Soccer World Cup 1998); Malaysia (Commonwealth Games 1996) and in Atlanta (Olympic Games 1996).

In every instance, the facility owners and developers are searching for improved methods of management and innovations to secure new sources of revenue, spectator entertainment, and user safety. The opportunities for multiple use is considerable. Perhaps the most significant potential exists in the development of sports-based visitor attractions.

Given the significant contribution of sport to cultural identity and heritage, it is remarkable that so few sports-based visitor attractions have emerged in these new facilities. In Britain, attractions at stadia are limited to museums at Manchester United, Liverpool, and Arsenal football clubs; the Wimbledon Tennis Museum and the Newmarket Horse Racing Museum. In Europe, FC Barcelona's Nou Camp Museum attracts over 500,000 visitors each year and remains the second most visited museum in Spain. Elsewhere, guided tours exist at some stadia but few are as complete as the Wembley Stadium Tour, sponsored by Coca Cola – the venue of 'Legends Tour'.

The examples from North America illustrate the most advanced application of the visitor attraction concept which uses sport as the dominant theme. However, the attractions are often very staid and traditional museum-style in presentation. Scope exists to develop and apply techniques, designs and technologies from the wider leisure industry to create a new generation of sports attractions for the millenium. The potential is enormous, the theme vibrant, the storylines evocative. Our sports heritage is the 'Sleeping Giant of Tourism' and a potent but neglected aspect of heritage.

The Author and Acknowledgements

Professor Terry Stevens is Dean of Faculty and Professor of Leisure and Tourism at Swansea Institute. He has recently completed a human resource strategy for the UK stadia and arena industry, and he was Director of the 1995 European Union COMETT Project *A Future for Europe's Past*.

The author would like to thank Diana Morgan and Heather Black for their patience in preparing the typescript.

References

Bale, J, *Sports Geography*, E and F N Spon, 1989

Balliet, W et al, *Gousha Sports Atlas*, USA Today, 1993

Birley, D, *Sport and the Making of Britain*, Manchester University Press, 1993

Borton, H T, *Ballpark Design*, Consulting Engineer Magazine, August, 1956

Burford, B, *Among the Thugs*, Secker and Warburg, 1991

Canter, D et al (ed) *Football in its Place*, Routledge, 1989

Catherwood, D W & Kirk, R L, *The Complete Guide to Special Event Management*, John Wiley & Son, 1992

Delfon, R, *The Master Plan*, Panstadia Vol 1 No 3 Autumn, 1993

Epperson, A F, *Private and Commercial Recreation*, Venture Publishing, 1986

Filger, S, *Sport and Play in American Life*, Saunders, Philadelphia, 1981

Filger, S & Whitaker, G, *Sport and Play in American Life*, WMC Brown – Dubuque, 1991

Ford, J, *This Sporting Land*, Times Mirror, 1977

Getz, D, *Special Event Tourism and Festivals*, VNR, 1992

Giulianotti, R et al (ed), *Football, Violence and Social Identity*, Routledge, 1994

Gruffudd, P & Herbert, D, *Heritage as National Identity*, in Heritage, Tourism and Society, Mansell, 1995

Grulich, T, *Prague: sports as History*, Museum Vol 170 No 2, Unesco, France, 1991

Gunn, C, *Tourism Planning*, New York: Taylor and Francis, 1988

Hall, C M, *Hallmark Tourism Events*, London: Belhaven, 1992

Herbert, W, *Creative Financing of Sports Facilities*, Panstadia Vol 1 No 1 Spring, 1992

Herbert, W, *Finding the Funds*, Panstadia Vol 1 No 3 Autumn, 1993

HMSO, *The Taylor Report: The Hillsborough Stadium Disaster*, Cmnd 962, 1990

Holt, R, *Sport and the British*, Clarendon Press, 1989

Horine, L, *Administration of Physical Education and Sport Programs*, W C Brown Publishers, 1991

Hornby, N, *Fever Pitch*, London: Victor Gollancz Ltd, 1992

Horne, D, *The Great Museum*, Pluto Press, 1984

Inglis, S, *The Football Grounds of GB*, Willow Books, 1987

Inglis, S, *The Football Grounds of Europe*, Willow Books, 1990

Inglis, S, *New Directions in Stadium Design*, London: Building Centre, 1993

Jarvie G & Walker, G, *Scottish Sport and the Making of a Nation*, Leicester University Press, 1994

John, G, & Sheard, R, *Stadia: A Design and Development Guide*, Butterworth, 1995

Jorgensen, P, *After the Event*, Panstadia Vol 1 No 3 Autumn, 1993

Indianapolis Chamber of Commerce, *Beyond the Games*, Indianapolis, 1992

Kitchen, T, *Manchester's Olympic Bid Review,* Proceedings Town and Country Planning Summer School, 1994

Lewis, T & Redmond, G, *Sporting Heritage: A Guide to Halls of Fame,* Barnes, 1971

Lipsitz, G, *Sports Stadia and Arenas,* Urban Land Institute, 1984

Lischer, M, *Herding Them In,* European Sport Vol 1, Sports Council London, 1992

Lowry, P, *Green Cathedrals,* Addison – Wesley Publishing, 1992

Luciani, R, *The Colosseum,* De Agostini, 1990

Murray, B, *Football: A History of the World Games,* Scolar Press, 1991

NSGA, *Sports Participation in the USA 1992,* NSGA Chicago, 1993

Neilsen, B, *Dialogue with the City: The Evolution of the Baseball Park,* Landscape 29, 1986

Mayne, J, *Cinema & Spectatorship,* Routledge, London, 1993

Pahud, J, *Combining Art, Culture & Sport,* in an Olympic Museum, Museum 170 No 2, 1991

Panstadia, *The Flame Still Burns,* Panstadia Vol 1 No 3 Autumn, 1993

Petersen, D D, *Convention Centres, Stadium, and Arenas,* New York: Urban Land Institute, 1990

Real, M & Mechikoff, R, *Deep Fan: Mythic Identification, Technology and Adventure in Spectator Sport,* Sociology of Sport Journal, Vol 7 pp 323–339, 1992

Redhead, S, *The Passions and the Fashion,* Avebury Press, London, 1993

Redmond, T, *The Changing Styles of Sports Tourism,* in Stabler M (ed) The Tourism Industry, CAB International, 1991

Stevens, T & Wootton, G, *Stadia as Attractions,* Leisure Management, Hitchin, 1995

Stevens, T, *Stadia – The Sleeping Giants of Tourism,* CHRIE 1992 Conference Proceedings. Washington, 1992

Stevens, T, *Unpublished Research for British Market Export Research Scheme,* Coventry, 1993

Stevens, T, *Theme Parks, J* (ed), Case Studies in Leisure Management Longmans, 1993

Sonderberg et al, *The Big Book of Halls of Fame in USA and Canada,* Bowker, 1977

Sugden, J & Bairner, A, *Sport, Sectarianism and Society* in a Divided Ireland, 1993

Taylor, R, *Football and Its Fans,* Leicester University Press, 1992

Thompson, L, *A Delphi Study to Identify Skills in the Commercial Foodservice Industry in the Year 2000.* CHRIE Conference Proceedings 1993, Washington, 1993

Thurmond, *Sports Museums and America's Passion for Sport,* North American Sports History Association, Maryland, 1978

Torkildsen, G, *Leisure and Recreation Management,* E & F N Spon, 1993

Twydell, D, *Football Grounds,* Aerofilm Guides, 1993

Walvin, J, *The People's Game,* 1994

Watt, T, *The End,* London: Mainstream Publishing, 1993

Weiller, B and Hall, C, *Special Interest Tourism,* Bellhaven Press, 1992

Williams, G & Smith, D, *Fields of Praise,* University of Wales Press, 1989

9

THE HERITAGE CONSUMERS
Identity and Affiliations in Scotland

Angela Morris, David McCrone & Richard Kiely

Heritage is a thoroughly modern concept and an important part of our modern consciousness.* As Raphael Samuel, writing in *The Independent on Sunday* (12 Feb 1995) points out:

> 'Heritage' is as popular with the general public in the late 20th century as the wonders of science and invention were in the 1870s when, on a Whit Monday, some 70,000 visitors are said to have flocked to Liverpool to see the new warehouses.

Samuel goes on to suggest that heritage:

> ...has given a new lease of life – and a new visual form – to what used to be called, in the 1890s and 1900s when it found expression in municipal libraries, swimming baths and bandstands, the Civic Gospel.

The past twenty years or so have seen the rapid growth of 'heritage' centres and heritage-based attractions. When the British Parliament passed the Ancient Monuments Act in 1882, it listed 68 monuments deemed to be significant. A century later, these numbered over 12,000. There were, in addition, 30,000 listed buildings, and in excess of 5000 conservation sites (Hewison, 1987).

This growth in heritage is largely a feature of the 1970s and 1980s. Half of Scotland's 400 museums have been opened since the late 1970s, and these attract around 12 million visitors annually (STB Visitor Attractions). Edinburgh Castle and Glasgow's Art Gallery and Museum attract around 1 million visitors each year, the Burrell Collection 750,000, and the People's Palace in Glasgow, and Edinburgh's Royal Museum of Scotland some 500,000. Next comes The Loch Ness Monster Exhibition, followed by Holyrood Palace with 350,000 and 330,000 visitors a year.

Our interest in heritage in Scotland started off as curiosity about the explosion in its local and national manifestations. In the words of George Rosie:

Scotland now has museums dedicated to a quite astonishing range of subjects. There are museums about coal mining, highland clans, fisheries, the Scottish rugby team, railways, slate quarrying, bicycles, motor cars, wirelesses, gaol conditions, aeroplanes, shipping, fossils, gem rocks, textiles, the Roman occupation, the savings bank movement, and the Loch Ness Monster. There is even a museum called The Cornice (in Peebles) which is all about the art of decorative plasterwork (1992: 158–9).

As we perused the heritage literature we became increasingly dissatisfied with the conventional, largely Anglo-centric, explanations to hand (Wright, 1985 & Hewison, 1987). We were particularly interested in the relationship between heritage and national identity and this received short shrift from both Wright and Hewison.

The nub of our argument is that heritage is significant in Scotland because it rests on a national and cultural dimension. By focusing on the consumption of heritage among those who have made a financial commitment to Scottish heritage, namely life members of the National Trust for Scotland (NTS), we will show that heritage is a reflection of nationalism in its widest sense. It may not, and frequently does not, carry political overtones, as the observations of life members of the NTS will make clear.

UNDERSTANDING CONSUMPTION

Consuming heritage is not simply a casual leisure activity. Heritage arouses passion and inspires zealotry. This is reflected in the large and important memberships of bodies such as the National Trust for Scotland (NTS) and Historic Scotland. In this paper we will be focusing on a sample of life members of the NTS, which by 1993 had over 230,000 members and an annual income of over £13 million. Of this over £3 million came from membership subscriptions.

Sociologists have traditionally neglected consumption, preferring to focus on production in contemporary societies instead (Miller, 1987). However, consumption is extremely important to an understanding of heritage (Urry, 1990). The Scottish Tourist Board (STB), for example, operates with a market-led consumerist concept of heritage, while the NTS epitomises a high-culturalist conservative one. The following comments by representatives of these bodies makes this tension crystal clear. The first is a comment made by the STB's new overseas marketing director in 1994: 'The first time I heard the Cairngorms (mountain range) described as a product, I thought it was a disaster, but in marketing jargon, that's what it is' (*The Scotsman*, 2 April 1994). Contrast this with the view of heritage with that enunciated by the recently appointed director of the NTS, (*Heritage Scotland*, 11 January 1994):

One of the enduring characteristics of the Trust has been described as 'perseverance', and whilst we may be regarded as having one foot in the past, we must also have an eye to the future in upholding standards, values and traditions which are important to the whole society. The Trust can be depended upon to 'persevere' as it preserves.

These comments reveal two contrasting views of heritage. To the STB heritage represents a product which is defined by the market. For the NTS heritage symbolises a wider and deeper set of social values which have to be revered and protected. The tension here is between market values and 'sacred' values. In our study of life members of the NTS our aim was to identify which set of values dominated among these self-defined heritage consumers.

CHARACTERISTICS OF NTS MEMBERSHIP

A random sample of life members of the NTS was taken from the lists held by the Trust. The survey generated 97 respondents, a 72% response rate of those approached. All respondents were interviewed face-to-face using a semi-structured questionnaire.

The members in our sample were overwhelmingly middle class and specifically from the professional classes (80%). Teachers formed the most common occupational group. A total of 35% of NTS life members in the survey were or had been teachers. A further 14% of respondents were currently or previously employed as civil servants, administrators or managers. A significant proportion (18%) of life members were or had been self-employed. There is then clear evidence to support the view that heritage has a particular appeal to those with high degrees of 'cultural capital'.

Respondents in the sample tended to come from stable occupational backgrounds. Only 35% of those we interviewed had changed career. A third of respondents had been in the same job since leaving school, and 31% had changed job but within the same profession. Only two respondents were unemployed, and only one in the whole sample had a manual occupation.

Most were highly educated, with 82% staying on after reaching the school leaving age (78% of men and 86% of women). The majority (57%) had received higher education at degree or post-graduate level, (59% of men and 55% of women). Only 25% had received no further education (27% of men and 22% of women). Over half were no longer in employment, yet income levels remained high. Over half (57%) had household incomes of more than £20,000 in the previous financial year. A further 20% earned more than 40%. Only 10% had a household income of less than £10,000.

ATTITUDES OF NTS MEMBERSHIP

Length of time as a life member ranged from four to 48 years. This made the average amount of time as a life member 16 years. Respondents were split equally between those who had joined directly as life members and those who had come in as ordinary members, before transferring to life membership.

Membership of other heritage bodies was very common among the life members in our sample. Over one-third (38%) belonged to local heritage associations. A further 35% of life members interviewed were also members of other national heritage bodies such as Historic Scotland, the Architectural Heritage Society of Scotland, and the Scottish Civic Trust.

Life members are active consumers of the NTS. On average, members had visited four properties in the last year, with a minimum of one visit and a maximum of twenty-three. The Culloden Centre proved to be the most popular site and was visited by half of the sample. The next most popular site was Culzean Castle on the Ayrshire coast (25%). Other popular sites visited in the previous twelve months were Crathes Castle and Falkland Palace (by 16% each), the House of Dun near Brechin (14%), Gladstone's Land (12%), and the Georgian House (11%), both in Edinburgh, as well as Kellie Castle in Fife (11%).

Life members in the sample regularly took holidays with 86% of respondents having had a holiday in the last 12 months and 56% having had more than one. They did not, however, tend to organise their holidays around heritage. Only 21% said that they regularly organised their holidays around heritage visits, while 36% never did so. Some admitted to occasionally visiting heritage sites when they were on holiday, but only 38% could be said to link holidays with heritage in any meaningful way.

Just under half of our respondents (47%) thought that heritage should remain in the hands of voluntary bodies like the NTS. This view was not shared by all respondents, with 37% believing that the state should be more involved, especially with regard to funding. A further 14% thought that a careful mix of the two was most appropriate.

Private owners of heritage properties received the support of a majority of life members, reflecting their overall preference for voluntary activity. A quarter (25%) thought that they should have a greater say in heritage, and only 6% that they should have less involvement. Just under a quarter (23%) thought that the balance was about right, and 19% thought it too difficult to generalise. A further 27% had no opinion on the subject.

There was a fairly strong feeling amongst life members that local government should be more involved in heritage, but with certain provisos. Those who felt that local government should be less involved (18%) were worried about the potential for political bias and control.

THE QUESTIONS ASKED

In our study, we attempted to do two things. Firstly, to identify whether NTS life members conceived of heritage as a product or as a set of 'sacred' values. Secondly, to explore the link between cultural nationalism and political nationalism. To this end the question we were interested in was to what extent does heritage in Scotland carry a political message?

To determine whether respondents conceived of heritage as a product or as a set of 'sacred' values we asked a series of five open-ended questions. These questions were:

We hear quite a lot these days about 'heritage'. Can you tell me what you understand by the term?

Do you think that there is a distinction between 'heritage' and 'history'?

As a life member of NTS, you obviously care about heritage. Can you tell me why you consider heritage to be important?

How would you describe Scotland's heritage in particular?

Are there any important differences between heritage in Scotland and in England?

WHAT IS HERITAGE ?

From the very beginning it was clear that 'heritage' was part of the normal vocabulary of NTS life members. Only 5% of life members considered it to have negative connotations. In very general terms, two broad senses of heritage emerged from our interviews. On the one hand, there were those life members who saw heritage in the fairly straightforward terms of buildings and artefacts. Here is a sample of comments:

> Heritage is a handy shorthand term attached to some odd artefacts. It gives people a sense of ownership.

> It's the buildings and artefacts of the past, down through the centuries.

Some included landscapes in their definitions as well. For example:

> It's places as well as buildings, literature and art, landscapes and forestry – all of that.

> The qualities and features of the physical landscape we have inherited, and which we have the duty to maintain.

Others hinted at a deeper set of values lying behind the artefacts. The other conception of heritage is much closer to the French word 'patrimonie', the possession of a much broader legacy of culture and values, what we might call 'inheritance':

> The visible material history, culture and roots of my being. The fascination of the past that is all around us. I want to pass it on to my grandchildren.

> The lifestyle of people in days gone by, but also how their lives affect ours. It's broader than buildings, extending to ways of living. It's part of our inheritance.

The key word here is 'inheritance'. For life members heritage is a broad concept which contains both cultural and personal dimensions. This interweaving of the cultural and the personal is the key to their commitment to heritage.

An important point to emerge from our discussions with respondents is that the concept of heritage represented a tangible link with a set of values which are crucial to a sense of identity. Some made the connection to 'national' aspects of heritage quite explicitly. For example:

> It's all aspects of human life which contribute to make Scotland what it is.

> I'm Scottish all the way through. Heritage relates to Scottish buildings, customs, traditions, everything relating to our country.

But while our respondents did articulate a strong sense of Scottishness, this, as we will see later, did not translate straightforwardly into political terms. Having asked our sample of life members what they understood by the term heritage, we asked them to distinguish between heritage and history.

HISTORY AND HERITAGE

A clear majority (75%) of our respondents thought that there was a distinction between history and heritage. Only 20% thought there was not. The remaining 5% did not know. For those who saw it, the distinction was at its most simple, the difference between artefacts (heritage) and events (history). Thus:

> Heritage is things that are left – artefacts; history refers to events and processes.

> History is something you read about in books; heritage is something you go and visit.

These comments reveal that heritage is frequently seen as more 'alive', more 'personal' and more connected to people's lives than 'history'. To elaborate:

> Heritage is an in-built thing, almost an attitude of people, their culture and way of life – like Burns's poetry; history on the other hand, is based on recordable facts – battles, kings and queens.

> Heritage is the living manifestation of history.

The distinction between heritage and history, therefore, is not simply between objects on the one hand, and events on the other. It is rather about the present and the past, in particular the way the past relates to and informs the present. This is evoked through buildings and artefacts, but it represents a much broader, connected process which appears to be more relevant to people's immediate lives.

The distinction between history and heritage is, therefore, about the distinction between the past and the present. History, especially with a capital 'H' – high history – is deemed, as the following comments suggest, to be remote and over:

History refers to political issues, battles and people, that is, things that happened. Heritage refers to the way people lived. This is much more interesting.

History is just about the 'past'. It's not necessarily a personal thing – it's not connected to you. Heritage on the other hand is 'your' past, 'your' personal details. It includes personal anecdotes and stories as well as buildings.

For life members it is, therefore, heritage rather than history which resonates with their own everyday lives. This helps to explain the significance of heritage today.

THE NTS AND HERITAGE

Having asked our respondents to talk about the relationship between heritage and history in abstract terms, we then related this to their NTS membership. We asked them to tell us why heritage was important. Once again we found ourselves tapping some deep and complex issues. It also became clear that heritage was more meaningful than history because it connects more intimately with everyday life.

Many of our respondents chose to answer this question not in terms of what the NTS did, but by drawing on their own conception of heritage. It was also interesting to note that respondents articulated a deeply personal sense of heritage rather than choosing to answer the question in terms of a specifically Scottish, that is, national dimension. Fully 50% answered this question in terms of their own need to give an account of their personal history, while 22% spoke in more orthodox ways of protecting and conserving the national past. The following comments illustrate a deeply conservative sense of heritage with respondents drawing strong lines of continuity between themselves, their predecessors and their children:

Unless you know your roots, you don't know who you are.

We are the products of our past, and we can only understand the present by knowing what's gone before.

It's what we have inherited, and it connects us with our ancestors.

For our respondents, heritage represented a chain of continuity between themselves and the past and was bound up with morality:

There is a duty on all of us to take care of the past to provide continuity for our children.

I feel we are custodians and I believe in the continuity of history. I'm very anti-revolutionary.

Heritage represents an oasis of stability in a chaotic runaway world:

I feel we are custodians and I believe in the continuity of history. I'm very anti-revolutionary.

Heritage represents an oasis of stability in a chaotic runaway world:

> Because the pace of life today is frenetic, and more gets lost, it's important to preserve and maintain what's gone before. It's easy to say that what's gone before has gone, but you need to know what you've come from.

As many of the above quotations reveal, heritage was to most of our respondents an intensely personal matter. It allowed them to express and articulate their deeply held beliefs and values, and their concerns about the direction and pace of social and cultural change. As an organisation, the NTS appeals to them because it gives expression, implicitly and explicitly, to these sentiments. Compare, for example, the observations of our respondents with comments made by the NTS's director in his editorial for its magazine:

> We live in an age when certain standards which ought to be timeless seem to have been turned on their head – both at an individual human level and in terms of corporate behaviour. ...That is why it is reassuring to think of the National Trust for Scotland as being a timeless organisation upholding traditional values but without acquiring a reputation as a rigid patriarch with a quaint and fuddy-duddy outlook.
>
> *Heritage Scotland*, Spring 1994

Both the NTS and its life members share an implicit set of social and cultural values which emphasise continuity, conservatism and roots. That is why the question about the importance of heritage to members elicits a strong sense of 'personal history' (50%), and a sense of continuity (33%), rather than a more conventional sense of nationhood (22%). Given the powerful image of Scotland which permeates heritage north of the Border, this is an intriguing finding. It came as a surprise that far fewer of our respondents than we might have expected connected this question about the importance of heritage with an explicitly Scottish national dimension. Those who did connect heritage with Scottish nationalism as such did so in the following terms:

> Heritage is bound up with Scottish culture and identity.

> If we lost our buildings we would loose a lot, that's why NTS tries to protect Scotland's heritage. But it's more than buildings, it's the preservation of the national outlook of the Scots, the need, if you like, to protect our moral fibre.

More generally, however, it was common to find heritage connected with a broad sense of nationalism:

> At an emotional level, it's pride in your country, you try to learn about your past and it's history. We must preserve the main elements, and we need to avoid sweeping away what we have inherited, to preserve the best of the past.

For life members then, the term 'heritage' is a vehicle for expressing a deeper and broader set of social values. It points to a world-view which is both conservative and personal, in which the past has distinct lessons for the future. Underlying it are deep-rooted fears that the icons of the past will be lost and that there will be no signposts for the future.

SCOTLAND'S HERITAGE

Moving away from their membership of the NTS, we asked our respondents to focus specifically on Scotland's heritage. By and large, they focused on physical characteristics rather than on cultural ones. The most mentioned characteristics of Scotland's heritage were the scenery (30%), it's geography (25%), and it's monuments, especially its castles (23%). Other non-physical characteristics were its culture of perseverance and hardship (18%), its language and culture (16%), the specific heritage of Highland clans and the Highland Clearances (10%), as well as its folklore (5%). Landscape and history were frequently intertwined as the following comments make plain:

It's highly influenced by its geography, the sense of persecution, the Covenanters and Highland Clearances, for example.

Features which are specific to Scotland such as the buildings which reflect the climate and environment. It's rugged. It also has links with Europe, unlike England which is rather insular.

Our respondents also tended to contrast Scotland's heritage, implicitly or explicitly, with England. Thus:

Scotland was a family-oriented society, with close-knit communities, unlike England.

Our history such as the clan system has some bearing on our lives. Culloden, for example, was a tragedy for the whole of Scotland. In the Central Belt there was a drift from the Highlands. Given the history of the Clearances the bitterness against the English is understandable.

The people of Scotland were also seen as an important part of Scottish heritage:

I think in terms of the toughness and resilience of Scottish people. Scots are very enterprising.

The spirit of perseverance over hardship.

Scotland's character and its people. The country is less populous and more rugged. This appears in the character of the people – tough and down to earth.

What starts out as a distinction between physical and cultural aspects of Scotland's heritage turns into something much more complex. Social values and physical landscapes are blended together. The result is a picture of Scottish heritage which contrasts strongly with England. Yet it was not uncommon for respondents to deny that there is a connection between heritage and politics as the following comments indicate:

> Well, it's not political, its not the SNP! I don't like them but I think of myself as a Scottish patriot.
> Being Scottish born, I stick up for Scotland, but the British should stick together. We should regard ourselves as British. We need to work to preserve Scottish heritage, though.

SCOTLAND AND ENGLAND COMPARED

To develop the point of comparison between Scotland and England, we asked our respondents to point out the important differences, if any, between heritage in the two countries. Most (62%) said that there was a difference. Only 35% denied that there is one. The majority of those who stated that there is a difference gave cultural reasons (50%), rather than geographical ones (17%). Respondents stated that England's heritage is characterised as consisting of grander houses (27%), on a larger scale generally (18%), and reflecting greater wealth (18%). On the other hand, Scotland's heritage is deemed to be more 'democratic' (26%), more varied (22%), and on a smaller and more intimate scale (11%). These themes emerged in comments such as:

> In England it's stately homes, and the riches of the upper classes. In Scotland heritage is more identifiable. The people who founded NTS were more socially aware and so they were concerned about the lives and the houses of other than the gentry.

> In Scotland, it's associated with the Clearances, the '45, the Jacobites. In England it's stately homes, Tudors, Windsor – with an aristocratic focus.

> England is wealthier. There are more grand houses, and country manors.

> English heritage is more about powerful people, the landed gentry.

This theme of greater wealth is also connected with the characteristics of the class systems of the two countries including social values:

> English heritage is less democratic.

> English heritage has a much stronger class bias in heritage, that sense of inheritance.

> There is a different cultural heritage, a different background. The attitudes are different, the thinking is different. Our educational standards are

higher. It's the English voices you hear in these parts these days, but our culture has firmer (if quieter) roots.

There is greater interest in life abroad because Scotland was and is a small country. England was rather inward looking.

The physical differences in heritage between the two countries were acknowledged, but, as we have seen, these are frequently judged to be expressive of more fundamental social and cultural values:

The (English) NT has more of a focus on property, whereas in Scotland NTS view land as a very important commodity.
England is more quaintly rural – the village green imagery. Scottish heritage conjures up harsher images in terms of the physical environment.

HERITAGE AND NATIONAL IDENTITY

A key part of the study was to explore the relationship between heritage and national identity. We wanted to find out how and in what ways an interest in Scottish heritage, defined by life membership of the NTS, was connected with our respondents' sense of nationality. For example, whether they feel more Scottish because of their involvement in Scottish heritage. To examine this, we used a question to tap aspects of nationality, which allowed us to make comparisons between our sample and the population as a whole.

The question we used was:

We are interested to know how people living in Scotland see themselves in terms of their nationality. Which of these statements best describes how you regard yourself ?

Bearing in mind the sample size of less than 100, we should not draw too many conclusions from the data themselves, but it is helpful to see these in comparative perspective:

	NTS members	People living in Scotland	Conservative Supporters
	%	%	%
Scottish not British	8	32	18
More Scottish than British	45	29	17
Equally Scottish & British	34	29	44
More British than Scottish	10	3	6
British not Scottish	4	6	15

The data shows that most of our respondents claimed dual identity, but that nearly four times as many gave priority to being Scottish (53% in categories 1 and 2) as to being British (only 14% in categories 4 and 5). This priority given to Scottishness cuts across the political affiliations of life members, with fully 42% of Conservative voters in our sample claiming to be

Scottish rather than or more than British. In our sample, Conservative voters were the most likely to give precedence to being British (24% compared with 15%). However, it is the claim to be Scottish rather than British which characterises the majority of NTS life members we interviewed. Scottishness was the norm. Respondents felt that they had to explain why they claim British identity.

POLITICS AND HERITAGE

Throughout this paper our argument has been that for life members of the NTS, heritage is a personal rather than a political issue. It comes as no surprise, therefore, that life members of the NTS are from our evidence, both culturally and politically conservative. Our question was:

> If there were a General Election tomorrow, which political party would you vote for?

The answers were as follows (voting patterns at the 1992 General Election in Scotland for the population as a whole are given for comparison):

	NTS life members	Scotland 1992
	%	%
Conservative	40.6	25.7
Liberal Democrat	26.0	13.1
Labour	10.4	39.0
SNP	4.2	21.5
Do not know/do not vote	18.8	N/A

In the study we have taken life membership of the NTS to indicate a commitment to Scottish heritage. On this basis we can conclude that there is virtually no connection, in our sample, between being a Nationalist and having a commitment to Scottish heritage. Fully 62% of life members had always voted for the party they mentioned and had a general commitment to its policies or agreed with its ideology. Disillusionment with their traditional party was the reason behind the minority's (35%) intention to change their vote.

The general tenor of our respondents' views was conservative. This can be gauged from the following comments which stress the link between conservatism and tradition. All are Conservative voters.

> They (the Conservative Party) have a love of the past and tradition.

> I've been brought up with and continue to believe in their ideals. And Conservatives value tradition.

> I'm not a political person. We've always been Tory here.

> We were brought up in the country, and farmers were aye Tory. Our parents voted that way, and so did we.

Our respondents had fairly strong views about what the political parties stand for. The Conservatives were deemed to stand for 'individualism and self-help' (18%), 'free enterprise' (18%), and 'tradition and the status quo' (13%). The Liberal Democrats represented 'consensus' (30%), 'idealism' (18%), 'sound social politics' (15%), and somewhat negatively, 'people who can't make their minds up' (by 15%). Attitudes to labour tended to be much more negative: 'equality' (24%), 'state intervention' (16%), and 'working-class interests' (16%). The Scottish National Party was regarded as standing for 'putting Scotland first' (20%), 'independence from Westminster' (20%)' and 'destructive nationalism' (17%).

Overall the Conservative Party attracted the most favourable comments (46%, to 23% which were negative), with the Liberal Democrats not far behind (43% and 20% respectively). Labour was viewed fairly negatively (40% to 20% who gave it positive mentions), but the greatest criticism was reserved for the Scottish National Party who attracted negative comments from 45% of our sample, and positive ones from only 15%. It was the SNP rather than Labour which drew the greatest degree of disapproval from our sample. This is interesting, given the plausible assumption between cultural and political nationalism. It was almost as if our respondents felt the need to deny the political implications of their commitment to 'Scottish heritage'.

Responses to the question 'Which political party in your opinion is most concerned about heritage'? reinforced the dissociation of politics from heritage. Few of our respondents thought that any party is more concerned about heritage than their political rivals. Nearly a third (32%) thought that none of the parties is particularly concerned. Just under a quarter (23%) thought that the Conservatives are the most concerned, and the same proportion could not say. Of those who thought that parties do make a difference most used their own experience as the basis of their reply. Those who thought it made no difference argued that this was because heritage has very little political pay-off for the parties. The following comments give a flavour of the responses:

> The Tories are letting stuff go down the drain, and I can't see that Labour would be able to give it a priority. But none of the parties can really be trusted on heritage. (Conservative voter)

> They (Labour) care for the people and the people are the heritage. (Labour voter)

> Lib Dems – because they think a bit better. The Tories are influenced by the landed gentry to preserve the land for themselves. (Liberal Democrat voter)

> The SNP because they are the only ones concerned about *Scottish* heritage. (SNP voter)

CONCLUSIONS

In our study, we sought answers to two things. Firstly, to identify whether NTS life members conceived of heritage as a product or as a set of 'sacred' values. Secondly, to explore the link between cultural nationalism and political nationalism. We were interested in finding out if heritage in Scotland carries a political message.

Our survey revealed that 'heritage' was an important word in the vocabulary of NTS life members. It was a term that virtually all our respondents used freely and easily. Heritage is not a trivial issue foisted on life members unwittingly or unwillingly. The majority of our respondents had little difficulty distinguishing heritage from history. History was most commonly seen as 'the past', as something remote and over. Heritage, in contrast, was regarded as more relevant, meaningful, and connected with their everyday lives. It conveyed a sense of lineage and inheritance in which the objects of heritage conferred identity and acted as vehicles for bringing the past into the present.

The second hypothesis we set out to investigate was the supposed link between politics and heritage. During the last thirty years there has been a revival of both cultural and political nationalism in Scotland. It seemed to us plausible that this should be expressed in and through heritage. This hypothesis was not supported by our evidence. The majority of life members in our sample (40%) were Conservative supporters. The Scottish National Party received the least support (4.2%). Indeed, the group's antipathy was reserved for the nationalist party and its seeming capture of the Scottish issue. Yet in terms of national identity our respondents saw themselves as Scots first and foremost, and pointed to major differences between Scottish and English heritage.

Our survey of life members of the NTS shows that the relationship between politics and heritage is far from straightforward. Life members in our sample had a strong and coherent sense of heritage both at a personal and a national/Scottish level but did not translate this cultural commitment into a political one in any simple way. Their political identity does not deny their cultural or national one.

The Authors

Angela Morris is a Rural Sociologist at the Scottish Agricultural College, Edinburgh. David McCrone is Reader in Sociology at Edinburgh University, and author of the acclaimed *Understanding Scotland: The Sociology of a Stateless Nation*. Richard Kiely is Research Fellow at the Research Centre for the Social Sciences at Edinburgh University.

*This paper draws extensively on material contained in *Scotland - the Brand: the Making of Scottish Heritage* (especially chapters 6 and 7) by David McCrone, Angela Morris & Richard Kiely, published by Edinburgh University Press, 1995.

References

Association of Scottish Visitor Attractions, *Visitor Attractions Survey,1992*

Hewison, R., *The Heritage Industry: Britain in a Climate of Decline*, Methuen, 1987

Miller, D., *Material Culture and Mass Consumption*, Blackwell, 1987

National Trust for Scotland, *Heritage Scotland*, NTS, 1994

Rosie, G., 'Museumry and the Heritage Industry', in Donnachie, I., and Whatley (eds), *The Manufacture of Scottish History*, Polygon, 1992

Samuel, R., in *The Independent on Sunday*, 12 Jan 1995

Urry, J., *The Tourist Gaze: Leisure and Travel in Contemporary Societies*, Sage, 1990

Wright, P., *On Living in an Old Country: The National Past in Contemporary Britain*, Verso, 1985

10

CLERGYMAN AND MERCHANT
An Iconography of the Dutch

Frans Schouten

A Dutch philosopher once said: 'The last thing a fish would find out is that it lives in water. Only on the fishmonger's slab will it discover what it is to be a water creature.'[1] Indeed, it is when we are out of our native context that we find out, often through others, the essentials of our own way of life. One can most easily describe the characteristics of a nation in a comparative way, and in comparison understand how others see us. Our relationship with the inhabitants of the UK is very revealing in this sense. For example, the adjective 'Dutch' in the English language tends to be used in a pejorative way, as in 'double Dutch'. This may have something to do with the fact that both countries have been competitors as traders or merchants on the high seas. There is some truth in this as the Duke de Baena, the Spanish ambassador to The Netherlands reports in an anecdote about the Dutchmen's lack of tact. He reports that at a lecture about the differences in character between the English and the Dutch. The speaker gave a large amount of historic examples of blunt, unmannered behaviour of the Dutch:

> What made his speech considerably more significant however was the fact that every time he cited these examples, the Dutch audience laughed heartily on hearing of the misbehaviour of their compatriots. Here the lesson was clear: the Dutch are not ashamed of their rough or impolite manners – they simply have no desire or intention to correct them. They consider this behaviour characteristic, even humorous, and can reach the point of being rather proud of it.[2]

As an Italian visitor to our country once observed: 'The Dutch are so low key about their own country that you only can interpreted it as the ultimate expression of pride.'

The main landmark of The Netherlands is water, both physically and mentally: water shaped our land and our characters. The struggle with both sea and rivers, claiming the land, and to protect the Low Countries has had a great impact on our frame of mind. It made us law-abiding, neat people with a strong sense of community and duty. The maintenance of dikes requests these qualities: it is a communal responsibility, it calls for good co-operation and everyone's involvement. An old form of local authority is the 'dijkgraaf' (dike count) an elected representative of the community to co-ordinate the maintenance of the dikes.

Our compliance with the authorities was strongly reinforced by the Protestant belief that the government is representing the Lord on earth. This compliance is diminishing, as it is everywhere else in the Western World. But the Dutch still live basically in a culture of consent. Put two Dutch together and you will have a commission, consensus is the ultimate goal. Even to the extent that discussion in parliament is often extremely dull because every bit of controversy is given to a commission of experts, and when it is really controversial it is given to a commission of wise men and women. But if consensus cannot be reached, the Dutch are in trouble, specially in religious matters. The historian Romein remarked:

> One Dutchman is a Conviction,
> Two Dutchmen are a Congregation,
> Three Dutchmen are a Synod.
> Four Dutchmen are a Schism.[3]

However, the Dutch compliance with authority does not specifically imply respectful behaviour. We have a tendency to treat everyone else as an equal, which can be very confusing for foreigners. A German observed in the 17th century:

> These people do not show much respect for their superiors. The subjects not only talk imprudently about the ones placed above them, they will even tell to their faces whatever pleases them. The lady of the house is hardly distinguishable from her servant, apart from the fact that the former may be found in the master's bed. At the dinner table no order is being kept, and the maid chatters and laughs at least as loud and as much as Madam.[4]

Traditionally, the Dutch have a twofold identity which is best described as 'clergyman and merchant'. The clergyman is the preacher, the missionary, the one who knows what is good for others, and who will endeavour to convince others of the correct faith or belief system. The merchant is the one who knows what others want, and who seeks ways to make a profit. The Dutch identity expresses itself in both ways. Most of our behaviour can be identified with one or other of these labels. Usually the merchant comes before the clergyman, when the market is established we will start to make converts to our own views.

The Dutch like to think of themselves as being very tolerant, and in a way we are, as long as it pays dividends. Due to our international trade background we respect anyone's belief systems as long as there is some mutual profit to gain. Our famous religious tolerance is partly based on that principle and partly on the principle of non-interference: if you leave others alone they will leave you alone. There are so many different Christian denominations in The Netherlands that such 'tolerance' has less to do with acceptance of different belief systems, than with co-habitation and consensus.

An important Dutch characteristic is the concept 'Pillars of Society'. These are socio-political groups with a specific identity formed around religious or secular belief systems. Their emergence dates back to the 19th century when the Roman Catholic Church, after centuries of 'illegal' practice, was again allowed in the public domain. The emancipation of the Catholics alongside the emancipation of the (liberal) bourgeoisie and the (socialist) lower classes, together with the emergence of other religious and socio-cultural groups laid a cornerstone in the formation of Dutch identity. This was the struggle for equal financial resources for pubic and private schools. In the early 20th century the battle was won in parliament in favour of those groups striving for equal opportunities to provide education in accordance with their religious beliefs. Major social divisions arose through every group organising itself with self contained provisions for almost every aspect of human behaviour. These groups, the so-called 'Pillars' looked after their flock in a most diligent manner with the support of government grants.

A multifarious network of services for all kind of denominations was established, such as Roman Catholics, different Protestant groups, Jews, liberals, socialists, etc. Each denomination acquired its own schools, hospitals, welfare organisations, homes for elderly people, leisure and sport clubs, broadcasting corporations, the list being far from complete. As a result the role of central government in The Netherlands is less centralised than in other European countries, and accordingly serves more as a facilitator of the private initiatives of citizens. Private initiative and the role of different associations and foundations are dominant aspects of almost any activity carried out in Dutch society.

This applies for any sector of the community, and particularly in the field of museums and heritage, although in this sector the role of the different interest groups are not as strong as in education and welfare. The reason for this is that the elite of the different socio-cultural 'pillars' share the same cultural value systems, and as the masses of their flocks would not participate in these activities there was no obvious reason for segregation in the cultural domain.[5] 'Apartheid' is after all a Dutch noun.

This system of segregation of provisions for different denominations is now eroding due to the general secularisation of society, but the role of private initiative is still very strong in every sector of Dutch society. There is a strong feeling that private foundations supported by government is a better vehicle for activities than direct steering from a central authority. So the sector of heritage institutions is generally scattered with a myriad of organisations at local, regional, provincial, and national levels. The advantage is a strong personal involvement by active members of groups. The obvious disadvantage is fragmentation of effort and a general lack of co-ordination. This problem is often dealt with by national organisations working for the common interest of a certain group of institutions, eg the national and provincial associations of museums and the Association for the Care of Monuments, etc.

This emphasis on the private sector is the prevailing trend in The Netherlands, and is reflected in the preference for foundations. The national and regional authorities are withdrawing from direct influence in the public domain. Everywhere we can see the tendency for central government to give more space for private initiative and less interference from policy makers on the national and local levels. Deregulation, decentralisation, and privatisation are the key words in the public sector. In the field of culture, including heritage and museums, this tendency is becoming particularly prevalent. This development conforms to a much older principle of cultural policy, that of government detachment. This has been implemented in various ways since Thorbecke, an influential 19th century Dutch liberal statesman. The present interpretation of his principles is that central government draws up the outlines for policy after due consideration of the key issues.

It is not just that authorities are withdrawing altogether from this sector, because there will always be some kind of link to government policy and subsidies, but the emphasis is shifting. Implementation is left almost entirely to the independent foundations.

The National Museums are a good example of this trend. Although they officially belong to central government, their raison d'être lies in society. Consequently, they are faced with a dual allegiance, and their problem in many cases is that the interests of the museum profession and central government do not coincide, causing serious strain in working relationships. For example, since the National Museums are part of central government, the Minister can be held politically responsible for actions by individual museums. It is the case that central government house rules make quick and decisive action on museum matters extremely difficult. The response has been for the state owned heritage sites and museums to be privatised in their operations. The collections and the sites and monuments themselves are still owned by the central government, but management has the freedom to operate in its own way like private foundations, deciding their own priorities and developing their product accordingly[6].

The old situation in the National Museums was as follows:

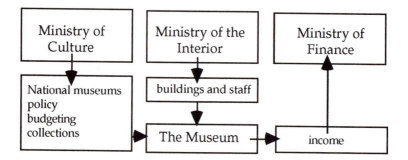

The museums had to deal with three ministries for different aspects of their functioning. At the end of the process, all the earned income from tickets, postcards, and catalogues went straight into the pocket of the Ministry of Finance. Under this system it did not matter to museum directors whether they had 1,000 or 100,000 visitors a year as no surplus remained with the museums. So no real incentives to improve the performance of the museums existed.

Although the collections are still owned by the state, the situation is dramatically different after privatisation. Museums are fully independent in their operation and their own money earning activities, but they have to adhere to policies set down by the Ministry of Culture. The situation in the UK is similar and is illustrated below:

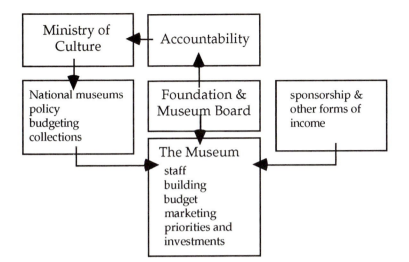

In these circumstances, it is of vital importance for any museum or heritage attraction to raise the level of its income. The successful operation of all its functions depends much more on the ability to raise funds and to find alternative sources of income. However, subsidies by government agencies are still a very important part of museum budgets, in particular with regard to collections in the care of the state or the community. But other ways of financing are becoming increasingly more important.

This tendency is also apparent in other museums. A recent survey of the provincial museums in Brabant[7] shows that although the volume of grants from local authorities has hardly changed over the last years, the actual budget of the museums have increased due to greater fund raising efforts, sales, extension of services, and the renting out of space in the museum for receptions, dinners and even weddings.

Alongside the ongoing deregulation of heritage policy and the increasing importance of foundations, there is another shift of emphasis apparent. Currently, the attention is focusing more on the care of collections, due to a report from the Netherlands Court of Audit in 1988 which identified neglect of museum collections. In 1990, the government decided to implement a 'Delta-plan' to deal with overdue maintenance in the collections and museum buildings within a short period of time.

Part of this operation was the assessment of the museum collections in terms of the value of the stored objects related to the theme and task of the specific museum. The collections were rated A (prime interest), B (secondary interest, but worthwhile keeping), and C (for disposal). In the last category disposal did not necessarily mean to getting rid of them, but trying to find out what other local collections would be interested to obtain the object. In the policy document on accessibility and conservation of the museum heritage, 'Kiezen voor kwaliteit' (Opting for Quality), presented in the Lower House on 21 December 1990, the Minister set the following conditions:

- the disposal of museum objects may only occur after it has been established that these are of lesser importance in relation to the museum's aims and objectives;
- disposal should be in accordance with the collection policy of the museum, which should be co-ordinated with that of other museums to prevent either overlaps or lacunae becoming prevalent;
- disposal will only be permitted after it has been clearly established that neither an exchange nor a permanent loan is possible;
- any revenues from sales should always be used for the purpose of acquisition to improve the quality of the collection.[8]

The government has made additional resources available both for National Museums and other museums to carry out these reviews. The scheme has been highly successful so far. However, resourcing collection reviews is ad hoc, and all the work is carried out in the form of projects and contracted to free-lance consultants.

Closely linked with the process of deregulation, institutions are required more and more to focus on their core functions and try to reduce their fixed financial commitments. Every aspect of professional museum work is increasingly carried out as a form of subcontracted labour. We encounter guest-curators employed on a fixed term contract to work on a specific part of a collection, or preparing an exhibition, for which the museum is unable to employ a permanent curator. In some museums, there are volunteer curators, mainly young graduates who seek work experience for their curriculum vitae. In-house exhibition designers are rare nowadays as specialised firms are contracted to do the job. Even functions that until recently were considered to be part of the core function of the museum, like educational programmes, are in many cases subcontracted. This tendency is caused by the insecurity of government funding policies, and greater dependency on income obtained from other sources .

The dichotomy between Clergyman and Merchant has become clearly visible in another aspect of policy at all levels in recent years. There has been a shift from regarding culture, specifically museums, as a heritage asset in its own right, to a commodity in economic development. Traditionally, public expenditure on culture was defended in 'Enlightenment' terms as being good for the education and well-being of the population. Financial resources were made available to ensure that everyone had equal access to the nation's cultural resources, and the emphasis was upon a policy of dissemination and optimal participation. The key word today is no longer 'participation' but 'marketing'. Cultural activities and resources like museums and monuments are now seen as key elements in the promotion of cities, the image building of an area, as promotional assets in the competition among local authorities to attract enterprises, new inhabitants and tourists as sources of income.

Very much like the British did earlier, Robert Hewison minted the term 'Heritage Industry' in 1987, the Dutch have discovered their heritage as an asset in the increasingly competitive world of tourism. Heritage professionals have to become accustomed to this new perspective, because they have to use a new vocabulary to write their grant applications, although they find it hard to see their institutions reduced to economic assets. In the world of museums, tourism is a rather demeaning prospect. Most museum professionals prefer to ignore the impact of tourism. They prefer to see their customers as lovers and connoisseurs of art and history and treat them accordingly.

Any person who reads Kenneth Hudson's *A social history of museums*[9] cannot avoid the impression that things have not changed much. Museums are still somewhat introvert institutions, distinguished and respected members of society, with a rather condescending attitude towards the general public.

There are several reasons why certain segments of society still feel that heritage is 'not for our kind of people'. First of all, the world represented by museums is not the world as perceived by the general public. It is a world structured by scientific laws, by taxonomy, and by a division in periods which is not at all common ground for the lay person. Museum professionals tend to forget that what is obvious for them is not clear to everyone else. In most museums, all the objects tend to look alike for the non-specialist, especially if they are piled up in large quantities.

Secondly, the communication in museums is rather conventional. Everyone is presumed to start form the same point and to undergo the same knowledge enhancing experience at the same pace. Thus, the visitor plays the passive role and museums the active role. Access to museums is highly structured, predetermined and controlled by staff so as to be 'correct, understandable, and educational'[10]. Such an explicit learning environment can be threatening. It puts a person in the situation of one who does not know, and it often makes a them feel stupid. The idea is persistent among museum people that the visitors come to learn something in the museum. However, a number of recent studies demonstrate that members of the public do not learn a great deal[11].

Related to this is the neglected fact that one of the most important reasons for visiting a museum is the opportunity for social interaction. Research done by Paulette MacManus shows very clearly that a visit to an exhibition is a social occasion. Visitors hardly ever come alone, they present themselves in small groups as a family or friends, etc. Visiting the displays is a means of interacting with each other[12].

Furthermore, museums do not always provide quality services for their customers. The assessment of the heritage attraction should not be entirely based upon the scientific correctness of the core product, but also on how effective the site or the exhibition is in raising curiosity, appealing to fantasy, and in providing a challenge. Neither should we neglect questions such as how clean are the toilets, how easy is it to park the car, the choice of items in the shop, and the quality of the catering.

The last challenge directed at heritage professionals by politicians is related to the traditional Dutch 'tolerance'. How do we deal with museums in a multi-cultural environment? Cultural and ethnic roots are becoming increasingly important, to quote Naisbitt:

> The more homogeneous our lifestyles become, the more steadfastly we shall cling to deeper values, we all seek to preserve our identities, be they religious, cultural, national, linguistic, or racial, the more worlds grow more similar, we shall increasingly treasure the traditions that spring from within.[13]

Is everyone entitled to their own museum, like the Anacostia Neighbour-hood Museum in Washington DC or the Museum of the Transvaal Neighbourhood in The Hague? The latter museum is depicting the life of ordinary people in an typical Dutch lower middle class setting, putting their lives into a broader historical and sociological perspective. However laudable these intentions might be, we probably can not go on providing every subculture and neighbourhood with its own museum as a focal point of local pride and identity.

Emphasis on one's own historical and cultural roots is an undeniable human right, but nobody can deny the role of museums to present a cultural identity, as well as emphasising the universality of human culture. A good example of this approach is the new Museum of Religions Life and Art in Glasgow where all major religions are presented and which is devoted to the universal search of mankind for the meaning of life. Although the representatives of 'minority' religions were very positive about the initiative, some comments from mainstream Scottish Christians were interesting. A Reverend from the Free Presbyterian Church refused to attend the opening of the museum because Christianity was portrayed as 'just another religion'.[14]

In a multi-cultural society museums have to be aware of the needs of 'minorities' among the population. Not so much in the creation of new museums for these groups, which are merely a political gesture, as the Moluccan Historical Museum in Holland. The Netherlands are providing a better example in the exhibition on the Chinese community in the Amsterdam Historical Museum as part of its overall policy to focus on the diversity that constitutes the actual city of Amsterdam.

By this example we are back were we started: with seeing our own culture through the eyes of someone else. To include in the presentations of our own heritage, the stories of other traditions that contributed to what we currently call 'The Netherlands' gives us a fresh look into our own culture. After all culture is about assimilation. Is the famous Dutch 'Rijsttafel' not an Indonesian dish called 'Nasi Goreng'?

The Author

Frans Schouten studied at the University of Utrecht, and he was appointed Senior Lecturer in Museum Education and Design of Exhibitions at the Reinwardt Academy in 1976 He was Director of this training centre 1981–90. From there he worked as a freelance consultant specialising in the management, presentation and exploitation of cultural heritage, being involved in projects such as new presentations in the National Museum of Natural History in Leiden, and of professional training for the Mediterranean area at the Centro Euoropeo del Patrimonio, Barcelona. He was assigned by UNESCO, to develop a cultural tourism strategy for Central Java and the Yogyakarta Area, an inventory of cultural tourist attractions and a prototype for site interpretation at Hindu and Buddhist monuments. He developed an operational plan for the cultural centre at the National Museum of the Solomon Islands and for a prehistoric hill fort on Fiji. He is now senior lecturer in heritage management at the National Institute of Tourism and Transport Studies at Breda.

References

1   Portman, H., *Wat is er met de mens gebeurd?* Bilthoven, 1971
2   Duke de Baena, *The Dutch Puzzle,* 1967
3   Romein, J., *Beschouwingen over het Nederladse Volkskarakter,* 1942
4   Benthem, H., *Hollandischer Kirch, Schuler, Staat,* 1698
5   Bevers, T., *Georganiseerde Cultuur,* Baarn, 1992
6   Lodder, G., *A Closer Look at Museum Policies,* unpublished document, 1988
7   Siderius, M, *BA Thesis,* NHTV, Breda, June 1995
8   Bloemberg, W., *Autonomy for the national museum in The Netherlands,* Ministry of Education, Culture and Science, Rijswik, 1994
9   Hudson, K., *A Social History of Museums,* London, 1975
10 Ames, M., *De-schooling the museums: a proposal to increase public access to the museum and their resources,* Museum 145, 1985, pp 25–31
11 Miles, R., *Museum Audiences,* International Journal of Museum Management and Curatorship 5, 1986, pp 73–80
12 McManus, P., *Communication with and between Visitors to a Science Museum,* Ph.D. Thesis, University of London, 1987
13 Naisbitt, J., *Megatrends 2000,* New York, 1990, p 120
14 The Late Show, 9 April 1993, BBC

11

THE OUTDOOR VIKING
How the Norwegians Do It

Per Frøyland Pallesen

Few other countries in Europe have a stronger bonding between people and the natural environment which finds expression in the nation's cultural iconography and identity. Norway has been described as a large country with a small population, ranked as number six in Western Europe when measured in terms of land area. It has a population of 4.3 million, giving a population density of 12 per square kilometre. Human settlement is spread over the whole of the country, and agriculture accounts for no more than 3% of Norway's total area. Only 1% of the country is urbanised, leaving the remainder in the category of woods and mountains. Some 70% of the total area is above the tree line and represents mountainous wilderness.

It was not until this century that Norway could honestly be described by the adjectives industrial and urban. Today some 75% of the total population lives in urban communities. At the turn of the century the equivalent percentage was 28%. These simple statistics clearly show that up until one or two generations ago, the majority of the population lived in close contact with nature and had to rely on the primary sectors of farming, fishing and forestry as the basis of their economic survival. Most Norwegians therefore have a close relationship to the primary sector. Many of us still have a close relative living 'in the country'. Therefore what is characterised as typically Norwegian in cultural terms often has its roots in farming, fishing and seafaring.

Norwegian natural resources are large when measured in terms of the possibilities offered by modern technology. However, until the outbreak of the Second World War, the country could only be classed among the poorer nations of Europe. In fact, large numbers of the population were not far from poverty. Dependence upon and the right to use the natural resources of the sea, land, forests and mountains have therefore for hundreds of years been a critical factor for the population and for our cultural activity. Demands on the landscape have therefore been considerable in order to meet the fishing, hunting and agricultural needs of a growing population.

From the time of the Vikings, laws have existed which give the individual rights to free movement in the countryside and on water. In addition, the right to harvest freely from what nature produces, with some limitations on hunting and certain areas of freshwater fishing is also laid down by law. This tradition is the basis on which the development of what can be called typical Norwegian leisure activities is founded.

Right of free access makes Norway an attractive tourist destination, but also creates pressure on the very resources which provide the attraction in the first place. The country now has to meet significant challenges, such as how can an expanding tourist industry use our beautiful natural resource assets within the rights of free access? Furthermore, how can we meet the demands of tourism development and industrial activity generally in a sustainable manner?

THE RIGHT OF ACCESS

The right of free access to the countryside is based on two fundamental concepts, the term 'innmark' (cultivated land) and 'utmark' (uncultivated land). This right of access is the foundation of the principle of 'allemannsretten' (all men's right), and the Open Air Recreation Act of 1957 gives everyone the right to free passage on uncultivated land all year round and on cultivated land between 15 October and 1 May when the ground is snow covered or frozen. In addition to walking, the right includes activities such as cycling, riding, picnicking, camping, bathing, landing and mooring of boats, etc. The right of access also includes the collection of wild mushrooms, plants, nuts and berries with the exception of cloudberries in Northern Norway. Certain restrictions do exist such as the distance to be kept from an occupied house or chalet and the duration of a camping visit. It is not permitted to use cultivated land for picnicking, sunbathing, staying overnight or the like without the owner's consent. In general, no activity under the right of free access must take place when it can result in significant damage to a young forest or cause damage to fences.

The right to free access has had, and still has, great significance not only for Norwegian outdoor recreation but also for the nation's cultural well being in general. The majority of Norwegians grow up in close contact with nature. The tradition of active use of the countryside is kept alive by outdoor family activities, the use of nature by schools, active pursuits by scouts and ramblers, as well as for hunting and fishing.

OUTDOOR RECREATION

There is a high level of outdoor recreation in Norway. The most widespread activity is recreational walking in which more than 80% of the population participate. Perhaps most striking is that over 60% go rambling in the summer and skiing in the winter, and 50% participate in boating activities.

The most uniquely Norwegian form of outdoor recreation is mountain hiking. Den Norske Turistforening (DNT) was founded in 1868 and is a nation-wide organisation for hikers. Today it is an umbrella organisation for some fifty regional mountain touring associations. These associations are responsible for building and running huts, marking trails and arranging tours in their respective districts. DNT maintain 19,000 km of signposted trails throughout the country and offers its members access to 330 huts and

Figure 1 Hiking on a marked trail.

Figure 2 Coastal landscape in Rogaland with traditional boathouse (naust).

lodges. Some trails are staked out in the late winter for cross-country ski touring from hut to hut. The main objective of the organisation is to promote a simple, healthy, sustainable and active outdoor life.

The association's aim is to reach all sections of the population, and especially the young, offering a wide variety of guided tours to meet different levels of proficiency. Tours are also available for the elderly and for young families. Although the majority of tours offered are for people with average good health there are also a wide range of services offered for specialist activities. These include glacier walking courses, courses in the basic principles of mountain climbing, dog sledging, skiing schools and in the basic principles of building and using snowholes. DNT has an approximate membership of 180,000. Annual membership costs £32 and includes a yearbook in full colour and a magazine which is distributed six times a year. These facilities and services are available for non-members at a higher rate. It has been estimated that approximately 5% of the population use the facilities offered by the DNT annually.

It can be argued that mountain hiking activity has a profound effect on the attitudes of Norwegians to nature and the natural environment and how to survive in the great outdoors. Activity is essentially at the level of the individual, summer and winter alike, where the signposted trails are essentially a guiding infrastructure for touring. One is expected to rely upon one's own capabilities by using maps and compass, for example, when the signposted trail is suddenly covered by snow.

This type of activity helps to create respect for the vicissitudes of climate so that the individual is able to cope with any weather conditions. It also stimulates an interest in flora and wildlife which encourage an understanding of the sensitivities of different species and ecosytems. For example, the knowledge hikers gain about the wild reindeer population is of fundamental importance in regard to the public debate concerned with measures for the culling and conservation of this species.

The fact that a large number of huts are run on a self-service basis is also of significance in terms of personal development. There is not only the need to make your own meals and wash up afterwards, but also in the development of social skills through activities such as providing fuel for heating, collecting water, digging snow and tidying up together before departure. Honesty is an essential requirement within the DNT system. To pay for the food and services used, one has to fill in a simple form, put it in an honesty box and the sum will be deducted from one's bank account. The system is naturally vulnerable and open to abuse and it is unfortunately under some pressure at the present time.

The DNT is also an active non-governmental organisation in the national environment debate. It plays a central role together with other important NGOs such as The Norwegian Society for Conservation of Nature and The Norwegian Society for Hunting and Fishing. Their contribution is important, not only in discussions concerning nature conservation policies, but also in terms of fundamental questions regarding sustainable development. They have an organised lobby for dealing with the government and they represent approximately half a million members (an eighth of the population). These organisations have to a large extent been able to dominate the agenda for environmental policies in fields such as preservation of rivers and waterfalls, creation of national parks and other conservation areas. They have led the

Figure 3 'Hytteliv'. Family laying a turf roof.

Figure 4 Recently improved footpath to Preikestolen in Rogaland.

arguments for the liming of rivers to combat acidification and operate as watchdogs to preserve the ban on motorised transport off the roads and on rivers. An example of this problem is the snow scooter, their use has increased dramatically, together with a growing demand for more liberal legislation. Attempts have also been made to begin heliskiing, where the transportation of tourists to the mountains by helicopter and plane has been proposed on many occasions. So far these proposals have met with no success. The guiding principal today is that transport off roads both on snow and on bare ground and also in the air should be limited to what is necessary to meet the needs of farming, provisioning of huts and other facilities. This covers the transport of both food supplies and other general provisions.

Snow scooter services are provided by farmers under licence. Snow scooter permits are issued by local municipalities to local inhabitants as a sort of taxi licence, in accordance with national by-laws. However, there is a degree of abuse which has caused increasing concern, both in regard to noise pollution that such traffic causes and in relation to the disturbance of the natural environment. This form of traffic exposes wildlife to needless stress, and the question of erosion in the summertime is also important.

Several other forms of outdoor recreation are also of major importance to the national way of life and influence people's attitudes towards the use of natural resources. Beside mountain hiking and hillwalking, boating is the next most important private means of recreation. The Norwegian coastline is some 20,000 kilometres in length, comprised of approximately 150,000 islands, a large number of fjords and sheltered waters offering perfect conditions for the use of almost 500,000 private boats. These vary in size from ten to approximately fifty feet. This fleet gives the owners the opportunity to reach islands and fjords of high quality which would otherwise not have been easily accessible. The demand from this sector creates a need to establish a large number of public recreation and conservation areas along the coast for boat-based weekend camping, as well as holidaying in bigger boats which generates substantial fishing activity. The maintenance and running of this recreation fleet develops skills of various kinds and creates self sufficiency and an awareness of the need to preserve the environment.

A similar analysis can also be made in regard to Norwegian 'hytte liv' – which is a term Norwegians use to describe what they do when staying at their second home in the country or seaside. This 'hytte liv' gives one a feeling of living close to nature and also strengthens one's identity with the location and area where the second home is located. There are approximately 400,000 of these in Norway, one for every tenth person in the population. Generally speaking they are on the coast or in the mountains, but they are also to be found scattered around in hills and woodlands. This large number of buildings, together with related infrastructure, naturally represents a substantial pressure on the environment and landscape. This pressure varies from area to area. Generally speaking, there is sufficient land available for this number of second homes as long as they are located in accordance with municipal plans and national guidelines. With the exception of the southern coastline and a limited number of mountainous areas, there are relatively few problems associated with this type of development.

Life and activities associated with a Norwegian's second home centres around a set of traditions, such as self-building activities (carpentry), general maintenance, wood cutting for fuel, fishing and many other forms of outdoor activities. 'Hytte liv' is therefore regarded as an important factor in developing public concern for conservation and protection of heritage assets.

PLANNING OPEN AIR ACTIVITIES IN URBAN AREAS

The right of free access does not cover all aspects of outdoor activity. Most towns and small communities in Norway have 'bymark' (common land) which is usually woodland close to urban settlements. Some densely populated areas, eg the Stavanger region are surrounded by agricultural land where the right of free access does not apply, even in the winter months due to the region's mild climate. In recent years priority has been given to the creation of areas in and around larger towns to stimulate outdoor recreation. This partly builds on the strong tradition in the population as a whole for outdoor activity, and it also has roots in socio-medical considerations.

The availability of recreational areas near to where people live will stimulate and increase levels of physical activity. Research shows that distance from paths where one can cycle, walk or jog is very important regarding frequency of use. Furthermore, the close relationship between recreational and policy goals are significant for sports authorities which view such paths as 'cheap sports facilities with a large capacity and minimal running costs'. This is even the case with artificially lit routes for use during the hours of darkness. Another argument which favours this type of development is connected with the cost of car transport. In urban areas, footpaths and cycle routes represent an environmentally friendly and sustainable alternative form of transport. Outdoor recreation areas in close proximity to residential areas will also reduce the need to travel to more distant parts.

As a result there is now public pressure to establish green lanes in and around urban areas. These areas are planned in such a way as to ensure variety and continuity throughout an entire urban area. In the Stavanger region such green lanes have already been planned and to a large extent realised in the same way as one would plan and build a sewage, telephone, water or road network. One criterion for such initiatives is that no housing unit must be further than 500 metres away from a green lane. This planning approach has been strongly supported at the regional level of planning, and has received financial support from both central and local government. It can be said that up to now this planning activity has been very successful, measured in terms of the increased use of existing green lanes which will hopefully improve the health and well being of those with access to such facilities.

All these aspects of Norwegian culture and outdoor tradition are in many ways the backbone of the Norwegian tourist industry. The facilities, the natural resources and cultural heritage are already present and can form basis for substantial growth. The difficult challenge facing us now is how this growth can be achieved without adversely affecting local attitudes to environmental conservation and the ability of local communities to meet their own recreational needs. The big question is how can tourism development be achieved in harmony with the national tradition of an active recreational life in natural surroundings? Or, put another way, how can a sustainable tourist industry be developed?

THE TOURIST INDUSTRY

The tourist industry is of great significance both at present and increasingly so for Norway in the future. This is partly due to the anticipated reduction in oil related activity, and tourism is viewed as an important alternative for economic development and increased employment. In 1993 tourism generated 4 billion pounds in gross national product. Total employment in the tourist sector is estimated at approximately 80,000 jobs. Norwegians account for some 65% of all overnight stays, but overseas visitors have shown the strongest growth in recent years. The annual growth rate for overseas visitors to Norway increased by 11% between 1993 and 1994, compared with 4% in Europe as a whole.

The majority are Europeans at 82%, and of these Germans account for 23%. Americans and Japanese are also important groups in the overall picture. The development of tourism is a priority area at all levels of government. Strategic plans are being produced where the development of communications, strengthening of education and professionalism in the tourist related sectors are main objectives.

The Government defines the main challenge in terms of meeting the growing international trend towards heritage based tourism. Norway's landscape assets coupled with an increasing awareness of its culture and lifestyle give Norwegian tourism a good basis to compete in this market. To meet the challenge of how to secure sustainable development demands an increase in know-how and quality of management so as to ensure that the natural and cultural resources on which we depend are properly maintained and not spoilt. In this way tourism can even strengthen the protection of our heritage.

Policy in this area is important and diffuse. There is a clear need to develop operational goals and criteria for a sustainable tourist industry, and we must formulate guidelines for how 'green tourism' can be developed in practice. However, there are large divergences of opinion and marked differences in perceptions among the sectors involved. There are those with interests in a technically based tourism product on one side. Then there are those who have their starting point rooted in Norwegian tradition and experience of nature conservation, for whom the environment, limited use of resources and individual activity are central ingredients and fundamental elements.

WHAT ATTRACTS TOURISTS?

The main attraction of a holiday in Norway is the landscape and enjoyment of the natural environment. Taking part in outdoor activities is therefore of great importance for large numbers of tourists. Research has shown that over half of car borne tourists participate in outdoor activities during their stay. In the case of North Cape some 90% of those interviewed reported that they had taken part in outdoor activities, primarily short walking trips. Even those who have experienced Norway through the car window, report that the view of an unspoilt natural environment was an important part of their stay. The majority of tourists visit the natural gems which have a high attraction level such as the national parks and special geological formations. These attractions offer mainly personal activity. An interview at one of these mass tourism areas, Briksdalsbreen, revealed that most visitors have a positive attitude towards active outdoor recreation and environmental considerations. Only 4% answered yes in reply to a question as to whether they would like to see improved accessibility to the area where one has to walk some 2km on a footpath to reach a main destination. In fact 80% were against an improved path.

Virtually all those interviewed were very satisfied with their visit to Briksdalsbreen and the reason for this response was quite simply, the natural environment. In comparison, on the North Cape, there has been improvements to accessibility at this site, but only 58% were satisfied with their visit. Dissatisfaction would appear to be related to the fact that accessibility spoils the visitor experience. As many as 25% were in agreement with the quote 'The location is spoiled by the modern and commercial tourist machine' and a further 50% agreed with the quote 'the physical tourist development reduces the special qualities and experience of nature on the site'.

There would appear to be a higher level of tolerance for measures to improve accessibility and services on the periphery of such attractions. These include paths and tours which are designed to channel visitors and reduce pressure on the environment in the area. A very interesting aspect of visitor perception of management is that foreign visitors seem to be aware of the difference in the way Norway tackles these problems as compared to how it is done in The Alps, and they cite this form of management as one of the very attractions of visiting Norway. These observations would appear to agree with other sources regarding international tourist trends. A Norwegian tourist expert with a background in the German market explains these preferences as follows:

– More unspoilt nature
– More of the original
– More warmth
– More mental stimulation
– More consideration for individual preference
– More comfort

This implies that holidays must increasingly be different from what one experiences at home. One must partake on both the physical and mental level while what one is experiencing must as far as is possible be real and unspoilt. At the same time high quality is of fundamental importance.

Horst Opaschowski, the German Professor at Freizeit Forschingsinstitut in Hamburg has formulated ten 'commandments' for quality vacations in years to come:

– Unspoilt nature
– Friendly atmosphere
– Tidy and pleasant

- Sun
- Healthy and comfortable climate
- Good culinary standard
- Quiet and little traffic
- Original and unspoilt surroundings
- Bathing possibilities in the sea, rivers or lakes
- A wide variety of restaurants, cafes and pubs

These commandments are in many ways a question of preference of lifestyle and will naturally vary from one individual to another and from one country to another. However they clearly signal an international trend which undoubtedly ought to be able to be considered in the development of a sustainable tourist industry. Norway would appear to be in possession of many of the characteristics outlined by Professor Opaschowski although the demand for sun and bathing temperatures can be problematic. However, there is evidence that the very experience of coping with bad weather also has an appeal in certain segments of the tourist market.

SOME PRINCIPLES OF SUSTAINABLE TOURISM

Norway has yet to formulate an official government strategy for the development of sustainable tourism, but the debate has begun. What follows is my own selection of some main points in this debate. In this context I should refer to our experience during the 1994 Olympic Winter Games in Lillehammer. A great deal of work lay behind trying to make the Games 'environmentally friendly', and to a large extent it is fair to say these efforts were successful.

What is meant by the term 'sustainable tourism' is still to be defined, and this in itself raises the question of whether large scale tourist activity combined with modern technology can possibly, under any conditions be viewed as sustainable. However, certain minimum requirements must exist if green, sustainable tourism is to be developed.

Nature's tolerance level or carrying capacity must not be exceeded, not only in the ecological sense of plant and animal life, but also in terms of waste control, pollution, erosion and in relation to the aesthetic qualities of the landscape. Research needs to be undertaken to determine carrying capacity for different habitats in relation to each type of recreational activity. The same principles must also be applied for sites of cultural interest, indeed cultural landscape in general. This clearly excludes a number of activities such as heliskiing, snow scooter safaris, guiding to wolverines dens and other types of polluting and resource demanding activities.

Sustainable tourism must be based on an understanding that natural attractions are to be experienced while respecting their vulnerability. Both planners, representatives of the industry and the visitors themselves must accept the principle that the level of use of an attraction and its surrounding habitat must not permanently affect the environment's capacity for recovery.

Accordingly we should plan and organise activity only up to the level that is necessary in order to make an attraction accessible, while at the same time allowing only acceptable wear and tear. A total approach for tourism 'in tune with the natural world' implies a certain degree of restriction on personal activity combined with a level of knowledge and awareness of ecological principles. This entails that one can not allow intensive tourist activity in core areas of natural beauty. One example of this type of problem is the debate surrounding plans to build a lift to the top of Preikestolen (the Pulpit Rock) plateau in Lysefjord, Rogaland. This proposed project is in direct conflict with the adopted land use plan for this area which assumes only basic tourist services and personal movement for access. The plan has been adopted by both Rogaland County Council and the Ministry of Environment, and fortunately it does not allow the development of what, in my opinion, will undoubtedly reduce in the long term the very quality of the attraction itself. This case also illustrates that. A sustainable tourist industry can not be based on maximum profit.

An important criterion which must govern all planning and management is that income should as far as possible be generated on the perimeter of an area or place of attraction and not at its centre. The planning and management of tourist activity must involve zoning for different activities and for varying levels of visitor use according to the physical conditions of the site. For larger groups the aim of a trip might be fulfilled by a small taste of an attraction, eg to walk on a footpath on the edge of a national park or conservation area. The possibility for generating economic activity on the edge of an attraction may be just as good without the necessity of visitors being transported deeper into a sensitive area.

Another requirement is that tourism must not impair the right to free access. This was attempted on the North Cape plateau where the viewpoint was fenced in and admission fees were to be paid at the visitor centre established nearby, a development which in itself was viewed by many as unfortunate. The fencing in of the area was contested by DNT as a breach of The Open Air Recreation Act. The Department of Environment concluded that the fencing in of the viewpoint was illegal, and the area is now open. This is only one of several similar attempts to charge for access, none of which have been successful to date. If the tourist industry attempts to challenge the right of free access by demanding payment for the right to enjoy sites and areas of natural beauty, it will most likely result in deep conflicts and public protest.

Another main principle is that sustainable tourism should not take on a dimension or form which will seriously damage or come into conflict with the heritage and lifestyle of local communities. Tourism has to be developed with respect for the identity and integrity of local culture, and this presupposes the necessary knowledge and information when developing tourism projects.

Sustainable tourism must seek to promote environmentally friendly transportation, including giving full attention to the role of public transport. Standards must also be set for environmentally friendly practice in all types of tourism accommodation, including the use of energy saving products. Indeed, the development of knowledge and skills in environmentally friendly management and planning is a fundamental prerequisite to future success for us all.

Another important prerequisite to achieving sustainability is that all products should be developed in line with national aims and guidelines, and within the framework of regional planning strategies. It is my firm belief that it is only in this way that we can secure the necessary high quality of development. Only thus can we establish the necessary infrastructure in an effective manner which will not be in conflict with the above principles of sustainability. The natural and cultural assets of Norway are sufficiently ample to sustain a far higher level of use than is the case today, provided this happens in a carefully planned manner.

The Author

Per Frøyland Pallesen was born in Stavanger and studied natural science and geography at the University of Oslo. He worked on the first national plan for river conservation in Norway, and in 1971 became Rogaland County Council's Conservation and Recreation Officer. He moved to planning in 1982 and became Director of Planning in 1988. He is member of a government committee dealing with national guidelines for environmental development of tourism in Norway, and serves on the Environment Committee of the North Sea Commission. A keen rambler, he has been a board member for both Stavanger and Norsk Turistforening (Mountain Touring Association).

Figure 5 Pleasure boats in a sheltered fjord.

12

RURAL VERSUS URBAN
Environmental Perceptions in Malta

Alexander Borg

Living in Britain has revealed to me that Malta is mainly famous here for two things: its sunny climate, nice bays and hospitable people, on one hand, and its notorious bird-shooting on the other. However, whilst glossy literature abounds on the former, very little, if any, is found which tries to explain the latter. For many Europeans, and sections of Maltese society too, the killing of birds is some abominable freak in Maltese nature. However, bird-shooting must be seen within the spectrum of traditional Maltese attitudes towards nature and the countryside.

My concern is not primarily with hunting, but with the wider dichotomy which exists in local perceptions and attitudes towards the environment. Two distinct viewpoints can be discerned which I call the 'traditional' and the 'modern environmentalist' perspectives. This paper seeks to show that there is more than what superficially meets the eye in the factioning of society between these two poles. Basically, the traditional and rural perception considers nature as something which must be overcome for the country folk to be able to make a decent living. The modern environmentalist perception emanates mainly from urban areas, being reinforced by a detachment of urban-dwellers from the harsh realities of Malta's working countryside. This divergence was induced by the insularity of the rural communities which stuck to a traditional way of life, and by the foreign orientation and international outlook of the urban economy and society.

This paper considers why the rural Maltese look at nature in an antagonistic light, and at how modern environmentalist attitudes evolved. It sets out to illustrate how this dichotomy is manifested on the ground. In conclusion, it looks at how environmental perceptions impact on the potential of tourism, and likewise how tourism, which is a mainstay of the local economy, can change attitudes to heritage.

This dichotomy in attitudes is very important when considering the sustainable use of Maltese heritage assets, which are in the long term of cultural and economic interest to local communities. Perceptions are important because they help form attitudes which in turn govern actions. It has been said that '...resource use should not be thought of solely as a routine controlled by physical media, but as a process in which temperament and attitudes of mind are involved', (Bowen-Jones et al, 1960). Indeed, recent theories define rurality not as a distinctive type of locality, but as a cognitive representation. In other words, the rural not as space, but as a perception of space. Thus, 'Space becomes imbued with the characteristics of these representations, not only at an imaginative level but also physically, through the use of these representations in action' (Halfacree, 1993).

EARLY HISTORY AND THE COUNTRYSIDE

During most of Malta's early history, as the Phoenician, Carthaginian, Roman, Byzantine and Arab civilisations controlled it, most of the population lived in, or close to, Mdina and the Cittadella in Malta and Gozo respectively. These two localities were very similar, located well inland on fortified hill-tops. The countryside outwith these forts seems to have prospered only during the heyday of Classical civilisation, when peace and stability reigned in the Mediterranean. Later, in 1090, the Normans conquered the islands from the Sicilian Muslims. In 1127, following an uprising by the latter, the local population was ousted from the fortified towns and made to settle in the countryside. Effectively this signalled the birth of Maltese villages.

The countryside was not a safe place to live in. The Normans introduced a strong system of feudalism, and Malta's position in the centre of the Mediterranean gave it tremendous strategic significance in the Middle Ages. It was situated at the confluence of the power lines and shipping routes of the Mediterranean superpowers of the time, eg the Normans, Genoese, Pisans, the Spanish Aragonese, the French Angevins and the Southern Muslim block. Malta was thus the subject of numerous intra-European political ploys, frequently being subjugated to warlords whose support the islands' rulers wanted. These feudal lords were only interested in using the islands as bases for their ships and from where to recruit sailors. Accordingly, agriculture became a fringe activity and was not invested in.

In these turbulent times, the dichotomy between the relative safe havens of the fortified towns and the vulnerability of country life, must have been very strongly felt. There were demographic shifts to safer inland locations. For instance, in the 14th century, the then hamlet of Hal Luqa gradually shifted to a nearby hill-top which enjoys open views of the coast, not for enjoyment of landscape, but to spot pirate landings. Early warning of such attacks would have enabled the locals to make it to one of the two fortified towns of Mdina and Birgu on the Grand Harbour.

The perception of the countryside by the medieval rural dweller must have been ambivalent. On one hand, they toiled to make a hard but rewarding living. On the other, they had to be constantly on the look-out for pirate incursions, whose despoilations often resulted in entire families and communities losing their homes, livestock and the crops which they had nurtured and which constituted their livelihood.

In 1429, 3,000 Maltese were lost out of a total population of 8,500 when the Moors invaded the islands and laid waste all in their path, killing so many beasts that the fields could not be worked for a long time afterwards. In 1450 and the preceding years, there was an acute drought which wrecked the cotton-growing industry upon which Malta relied heavily, leading to the

Figure 1 Medieval chapel at St Thomas Bay.

starvation of many. Later, plague hit the islands, and in 1473 another severe drought nearly led to a mass migration from the islands.

With the coming of the Knights in the 16th century, the political situation gradually grew more stable. However, there was only limited change in agricultural practices and rural life. From the end of the 19th century, new technology was available to Maltese farmers, but the small size of the agricultural holdings, stemming from the law of inheritance, and from the often steep terrain, precluded mechanisation on an extensive scale. The small size of land holdings thus dictated the perseverance of labour intensive agricultural practices.

The natural environment of the islands is not particularly conducive to cultivation. In most cases, apart from valley bottoms, there is insufficient soil-depth for agriculture. The farmers had to obtain soil by carrying it to their plots, digging in the bedrock to increase depth and adding quarried material or wastes to get sufficient volume. All of this was then mixed together, and manure, domestic wastes, dry vegetation and fertilisers were subsequently applied to enhance the nutrient content of the soil.

Since many parts are hilly and steep, the farmers had to terrace the hillsides to form fields. Even steep hillsides were terraced into narrow strips which were intensively worked. The backwalls of the terraces were cut into the solid rock and the resulting rubble used to bed the fields and to construct drystone rubble walling for the outer edge of the terraces. These walls were very skilfully constructed and, when well-maintained, serve as excellent retaining walls allowing rainwater to percolate but simultaneously holding the precious soil inside the terrace. Unfortunately, the labour involved in constructing and maintaining such walls is hard and other less effective forms of walling requiring less effort are being adopted to the extent that traditional wall building is fast becoming a dying craft.

The annual rainfall pattern is basically a rainless summer and a wet winter with circa 85% of the total annual precipitation falling during the six-months of October to March. But the monthly rainfall varies widely, particularly in the wet winter months. The least predictable month is October, which in some years has no rain at all, whilst at other times it has more than the annual mean. Farmers are thus confronted with situations of limited precipitation, with practically rainless summers and widely varying rainfall in the winter months, and with a tendency for uncommon but severe droughts. Therefore, substantial efforts are made to secure as much water as possible. Wells and cisterns have been constructed since prehistory and drainage off the fields is impeded to retain maximum soil moisture at the beginning of the dry season. Practically all of the few existing perennial springs have had their water re-routed, whilst fields are even inserted in the dry valley-bottoms where water is channelled after rainfall.

However, whilst farming is mainly geared to arid climatic conditions, heavy storms with intense rainfall and gales, inducing flash floods, are regular in autumn and can have devastating effects. The worst effects of such flash storms are erosion related. They frequently occur at the end of the dry season, months after the last rainfall, and with the soil completely parched. The terraced fields consequently lose a lot of the soil which the farmers had diligently nurtured over the centuries, particularly when the rubble walls are not maintained properly. In the valleys, the torrents sweep off anything in their way.

114

Another aspect influencing water-supply is the geological structure. Maltese rock is basically limestone, with the sole impervious stratum being a blue clay layer which is absent in most areas. Two basic types of aquifers are found. The first is formed where water seeping down the limestone is blocked and gathers on the clay stratum, and the second occurs where the water percolates down to sea-level and floats on the denser marine water. Some fields have the advantage of being located in areas where the water table is not too deep, and hence wells, traditionally using wind-powered pumps, can extract this valuable resource. However, the eastern side of Malta has no water for ready irrigation and farmers there must rely heavily on rainfall.

Agricultural land (*raba'* in Maltese), is classified into two categories: *raba' saqwi* and *raba' baghli*, the former being irrigated land and the latter having no ready supply of water for irrigation, its productivity being thus dependent on rainfall. The value of *raba' saqwi* is much higher than that of *raba' baghli*, it is much more productive, much more protected and most full-time farmers own such land. It allows farmers to invest in better techniques, like drip irrigation and greenhouses, since all-year production enables them to get better prices from early or out of season crops. The most prosperous farming communities are found in western Malta.

The introverted character of the vernacular architecture is a reflection of this history and Malta's climate. The austere walling of the houses, with few apertures, blocks out the harsh world outside, while all rooms look into the central courtyard which provides shade and relief in the form of fountains, vines and citrus trees. The external world represents hardship and danger, as opposed to internal private spaces, which convey safety, repose, comfort and delight. The stark walls stand between what is perceived as positive and pleasant, and what is harsh and fraught with danger.

TRADITIONAL ATTITUDES AND PERCEPTIONS

In this harsh environment man created the land on which he could live.
...The principal conclusion is that everything one sees in Malta, other than the major topographical features, is man-made and man-maintained in existence.

These remarks by Bowen-Jones *et al* (1960) hint at what this paper considers as being the underlying notion in the traditional Maltese perception of the countryside and natural environment. Throughout history, Maltese farmers have had to endure the entire range of adverse conditions with which the countryside continually confronted them. Hence, they grew to rely on personal effort. Man-made environments signified hard toil and were of value and therefore respected, natural ones were not. Chronic failure in food self-sufficiency exacerbated the situation, making Maltese society traditionally perceives pristine and virgin countryside as wasteland. The natural environment is traditionally seen as being of little value unless it has been worked by humans. There were no qualms whatsoever in completely altering the face of nature to be able to produce or extract something of perceived value. The excessive dumping of litter alongside country-roads is

Figure 2 Terraced hillside with drystone walling to prevent erosion.

Figure 3 Small fields are worked by hand and parched in the growing season, unless within reach of spring water.

clear testimony to this lack of appreciation. Such attitudes are widespread in many sectors of society, particularly in rural areas.

Thus local agricultural authorities still classify garigue karstland as 'wasteland' although ecologists point out that, despite their barren appearance, such habitats support Malta's highest levels of biodiversity. Prior to the 1992 planning legislation, farmers were actually encouraged to reclaim such wasteland for agriculture.

Conversely, attitudes towards cultivated land were always much more protective. Legislation has been in force for a long time to minimise soil loss from fields given over for non-agricultural development. These perceptions of the natural environment are part of the mainstream traditional culture, particularly in rural areas. By comparison, whilst English industrial workers were engaged in a mass trespass on Kinder Scout in the 1930s to secure access to the countryside for recreation, the industrial worker in Malta bought a shotgun and tried to relax whilst extracting something judged as useful out of the countryside.

The now notorious hunting in Malta started mainly as an effort by the less well-off to supplement their kitchen with some fresh meat. Hunting must then have had little impact on the large numbers of migratory birds. Indeed, the bird had a very fair chance of getting away, as the local hunter was usually only equipped with a very primitive shotgun and a couple of dogs. Matters are very different now when hunters are equipped with sophisticated rifles, other paraphernalia such as decoys, bird-whistles and recorded mating calls. Four-wheel drive vehicles can take them to remote parts of the islands in very little time, and the main aim is not to get extra food, but to gather as large and varied a collection of stuffed birds as possible. The rarer the bird, the more valuable it is in the showcase, and the laws specifying protected species are blatantly flaunted. Today, bird shooting 'for kicks' with utter disregard for the law epitomises the insensitivity traditional attitudes towards the natural environment can lead to.

However, this nonchalance towards appropriating for oneself anything which nature occasionally makes available is not restricted to hunters or song-bird trappers. What may be considered as even more worrying is the large number of children engaged in their own versions of hunting. Catching robins with a *trabokk* (a small cage devised especially for trapping robins) is very popular. When the countryside is ablaze with the colours and aroma of the *narcissus tazetta* flowers, they are cut down by the thousands to be sold in large bunches at nominal prices by children. A common practice in the rainy periods is to collect edible snails, which often seek shelter from the sun between stones in rubble-walls. These sustain considerable damage when pulled down by visitors in search of snails with obvious repercussions for farmers who occasionally resort to poisoning the snails to stop the damage.

A favourite pastime on family visits to spring-side areas in winter is for small children to be taken tadpole catching by their parents. The creatures are later taken home in jars to die. Hikes by boys to the popular Bahrija area, one of the rare localities where a perennial spring still runs in its natural state, often end in massive hunts for the extremely rare (due to dwindling habitats) Mediterranean Freshwater Crab, *Potamon fluviatile lanfrancoi*, which is taken home to die in a bucket or garden pond.

There seems to be an innate instinct ingrained even in children's minds, that whatever they fancy in the countryside, be it colourful flowers, orchids, nestlings, butterflies, ladybirds, chameleons, frogs and tadpoles, sea-crabs, shrimps, molluscs or snails, they are entitled to capture and take home, even in the knowledge that they will soon perish. Such gathering instincts are often fostered by parents who ingrain these traditional attitudes to nature in the still pliable perceptions of Malta's future generations.

COMING OF THE KNIGHTS AND URBAN SOCIETY

The granting of the Islands by the Spanish monarchy to the Order of St. John in the 16th century was a very important milestone in Malta's history. The Order had a long and chequered history. Originally established and based in the Holy Land to provide defence and shelter for pilgrims, it was ousted from Jerusalem, as well as from its subsequent base in Rhodes by the Turks. It had thus undergone a major metamorphosis, becoming a very powerful naval power at the forefront of Christendom's lines against the Ottomans. As a consequence, Malta suffered from some acute reprisals by the Turks, but the prospects for Malta were very different from its previous experiences. This time, the rulers were actually dwelling on the islands and they were a powerful and rich body. Malta was thus no longer being drawn into explosive politics and then left to face the music. It had become the home of its own Knights, and from its erstwhile fringe political position, it suddenly shifted to centre-stage in its new rulers' domain.

Cash flowed into the island and the Knights' maritime inclination soon instigated fundamental changes, the most significant of which was the immediate replacement of landlocked central Mdina, by the then fishing township of Birgu as the capital city. The Knights fortified and enlarged the town, and later erected fortifications around much of both the Birgu and the Valletta sides of the Grand Harbour. This induced a complete re-structuring of the Maltese economy, hitherto overwhelmingly agrarian. The Order's galleys needed maintenance and repair, ancillary industries were required and seamen were in constant demand. Furthermore, the aristocratic Knights and their retinue expected high standards of living, promoting a wide spectrum of service industries. The building of new palaces, auberges, houses and fortifications created a large market for the building trades. Indeed, the era of prosperity and stability saw the emergence of a trade-oriented bourgeoisie based in the harbour area. These trends were later enforced by the British, who also based Malta's civil authorities in the area. The relative security and prosperity also induced the population to expand at un-precedented rates. The harbour area acted as a magnet, attracting people from all over the island by the promise of new economic prosperity.

The divergence in character between Malta's urban and rural societies took on proportions completely out of scale with the small size of the islands. Perception and attitudes towards the countryside gradually changed for several reasons. One was that urbanisation was intimately associated with an era which ushered in prosperity and stability, both politically and economically. This modified the self-centred reasoning which country families and communities had been forced to adopt in order to survive in less prosperous times.

Figure 4 Anti-environmentalist slogans daubed on the remains of an ancient temple at Borg In-Nadur.

Figure 5 Vandalism defaces the crumbling walls of a fine example of 17th century architecture.

Another reason was that urbanisation took people from the agrarian way of life, and their links with the countryside and natural environment became much less intimate. This distanced them from attitudes to nature fostered through the hardship of procuring a decent living in the country. There was also the creation of extremely crowded, unhealthy, unplanned and unserviced slum areas. The problem was exacerbated since the harbour towns were fortified and could not expand. The Mandragg area in Valletta and the It-Toqba (literally, The Hole) area in Birgu were both unattractive. They were on low-lying land which was occupied and transformed by the poorer workmen into squalid slums. People living in such oppressive environments obviously relished the openness, tranquillity and unpolluted atmosphere of the countryside. Indeed, traditional acquisitive instincts prevailed and visits to the country often included occasional shooting or trapping. Even now hunters and trappers genuinely value the sense of peace and relaxation they experience as they hunt with their dog in the clean country air. The birds they catch may not even feature in their perception of nature.

Rural life continued to be introspective, the farmers toiling to provide sufficient food to make a living. However, the majority of urban activities were mainly foreign-oriented. Thus the countryside dwellers stolidly adhered to established tradition, whilst insular attitudes in the urban areas were considerably modified. The interchange of ideas with the outside world increased and cultural differences between the Maltese and their European counterparts were progressively reduced. Indeed, by the time of the Knights, 'the townspeople became largely indistinguishable in outlook from the inhabitants of the other towns of Southern Europe. Their standard of living, ...education, ...food, ...houses and home life ...were probably also much the same. In the countryside, however, old forms ... remained very much the same', (Wettinger, 1989).

The extent to which foreign culture impinged on urban life was evidenced by the language of town people which showed an extensive sprinkling of Romance words not found in rural Maltese. The more highly educated renounced Maltese for Italian (and later English) and considered use of the indigenous language uncouth. There was always a lot of mixing with foreigners in the harbour areas and this is reflected in the large number of foreign surnames to be found there.

RISE OF THE MODERN ENVIRONMENTALIST

Urbanisation and associated development thus had the effect of modifying urban dwellers' perceptions of the natural environment, and the hold of traditional attitudes was relinquished, thereby rendering townsfolk more receptive to change. But the rise of environmentalism, which contrasts starkly with traditional mentality, is a recent phenomenon and it only now seems to be gaining ground. This may be attributed to widespread education and an increased affluence and stability in the political climate.

Education is a prerequisite for environmentalism. It gives insights into the intricacies of nature, ecology and ecosystem beyond the superficial views previously held, and thus provides an appreciation of the countryside in its totality. Education also exposes the sensitivity of nature, the adverse impact of human meddling and engenders a more responsible attitude. It also demonstrates that humans are just one component in the wider ecosystem, and anything happening in the natural environment will somehow reverberate to affect human existence.

Standard of living is another parameter which governs the growth of environmentalism. The more affluent a society, the higher environmental issues are placed on the political agenda. Thus, according to O'Riordan (1981), in the political framework, environmental quality tends to be awarded third priority, trailing behind security, health and economic growth (first priority). Regional development, redistribution and equal opportunities follow as second priority. Even on an individual basis, it is quite reasonable to assume that people are generally concerned about the quality of the environment only when they have attained economic and physical security.

The attainment of a high profile by environmentalism in the last decade may thus be attributed to a combination of more people reaching higher education levels and stability being experienced in the political climate. Between the late 1960s and early 1980s, Malta was still struggling to come to terms with its new independence which thrust it into an unfamiliar economic situation. Unemployment was rife and political turbulence further pushed environmental concerns down the priority list.

Subsequently, with unemployment rates drastically reduced, a calmer political climate and a general increase in affluence, environmental issues became more important. Awareness increased, various environmental NGOs flourished, enforcement of conservation law in the countryside started being felt, and a small Green Party was established.

THE DICHOTOMY OF PERCEPTIONS

The dichotomy between traditional and modern environmentalist perceptions of the countryside is very strong, and is perhaps best epitomised by the heartfelt rancour which exists between the hunters and the Malta Ornithological Society (MOS), Malta's largest environmental NGO. This conflict pervades the entire environmental debate in the islands.

However, with the widespread increase in affluence, higher education and mobility, various shades of grey are emerging, but the picture is unfortunately still extremely polarised. The extreme ends of the spectrum tend to be urban white-collar workers, on one hand, and rural agricultural and blue-collar workers on the other. Their backgrounds and perceptions are so disparate that they often speak different languages and very little effort is made to communicate. This, coupled with the intransigence and the constant verbal abuse between the hunting and the environmental lobbies, has created an aura of deep mutual mistrust, which often affects any countryside initiative.

The environmental lobby needs a better communications strategy. Although their line of reasoning may be perfectly logical, they often tend to ignore the background of those steeped in the traditional perception of nature. Condemning the shooting of birds because it is cruel is logical to many, but a farmer who breeds livestock may find it difficult to accept.

Furthermore, the whole environmentalist movement seems to have taken many by surprise, and they instinctively react warily to it. Efforts to overturn the established order make them all the less trustworthy in the eyes of a conservative rural society. Attacks levelled at the Church for not condemning hunting, and the Green Party supporting the legalisation of divorce, probably did not help matters in the deeply religious countryside. Moreover, country people resent interference into what they should or should not do by groups of urban youths who may never have seen a day's work in the fields. In other words, the failure of the environmentalist movement to express itself in an easily understood language has bred mistrust in the countryside.

The Association of Hunters, Trappers and Conservationists (AHTC), on the other hand, knows that as long as it maintains its large support base, which currently exceeds the environmentalists', politicians will be very reluctant to do anything which goes against their interests. Malta has two main parties contending for power and the difference in votes polled is only a few thousand. Both parties and the AHTC are well aware that a block vote by the hunters and their families would signify an electoral victory for the party receiving them, and the AHTC has no qualms in pointing this out very lucidly to politicians. To the hunters' credit, they have always maintained a united front, which is more than can be said of the environmentalists.

Secure in their numbers, the hunters have at times threatened forming their own party, and they expressed themselves against Malta joining the EU because of its strict hunting laws. The introduction of stricter hunting regulations in 1994 saw some massive protests, and the final legislation was a scaled-down version of the original proposals which would have banned spring hunting altogether. The aftermath saw intimidatory action and abuse towards officials and politicians. Prehistoric monuments, historic buildings and newly installed road-signs were vandalised and painted with obscene slogans. This rift in the Maltese society is showing no signs of healing, and this obviously puts the Maltese authorities in a quandary. The local ecclesiastical authorities tend to avoid expressing themselves on the matter, whilst government bodies often find themselves treading a tightrope.

Older civil servants are often not conversant with the new environmental agendas they are faced with. Departments may have good intentions, but may not have the expertise to make sound environmental judgements. This is compounded by fear of being unwittingly drawn into some hunting versus environmentalist polemic. Many environmentalists also seem to judge development proposals exclusively in the light of the natural environment, without due regard to socio-economic aspects. Sometimes, government officials try to work out impossible compromises or apply cosmetic surgery in cases which call for more categorical resolve. Fortunately, recent planning and environmental legislation provides a more rational and transparent system of decision-taking which should cope better with these problems, and it will open debate where all parties, whatever their convictions, may express themselves and expect to receive an impartial and objective hearing.

THE POTENTIAL OF TOURISM

Tourism has the potential of inducing changes in the way many perceive the natural and other heritage in the countryside. Since the closure of the last military bases in Malta in 1979, tourism was targeted as the best means to make good the loss of revenue and service industries which the armed personnel and their families had generated. Most of the tourists were attracted by the sun, sea and sand, and their numbers have been steadily increasing until they exceeded the one million mark in 1992. This is very large for a host population of circa 360,000 and a land area of less than 100 square miles. Consequently, the authorities have shifted their strategy to target upmarket tourists, and countryside and heritage are now seen in a different light.

Die-hard hunters, on the other hand, see tourism as a potential threat. They realise the economic prowess of tourism may undermine their present stronghold on Maltese politics. It may have been no coincidence that heritage assets were vandalised in reaction to the introduction of measures seen as contrary to hunters' aspirations. The AHTC denied any involvement whatsoever, and others claimed that the sabotage was a subtle ploy to sully the hunters' reputation with the public. Indeed, many hunters and trappers are fed up with foreign visitors trying to impose their views on them.

However, tourism can be very useful in changing traditional attitudes. A considerable number of fishermen, for instance, are already tapping into tourism and using their boats on tourism-oriented activities in summer when fishing is not so rewarding. If types of tourism products can be found which would be suitable to the local farming scene, then farmers may start placing a value on the environment too, as long as income filters down to them. Unfortunately, almost all agriculture is intensive, time-consuming and arable and these characteristics are not so conducive to combining agriculture with tourism.

Malta is richly enough endowed to host various forms of cultural tourism, its main assets being a heritage rich in history, archaeology, architecture, geology, botany and wildlife. Making better use of these assets for tourism would improve local perceptions of the environment. The current state of affairs unfortunately renders the islands unsuitable for bird-watching, which is unfortunate, considering the large number of migratory birds which make it to Malta (the number which manages to leave may not be so high). If Utopia were to arrive in the Maltese countryside, then hunters would undoubtedly be amongst the best guides for visiting bird watchers. Their views on shooting down the birds may be quite different if they were suddenly able to translate them into hard cash.

The attempts by extreme environmentalists to tarnish Malta's image in the tourist markets is as tragic as it is socially unethical. If the environmentally conscious tourist market is lost, then it would be replaced by less discerning visitors. If we encourage tourists who demand and expect greenness in the local product, then pressure will mount on the authorities to accommodate them, and traditional perceptions of the countryside will hopefully adjust accordingly.

The different parties should now start to communicate with each other in a commonly agreed language. Unless they try to understand each others' diverse perceptions, trust can not be built up and intransigence removed, and no real progress will ever be achieved. It is incumbent on all countryside users to stop, reflect, look at what is happening around them, rise above the mire of entrenched interests, and objectively debate in a constructive manner how the rich heritage of Malta's countryside can be left to future generations to enjoy as much as by us today. Tourism can certainly be a major means by which such sustainability is achieved. A basic prerequisite for its success would certainly be that global culture respects local identity, and that local perceptions respect global concerns.

The Author

Alexander Borg is an architect and civil engineer, with an honours degree from the University of Malta, where he majored in Urban Design and Planning. He was the first local professional officer to be employed by the Malta Planning Authority in its Environmental Management Unit. With a long standing interested in heritage management and conservation, he has participated in and helped organise a number of village inventories. From within the Planning Authority, he has established and run the scheduling process for the listing of heritage sites. He is currently completing a masters degree in Rural and Regional Resources Planning at the University of Aberdeen and The Robert Gordon University, where he is focusing on the management of Malta's rural heritage resources and countryside recreation.

References

Azzopardi, A. E., *Fatal Flight: The Facts,* Association for Hunting, Trapping and Conservation (Malta)- GH.K.N.K, 1992

Bonanno, A., *Distribution of Villas and some aspects of the Maltese Economy in the Roman Period,* in Journal of the Faculty of Arts, (University of Malta), Vol. 6, pp 73-81, 1977

Borg, A. L., *A Planning Study of Bingemma: The Basis for a Rural Local Plan,* unpublished B. E. & A. (Hons.) Dissertation, University of Malta, 1993

Bowen-Jones, H., Dewdney, J. C. and Fisher, W. B., *Malta: Background for Development,* Department of Geography, University of Durham, 1960

Brincat, J. M., *Language and Demography in Malta,* in Fiorini, S. and Mallia-Milanes, V. (eds.), *Malta: A Case Study in International Cross-Currents,* University of Malta, 1991

Camilleri, F., *La Lettura del Paesaggio: Studio per la Pianificazione del Settore Nord-Ovest dell'Isola di Malta,* unpublished thesis, University of Genoa, 1989

Chetcuti, D., Buhagiar, A., Schembri, P. J., and Ventura, F., *The Climate of the Maltese Islands: A Review,* University of Malta, 1992

Department of Statistics, *Demographic Review 1990,* Government of Malta, 1991

Fenech, N., *Fatal Flight: The Maltese Obsession with Killing Birds,* Quiller Press, London, 1992

Gauci, V., *Supply of Irrigation Water in a Semi-Arid Area,* in Mizzi, L. and Busuttil, S. (eds.), *Options méditerranéennes: Malta – Food, Agriculture, Fisheries and the Environment,* Centre International de Hautes Etudes Agronomiques Méditerranéennes (CIHEAM) and Institut Agronomique Méditerranéen de Montpellier, 1993

Halfacree, K. H., *Locality and Social Representation: Space, Discourse and Alternative Definitions of the Rural*, in Journal of Rural Studies, Vol. 9, pp 23-37, 1993

Horwath & Horwath (UK) Ltd., *The Maltese Islands Tourism Development Plan*, Ministry of Tourism, 1989

Kalchreuter, H., *On Bird Hunting on Malta*, F.A.C.E., 1992

Luttrell, A. T., *Approaches to Medieval Malta*, in Luttrell, A. T. (ed.), *Medieval Malta: Studies on Malta before the Knights*, The British School at Rome, London, 1975

Micallef, G., *Hal Luqa: Niesha u Grajjietha*, Bugelli, Malta, 1975

O'Riordan, T., *Environmentalism*, Pion Limited, 1981

Richardson, D., *The Green Challenge: Philosophical, programmatic and electoral considerations*, in Richardson, D., and Rootes, C. (eds.), *The Green Challenge: the development of Green parties in Europe*, Routledge, 1995

Schembri, P. J. and Baldacchino, A. E., *Ilma, Blat u Hajja: Is-Sisien ta' l-Ambjent Naturali Malti*, Malta University Services Limited, 1992

Schembri, P. J. & Lanfranco, E., *Development and the Natural Environment in the Maltese Islands*, in Lockhart, D. G., Drakakis-Smith, D., and Schembri, P. J. (eds.), *The Development Process in Small Island States*, Routledge, 1990

Sisman, D., *Green Tourism in Malta: Issues and Opportunities*, Green Flag International, 1991

Wettinger, G., *Aspects of Maltese Life*, in Mangion, G. (ed.), 'Maltese Baroque', Ministry of Education, Malta and Council of Europe, 1989

Figure 6 Mdina. Courtesy of Richard England.

13

ROUTES TO CULTURAL IDENTITY
A European System of Networks

Michel Thomas-Penette

The Council of Europe's Cultural Routes programme was inaugurated in 1987 on the initiative of the Council for Cultural Co-operation (CDCC). Its purpose was defined as encouraging Europeans to explore the routes where the European identity has been forged. It also aimed to point them towards new recreational opportunities in the form of alternative and cultural tourism. Its mission was to organise thematic routes which would link different countries or regions of Europe.

In the course of five years a dozen or so routes reflecting the primary aim were explored and launched. But in view of the exemplary, symbolic value of the Cultural Routes, and their real success, reflected outside the organisation by the proliferation and popularisation of local routes, it became necessary to make it clear that the initiative had originated with the Council of Europe, to make renewed efforts to ensure that the organisation's message to the citizens of Europe through the Cultural Routes was getting across, and to redefine themes and methods.

The urgency of this fresh appraisal was further accentuated by the fact that, in a radically changing Europe, the values upheld by the organisation - human rights, democracy, tolerance and the rule of law - had to be constantly and actively promoted. The Cultural Routes offered a prime living example of the virtues of transnational co-operation, in which all the main strands of the Council of Europe work were forged together to form a coherent whole.

Thanks to the positive outcome of the methodological work now being completed on the themes of Monastic Influence and Parks and Gardens, it was possible to redefine the entire programme as part of cohesive strategy in which the respective roles of the Council of Europe and its network partners are clearly defined.

ROUTE THEMES

In order to give consistency to the themes, they were arranged in caJ Purserre concerning dynamic processes of intermingling and cross-fertilisation which helped to shape Europe: at first, the peoples and migratory flows of Europe and, secondly, the dissemination of ideas in Europe: those emerging from religious or artistic movements, those which accompanied economic or technical trends, and also those associated with scientific discoveries.

The Cultural Routes on the Celts and Vikings belong to the first group, as does the new route on Gypsies, currently being prepared. The chosen themes must be able to illustrate these peoples' specific contribution to European civilisation and the deeply rooted traces of their influence, whether revealed by archaeological or historical research. It goes without saying that the story of their migrations and the cultural intermingling which resulted will also cover recent periods right up to the present.

The Santiago de Compostela and the Francigena Pilgrim Ways, Monastic Influence, the Hanseatic Cities, the European Cities of the Discoveries, the Silk and Textile Routes, the Baroque Routes, Parks and Gardens. The Rural Habitat and Mozart/Music Routes belong to the second group.

The chosen themes are based on dissemination and movement within Europe, on identification with specific places in several European countries and on the possibility of developing practical network projects. The themes could take, as a starting point, a commemoration or a specific event with a European dimension, if this is of sufficient significance to bring about the setting up of a long term route initiative.

These two main focuses are illustrated by themes which might be placed under the headings of:

- collective or individual linear routes: pilgrim ways, the establishment of monasteries, staging posts during the Viking expeditions, and Mozart's travels;
- transfrontier routes forming a circuit: Architecture without Frontiers or Rural Habitats;
- networks of regional and local routes which are geographically separated but share the same themes and history of exchanges within Europe. This shared history can come to life today through exchanges of experience: the Silk and Baroque Routes;
- networks of towns or sites: the Hanseatic Cities, the Cities of Discovery, the Towns of the Schickhardt Route, Parks and Gardens.

ROUTE FUNCTIONS

The cultural routes have several complementary functions which are all part of a cultural co-operation process:

- exchanging information and experience: this makes the routes a dynamic observatory of identity markets and hence of the diversity of European identities, resulting in practical cultural co-operation embracing the whole range of participants from the researcher to the cultural or tourist operator;
- protecting the cultural values of Europe by taking account of tensions between local, regional, national and European identities;

- an experimental function by allowing new forms of work to be implemented between different complementary scientific fields and creating synergies between those involved in all the stages of a project, including the various departments of the European institutions.

COMPLEMENTARITY OF TOURISM AND CULTURE

In the Council of Europe, the idea of complementarity between tourism and culture is based on combined action at five different levels, including and reinforcing cultural tourism and thus preventing the programme from becoming only a series of cultural or tourist products. In this constantly changing process, involving both research and action, the emphasis is placed on the following five complementary fields:

- research exchanges, which secure the scientific bases for the themes;
- educational encounters, which provide awareness of the major European issues for European citizens who will, in the long term, become spokespersons for the values defended by the organisation ;
- protection and enhancement of lesser-known, diversified heritages, which guarantee the discovery of original sites off the beaten track of mass tourism;
- contemporary creation, which provides a vital imaginary dimension by means of live spectacle, story-telling and music;
- cultural tourism which involves laying out real routes based on themes of encounter, sharing and reception.

THE SUPPORT SYSTEM

There is a Resource Centre, a Strasbourg-based information unit, which houses all reports, articles, audio-visual products and maps concerning the Cultural Routes. It also keeps the files of partners actively engaged in projects and maintains relations with specialist documentation centres.

The Cultural Routes' Secretariat is responsible for the publication of an information Newsletter (ROUTES) which provides a link with experts and networks. The information on current developments in the networks and routes conveyed in this bulletin is subsequently published in the form of brochures which regularly accompany new initiatives. These publications are now supplemented by a Practical Guide to Cultural Routes. The way they are organised is designed to help project organisers integrate their proposed routes more effectively into the programme. The Resource Centre works with private networks and partners to prepare general or monographic publications and audio-visual productions on the routes.

After cases have been examined by the Secretariat General, an Advisory Committee assesses proposals and the state of progress of the network's activities. It gives an opinion on new proposals and their classification in groups and categories. As new files or proposals are submitted, it allows the Secretariat to liaise with any other Council directorates which may be affected. The Committee consists of representatives of the CDCC committee (Culture, Education & Cultural Heritage) and representatives of the Council of Europe's Secretariat General. It also comprises external experts, who are chosen according to the subjects under examination or are contracted for work assessment purposes.

As the role of the Advisory Committee is not to dispose but to propose, the Secretariat transmits its opinions to the Culture Committee. The final programme is subject to the political and financial decisions of the Committee of Ministers, which are based on proposals submitted by the Council for Cultural Co-operation (CDCC) and its specialist committees.

THE OPERATIONAL METHODOLOGY

The methodological study on the two themes of Monastic Influence and Parks and Gardens has shown that the Council of Europe must draw on operational networks, involving national and regional public authorities and the community at large. Each network has a different theme, activity, mode of functioning, mode of internal co-ordination between members and mode of co-ordination with the Council of Europe.

These networks will take charge of the routes and be responsible for the following tasks:

-   guaranteeing their financial and functional viability;
-   establishing forums for exchange and practice by encouraging, in particular, co-operation between countries in Western Europe and Central and Eastern European states;
-   putting forward proposals and establishing a programme of pilot schemes carried out with the Council of Europe European Civilisation Classes, arts classes, higher training academies, forgotten or unusual heritages, exhibitions, publications, etc;
-   promote network-specific inter-regional co-operation projects and network-specific regional schemes for local development.

Some initiatives existed even before the inception of the programme and others were generated under the new impetus created by the methodological study. Among the latter, artistic and cultural networks adopt a transverse approach to implementing artistic research and dissemination projects between towns and regions.

Some networks already exist and others are being established:

-   The Monastic Influence and The Parks and Gardens Networks were launched in 1992–93.
-   The Inter-Regional Co-operation Association for the Santiago de Compostela Pilgrim Ways was launched in 1989 and is made up of three groups: first, a group of active members, regional councils and four representative from each of the participating regions; second, a group of active members, each from the

communes in those regions designated as resting places on the Santiago-Pilgrim Ways and represented by the mayor; and third, a group of associate members, including the European Centre for Compostela Studies, several St James' Societies, the French Ramblers Federation and Universities etc.
- The Rural Habitat Network (Architecture without Frontiers Routes) was launched in 1987 and is made up of active members from 15 European countries.
- The European Textile Network (Silk and Textile Routes) was launched in 1991–92 and is an association joined to a Foundation with both working in the 43 countries which are part of the Cultural Convention of the Council of Europe.
- The Academy of Gestual Arts (Les Transversales) was launched in 1992-93 and is an association of artists, scholars and theatre venues.
- The Network of Cities of Discovery was launched in 1994 and is an association of more than 20 European towns, among them Lisboa, Sevilla and Antwerpen.
- The Baroque Network was launched in Malta in 1994.
- The Viking Route and Hanseatic Cities networks are currently being established.

These are the main features of the Council of Europe's pilot schemes, the methods of pooling operators' resources, their relations with the public authorities, the information material provided and the cultural and tourist products on offer. In the next chapter, Moira Stevenson gives an account of the Silk and Textile Route. What follows below is a brief description of one pilot scheme developed to reach young Europeans at the beginning of their university careers.

THE EUROPEAN CIVILISATION CLASSES

During the meetings that defined the Monastic Influence theme, the experts set priorities for the Council of Europe pilot schemes. Their aim was to target young people to bring about long term contacts between students from different disciplines and religious backgrounds. These meetings would take place in a monastery and be accompanied by an introduction to the monastic heritage of neighbouring countries and regions.

The Monastic Influence Network immediately adopted the recommendations and proposes to mount, over four years, an itinerant Civilisation Course on the theme of monachism, with participation by France, Portugal, Romania, Greece and a Nordic country which has not yet been determined. The course will bring together twelve students from each country. It will also be open to students from various university disciplines, including the anthropological sciences. Its objective will be to study questions relating to the theme of monachism and to bring out their contemporary relevance. This will be done by a combination of structured learning and an open exchange of views among participants involving both students and teachers. In each country it will take place in a monastery which has preserved the atmosphere and authenticity of its original function intact.

The students will be selected on the basis of a written application and the course will be monitored by a Scientific Committee with the task of designing the application form and suggesting the programme of study for the three years. Teachers will be drawn from different disciplines in order to contribute points of view other than those of historians. Each student will be required to write a dissertation to be handed in at the end of the course. They may also be required to engage in the dissemination of information and instruction in high schools in their respective countries. The course must be of a sufficiently high standard to give it significant weight in each student's curriculum vitae, a par with other forms of extra-curricular activities at university.

It is also expected that the teachers, researchers and specialists from different countries will, in addition to the questions debated with students, undertake their own research and discuss it with their peers. Countries will organise national programmes of continuing education workshops for teachers, socio-cultural instructors and tourism executives. They will also organise meetings on monastic heritage for elected representatives and local authority cultural officers, including specific activities for technical high schools.

The Council of Europe will establish the Scientific Committee and be responsible for the contact, briefing and development work in each country. Each country will be responsible for travel by its own students and teachers. Host countries will be responsible for organisation and accommodation expenses, for discovery sessions and workshops and associated cultural activities. Session programmes will be designed through a co-operative effort by several ministries, ie Culture, Education, Tourism, Youth, Occupational Training, etc. It will also include local authorities, cultural and religious bodies which are part of the Network.

CONCLUSIONS

Europe is both one and multifarious. It would therefore be a worthwhile exercise to consider what unites and what divides her, to explore the diverse proclivities that make her what she is, the good and not so good passions coursing through her - not only because it is a comforting activity but also because it reveals any sensitivities and enables us to be better prepared to the future.

This quotation from Georges Duby's Introduction to the book published by the Council of Europe *Pushing back the Horizon: European Cultural Itineraries and Explorations for the Third Millennium*, summarises the main aim of a programme that intends to eliminate prejudice with history teaching, by bringing to the fore the mutual and positive influences between different countries, religions and ideas in the historic development of Europe.

The Author

Dr Michel Thomas-Penette is Professor at Paris VII University and has been Programme Adviser for the Council of Europe Cultural Routes programme. He was the Director of Textile/ Art magazine and of a Documentation Centre on textiles in Paris. His exhibitions have included one in the Museum of Decorative Arts and one in the Cite des Sciences et de l'Industrie in Paris. He is the author of a book on Textile Art published by Skira-Rizzoli. Following establishment of a Silk Route in Europe, he is now managing the whole programme and takes part in the launching of European Networks on such diverse themes as Parks and Gardens, Pilgrim Ways, Rural Habitat and Monastic Influence.

References

Various authors, *Pushing Back the Horizon, European Cultural Itineraries and Explorations for the Third Millennium.* Council of Europe, Editions du Rouergue, 1994

Various authors, *ROUTES: Newsletter on the Council of Europe Cultural Routes*, Nos 1, 2 & 3, Council of Europe, 1993–1995

14

SILK AND TEXTILE ROUTES
Council of Europe Cultural Itineraries

Moira Stevenson

The Silk Routes Cultural Itineraries Programme of the Council of Europe was initiated in 1987 and launched with a meeting in Como in 1988. This was followed by meetings in Nîmes, France in 1989, Bursa, Turkey in 1990, Barcelona, Spain in 1991, Macclesfield, England in 1992, Soufli, Greece in 1993 and Portugal in 1994.

At each of these meetings academics and museum, heritage and tourism professionals presented material on the silk industry and how it was, or could be, used to benefit the local community, schools, visitors and the economy of the European regions through tourism. Each country has a different experience and case history which has been determined by the participants and the organisational structures of heritage organisations and tourism in the different regions of Europe.

I first describe the case histories of each of the participating countries, then look at the wider issues and networks which have developed from the Silk Routes Initiative. Taking each country in turn, from the initials meeting in 1988, I will attempt to describe the progress made in developing the itineraries.

ITALY

It was appropriate that the first programme meeting was held in Como, Italy, since Como is arguably the most important centre for silk manufacture in Europe today. The meeting was hosted by the Council of Europe and Fondazione Antonio Ratti. Ratti is the largest silk manufacturer in Como and well known in the silk trade internationally. The meeting brought together manufacturers, textile experts, academics, industrial archaeologists and museum curators from five countries.

The silk industry was well established in Italy by the 14th century and the technology developed there was to influence manufacture throughout Europe. Today, the legacy of this technological innovation can be seen both in the communes of Como and Lecco and the territory of Lariano. In addition, buildings and other activities related to silk can still be found in Bologna and in the Piedmont region. Architects, historians, industrial archaeologists presented research at this first meeting. The surviving heritage and its potential for tourism development was discussed.

A number of influential temporary exhibitions were staged in the following years and research proceeded at the Universities of Pisa and Turin. Claudio Zanier, Professor of Modern History at Pisa University and an authority on the development of the silk industry, was very active in initiating research, co-ordinating the work of others and working with industrialists to make practical progress with the establishment of an itinerary.

In 1992, he worked with the Como Chamber of Commerce, Industry, Craft and Agriculture and the Commune of Lecco to host a meeting at the Villa Olmo which brought together industrialists with academics and local government officers to lay the ground for establishing the itinerary for the Como and Lecco communes and the territory of Lariano.

Two publications resulted from this meeting. The first publication was the papers presented at the meeting and the second a pocket guide to the sites related to the silk industry. The guide included photographs and descriptions of museums, sites of industrial archaeology and modern factories. It was published in Italian, French, German and English.

Research work on the silk industry continues at the University of Pisa and elsewhere. At the University of Turin, architectural research into the silk mills of the Piedmont region is ongoing and proposals for their restoration are being developed. The Musei Civici de Cuneo and Musei de Bologna are also active in research and interpretation of the silk industry.

FRANCE

The areas of France one first thinks of when one mentions silk is Lyon or Tours which are the centres of silk weaving. However, it was not Lyon or Musee des Tissue in Lyon with its wonderful collection of historic textiles that was the first to use the theme of silk to promote tourism, but the Cevennes, a region west of the Rhone and south of Lyon. It was in this area that sericulture became well established to supply the weavers in Lyon with their silk until two events beset the industry. The first was pebrine, the bacterial infection of silk worms which hit the silk worm nurseries of the Cevennes in 1849 and caused untold havoc in the industry until it was eventually brought under control in 1875 by techniques developed by Pasteur. The second was the opening of the Suez Canal in 1865 which improved transport links with China and provided the Lyon silk weavers with an alternative source of supply of their raw material.

Despite subsidies brought in by the French Government in the 1890s the Cevennes never again enjoyed the same prosperity and the industry went into decline. The introduction of synthetic fibres after the second world war took the final toll and, despite a short lived attempt at revival, the last mill closed in the early 1960s. The mountainous nature of the Cevennes made diversification into other forms of agriculture difficult. The mining industry in Ales was also in decline. Employment opportunities were limited and the economy of the area was threatened.

In the 1970s two initiatives were launched with the aim of reviving the silk industry and generating economic benefit to the area. The first was Societe d'Interet Collectif Agricole – Soie Cevennes (SICA-Soie Cevennes). This was a co-operative of silk manufacturers which aimed to cover all processes in the production of silk from 'Soil to Fabric'. It included mulberry cultivation, rearing of silkworms, spinning, dyeing and weaving.

The second was the Association pour le Development de la Sericulture en Cevennes Manobet (ADSC). This worked in association with Sica and was involved in promotion, training and manufacture. It was responsible for establishing and maintaining a silk museum collection and archives and mounting temporary exhibitions. They were also involved in the organisation of training courses in cultivation, techniques, rearing of silk worms and silk manufacture also feature in their activities.

In 1984 the Languedoc Association for Sociological, Ethnological and Documentary films and CNRS research team proposed a project known as 'Chemin de la Soie' or 'By-roads of Silk' which was accepted by the French Ministry of Culture in 1986 and the project began in January 1987.

In addition to the two initiatives established to revive and promote the silk industry of the Cevennes in the 1970s, the 'Chemin de la Soie' project included a wide range of heritage, cultural and environmental organisation. There were 12 partners in all, including museums and the Cevennes National Park, local cultural and historical associations and national research organisations. The project was concerned, not only with historical research and documentation of the silk industry of the region, but in the use of this information to raise contemporary awareness of the factors which have shaped the character of the Cevennes. The project linked cultural heritage and traditions with agricultural and manufacturing for the economic benefit of the region. The increased publicity and profile given to the broad based nature of the project helped to promote the silk woven products manufactured in the Cevennes and increased the marketing opportunities.

The publication of a full colour hard bound volume entitled *Les Chemins de la Soie: Itineraires Cultivels en Cevennes – Bas Langedoc – Cevennes – Vivarals* in 1993 draws together much of the historical research with contemporary practice and presents it in an attractive form together with other tourist information on regional foods and places to visit. This makes the book a combination of reference work, coffee table book and informative tourist guide to the region of the Cevennes.

The Chemin de la Soie initiative provides an interesting model for using cultural heritage to promote economic development and industrial regeneration. It brings together historians, ethnologists, museum curators, heritage professionals, agriculturalists, scientists and industrialists with tourism professionals and regional government agencies. The cross fertilisation of ideas from such a partnership can generate new and creative models for economic regeneration.

Elsewhere in France, there are plans for a regional textile guide as part of the series of European Regional Textile Guides. In the Picardy and Pas de Calais regions, Claude Fauque is working with textile experts and regional government to develop the first of a series of guides. This project is a tripartite project which involves the publisher, Syros Alternative, the Council of Europe and the regions concerned. These guides will be targeted at a popular market and aim to stimulate visits to the European region among people with an interest in the subject through excellent presentation and design of the volumes.

TURKEY

The Council of Europe Cultural Itinerary meeting for silk was held in Bursa, Turkey, in 1990. Bursa was not only a major silk manufacturing centre in the 15th century, but is the centre of the silk industry in Turkey today and home of the centre for scientific research on sericulture. All processes on the manufacturing of silk take place in Turkey, and collections of silk textiles can be seen on display both in Bursa and at Topkapi Palace Museum and The Museum of Oriental Art in Istanbul, The Melvan Museum, Konya and elsewhere. However, the strongest interpretive story is perhaps that of The Silk Road and the caravanserai.

The caravanserais were a network of fortified inns, where traders, and the goods they carried, could safely shelter on route across Central Asia to the Mediterranean. All kinds of precious goods and ideas were carried in both directions along a network of trade routes which in the 19th century were named the Silk Road by Baron von Richthoven. Caravanserai were built throughout Central Asia and the Middle East not just in Turkey. Today there is considerable interest both in the restoration and documentation of these sights and in their development as a potential mechanism to encourage cultural tourism.

The first step undertaken by the Turkish Ministry of Tourism was to create a high profile for the idea by inviting over 100 international journalists to participate in a symbolic journey in motor caravans along the Silk Road. This was a highly photogenic spectacle, but much more research is necessary before the caravanserai might be developed as a mechanism to achieve sustainable, non-intrusive tourism which will help to provide sustainable economic growth in areas not traditionally associated with tourism. Research is needed to establish:

- what type of product is needed;
- what kind of infrastructure is necessary to support it;
- how it will be marketed and to which target markets.

A complete survey of both the Seljuk and the Ottoman Caravanserai is necessary (there are about 200 of each). Full archaeological and architectural surveys, including plans and photographic documentation, will be necessary. From such a survey it will be possible to identify those sites which should be:

- left to decay in their natural state;
- preserved in present state;
- restored as museums;
- restored and converted to other uses.

The criteria to determine which course of action is selected for each site needs to be established. Those sites which are not of the primary historical and archaeological importance and which are geographically well placed to serve the touristic strategy might be developed as:

- interpretation centres;
- museums;
- cultural centres for performing arts;
- restaurants and hotels;
- retail centres along the route for the sale of local crafts and goods, including silk.

Which option is selected would be determined by the architectural qualities of the building and its suitability for the new use matched with the requirements of the tourism strategy. In the week following the symbolic journey along the Silk Road by the international journalists, the Minister for Tourism presented the idea at the World Tourism Conference in Tashkent. Articles have subsequently appeared in the international press and we look forward to seeing further proposals for the development of the theme and the realisation of a viable and sustainable tourism product.

SPAIN

The fourth programme meeting was held in Spain. The first evidence of woven silk imports appears in Spain during the Visigothic period when silk was imported for use by the clergy and nobility. The cultivation of mulberry trees and breeding of silk worms was introduced into Andalusia by the Arabs. Documents of the 9th century record silk production in Almeria, Cordoba and Granada. The main silk production centres of Murcia, Valencia and Toledo all have strong relationships with the Arabic traditions which was perpetuated by the presence of the important Moorish population which was expelled at the beginning of the 17th century. A silk industry was also established in Catalonica in the 18th century and Barcelona, Manisa and Malaro were significant centres of production.

Proposals for a cultural itineraries based on silk were co-ordinated by Eulalia Morral-i-Romeu, Director of the Textile Museum in Terrassa, a textile manufacturing centre north east of Barcelona. Proposals for two major itineraries were drawn up in 1987. The first proposal linked the main silk manufacturing areas of Andslusia, including Cordoba, Granada, Almeria and Malaga and the collections and manufacturing centres in the Catalan region. The second concentrated on the areas of sericulture and production in Toledo, Murcia and Valencia.

The initial proposals were developed further and an association was established which brought together commercial manufacturers, researchers, academics, museum curators and tourism operators to undertake the necessary research and established the logistics of a tourism itinerary.

The Council of Europe meeting was held in Barcelona in 1991, and an itinerary was launched. The delegates visited the Textile Museum in Terrassa, mulberry plantations and a sericulture research station in Murcia and a college of design in Valencia. The itinerary ended in Granada at the Alhambra. Since 1991, further research and development work has been undertaken and a model for a realisable tourism product has been established. The Catalonia region is also collaborating with the area of South West France, an area which has similar cultural traditions. Together, they are developing a strategy for a trans-national cultural tourism initiative which involves silk and textiles as one of the themes.

SILK AND TEXTILE ROUTES IN BRITAIN

Since the first programme meeting, held in Como, Italy 1988, the Silk Museum in Macclesfield has worked with other partners in Britain to raise the profile for cultural tourism on the theme of silk. The Silk Museum in Macclesfield, as the only registered museum in Britain devoted to silk, is a natural focus for these activities, and the Council of Europe initiative has provided a catalyst for furthering this work.

The itinerary in Macclesfield predates the Cultural Routes Programme and the Silk Trail. An urban walking trail interpreting the heritage of the silk industry in Macclesfield, was published in 1984 to coincide with the opening of Paradise Mill working silk museum. This was followed in 1987 by the Silk Museum within the Heritage Centre building. Since 1988, and prompted by the Council of Europe initiative, the Museum has compiled documentation on other museums and institutions related to the theme of silk which could provide the basis for an itinerary or itineraries in Britain.

Included in these itineraries are museums of textiles and costume, country houses (where silk was used extensively in interior decoration and furnishings), galleries with collections of paintings depicting costumes made from silk, silk mills, warehouses and houses where silk merchants and weavers lived and worked (for example, Spitalfields in London and the weavers garrets in Macclesfield, Congleton and Leek).

Over 40 visitor attractions or museums with material or exhibitions on silk textiles or fashions have been identified. This list does not include country houses, galleries, or industrial and architectural/archaeological sites. Four separate itineraries were drawn up linking a group of attractions which gave a representative selection of sites. These proposals were sent to two regional tourist boards, the English Tourist Board and the British Tourist Association, but the response from these organisations was that while they considered it to be a good idea it was too specialised for the markets they were trying to attract. However, the climate is now more receptive than when the initials approaches were made.

Approaches were also made to individual special interest tour operators which met with greater success. British Heritage Tours, an independent special interest tour operator based in Chester, did show interest, and since 1992 they have offered a special interest short-break package titled 'The Silk Road to China'. This markets the Silk Museum and Trail in Macclesfield, together with visits to china factories in Stoke on Trent and followed on from a highly imaginative promotion by the Stoke on Trent Council 'Do China in a Day'. Neither the Macclesfield nor the Stoke areas have been traditionally perceived as tourist destinations and are identified in the public mind as industrial/manufacturing towns. The promotion of special interest or cultural tourism has therefore been significant not only in generating economic benefit but changing the image and profile of an area. This can have both social and economic benefit beyond that generated purely by the tourism industry.

A further example of a special interest tour company using a textile theme in Britain was the Rowan Travel Company, a subsidiary of Rowan Knitting Yarns. Using the opportunity offered by the Kaffe Fassett Exhibition held at the Victoria & Albert Museum in London, Rowan Travel offered a package targeted at craft practitioners and those interested in textiles. The package included time in London to visit the exhibition with an opportunity to meet and hear Kaffe Fassett lecture, followed by knitting workshops selected by other practitioners at the Rowan Yarn Mill in Yorkshire.

The success of this led to a two week package titled 'Wool and the Wonders of Scotland' which visited practising weavers and knitters, sheep breeding stations, museums and exhibitions. The product was marketed through yarn suppliers and promoted mainly in the USA and Canada, Australia and New Zealand, Holland and Scandinavia.

Unfortunately, the company was hit badly in the recession and was affected by the decline in business from America due to the Gulf War and are now trading on a much smaller scale, ie 12 –15 textile craft courses each year in association with Rowan Yarn concessions in deportment stores like Liberty's in London. In addition courses are held at the Rowan Yarn Factory in Yorkshire and occasional courses are also offered in association with National Trust properties. Accommodation is no longer provided in the package, and the company no longer offers the 5–14 day options like 'Glorious Colour' and 'Wool and the Wonders of Scotland' which were offered in the late 1980s. Their activity is now more related to Rowan Yarn's marketing than cultural tourism.

'Wool and the Wonders of Scotland' is not the only promotion in Scotland. The Scottish Tourist Board, not in a position to offer visitors a Mediterranean climate, have been active in promoting cultural and special interest tours for many years and the Woollen Trail was only one of a number of themed promotions which included castles and whisky among others. The Scottish Borderers Woollen Trail promoted by the Scottish Borders Tourism Association and the Scottish Tourist Board was first published as promotional print in three languages (English, French and German) in 1982. This Trail aimed to encouraged visitors to stop off in the Scottish Borders en route to Edinburgh or the Highlands and marketed the visitor attractions of woollen mills, museums and retail outlets for woollen products produced in the region.

Greater detail on this is provided in a paper delivered by Riddell Graham, Director of the Scottish Borders Tourist Board at the Council of Europe Meeting in Nîmes in 1989. Further evaluation of the effectiveness of the trails in economic terms was explained at the meeting in Macclesfield in 1992. I understand from a recent conversation with the Director of the Scottish Border Tourist Board that it has been decided to withdraw the trail for the present time, since the quality of the product offered by the visitor attractions has deteriorated through the lack of capital investment. The Board do not feel that it is appropriate to invest more in promotions which could lead to customer dissatisfaction through overselling of the product and would ultimately damage the image of tourism in the region. A strategy which involves capital investment as part of a single regeneration initiative for the

River Tweed is currently being worked on and there is a plan to relaunch the Woollen Trail following significant capital investment.

Since 1992, when the European Textile Network became the carrier network and the Council of Europe have broadened the theme to include Silk and Textiles, the opportunities for funding a textile itinerary in Britain are more optimistic because the woollen and cotton industry were much more significant to the British economy and there is a greater legacy of heritage and visitor attractions related to this theme.

The number of museums and visitor attractions which can be linked to the textile theme far outnumbers those which can be linked to silk. In the North West region of England, where the cotton industry was fundamental to the economy in the 19th century and the basis for Manchester's prosperity, it will be possible to collaborate with many more institutions to compile and fund a regional textile map which could be used in both a promotional and interpretative context. It is anticipated that this will be available for the ETN Conference to be held in Manchester in March 1996.

It is also the intention to collaborate with the Council of Europe in the production of a regional textile guide to the North West region as part of the series of European Textile guides to be published with Syros-Alternative.

GREECE

In Greece, the silk industry dates back to the Byzantine period, and silk first appeared in the Greek Islands after the 7th century. Centres of production at this time were Thebes and Mystras. Production was for local consumption supplying Constantinople and other places. During the Ottoman period, new markets were opened up and there are similarities between Greek centres of manufacture and the Ottoman Silk manufacturing centre of Bursa. In the modern period, the industrialisation of the silk industry took place in centres from Morea to Soufli.

Today, the industry is much smaller and the links with the Council of Europe have focused upon the town of Soufli, which is located in the north east of Greece. Here there was a flourishing silk industry in the 19th century with many factories. Today, there is a small museum developed with the sponsorship of one of the Greek banks. The itinerary is largely focused upon the town and the Mayor of Soufli has actively encouraged its development. Links have been established between the Cevennes in France and Soufli. An agreement has been drown up between the two areas which have similarities both geographically and economically and exchange visits have taken place to compare experiences and learn from each others practice. Soufli is one of the few examples which demonstrate significant private sector sponsorship in the development of the tourism product since it was the bank which provided a substantial contribution to the museum development.

PORTUGAL

The last meeting of the Silk Routes Programme was held in Portugal in November 1994. Portugal already has a strong tourism industry, but it is largely focused on the Algarve and the coastal areas. Interest has recently focused on ways of developing sustainable tourism in the poorer and more remote regions, particularly in the north of the region Tras-os-Montes. The Silk Route is centred on the district of Braganza, which is located on the Spanish border at the north east corner of Portugal.

The capital of the district is Braganza which was an important centre for silk manufacture. However, the centre for the meeting of the Silk Routes Programme was in Mirandella where in 1891 a sericulture station was built to undertake research on sericulture with the object of detecting and treating the infection Pebrine which affects the silk worms. Material from the sericulture station formed part of a display in the Museum and Cultural Centre in Mirandella and was the basis for one of the stops on the proposed itinerary. One of the principal points of interest on the Silk Route Itinerary in Portugal was at Chacim in the department Macedo de Cavaleiros. The Royal Manufacturing which was built in 1788 and introduced the Piedmontese technology to Portugal. Other points on the Itinerary included Freixo de Espada a Cinta, and Braga and Oporto in the north west.

Clearly, the area of Braganza would benefit from the development of cultural tourism. However, significant investment would be required both to develop the visitor facilities and attractions and the tourism infrastructure. The eligibility of this area of Portugal for European Union resources for economic development could be of great significance in implementing both the tourism product and the itinerary.

HOLLAND AND BELGIUM

Although Portugal hosted the last major meeting in the Silk Routes Programme, a new model of smaller meetings has been developed by the Council of Europe which aims to progress the itineraries on the ground. Michel Thomas-Penette, working with the partners in the countries represented, has been involved in organising small working groups in order to progress the development of regional textile guides. The first of these meetings was held in Belgium and Holland, which are to be the basis of the second European Textile Guide, the first being for the Picardy region of Northern France.

The second guide involves collaboration with local government in Belgium to promote a group of textile museums in the Flemish speaking region of Belgium and the Netherlands Museum of Textile in Tilburg, Holland. The sites include the Museum of Tapistrie in Tournsi, Musee de la Rubanerie Comines, the Linen Museum in Courtai and the Museum of Bonnetterie. Financial support will come from regional government and tourist organisations surrounding Muscoran and the Museum of Textiles in Tilburg. The publication will form part of the series developed by Claude Fauque of Syros-Alternative and the Council of Europe. The programme of small working meetings is a model which is being developed in parallel to the major meetings organised by the carrier network system which arose from the changes in operation initiated by the Council of Europe.

A CHANGE OF OPERATION AND EMPHASIS

The conference in Portugal was planned to be the last in the series devoted to the promotion of the Silk Routes Programme since Portugal was the last of the initial grouping of countries to launch an itinerary. A number of factors were to influence the changes in the operation of the Programme:

- the need to have a broader geographical base for the itineraries in order to accommodate the greater involvement of the Northern European members who were becoming more active within the Council of Europe;
- following the fall of the Berlin Wall, greater emphasis was being placed on collaboration with the Eastern European countries;
- the adoption of carrier networks by the Council of Europe as a means of furthering and promoting the cultural itineraries generally.

THE CARRIER NETWORK: FROM SILK TO TEXTILE ITINERARIES

In line with the methodology adopted by the Council of Europe for the other cultural itineraries, the European Textile Network (ETN) became the carrier network for the Silk and Textile Itineraries in 1992. The theme was broadened from silk to include other textile fibres since it was necessary to broaden the theme of silk to accommodate the Northern European members where wool, linen and cotton are more important to the textile economies.

ETN was founded in 1989 by Beatrijs Sterk and Dietmar Laue, a couple based in Hannover who run a magazine called Textile Forum. Disturbed by the rise in nationalism which arose in Germany after the fall of the Berlin Wall, they sought a way in which they might encourage European unity and a stronger awareness of a single European identity which would help to override nationalistic tendencies. With their extensive contacts among textile practitioners they proposed the idea for a European Network based on textiles.

ETN now has 255 individual members and 151 institutional members within Europe, and a further 72 members outside Europe, making a total of 478 members in 34 European and 19 non-European countries. Membership is open to both individuals and institutions. Embodied in the constitution is the principal of strong representation from Eastern Europe to the extent of subsidising their membership. The membership of ETN was initially mainly drawn from textile practitioners and people involved in textile education.

There are now five specialist areas, ie textile design and fashion, textile education, textile artists, textile media and cultural heritage. Conferences were held in Erfurt in 1992, Lousanne in 1993, Budapest in 1994 and St Petersburg in 1995. Meetings are planned for Manchester in 1996 and Spain in 1998. At the meeting in Budapest, the Council of Europe Silk Itineraries Programme was broadened to accommodate textiles and the Eastern European possibilities were explored. This was further extended at the meeting in St Petersburg.

The Cultural Heritage Group is mainly responsible for furthering the work of the Council of Europe Silk and Textile Cultural Itineraries Programme, since the membership of this group is made up of people representing museums and heritage organisations which are likely to form the basis for the Textile Itineraries. Other collaborative activities have arisen both with the education and artists groups which have led to bi-lateral projects and the exchange of students and ideas.

THE EUROSOIE RESEARCH NETWORK

However, ETN is not the only network. Since 1991, Eurosoie, an association registered under French law, was established to encourage research, collaboration and the promotion of silk as a theme for cultural itineraries. Representation is essentially made up of the partners brought together through the Council of Europe Cultural Itineraries programme and has resulted in research collaboration between Portugal, Spain, Italy, France, Britain and Greece. The membership is essentially researchers, academics, museum curators.

It is the collaboration between individuals through the Eurosoie Network which has added to the body of knowledge we have on the development of the silk industry in Europe. The generous sharing of research has uncovered sources which were previously unknown to some of the partners and lead to new avenues of research. Trans-national relationships have been uncovered which establish historical trade links between communities which we are now attempting to re-establish through tourism and exchange. The research undertaken by the membership of Eurosoie will inform and contribute to the quality of the implementation of the silk routes cultural itineraries throughout Europe.

METHODOLOGIES FOR IMPLEMENTATION

A wide range of methodologies and approaches have been employed to implement the itineraries but clearly the full range of the media available for implementation has not been exploited. The preferred option, whether for logistical or financial reasons seems to fall within the category of printed guides, whether they are used as free promotional print or substantial guide books:

- road signs, while considered, have not yet been implemented on a scale to be significant in relation to silk/textile itineraries, although this has been considered in the Scottish Borders and has been implemented elsewhere on other trails/cultural routes;
- personal tourist guides have long been a cost effective option for group itineraries, but are not so easily adaptable to the individual or independent tourist, although for group and education visits, tourist guides have been used in Macclesfield and the Cevennes;
- tour operators offering special interest packages employ trained guides to escort groups round, and hotels offering short break

themed packages, often build in some kind of introductory lecture as part of the programme;
–   transport authorities have used themed promotions as a means of marketing their service, but this has yet to be applied to silk and textiles;
–   the media can also be used for both promotion and interpretation, whether this be through printed editorial in magazines or feature broadcasting for radio or TV.

CULTURAL TOURISM

Cultural and special interest tourism represents only a small sector of the total tourism industry and is often neglected in tourism promotion since it is not perceived as bringing the significant economic returns that mass tourism can generate. While it is true that the economic benefits cannot be measured on the same scale as the 'Sun and Sand' market. If one considers performance in relation to issues of cultural traditions, community, environmental and heritage preservation and sustainability, the picture is very different.

The scale of cultural tourism is such that it can be sustained and need not demand the same scale of capital investment in tourism infrastructure although without investment to develop and maintain the product it will not be sustainable. However, this investment should be spread between the conservation of the cultural heritage and the visitor management and facilities to ensure visitor satisfaction, without causing such environmental and social impact that it diminishes or destroys the cultural or environmental feature which is the focus of the tourism.

Cultural Itineraries provide a vehicle which is useful both in the promotion and management of cultural tourism. It can also provide a focus which can integrate manufacturing and tourism initiatives for both social and economic benefit. The initiatives in Macclesfield, the Cevennes and more recently Soufli are models which explore different aspects and partnerships which have impacted on tourism and economic developed in different regions of Europe.

CONCLUSIONS

Of all the cultural itineraries adopted by the Council of Europe, Silk and Textiles offers the most exciting possibilities for linking communities, cultural heritage and traditions with contemporary manufacturing and tourism for the economic and social benefit of a region.

Although it could be argued that 'Gardens' and 'Architecture without Frontiers' still engages with current industrial or craft practises through horticulture and the building industry, it does not offer all the possibilities of engagement offered by textiles. Although gardening and the love of gardens is popular throughout Europe, it does not transcend all cultural, educational and socio-economic boundaries and few of us get involved in designing and building houses, but all of us make personal choices about textiles through the clothes we buy and wear. Many, particularly within the female population, become involved in the production process of both textiles, fashions and textile manufacture. Whether as a craft or industrial practice, it transcends all cultures.

A number of interesting models have been adopted which use textiles as a basis for economic regeneration and tourism, but there are many more opportunities for development of creative partnerships which bring together the expertise and energies in cross-disciplinary groups. I would commend the theme of silk and textiles as a vehicle for exploring new models of community, cultural and industrial practice as a means of economic and socials regeneration.

The Author

Moira Stevenson graduated from Bath Academy of Art, followed by a postgraduate qualification in Art Gallery and Museum Studies from the University of Manchester. A Fellow of the Museums Association, she is currently a Council Member representing the North West Region. She has worked in museums since 1973, starting her career as a designer in the Royal Scottish Museum, Edinburgh. She is currently Director of Macclesfield Museums and Heritage Centre with responsibility for three museums. Two related to silk have achieved local, national and international awards for a wide range of activities, including the Come to Britain trophy and the Sir Mark Henig Award for Tourism. She has been involved with the Council of Europe Cultural Itineraries Silk Routes Programme since its inception in 1988.

Figure 1 Hamish Moore playing the Triple Pipes.

15

ON THE TRAIL OF MUSIC
Origins of the Scottish Triple Pipes

John Purser

Scotland is irrevocably associated with the bagpipes, yet their early history in this country is very obscure. The triple pipes carved on three Pictish/Scottish stone carvings are not only possible fore-runners, but represent a type of instrument so rare that it is otherwise known only in Sardinia. Like the Sardinian pipes (the launeddas), the Pictish pipes include a drone and were probably played using the esoteric technique of circular breathing, which produces a similar effect to pipes where the air is supplied continuously from a bag. Modern bagpipers use this technique on the practice chanter.

The reconstruction is necessarily speculative, but the carvings are clear enough to indicate not only the size of the pipes in relation to each other, but also in relation to the player, and the position of the fingers is also fairly clearly shown. The research for the reconstruction was undertaken in consultation with experts in the fields of archaeology, ethnomusicology, and other related disciplines.

The appearance of the pipes in close association with the Pictish clarsach (triangular framed harp developed by the Picts) echoes ancient classical Greek association of the aulos (a double pipe) with the lyre. In essence the Pictish clarsachs and pipes are developments of these simpler instruments, and their reconstruction is of immense significance to the history of pipe playing in Scotland; to Scottish music in general; and to the history of early music internationally. The fact that the pipes were clearly designed to play in more than one part with a drone gives them a special significance in the early development of part-writing, with which they are contemporary.

THE EARLIEST MULTIPLE PIPES IN SCOTLAND

The earliest depiction of any instrument in Scotland is that of the double pipes on a Roman distance slab from Bridgeness on the Antonine Wall (now in the National Museum of Scotland). It dates from 142 AD and the right hand panel depicts a *suovetaurilia* – a purificatory sacrifice of a pig, a sheep and a bull. A musician (shepherd or herdsman) is shown clearly playing a double pipe, the two pipes being held at one end in the mouth but splaying out quite widely and held in separate hands in which the fingers are clearly shown.

The way the fingers have been placed suggests strongly that both pipes were melody pipes with finger holes. The pipes are conical and appear to be of equal breadth and length, though one is cut short by the clothing of one of the figures. This is a Roman ceremony, conducted by officers of the Second Legion; and neither the stone nor the ceremony it shows will have gone unobserved by the ancestors of the Picts who raised the Lethendy stone some 800 years later. It is possible that this instrument was introduced to Scotland by the Romans, or reinforced the use of an existing instrument, and that a third pipe in the form of a drone was added by the Picts or their ancestors. The Sardinian launeddas was as old as the late bronze age, but, apart from one representation in a 13th century Spanish manuscript, there is no evidence of their having spread to the rest of Europe.

It is important to keep this situation in mind when it comes to discussion of transmission of instruments between Scotland and Ireland. It should also be kept in mind that the Irish had very little direct contact with the Romans – such as they had, being in the form of sporadic raids. They could have obtained instruments from the Romans and learnt how to play them at their leisure back in Ireland; but on the basis of the present evidence, the natural conclusion with respect to any possible Roman influence upon the development of double and triple pipes in Ireland and Scotland, is to assume that the Scots had a greater familiarity with the Roman double pipes and better opportunity to imitate their manufacture and playing technique.

Collinson argues that the divergent Roman double pipes are a basically different type from the parallel pipes, and he suggests that the Roman pipes left no descendants in Britain, but the divergence or parallelism of double pipes is of little morphological or musical significance since the player can move them apart or bring them (even bind them) together at will. However, it is clear that when it comes to triple pipes, keeping them close together and at least partially bound, makes them easier to play. If the triple pipes were indeed a development from double pipes (see below), the bringing of the pipes together so that they are more nearly parallel is only a minor aspect of the development. There is no written evidence for, or oral tradition of the use of triple pipes at any period in Scottish history or pre-history. The sole surviving evidence for the presence of these instruments in Scotland is to be found on three carved stones. One is situated at Lethendy in Perthshire, another is at Ardchattan in Argyllshire, and the third is on St Martin's Cross on Iona.

THE LETHENDY STONE

This stone is fully described in PSAS Vol 104 by Fisher and Greenhill, *Two unrecorded carved stones at Tower of Lethendy, Perthshire* (hereinafter Fisher and Greenhill) who ascribe the stone to the 10th century AD, calling it a 'Picto-Scottish Relief Carving'. The musicians on the stone are also discussed by Porter in *Selected Reports in Ethnomusicology 4* (1983) *Essays In Honour Of Peter Crossley-Holland*, (hereinafter Porter) and Isobel Henderson discusses them in *The 'David Cycle' In Pictish Art* in *Early Medieval Sculpture in Britain and Ireland* ed John Higgitt in *BAR British Series 152 1986* (hereinafter Henderson). Collinson makes a surprisingly brief reference to it in *The Bagpipe*.

There are three pipes. The two shorter ones appear to be the same length, the third is considerably longer and is probably a drone. The ends of all three are in the player's mouth and any divergence between his mouth and the further ends of the pipes is slight. There seems no more reason for supposing that any of the pipes ends with an attached horn than there is for the triple pipes found on two Irish crosses. The suggestion is made by Baines in *Bagpipes* and endorsed by Fisher and Greenhill; but such an important feature would surely be depicted unequivocally. There is not even a hint of such a device on any of the carvings, the continuous lines of the pipes being unbroken and any slight conicity being even throughout their lengths.

A lot of information can be got from the Lethendy stone and the structural details will be taken up below. However, the context is equally important. It is not possible to tell whether this slab is part of a cross-slab, but it is clearly Christian. Two clerics hold, respectively, a book and a sceptre. Below them are two musicians facing each other. Both are standing. One is holding a small triangular framed harp with a prominent sound-box and seven strings. It is sufficiently small for it not to touch the ground. No means of support is shown, but it was possibly supported by being attached to his waistband or other clothes fastenings – the early Celtic monks were known to travel with small harps suspended at the waist (see Purser, *Scotland's Music*).

The other musician is playing triple pipes. The detail of these pipes and their fingering will be discussed below, but it is clear from the carving that the player has his mouth extended by the presence of the pipes, and his cheeks extended by the effort of blowing, and this forms a striking contrast with the mouths and over-all facial expressions of the other figures, the triple pipe player being the most obviously active and conveying a sense of energy. The two musicians are similarly dressed in tunics loosely belted either at the waist or the hips. In between them is what is quite probably a barrel drum, and beneath the drum and the harp there is an animal with a collar, possibly a dog, as Fisher and Greenhill assert with confidence. However, the details they point out – the pointed ears, a curled tail and clawed paws – are at least as suggestive of a cat, and this identification is reinforced by the arched spine, and by the fact that a cat is clearly shown in a parallel situation, beside a triple piper and a harpist, on the cross at Clonmacnoise in Ireland.

The basic facts to be deduced are that triple pipes and clarsach were played together, possibly with the addition of a drum, and that this playing could find a place on a Christian monument, suggesting that the music being played is itself religious in some way or another. The usual interpretation of scenes involving musicians is that they represent King David of the psalms, either as poet-king, or as shepherd. The piper then represents the shepherd with his pipes and the dog becomes a shepherd's dog. However, the undoubted cat at Clonmacnoise does not fit in with this scenario, and alternative explanations should be considered. The psalms were of particular significance in the early Celtic church, and the figure of David as both King and Musician was a naturally appealing one, especially in Ireland and Scotland where the bardic traditions and status had not been replaced by Roman social structures. We should therefore be prepared to find some native contributions to the David iconography, the most obvious of which is the Pictish triangular framed harp, but of which creatures like the cat may be further examples.

If the Lethendy animal is in fact a cat, what might be its significance? The Gaelic for cat was and still is 'catt'. The name of the son of the founder of the Picts was Cat, from whom Caithness and the Clan Chattan take their respective names. The names are still taken to be derived from the creature, so we may assume that the Picts either used or welcomed the word 'cat' with its accepted meaning. An image of a cat in Pictland could then represent both a people and a place.

On the other hand, there being no such associations at Clonmacnoise, it might be more meaningful to think of the cat in its symbolic role as a creature of the dark, to be found perhaps at the entrance to the other world. The music would then be funerary – perhaps a dirge for any person for whom the stone had acted as a grave marker, or a lament for some biblical figure such as St Paul the hermit, whose burial is said to be honoured in the scenes next to the triple piper at Clonmacnoise, and who (with St Anthony) features regularly on Pictish cross-slabs.

If this interpretation is correct, then the cat's attitude, licking its belly, is one of indifference, which can be somewhat lamely explained by the thought that St Paul's other world is not going to be the dark one in which cats feel so free. The cat was popular in early Gaelic literature. As a domesticated creature, a pet of the priests, cats perhaps represented the taming of wickedness. The white cat of the famous early 9th century poem *Messe ocus Pangur ban* may be white to add to his other virtuous characteristics as a diligent hunter of mice, paralleling the Scholar's hunting out of obscure meanings.

It may be significant in this connection that on the Ardchattan stone and possibly on the St Andrews sarcophagus fragment (where the presence of a harp is uncertain), David is shown in a context which may suggest he was taming the wild beasts with his harp, as Orpheus did with his lyre (Henderson). In the light of such evidence, the cat could be thought of as a parallel theme – the creature of the dark tamed.

ARDCHATTAN CROSS SLAB

Although from the west of Scotland, this stone is essentially Pictish in design, the cross being carved in relief on a much damaged rectangular stone, the parts surrounding the cross being heavily decorated. A warrior figure unique to Pictish sculpture, with spear and shield with central boss, is shown on this stone. On the right hand edge are clearly carved three hooded figures, probably clerics, one above the other. The top figure is playing a harp – almost certainly a triangular framed harp. The central figure is blowing triple pipes but, interestingly, no attempt has been made to show the altered shape of the mouth required to make the manner of playing explicit. Instead the pipes merely terminate at the front edge of the player's lips and nose. The third and lower figure is holding what may be a bone or rattle of some sort. Romilly Allen describes this combination of musicians as suggestive of Revelations Chapter 4, but there seems little or no justification for the notion, even accepting that the lower figure may be holding a crown rather than a musical instrument.

ST MARTIN'S CROSS ON IONA

Here again, what may well be triple pipes are associated with a stringed instrument, and below the triple pipes themselves is a rectangular object which may be a drum. This cross is described by the Royal Commission on the Ancient and Historical Monuments of Scotland in their Vol 4 *Argyll an inventory of the monuments* published in 1982, hereinafter RCAHMS.

The presence of pipes and a probable drum alongside the harp has been commented on by Porter and others as untypical of early Christian practice in the rest of Europe. Fisher and Greenhill suggest it is a native response to the frequent mention of these instruments in the Old Testament. It implies a lack of concern with the classical role model for these instruments, in which the lyre was considered superior and Apollonian, the pipe of Pan inferior and Dionysiac (see below).

DATING OF THE STONES

No strictly scientific technique has yet been found which can date the carving of any of the stones referred to. No dates are inscribed on them, nor are persons who could be clearly identified referred to on them, other than Biblical or early Christian figures. Dating is therefore dependant on analysis of design elements and their possible lines of influence. This is an area so dogged by nationalist prejudice, speculation and muddled thinking, even among scholars of repute, that one is hesitant to enter the fray. One of the most prevalent assumptions is that the sculptors virtually always had earlier iconographic models for their work. This is accepted without question, though there are many counter-indications, and these counter-indications include most notably the scenes with musicians where, it will be argued, they most likely had actual instruments and musicians as their models.

Strictly speaking, the earliest possible date for any stone depicting Christian scenes is the arrival of Christianity in the area. This in itself is not a straightforward matter but, as far as Scotland is concerned, could in certain areas, be any time from the 5th century on, and in the areas in which triple pipes are shown, any time from the 6th century on. The latest possible dates are even harder to establish.

An example of the difficulties in assigning such dates is found in one of the reasons offered for a latest date of 800 for the Iona crosses. Iona was recorded as being attacked by the Vikings in 802, 806 and 823 or 824. These attacks were still occurring as late as 985 and, from the start, were so severe as to have caused the relics of St Columba to be taken to Dunkeld in the mid 9th century. The argument is that the carving of such major works was unlikely after such turbulent times (Henderson). On the other hand, the survival of these crosses without any sign of vandalism, despite the Vikings, might suggest that it was the one Christian manifestation which could not be slaughtered, stolen, sold, melted down or burnt, and would therefore have been continued. What is more, it is perfectly obvious from the very continuance of the Viking raids, that there was still something worth raiding. In other words, the community recovered and no doubt made good its losses as best it could. Even the removal of St Columba's relics has the alternative explanation that Kenneth MacAlpin wanted to centralise and unify Christian worship at the heart of the kingdom rather than on its Irish-influenced western edge.

Stylistic grounds are also offered for dating the Iona crosses to the 8th century, St Martin's cross being regarded as late 8th century work (RCAHMS *Argyll* Vol 4 Iona, 1982). If this is the case, and if, as Henderson suggests, the St Andrews sarcophagus David scene is closely analogous to the Ardchattan stone and is late 8th century itself, then a late 8th century date is possible for Ardchattan also, except for the assumption that the triple pipes were imported from Ireland which, it seems, Henderson has adopted from Fisher and Greenhill.

The first reason for dating the Lethendy stone as late as the 10th century is given by Fisher and Greenhill as being the presence of the triple piper which they assume has been adopted from Ireland. No reason for this assumption is given. They further implicitly assume that any such influence was later than 843 which is extraordinarily late, considering that it is an indisputable fact that much of northern Pictland was converted to Christianity by Irish missionaries from the 6th century onwards and that the influence of Adomnan reached into Perthshire in the 7th century.

These problems of dating refer also to the Christian carvings in Ireland and England and the most elaborate studies and explanations have been produced to explain the sources of the iconography and of the idea of translating that iconography into stone (Peter Harbison, *The High Crosses of Ireland* Bonn 1992, hereinafter Harbison). Two salient facts with respect to all these theories are, however, the two least considered. The first is that only in Pictland is there clear and extensive evidence of an immediately pre-Christian school of stone-carving. The second is that the record in stone from this period in England is singularly poor by comparison with Ireland and Scotland, and within that record, David iconography makes only two appearances.

Clearly the Christian iconography must have its source ultimately in the Bible and other Christian writings originating in the Mediterranean countries, but the notion that this iconography was most likely to have been transmitted via England is a constant stumbling block to any kind of rational assessment of the problems. It stretches credibility that so much iconographic material could have passed through England and left so little trace by comparison with Ireland and Scotland. What is more, the bulk of those traces in England is to be found in Northumbria which was not only Christianised from Iona, but was in close communication with the Picts, its main early Christian centre at Lindisfarne being only ten miles south of the present Scottish border. Given that the northern Picts (who were the producers of the pre-Christian stone carvings) were Christianised from Ireland, a natural conclusion to draw is that the Irish got much of their iconography direct from Mediterranean sources; the Picts got much of their Christian iconography from Ireland; the Irish got their interest in stone-carving from the Picts, and the two of them acted as a major influence on the Northumbrians.

Of course such a model is simplified, but the fact that it has only been peripherally considered is deeply to be regretted and has led to manifest absurdities such as the proposal that all the Pictish depictions of triangular framed harps (of which there are at least three different types) are derived from one possible (and scarcely decipherable) triangular framed harp on a stone at Masham in Yorkshire (Henderson).

THE SIGNIFICANCE OF IRISH AND SCOTTISH TRIPLE PIPES

The same assumptions affect our consideration of triple pipes. It is boldly stated by commentators that these were adopted by the Picts from Irish models (Henderson, Fisher and Greenhill, RCAHMS, and implicitly accepted by Porter). No evidence for this notion has ever been offered, save that there are two examples of triple pipe players in Ireland. In fact, if the Ardchattan and Iona stones are dated to the late 8th century then they probably pre-date the Irish stones at Clonmacnoise and Monasterboice which are usually described as 9th century (an example of triple pipes suggested for Roscrea and assigned to the 12th century by Harbison, is too worn to be meaningful). Of vital significance in the relationship between the Irish and Scottish triple pipes is the presence or absence of the triangular framed harp. I and others have argued (Purser, *Scotland's Music*, Sanger and Kinnaird, *Tree of Strings* and Porter, op cit) that the Picts were the originators of the triangular framed harp. This accepted, it means that the sculptors could, and probably did work from original instruments which they had seen played by live musicians. This certainly seems to be the case with the Lethendy triple pipe player, as well as on the two Irish examples, where the piper is shown with an attention to detail. As for the triangular harps, these are carefully observed and indicate the presence of different types, for which no earlier iconography has ever been produced.

What this association between the triple pipes and the triangular framed harps would naturally suggest, is that the triple pipes were just as likely to have been initiated by the Picts as by the Irish. However, on the Cross of the Scriptures at Clonmacnoise, the triple pipe player is on a different face of the cross from the other musician whose instrument is a typically quadrangular one of lyre type, and at both Monasterboice and Clonmacnoise the scenes in which they appear are decidedly different (see below) so it may be that we have two parallel but distinct traditions of triple pipes usage in Scotland and Ireland. There is one other example of a pipe player on an Irish cross at Durrow, in association with the lyre, but they are not triple pipes.

On the evidence available, the most likely scenario is that the triangular framed harp was invented and exported by the Picts: that the triple pipes were known to them at the same period but that the Irish also knew them at, or a little after the same period: and that this combination of harp (or 'lyre') and pipe (and occasionally drum) was known in both countries and accepted as appropriate for Christian worship. Such associations were not accepted and are not shown in any other European Christian iconography, to my knowledge, although the Sardinian launeddas was regularly played in modern times, in or around church services, not always to the pleasure of the priests (Andreas Bentzon, *The Launeddas*, Acta Ethnomusicologica Danica 1, Copenhagen 1969, hereinafter, Bentzon).

The important difference between the Irish representations of these scenes and those of the Picts is that both at Durrow and Monasterboice the two musicians are part of a Last Judgment scene, and are together on the right hand of Christ, or flanking him. In this assessment I do not follow Helen Roe (*Monasterboice and its Monuments* County Louth Archaeological and Historical Society, Longford 1981) in declaring the large seated figure on Christ's left hand side to be the archangel Gabriel sounding the last trumpet, preferring Harbison's suggestion that it is a triple pipe player. In fact in good light the triple pipes are very clear. There is another piper (whose instrument appears to be a single pipe) behind the quadrangular lyre player and he is described by Harbison as a flute player.

The importance lies in the fact that the tradition bequeathed by the Greeks to the rest of Europe, and still sustained to this day, is that the harp, or similar plucked stringed instrument is the Apollonian, heavenly, godly instrument; whereas the pipe is the Dionysiac instrument of the minor god, Pan, and is considered inferior. This distinction of quality is enshrined in the story of King Midas, who is given asses ears for preferring Pan's music to that of Apollo. The story was widely known by musicians through the ages and was delightfully described in a secular cantata of J. S. Bach. It was also known in western Scotland, but the version I was personally told by John MacKinnon in Skye did not include any competition between instruments. The King did indeed have asses ears from birth, and although the rest of the story concerning the discovery of the King's deformity (which he hid under long hair) is broadly similar, it is the harps which betray the secret, rather than the reeds.

One can not draw certain conclusions from this evidence, but it suggests that the native tradition did not accept denigration of the pipes as inferior to or inappropriate with the harp in a musical or Christian context, although in post-reformation times the pipes have been vilified by some churchmen.

If we take this evidence along with the broadly accepted interpretation of all these musicians as representative of King David of the Psalms in various manifestations, then we have to remember that to the psalmists all sorts of instruments were equally acceptable for worshipping the Lord, even though David himself played a lyre. What this means is that the triple pipes could have a place in the heavenly rather than the hellish music. They could tame the cat (see above); they could play a lament; they could play alongside the harp or lyre for the souls of the righteous; and they could just play along, as they do at Lethendy.

THE TRIPLE PIPES IN THE REST OF EUROPE

With respect to the triple pipes elsewhere in Europe, it is worth remembering that in Sardinia they date back to the bronze age and that there is one 13th century depiction of them in Spain, and that is the sum total of the evidence. They are said to derive ultimately from ancient Egyptian double pipes (Bentzon). Bentzon's exhaustive study of the launeddas does not concern itself too deeply in its ancient history, no doubt because it is difficult to prove anything. Sadly, he appears to have been unaware of the Pictish and Irish triple pipes. Suffice it to say that double pipes are common in ancient and modern times, and triple pipes are exceedingly rare – quite possibly because it is very much harder to keep blowing three pipes simultaneously than it is two. But that the triple pipes are a development from the double pipes, seems as natural an inference as that bags were attached to pipes rather than pipes attached to bags, though one can make some sort of a noise with a bag alone.

CONCLUSIONS ON THE ORIGINS AND DATING OF THE PICTISH PIPES

There is no reason for supposing that the Pictish triple pipes were derived from Irish models – if anything, the reverse. There is no obvious route of transmission for the Pictish and Irish triple pipes to have been derived from the Sardinian launeddas. There is every reason to believe that triple pipes are a development from double pipes. There is evidence for double pipes on a Roman stone on the borders of Pictland. It is therefore entirely possible that the Picts developed their triple pipes from Roman double pipes. If this is the case, it implies a higher degree of musical skill and perseverance on the part of the Picts, as the instrument is exceedingly difficult to play and control. There is no evidence that the Romans had triple pipes and, given the vast quantity of iconography they left behind them, it seems very unlikely that they had them.

One final possibility should not be ruled out, and that is that there were Sardinians in the Roman army who brought triple pipes to Scotland with them. If this is so, they left no trace of their influence on their way from Sardinia, although this could be explained if their journey to Scotland was largely by sea.

METHODOLOGY OF RECONSTRUCTION

Hamish Moore undertook the manufacture and first performances of the Pictish triple pipe reconstruction. He is internationally known as a pipe maker and player, with expertise on several different kinds of pipes. A further reason for his involvement with the project was his developed technique of circular breathing (see below).

Although cane is the material used in Sardinia, some of the canes used for parts of the launeddas are rare even there and their locations are closely guarded secrets. There has never been a supply of comparable or useful cane in Scotland, so it was decided that the Pictish pipes must have been made of wood. There is evidence for the use of wood augurs and spoon bits, and the native woods in use at that period were alder, birch and cherry (information from Anne Crone of the Archaeology Unit in Edinburgh). However, the most suitable native timber for making pipes, available at the relevant period, was yew; so it was decided to use yew, notwithstanding the lack of any surviving artefacts made from yew at that time. The reasoning behind this decision was as follows:

1. Almost any kind of musical instrument is a special case and as there are no relevant surviving musical artefacts using wood to

guide us, there were no counter-indications of a musical nature for the use of yew.

2.   The absence of yew in non-musical artefacts could be interpreted as a significant counter-indicator in that it might suggest that yew was a sacred tree or had some taboo attached to it which prevented its use. The reason for ignoring this very real possibility was that a musical instrument depicted in a religious context would be precisely the sort of artefact which would be worthy of yew. In other words, I would suggest that if there were any taboos or restrictions with respect to the use of certain materials, these would most likely apply to their use for the sort of everyday objects that tend to form the bulk of the archaeological evidence, the sacred wood being reserved for sacred tasks. That the triple pipes were used for sacred purposes is indisputable.

3.   The reliability and good turning and boring qualities of yew make it the best candidate for the construction of pipes and it is hard to believe that it would have been by-passed in favour of a less suitable or readily available wood.

4.   Yew was used in Ireland at this time and, since the triple pipes appear in Ireland and Scotland, and there are many other cultural connections between the two countries, including the monumental sculpture on which the pipes appear, it seems reasonable to suggest that its potential was known in Scotland and that its absence in the archaeological evidence is not necessarily significant. The actual timber used was heartwood from midway up the trunk of a yew from the Dunkeld area that was at least 500 years old. This timber had been seasoned for more than ten years.

A set of reeds made from native elder (commonly used by the travelling folk for bagpipe reeds) will be available, but cane from central France was used initially for the reeds as reed cane could have been readily imported and gives the best results. Reeds could also have been made from oatstraw, but these are not very stable or long-lasting. The other materials used are a blend of beeswax and oil to assist in tuning and adjustment of reeds and finger holes, and thread to bind the pipes together.

The longest pipe is the drone (610mm overall) and it is made in two sections, the lower section being 365mm long and the upper one 245mm long. The drone is pitched in A. Its external diameter at the bottom end is 25mm. The bore of the first section is divided evenly between the mouth end at 5.5mm and the rest at 6mm. The lower section is similarly divided with bores of 6mm and 7.5mm. They are not therefore strictly speaking conical; but the effect is so similar to a conical bore that it would take great expertise to detect any difference. The chanters are absolutely cylindrical and have a bore of 5.5mm. At their bottom ends the external diameter is 13mm. All these dimensions are decided by a number of factors. A fairly wide bore allows for a good airflow and increases the volume. Because the reeds have to be relatively small to fit into the mouth, they are not in themselves as loud as they might be, so any increase in power from the chanter itself is to be welcomed.

The two chanters are 395mm long, but the holes are positioned so that the outside chanter (lower hand) produces the notes A,B,C,D; and the centrally placed chanter (upper hand) plays the notes D,E,F-sharp,G,A.

These pitches are the natural consequences of two simple decisions, derived from the stones. The basic pitch is decided by the lengths of all three pipes, and these lengths are determined by their size in proportion to the people playing them. The pitches of the fingered notes are decided by the principle of boring the holes at even spaces on the chanters – a common practice, and one supported by the Lethendy stone where the player's fingers are widely and evenly spread (this was the custom among old fiddlers too). These pitches relate closely to the old Highland bagpipe scale when the bagpipes were played with open fingering and with a fairly flat C sharp. They are not rigidly determined, however. As the pipes warm up and the reeds bed in, so the pitch tends to rise, and this has the advantage of allowing the reeds to be pushed further into the pipes, thus giving more space in the mouth. Tuning can also be adjusted (while still playing), by adding or subtracting small quantities of specially prepared wax to the finger holes. This is a widespread practice, especially among launeddas players.

The fingers of the left hand reach across the drone to the centrally placed chanter. This seems to be the case with the Lethendy musician, though it may well be that the Clonmacnoise player (the only other carving with much clarity with respect to the fingers) is fingering all three pipes, his left (upper) hand fingering the longest pipe; and his right hand fingering the two others. The thumbs are used to support the chanters, but it is possible to introduce a thumb hole, though neither tradition nor iconography support it.

The truth is that we cannot be certain about these fingerings. The only living examples to draw from are the launeddas players, and they use several different combinations of pipes and tunings, with various fingering consequences. We are therefore reasonably justified in trying out different combinations of pipes and tunings for the Pictish and Irish triple pipes. Once you have the potential for a variety of harmonic effects and combinations of partial scales, the temptation to experiment is much greater than it is with instruments confined to one note at a time, or one note and a drone. For the moment we have settled upon the arrangement outlined above, but may well change this in future.

One other factor influencing the choice of pitches was the traditional tuning of the Highland bagpipes which, however, can be securely based on evidence from no earlier than the 18th century. Even so, it proved impossible to include the low bagpipe g on the triple pipes as the stretch for the fingers was too great.

One problem encountered with fingering the pipes was that of reaching the centrally placed chanter without being inhibited by the drone. The solution was to bind it so that it lies a little proud of the plane of the three pipes. The launeddas players bind their pipes.

BLOWING THE TRIPLE PIPES

The breath control is no easy matter on the triple pipes. The mouth is well filled with the reeds and this almost induces a desire to gag when taking breath. It is not easy to control the amount of air wasted by escape round the sides of the pipes. It takes quite a bit of air to keep three pipes blowing. To this has to be added the difficulties of circular breathing with relatively little space left in the mouth for a reserve of air.

That circular breathing was used is virtually certain. Not only is it the technique used on the launeddas, but it is a technique used by Scottish pipers on the practice chanter (obviously without the bag), and it is virtually essential if anything approaching sustained playing is to be achieved. Without circular breathing, three pipes simply exhaust the available air supply too rapidly to allow of good music making.

At first Hamish Moore did not expand his cheeks when circular breathing the triple pipes, but the launeddas players advised him to do so, and this is supported by the clear indication of the musician's expanded cheek on the Lethendy stone.

The circular breathing involves drawing in air through the nose while keeping the flow outward through the lips. Sustained playing seems to have a similar effect to hyper-ventilating. The player may become a little confused and light-headed – indeed an almost trance-like state can be achieved and, paradoxically, can leave the player feeling totally relaxed, although it looks and is strenuous to play triple pipes – more so than, say, didgeridoo.

Hamish Moore at first played the instrument with the single reed downward cut and facing down inside the mouth. This avoided any interference of the lips with the reed, but allowed the tongue to control, even stop the reeds vibrating. However, the launeddas players advised against this practice, declaring that with the reeds near the tongue they become too moist and it makes it much more difficult to keep the instrument in tune.

They also used reverse cut and harder reeds and Hamish Moore found that as his playing strengthened so he too could do the same. The advantage of harder reeds was both in volume gain and in greater pitch stability.

THE REPERTOIRE

No music for Pictish or Irish triple pipes survives in any form whatever. The instrument itself had to be the guide to any exploration of music for voice or other instruments that could be considered relevant.

A number of initial choices had to be abandoned because it became obvious that they were quite inappropriate to the instrument even though they were nearly contemporary with it. In particular, remnants of chants for St Columba were essentially unsuited because of their wide range. Much the same applied to the probably Scottish items found in *The St Andrews Music Book* (W1). The solo lines were too wide-ranging, and the two-part music rarely came anywhere close to the available range of combinations on the triple pipes.

The triple pipes, as reconstructed, have a range of eight notes; but because the three pipes sound continuously, when any melody goes onto the lower hand, the higher chanter is still playing and tends to obscure the melodic outline. Skilful choice of the appropriate combinations of notes can help to clarify the melody when on the lower hand, but it is clear that the instrument works best when the melody is on the upper hand, or when the music is determined more by harmonic and rhythmic combinations than by pure melody itself. This means that the best melodies for the triple pipes are narrow in range.

The first tune chosen was that of the 'Pilililiu' (see Purser, *Scotland's Music*). This pre-Christian lament has associations with the bagpipes, with birdsong and with Ireland as well as Scotland. Given that the triple pipes were probably used, among other things, for laments (see above) and that they appear to have been native instruments brought into a Christian context, this seemed a reasonable choice.

Another tune chosen was a very simple repetitive Gaelic chant to stop a hail shower (see Purser, *Scotland's Music*). This probably pre-Christian chant has been Christianised and seemed appropriate to the period of the pipes which were carved at the time of or shortly after the Christianisation of the Picts.

A further choice was not so much that of a tune as of a style – the style of Gaelic psalm singing. Although Gaelic psalm singing utilises tunes composed from the 16th century on, it so alters and embellishes them that the result is closer than anything else in Western Europe to forms of Christian chanting thought to be as old as Christianity itself, and still practised in the Middle East. The fact that this style is used for the Psalms emphasises the David connections with the triple pipes, which lend themselves very well to this sort of embellishment, even matching the nasal reedy tone the singers deliberately produce.

The potential repertoire is still being explored. At the time of writing, the possible use of the pipes to accompany dance had yet to be followed up, and there are other sources to be explored. Much work has also yet to be done on their role as an accompanying and partnering instrument in ensemble. However, the triple pipes are of such an unusual nature that they probably used mostly a repertoire specifically designed for them or their inclusion, and it also seems probable that (as with the launeddas) improvisation was a major factor in the development of repertoire.

Finally, with respect to repertoire, it should be remembered that the choice of pitches for the chanters and for the notes available on them was most likely a wide one. There are over fifty different types of launeddas, for instance, even though the instrument is wholly confined to Sardinia. What is more, any one player is likely to possess several different types. In addition, it is possible to retune the instrument with wax, even while performing, and this is not an uncommon practice. If we allow these variables to apply to the development of the Pictish triple pipes then we are, in truth, only at the very beginning of a long journey of adventure. But we are confident that the basic structure and sound is correct; that the principles underlying the manner of performance have been the right ones to adopt; and that the greater dissemination of this instrument is to be encouraged. The Sardinians were thrilled to find at long last evidence of an instrument similar to their own, and we believe pipers all over the world, and especially in Scotland and Ireland, will welcome this extraordinary and virtuosic addition to the world of sound.

The Author and Acknowledgements

Dr John Purser is a polymath of Renaissance stature. A highly respected composer, musician, poet, dramatist, broadcaster, writer and university lecturer, he is most widely known for his BBC Radio Scotland programmes on the history of Scottish Music, and he wrote *Scotland's Music* (1991).

Hamish Moore and the author are particularly grateful to the Glasgow Royal Concert Hall for having had the courage to commission this reconstruction for the '1995 Celtic Connections'. Few such bodies would undertake to support so whole-heartedly such a strange venture – but it is an exciting one from which much has been and has yet to be learned, and we hope it will give as much excitement and pleasure to others as it has to the author of this paper.

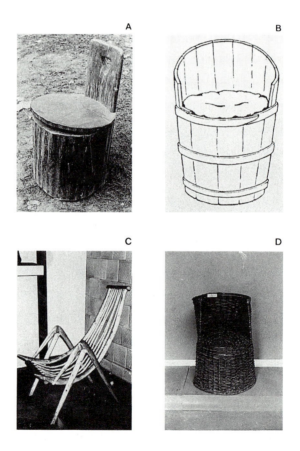

Figure 1 (A) Latvian tub chair made from tree trunk. (B) Barrel stave chair from Isle of Skye, after photograph by Sigurd Erixon circa 1920. (C) Transylvanian chair constructed from natural knees of timber. (D) Wickerwork chair from Isle of Skye circa 1920.

162

16

ON THE TRAIL OF FOLK FURNITURE
A Highland Heritage Shared Across the Seas

Ross Noble

For me, it began before I was born, and I have no doubt it will continue to be a surprising discovery for many yet unborn. For some people, however, it will remain an undiscovered, or certainly unexplored, concept throughout their lives. Others would die rather than admit its validity, and during this 20th century in Europe many have.

We can accept the idea of world culture: plastics and plutonium; convenience foods and Coca Cola; the global village and the internet of cyberspace. What is harder to comprehend is that the common everyday objects of our traditional culture, those very things which we use to enhance our national identity, are shared with strangers. Worse still, they may have originated with those strangers, or at least their distant forebears.

Growing up in a Scots/Irish family, and spending several years studying cultural interaction in Africa did little to disillusion me in my deeply held preconceptions of the uniqueness of Scottish culture. Indeed, it was largely my enthusiasm to communicate this which led me to a career in museums.

This in turn led me to the prenatal event which helped to change my perception. As a fledgling curator, I was encouraged by one of my mentors, Alan Gailey of the Ulster Folk Museum, to read the works of a Swedish scholar, Professor Sigurd Erixon. It was particularly his essay, *West European Connections and Culture Relations*[1], published in 1938, four years before I was born. Here, at a time when most of Western Europe was turning in on itself, becoming obsessed with national identity, was a paper coming out of Scandinavia boldly proclaiming a common folk culture for Western and Northern Europe, and perhaps even West Africa.

From this starting-point, I came to realise how important a role Scandinavia, and especially Sweden at this time, played in advancing the concept of European ethnology and comparative geography. But it was Erixon's essay that I returned to over and over again as he wove a web of tantalising threads between the simple artefacts, pack-saddles, bake-stones for oatcakes, and especially folk furniture of Spain, North-West Africa, France, Germany, Ireland, Scotland and, of course, Scandinavia. The result was not a piece of worsted, tightly woven and hard-wearing, but a piece of gossamer, all too easy to pull to pieces.

Erixon raises at least as many questions as he answers, and some of his postulations have not survived the test of time and subsequent research. But that in no way belittles the contribution he makes, for it is in such attempts to explore the most fundamental of human connections that ethnologists are still engaged today, and are finding it no more simple. Fifty-five years later, Jonathan Bell writes of comparative studies between Ireland and Scotland:

> The following small case study is intended to show that even at an empirical level the search for connections cannot avoid baffling complexity.[2]

In the field of furniture studies, the interaction of design and stylistic decoration across Europe and beyond has long been a subject of interest as far as fashionable furniture, both metropolitan and provincial, is concerned. But very little detailed work has been carried out to build on the work begun by Erixon and his contemporaries on simple folk furniture. This paper lays no claims in that direction. It is rather an attempt to explore, in the footsteps of Erixon, some of those tenuous interconnections, as seen from a Highland Scottish perspective, and to see how they relate to the theme of 'Local Identity in Global Culture'.

Perhaps the most easily accepted evidence of interconnection is linguistic. The common terms for basic furniture items such as stools, benches, tables (boards), larders, provide links across many of the European languages and across the centuries too.

From a very early stage in his development, man has always sought to have a place within the dwelling, or indeed when travelling, where the most precious possessions could be secured and kept out of the reach of predators, human or animal. One of the simplest solutions to this age-old problem is the box. Relatively simple to make, versatile in its functionalism, it can be a seat or a work surface as well as a store, capable of storing food, or documents, as well as textiles or coinage, the box is one of the most basic pieces of furniture in Europe, if not the world. The Romans called it 'cista', the Vikings 'kista'. In Old English it was 'ciest', later to become 'chest', and in Scotland it is a kist (Gaelic 'ciste').

Similarly, words for seats have an ancient provenance, which brings them into many of the European languages in remarkably similar form. The word 'chair' stems from 'cathedra' (throne), and can be seen in French 'chaise', Irish or Gaelic 'cathair', while the more general word 'seat' matches the Norse 'sess', German 'sessel', Gaelic 'seisach', English 'settle'. 'Bench' and its Gaelic counterpart 'being' come again from a Old Norse word 'bekkr'.

The foregoing only dips into the richness of linguistic evidence for the commonality of basic furniture across Western Europe. In a recent study into the Highland kitchen dresser, whose plate-rack in Caithness was traditionally known as the 'aumry', I was led back on a linguistic trail through 'aumbrie', the piece of furniture in Scotland which preceded the dresser in terms of function, to 'ambry', the little altar cupboard in an episcopal church where the Host is stored, to 'almarie', the Old French forerunner of 'armoire', and eventually back to the Roman 'armarium' or larder. The form and style of the piece of furniture had changed radically over the centuries, but the age-old name referred back to the basic function of storing food and the utensils for its preparation.[3] It could be argued that a very similar pattern can be traced

Figure 2 (A) Welsh stickback chair from Welsh Folk Museum. (B) Stickback chair from Easter Ross. (C) Stickback chair from Argyll built round a natural tree fork. (D) Latvian stool built round a natural tree fork.

Figure 3 (A) Cape Breton chairs, showing constructional links to 'Northern Tradition' chairs, Highland Village Museum, Iona, Cape Breton. (B) Cape Breton chair of Northern Tradition construction, Sydney Museum, Cape Breton. (C) Chair from Grantown-on Spey built round a natural tree fork circa 1770. (D) Stickleback chair from Wester Ross built round a slab of timber.

166

Figure 4 (A) Caithness armchair built round natural knees of timber, early 19th century, National Museums of Scotland. (B) Caithness chair. (C) Open dresser from West Coast Mainland. (D) Open dresser from South Uist.

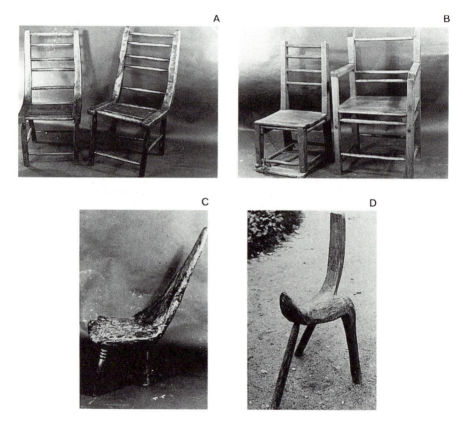

Figure 5 (A) Sutherland chairs of the Northern Tradition made from natural knees of ash. (B) Nothern Tradition chairs. (C) Natural knee chair from Harris. (D) Natural knee chair from Latvia.

from the Norse base 'bekkr' to the Scots 'bink' which was not only a seat but a bench for preparing food, and, by the early 19th century, the dresser again.

Style as an imported feature is much more commonly associated with fashionable furniture, but it cannot be ignored at the vernacular level either. As words and concepts travel and are absorbed into new languages, so too do good design or style. Sigurd Erixon showed this with the widespread popularity of barrel-stave chairs, which can be traced throughout Northern Europe in the Middle Ages, and archaeological evidence points to their earlier existence (pre-historic) in the Mediterranean area.

These barrel-stave chairs, argued Erixon, were a development from a more basic chair, now found only as relics in the northern regions of Norway and Sweden, in Finland and Latvia, made from a hollowed-out tree trunk (Fig 1A)[4]. However, more recent research by Victor Chinnery reveals evidence that this more primitive form was known in Britain, as well as the more sophisticated staved chairs.[5] Incidentally, Erixon's own fieldwork in Scotland in 1936 provides the only evidence I know of staved chairs of this type in the Scottish Highlands.

Norway may well have been the source of inspiration for the 'branderback' chairs so popular in the Highlands, and especially in Caithness (Fig 4B), while France or the Low Countries probably introduced Scottish craftsmen to the curved arms of the 'caqueteuse' style of armchair.[6] This affectation can be seen quite commonly on Highland vernacular chairs of the 18th and 19th centuries.

It is often difficult to discern whether a 'style', or at least a stylistic element, in a piece of vernacular furniture has been borrowed from another place, or whether that element emerges from the design limitations imposed by the material or the function of the piece. Plate racks on Highland dressers are a case in point.

The normal way to display a plate on an English or Welsh dresser, is to stand the plate on its edge, and allow it to lean backwards slightly against the backboard of the dresser. In most cases there is a central groove or a raised bead running lengthwise along the shelf to prevent the plates slipping forward and crashing down to the floor. On a Highland dresser, the plates lie forwards and rest on a wooden spar which is placed at the front of the rack, at approximately the middle point between each pair of shelves. The rim of the plate, in this instance, touches the backboard, and extends beyond the front of the dresser to a point beyond the line of the shelf above (Fig 4C).

This technique of display has several advantages in the context of a Highland house. More can be displayed in a given space, as the shelves are closer together. With the restrictions on good timber facing most Highland furniture makers, a shorter run of planking would be desirable. Equally, given the low wall height of most vernacular houses in the Highlands, as compared with English or Welsh farmhouses of a comparable period, the distance between shelves would be a limiting factor in the overall capacity of the dresser, which would probably be the tallest piece of furniture in the house. Moreover, chairs and stools in Highland houses tended to be lower than those in the south. This stems from the tradition of a central open hearth and a rudimentary or no smoke hole, which meant that folk sat low, under the level of the almost permanent bank of peat smoke which lingered in the upper reaches of the room. From such a low angle, a vertical or backwards-leaning plate would not be seen to advantage, while the highland system provided the ideal line of sight for these prized pieces of china or stoneware.

In Ireland, many dressers have the characteristics outlined above, together with a distinguishing feature that the base unit and plate rack is often constructed as a single unit, unlike those of England, Wales, and, generally, Scotland.[7] The fundamental question is whether the Scots and Irish each developed independently a style of dresser rack which varies from the older tradition in England and Wales, or did one copy from the other?

Many of the criteria which led to this style of plate rack in a Scottish Highland context are equally applicable in Ireland, scarce timber, low walls, low seating and perpetual peat reek. There are Highland dressers, such as that from South Uist (Fig 4D), which are made as a single unit. There is no strong evidence either way, and a whole field of research lies awaiting an eager PhD student, but since dressers are a feature of the Irish house earlier than in the Scottish Highlands, where they only appear in the closing year or two of the 18th century, it is more likely that design ideas flowed eastwards across the Irish Sea, rather than the other way round.

Design concepts and style are secondary in analysing folk furniture to questions of form or structure. This is in part because that too was the thinking of the vernacular furniture maker. It is not that design, or perhaps rather decoration, is absent from such pieces, but that it is often superficial decoration and equally often borrowed from the (at one time) fashionable furniture of the professional or gentry homes. The 'Queen Anne' flavour of the some chairs can suggest an early 18th century date (Fig 3C), but the museum has examples which were in fact made in the 1770s in Grantown-on-Spey. Their real interest to the furniture historian is that they are each constructed round a central element comprising a naturally-forked branch of a fruit tree.

More fundamentally, one must look at form and structure because it is in these that the furniture historian can properly find the basis for a system of classification of vernacular pieces. It is through studying form and structure that one will discern how widespread are some of the techniques of folk furniture-making, and begin to realise how far back in European history lie these common roots. One of the strengths of Erixon's work is that he saw beyond the design or decoration which marked a piece Spanish, or Finnish, or Turkish to the basic structure which showed their interconnection.

Such studies do not sit well alongside cultural chauvinism, where the uniqueness of a nation's heritage is promoted. Indeed, in extreme cases the potential for debate is removed for the chauvinist argument becomes a closed circle. The uniqueness of the cultural heritage becomes a pillar in the case for nationhood, and national identity requires the guarding of the uniqueness of the cultural heritage.

To illustrate the ethnological viewpoint, one can take the example of traditional chair types in the Scottish Highlands. All are primitive, in the sense of requiring no sophisticated technology for their production, although many are far from crude in their execution. All are firmly rooted in the physical landscape of Scotland, with regional variations reflecting the availability or otherwise of raw materials. All but one feature in the furniture gallery at the Highland Folk Museum as prime exhibits of 'Highland' identity. And yet, all are firm proof of a common European heritage, and all have played a part in putting a Scottish stamp on the cultural heritage of North America, Australia and elsewhere in the world.

The most common survivor and most widespread type of Highland chair is that formed from a core structural element of a slab of timber, a slice of tree. To this is added three or four branches which are socketed into holes gauged, drilled, or burned out of the slab, thus forming a basic stool. Further holes for further branches, and a roughly shaped branch as a top rail and one has a stick-back chair (Fig 3D). Such chairs are provenanced from all over the West Highlands and in parts of the Central and East Highlands. They have local names. In Argyll they are 'Kenmore chairs'. Further north they are known as 'Ross-shire chairs' (Fig 2B).

This traditional 'Scottish' chair, is also a traditional 'Welsh' chair (Fig 2A), and a traditional 'Irish' chair. Brittany, Andalusia, and other parts of Europe on the Atlantic seaboard can also lay claim to this chair type. I have been tempted to speculate in earlier writings that this may be the quintessential 'Celtic' chair type, making some sort of ethnic claim on it even if a national claim is insupportable. However, in my travels and researches, I have now noted this construction used in chairs in Scandinavia, in Slavic Europe and in the Eastern Mediterranean countries. It has to be accepted that this is one of the simplest forms of chair construction, requiring no joinery skills, and is part of a very ancient common European, or even Indo-European heritage.

This acceptance of a common heritage does not always come easy to furniture historians. For many decades all these 'stick-back' or 'comb-back' chairs, from any part of Britain or Ireland, have been regularly classified as 'Windsor Chairs' or 'primitive Windsor chairs'.[8] In 1979, Victor Chinnery recognised the inaccuracy of this approach, and suggested that Windsor chairs were a progression in the eighteenth century from an earlier chair type.[9] But as late as 1993, Bernard D. Cotton, president of the Regional Furniture Society, could write of traditional 'Manx' chairs of this type:

> The term Windsor chair is applied, as a definition, to all chairs which have a wooden seat into which legs are mortised from below, with back uprights mortised into from above... distinct Windsor chair making traditions developed in the Celtic areas of Britain, including Scotland, Ireland, Wales, Cornwall and the Isle of Man.[10]

A variation of the above structural technique is the use of a natural fork of a tree or a branch as the unifying element, rather than a slab. This has already been seen in a sophisticated form disguised by design. But a number of simpler, more honest, versions are held in the collection at the Highland Folk Museum. Again, I have written of these chairs in the past as a Scottish, indeed Highland type, and have linked it to the area of the Caledonian Pine Forest, whose trees produced such distinctive and suitable natural forks (Fig 2C).[11] However, recent research by Cotton has revealed a series of natural fork stools on the Isle of Man, which he himself links to this Highland tradition[12], while a colleague in Latvia has recently sent me a photograph of a natural fork stool (Fig 2D).

Erixon postulates the strong possibility of a West European chair type with a simple ladder-back and a seat of woven grass or straw. He sees this as a Mediterranean type which spread as far north as Scandinavia. Again more detailed examination of the evidence across Europe suggests a wider distribution than perceived in 1938. The Baltic States again provide examples as does Russia and Slovakia.

I. F. Grant, the founder of the Highland Folk Museum, well acquaint with Erixon's work, suggests two sub-types of this chair for the Scottish Highlands, a 'West Mainland' type with the weave running diagonally across the seat from the corners, and a 'Western Isles' type with the weave running from front to back and side to side.[13] However, all the chairs of both sub-types in the collection at the museum are fairly sophisticated, with turned legs, or mortise and tenon joints or some other evidence of being made by craftsmen. I know of no extant examples of truly vernacular pieces in this form, although circumstantial evidence, (discussed below) points in that direction. Thus it is really only the acceptance of the wider common heritage which can truly allow the Scots to claim this chair type as part of their ancient domestic culture, rather than a late importation through the craft guilds.

Erixon's own fieldwork provides the only evidence of which I am aware that the Scottish Highlands were part of the very wide distribution area for staved tub chairs, 'kubbstol'. His drawing of a chair (Fig 1B) seen in a house on Skye puts it firmly in the tradition which, Erixon argues, takes it back to a basic European tub chair which was either hewn out of a log or tree stump, or built up out of plaited grass, the 'lipp-work' tradition. This latter form is traceable in England and Wales back to Romano-British culture, and continues into the recent past, although survivors are all of 18th or 19th century origin.[14] The only physical link extant in Scotland is the basketwork chair, from Skye, in tub-form, dating from the 1920s and made under the auspices of the gentry-led Highland Home Industries (Fig 1D). Again, without the supporting evidence of a common European tradition, this basket chair can be dismissed as romantic invention.

Much of my own fieldwork in recent years has been targeted at an equally romantic-looking form of chair, and one which almost certainly influenced Charles Rennie Mackintosh in his revolutionary modern chair styles. These chairs, which I have called the 'Northern Tradition' of chairmaking,[15] perhaps bring together many of the ideas and arguments postulated in this paper. They point out how much work requires to be done before we can say we understand such a simple element in the make-up of the Highland heritage as a domestic chair.

Northern Tradition chairs have as their main structural element two natural knees of timber, or in some cases one knee cleft longwise to give two complementary shapes (Fig 5A). These knees are held apart, and in place, by a series of round spars (often rough branches) socketed into the main timber and back wedged. The legs are attached in a similar fashion. The seat board is loosely fitted into rebates roughly gouged out of the inner faces of the knees, and again held in place with round spars.

This structure apparently stemmed from the virtually treeless nature of the Northern Highlands, and the tendency of whatever scrub timber, that succeeds in growing at all, to grow horizontally after the first few feet of height under the incessant pressure of the winds which scour the land. In this highly unlikely structural solution to making a chair, I had surely found a distinctive, probably unique, part of Highland material culture.

The first disillusionment came quickly. My 'unique' chair was known in Northern Ireland, and there were several in the collections at the Ulster Folk and Transport Museum. The environmental conditions in North West Ireland are not dissimilar to those in Sutherland and Caithness, so that stunted scrub timber would be an important local source of material for folk furniture.

The discovery, in the stores of the National Museum of Antiquities of Scotland of a brander-back armchair with natural knees of timber as the main structural element (Fig 4A), and an early 19th century provenance from Caithness, made me revisit the question. Until then I had happily associated these Caithnesian brander-backs with Norway. Did I now have to look to Scandinavia for a link with natural knees? I questioned all my Scandinavian contacts without success. After all, the timber quality in Norway and Sweden would seem to preclude any recourse to scrub thorn trees. But a Latvian colleague said such chairs were known in the then Baltic Republics of the Soviet Union.

When I next went into print on the subject of the Northern Tradition, I made mention of a possible Baltic connection, although I had seen no evidence to back up the assertion.[16] When photographs arrived, the chair type was structurally quite different, since it used a much more substantial knee for the whole seat and back (Fig 5D), a technique not unknown in the Western Isles (Fig 5C). However, as that door closed another opened with the reporting of natural knee chairs in Transylvania (Fig 1C). Much more research will be required before common ancestral links between these two chair types is postulated in print.

As work on the Northern Tradition chairs in the collection at the Highland Folk Museum and elsewhere continued, another group of chairs came into focus. These were simple ladderbacks, like the previous group, but with the back and back legs being the structural element, as with most 19th and early 20th century wooden chairs. The unusual features were, firstly, the seat which tended to sit rather unhappily into the form of the chair, and, secondly, a set of stretcher spars just below seat height. If the solid wooden seat were removed, this chair type would closely resemble the form, if not the structure of Northern Tradition chairs. The examples recorded all come from the North-West Highlands or the Western Isles (Fig 5B).

One possible explanation for the enigmatic upper stretchers is that they are a carry-over, a relic of the natural knee construction, in the same way that Caithness chairs have kept elements which are structurally unnecessary. Another possibility is that the wooden seat is the extraneous element, and that we are here looking at the vernacular construction of chairs with woven grass or straw seats. That explanation then opens up the question of woven seats on the natural knee chairs.

This very technical and somewhat tortuous digression is not irrelevant to the main thesis of this paper. For during field studies in Cape Breton in Nova Scotia, I came across numerous examples of this sub-type of the Northern Tradition, if that is what they are (Fig 3A & B). There is, of course, a very direct link between the Cape Breton community and areas like the Uists and North West Ross, from where these chairs have their provenance. The wooden seats sit as uncomfortably on the Canadian examples as they do on the Scottish ones, especially where New England design features have been incorporated as well.

These chairs, whether in Scotland or Nova Scotia have the appearance of a piece of furniture in the process of transformation from one form to another. Did such chairs go out to the New World in this hybrid form two centuries ago? And did the desire to cling to all things Scottish lead to them being copied and adapted by the Cape Bretoners, preserving what might well be no more than a piece of ephemera in the history of Scottish folk furniture? I have found no evidence of natural knee chairs in Cape Breton, but one has been recorded in Australia.[17]

Other examples of folk furniture are found among Scottish emigrant communities, as is true of most emigrant communities around the world. Kists, reputed to have travelled with the first migrants are almost venerated. Highland dressers and aumries crossed the Atlantic and played their part in developing North American furniture design. Simple slab seat chairs are claimed by the Scots, the Irish, the Welsh, the Norwegians and the Germans, all with justification. And, of course, the more sophisticated ones became 'New England Windsors'.

Thus did some of the cultural prejudices about simple folk furniture spread across the oceans along with the pieces themselves. Can we see in this a parallel with the transmission of material culture back in the great migrations which led to the peopling of Europe? Does a society on the move cling to homely, comforting artefacts from the past at the same time as it is grasping and exploiting new technology which will give it the edge in the environment it is entering, be that technology the bronze axe, the iron spear, the McCormick reaper or the Colt 45?

That is a question which cannot be answered, but, as a premise, it perhaps helps to bring some understanding of the dichotomy with which this paper began. When a society is changing and developing, and especially when it faces new frontiers like cyberspace, or the dissolution of old frontiers, like the nation states of Europe, new technologies are eagerly grasped, and new social and political norms established. But at the same time, these strong and forward-looking pioneers are equally concerned with issues of 'heritage' and 'conservation'. These are not the last bastions of conservatism, the refuge of those who wish to hide from change. Rather 'heritage' is an underpinning reassurance that man can go forth into the unknown and survive.

When I. F. Grant founded Britain's first folk museum 60 years ago, and began collecting the pieces of folk furniture currently under discussion, she saw a culture under threat, and termed her museum 'Am Fasgadh' (the shelter or refuge).But she quickly came to recognise that the culture was stronger than the threats raised against it, and changed the name to 'The Highland Folk Museum'. Today we are tending to treat the wider issue of heritage to the 'am fasgadh' approach, something which requires cosseting, and protecting from the threats of outsiders. Perhaps we have to recognise that just as our folk furniture is truly a common heritage, so to is our wider relationship with our environment. Such recognition in either case does not diminish its status or its bond to us as individuals. It only places it on a larger stage, and makes it the concern of a global audience instead of a local one.

The folk furniture of the Scottish Highlands is the folk furniture of Europe, and of much of the rest of the world. As such it is worthy of respect. It is worthy of respect from all of us, wherever we come from, for it is not apart from, but is a part of Global Culture.

The Author

Ross Noble was born in Ayrshire and educated at Ardrossan Academy and at Aberdeen University, where he specialised in studies into cultural interactions, particularly in East Central Africa. He pioneered the concept of 'travelling curator' with the Scottish Countrylife Museums Trust, assisted by the Carnegie UK Trust. In this role he helped to develop Auchindrain Museum in Argyll, and to write the interpretive plan for Biggar Museum Trust. Since 1976, he has been Curator of the Highland Folk Museum, and Regional Curator for the Museums Service of Highland Regional Council. During the late 1980s he has developed the concept of 'Heritage in Action' programmes, whereby traditional crafts, skills, music etc. become a daily part of the museum's interpretive techniques. Special heritage programmes for schools have also been developed, where children can participate. He is a member of the Association of European Open-Air Museums, and is currently President of the Society of Folk Life Studies.

References

[1] Erixon S. *West European Connections and Culture Relations* in Folk-Liv No. 2 pp 137–172 (Stockholm) 1938

[2] Bell J. *Farming in the Outer Hebrides and North-West Donegal: The Problems of Comparison* in Cheape H. (ed), *Tools and Traditions*, National Museums of Scotland, 1993

[3] Noble R. R. *Highland Dressers and the Process of Innovation* in Regional Furniture Vol. VI pp. 36–46, 1992

[4] Erixon S. Op.Cit.

[5] Chinnery V. *Oak Furniture: The British Tradition* Antique Collectors' Club, 1979

[6] Ibid.

[7] Kinmonth C. *Irish Vernacular Furniture 1840–1940*, unpublished thesis, V&A/RCA 1988

[8] Sparkes I.,*The English Country Chair* 2nd edition, Spurbooks, 1977; Ayres J., *The Shell Book of The Home in Britain,* Faber & Faber, 1981; Toller J., *Country Furniture*, David & Charles, 1973

[9] Chinnery V. Op. Cit.

[10] Cotton B. D. *Manx Traditional Furniture*, Manx National Heritage, 1993

[11] Noble R. R. *Chairs, Stools, and Settles*, in Cruickshank G. (ed) *A Sense of Place*, Scotland's Cultural Heritage, 1988

[12] Cotton B. D. Op. Cit.

[13] Grant I. F. *Highland Folk Ways*, Routledge & Kegan Paul, 1961

[14] Chinnery V. Op. Cit.

[15] Noble R. R. *The Chairs of Sutherland and Caithness: A Northern Tradition in Highland Chair-making?* in Regional Furniture Vol. I pp. 33–40, 1987

[16] Noble R. R. *Chairs, Stools and Settles*, Op. Cit.

[17] Cornall G. *Memories: A Survey of Early Australian Furniture*, c. 1990

Cotton B. D. *The English Regional Chair*, Antique Collectors' Club, 1990
Gailey A. *Kitchen Furniture*, Ulster Folklife Vol. 12 1966
Gilbert C. *English Vernacular Furniture 1750–1900* Yale University Press, 1991
Kinmonth C. *Irish Country Furniture 1700–1950*, Yale University Press, 1993
Shea J. G. *Antique Country Furniture of North America*, Evans, 1976

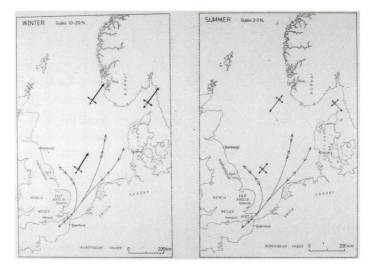

Figure 1 Prevailing winds in winter and summer.

Figure 2 4.4 m long rock carving at Bjørnstad in Norway.

Figure 3 The 'Nydam' boat from Denmark of the klinker built type used for both trading and raiding in the 3rd century onwards.

17

THE NORTH SEA HIGHWAY
Cultural Arena or Political Barrier

Martin Carver

The inhabitants of an extended coastline alternate between an intense exploitation of the sea and a complete neglect of it'.

A Brøgger, 1928

Britain's problem with its identity seems to have begun about 8000 BC. Up to that time, (the Mesolithic period) the places that were to become Scotland, England, Scandinavia and France shared a land and a cultural repertoire. As the ice melted (in the last global warming), the land became covered initially with shallow water you could walk across, then ever deeper until Britain became an island. Mesolithic settlements still occasionally snag the nets of fishermen over the Dogger Bank.

From this point on the peoples of Britain, France and Scandinavia faced each other across an expanse of water. Was that water a barrier or a thoroughfare? Did cultures develop separately or together? Were the North Sea countries always in contact, sharing their ideologies and their destinies? Or were they always in conflict, irredeemably separatist and adversarial?

The evidence of archaeology for the cultures of the countries that bordered the sea since the ice age ended, is now quite good. We also have quite a lot of information, some of it speculative, about how the sea might have been used. The technology for sea travel, including travel out of sight of land (blue water crossings), existed from bronze Age and arguably much earlier. However, that does not mean that people actually crossed the sea. Our evidence offers rather the story of an island that blew hot and cold about sea travel; one that was constantly wooed by its neighbours, but simply could not make up its mind between them. The North Sea was potentially a thoroughfare, but was made into a barrier by ideology and economics, often through the use of force.

COULD THEY CROSS THE SEA?

The North Sea is a shallow sea, and for that reason, one of the most dangerous in the world; it is quickly worked into short, steep waves by the mass of water from the neighbouring Atlantic (Makepeace, forthcoming). Its climate and geography as derived from modern admiralty charts, shows that there are four times as many gale-force winds encountered in winter as in summer. Admiralty data also show that, while the wind direction varies from day to day, from May the net effect is south-westward-driving, and from October, north-eastward (Brøgger 1929, 24; Carver 1990, fig 15.2). This implies that, while the North Sea can be crossed in open boats at any time from May to September, the winds favour boats travelling from east (Scandinavia) to west (Britain) and back before the winter gales return. The coastal character of Norway, as compared to Britain, suggests that boats there would always be a favoured method of transport, and that the development of boat technology would usually be more advanced in that region. Scandinavian rock-carvings show that the boats constructed by the coastal countries are first made of skins stretched on a wooden former, possibly in imitation of seals, and they were rowed and could be quite large. Trials of replicas based on the carvings show that such boats were perfectly sea-worthy.

Sail is known from the Bronze Age in the Mediterranean and was used in the North Sea by the Roman period, when the Romans made a tour right around the island, including Orkney, and routinely supplied their garrisons up to the Firth of Forth by sea. In the great period of Germanic unrest, which threatened the Empire from the 3rd century AD, the raiders habitually arrived unannounced (i.e. from deep water) across the sea and the coast of Britain was fortified accordingly. Although portrayed as raiders, it is likely that the aim of these seafarers was not so much to raid as to avoid Roman customs by landing on unattended beaches. Such expeditions also led to settlement. The Anglo-Saxons crossed the North Sea, so did the Franks, the Frisians, the Danes and Norwegians, while in the Baltic there was a similar lively traffic. The boats were clinker built and keeless and were at first rowed or sailed with a favourable wind.

In the 9th century, the North Sea raiders acquired the nickname of Vikings, (which is not an ethnic label but a type of activity – analogous to 'bikers'). There were Irish, Pictish and English Vikings too, but the majority were from Denmark, Norway and Sweden. Their ships were generally bigger and more manoeuvrable under sail (Crumlin-Pedersen and Vinner 1986, passim). The driving force in Viking politics, as in Saxon, was probably to break the trade cartel of Christian Europe, and they had the ships to do it. My own experience of sailing (and sinking) in a Viking ship, convinced me that the Vikings' principal contribution to technology was not sail itself, but how to tack (Carver 1995).

By the 12th century and after, the repertoire of ships included the flat-bottom cog, the design of which was owed at least partly to economics. These ships did not beach, as had been the case up to them; that was now forbidden by trade regulations and called 'smuggling'. Ships had to dock in designated harbours where they could unload commodities destined for specific markets, and be relieved of the appropriate tax. The old freedoms probably continued longer in the northern lands, – the northern isles of Britain and in Scandinavia where they were always most fiercely defended.

The way these craft found their way about in the days before instruments has been discovered both from archaeology and from consultation with surviving practitioners. Direction and position in summer can be divined approximately from the position of the sun and its height at midday, but in any case since land flanks the North Sea on both sides, it is possible to leave

Norway anywhere within a 60 degree arc and still hit Britain. More refined navigation was effected through the old techniques collected by Taylor (1956) and Binns (1980); the mother swell, the migrating geese, and when near land, listening to the gunwale for the characteristic barks and howls of the sea hitting a coastal feature – a feature, which, for that reason might be named 'the dog' or 'the goose'. We know that travel from Norway to Scotland in open boats was perfectly possible, because it happened in the war, complete with animals and families. Arne-Emil Christiensen, now Director of the Viking Ship Museum, witnessed such voyages himself in boats no bigger than the 9th century Gokstad faering.

How fast were such journeys; were they just for refugees, one journey in a lifetime? Or routine? Arne-Emil took five days and four nights in a rowing boat. Brøgger in 1927, sailing to give his Rhind lectures in Edinburgh, left Skudesnes at four o'clock on Wednesday afternoon and at seven o'clock on the Friday morning sighted Noss Head off Bressay on Shetland (Brøgger 1929, 31). But a Viking sailing ship could move a lot faster than that. from experiments, one can reckon, as a working average, on 40 miles a day under oars and 80–300 miles a day sailing, as a working average. Compare this with travel on foot or with a laden cart on an unmade road, where 15 miles a day would be good going. In pre-16th century Europe, therefore, the jet set travelled by water, and allegiances would develop accordingly. For a seafaring native of Inverness, Iona or Bergen are nearer than Kingussie or Stirling.

Sea travel in the middle ages and earlier, therefore, was not only possible, but quicker. In theory, those living on the coast or navigable rivers, the majority, were users of a common infrastructure. There was nothing to stop them and everything to encourage them finding markets and owning land across the water, rather than in the muddy outback. We might visualise, again in theory, the North Sea as a cultural arena, in which ideas were freely exchanged and culture was shared and developed. If cultural distinctions were to appear and harden, they would be more marked between the coast and the hinterland, rather than between coast and the coast. In theory yes, but is that was actually happened? And if not, why not?

TURNING TO THE SEA AND TURNING AWAY

The story in prehistoric and medieval times is largely told from the material culture itself, but it is generally only the material culture found on land that we can use. Ships with cargo are sometimes found, but even so their cargoes report only on a single voyage. On land, buried settlements and cemeteries capture examples of exotic cultures, telling us when and in what context the people of Britain were importing or emulating the customs, tastes, fashions, and symbols of an overseas country. from this we assume that there is an association between them – but what kind of association is still hotly debated. When similar objects are found in Britain and Norway, for example, this can be held to mean migration, or trade or religious mission or political affiliation or conquest. This uncertainty it not new, however, as we shall see, until the advent of systematic written records, speculation about contact across the sea was not only rife, but very influential, forming unshakeable opinions among the British, even when widely inaccurate or completely incredible.

PREHISTORIC TRAFFIC

I shall now attempt to chronicle the cultural traffic to and from Britain over the last 3,000 years according to archaeology, concentrating on the pre-modern era. I shall stick to the current consensus on migrations, while mentioning some of the minority theories which might well yet carry the day.

After the land of the Channel and the southern North Sea disappeared under salt water, the Mesolithic cultures of the east coast of England and the west coast of Denmark slowly grew away from each other. The agricultural revolution, introduced into continental Europe from c 5000 BC, appears to have come overland along the corridor of the Danube. The early Neolithic cultures of Britain were at first discrete, then shared some attributes with the area of France. The builders of megalithic monuments were active along the maritime corridor from Spain to France, Ireland and Western Britain as far as the Shetlands. The same maritime zone, expanded to include all of Britain, but excluding most of Scandinavia, saw the arrival of the 'Beaker Culture' in the late 3rd millennium BC, laying the foundations for a British population that looked south for most of the bronze age (Piggot 1965, figs 27–29, 54).

THE CELTIC EXPANSION AND ROME

But in the early Iron Age, Britain became a partner in a quite different culture-zone which spread across central and northern Europe, one defined by the first people to be described by history – the Celts. The term 'Celts' refers to a confederation of peoples, who shared the roots of a common language and are considered by history to be the ancestors of the Britons, the Gauls, the Irish and (more controversially) the Picts. Throughout the period of Celtic domination, which endured until the Roman conquest, the peoples of Britain appear to have continued to look mainly south and east across the channel to the Rhine. Only the Arras culture of Marnian France, with a burial practice featuring chariots under square mounds, was strangely echoed in eastern Yorkshire, and perhaps in Scotland too. Does this represent an experiment in the use of the North Sea as a thoroughfare? If so, it was a brief one; the Celts, when then expanded, went south too, into north Italy and Greece, and from the Mediterranean came the riposte in the form of Greek and Roman merchants and eventually conquerors.

Britain was visited in the 6th century BC by the Carthaginian Hamilcar, and some time later by Pytheas from Greek Marsalia, who got to the Orkneys and confirmed that Britain itself was an island. The geography of the place was not unknown to Julius Ceasar or Claudius, whose route was nevertheless terrestrial rather than maritime. It took them through conquered Gaul, and then, strangely and crucially, not to Ireland – which had as much potential as a fertile source of tribute payers – but to the south east of Britain, then into the interior of the British island north and west, laying a system of inland communication, which for the first time was quicker than the sea.

It can be seen, therefore, that up until the Roman period, the cultural exchanges of Britain are running largely south and south-west. The island can be seen as having three maritime zones: the Channel (south), the Irish Sea (west) and the North Sea (east). In the earliest civilisations, of the Neolithic and the Bronze Age, it was the sea zone which received most of the attention and investment and which formed the busiest cultural highway. In the Celtic and Roman periods it was the Channel which appeared to have carried most of the traffic – and became the arena of the political and the cultural debate. The North Sea, in contrast, seems to have been a dead space; if anyone went on it, they were creeping round the edge or confined to territorial waters.

THE NEW AXIS OF THE GERMANIC SEA

But its time was about to come. During the 3rd and 5th centuries AD as the Roman Empire first went Christian and then broke up, the North Sea became the cultural highway of the Germanic people living in northern Europe and Scandinavia. Shared cultures are seen in the many cemeteries of this period, between east England and south Denmark in the 5th century, and east England and southern Norway in the 6th century. This shared culture extends visibly no further to the north than the Tyne, so that at present it is only the southern part of the North Sea that is seen as an active scene of Germanic cultural exchanges. Supremacy in this southern sea was disputed among the Germanic peoples, although their detailed deployment is very hard to know. Saxons, Frisians and Franks all have their modern champions to claim the prize of most successful seafarer (McGrail 1988). Of these peoples, the most disruptive were probably the Germans who had settled furthest south, and adopted a quite different, non-German, culture – that of the Christian Romans. These were the Franks. Like the Celts and the Romans before them, their political task would be to sever the valencies which linked Britain and Scandinavia across the sea, and claim the cultural domination of Britain for herself (Wood 1983).

THE WESTERN SEAWAY

Meanwhile, the Irish sea zone had also been reactivated, and for the first time probably since the Bronze Age, the Irish sea territories were sharing cultural attributes with each other and directly with the Mediterranean. The 6th century pottery known as 'Red Slip Ware' has recently been said to come from Byzantium itself at the east end of the Mediterranean. Britain at this time therefore went through an intensely maritime phase, and the spine of the island was almost a frontier zone, the west of the country looking west, the east looking east and the south looking south, as Irish, Romans, Franks and Scandinavians vied for cultural supremacy.

The course of this battle for the soul of Britain can also be followed now in documents since it was essentially expressed as a battle of ideologies, with Christianity as the major source of propaganda. The east preferred an ideology which was natural, heroic, self-sufficient, without kings or the state, in which enterprise and derring-do were pre-eminent. The south favoured

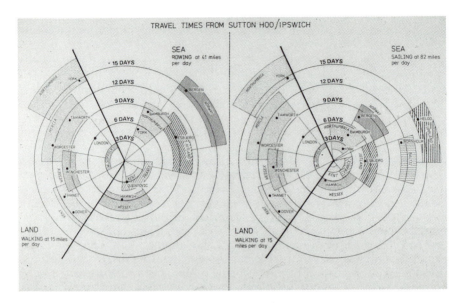

Figure 4 Travel times from Sutton Hoo/Ipswich by sea and land.

Figure 5 King Raedwald 'the compromiser' and the Sceptre of 'intertextuality' from Sutton Hoo.

the pastoral care of Roman Christianity with its urban network, provision of public amenity and belief in the supremacy of coded law, both in life and afterwards. The west preferred a Celtic version, which was a mixture of the two, regulated and Christian on the one hand, non-urban and non-imperial on the other (Carver, 1993).

SUTTON HOO

An example of this ideological battleground is provided by the Anglo-Saxon Royal cemetery at Sutton Hoo, initiated by the people of East Anglia at the end of the 6th century, just as the mission of Augustine arrived in Kent. Attracted on the one hand by the political opportunities presented by the concept of Christian kingship, and by the economic opportunities offered by the market of Christian Europe, they were nevertheless repelled by the central European lifestyle and the loss of autonomy implied by orthodox religious practice and the Pope.

The solution under King Raedwald was a grand British compromise. The gifts of the Franks and Romans, and the symbols of the Britons were accepted, and kings were created, but with a new pagan, instead of Christian design. Ritual killings, whether sacrificial or judicial, surrounded the mounds, and the burial practices: cremation in bronze bowls, or burial in a ship, were purely Scandinavian. The sceptre is a marvellous example of 'intertextuality', a Byzantine emblem carrying the faces of German gods, with a Celtic stag on top. Raedwald himself is said to have attempted the ultimate compromise in religion too, erecting an altar to Christ in the temple constructed for his pagan gods (Carver, 1992).

Then as now, therefore, the problem of British politics was whether her alliance should be to the dominant centrist ideology of the continent, with its anticipated mercantile advantages, or to the desired and imagined autonomy of an island people, in alliance with similar peoples in the islands and fjords of the northern seas. In the 7th century, the politics of the continent won, as is graphically illustrated by the dramatic switch in the maritime axis. It is reflected in the distribution of glass claw beakers (a Kentish and East Anglian speciality of the 6th century, much demanded in Sweden and Norway). The pattern changed barely a century later; the distribution of coins minted in Britain is directed at the Rhineland. Britain, or at least its south and eastern parts, had turned its face from the North Sea to join hands with the new Christian Europe.

VIKINGS

The episode in which Scandinavia fought back was brief but famous. The Vikings as raiders, traders and settlers dominated the north from the 9th to the 11th centuries, creating a cultural zone which included Scotland, northern England, eastern Ireland and the Isle of Man and penetrated as far south as Sicily. A Scandinavian cultural redolence has remained in these areas, and in Yorkshire and East Anglia, until the present; but the political projects which dominated the island from the 11th century rarely involved Scandinavia.

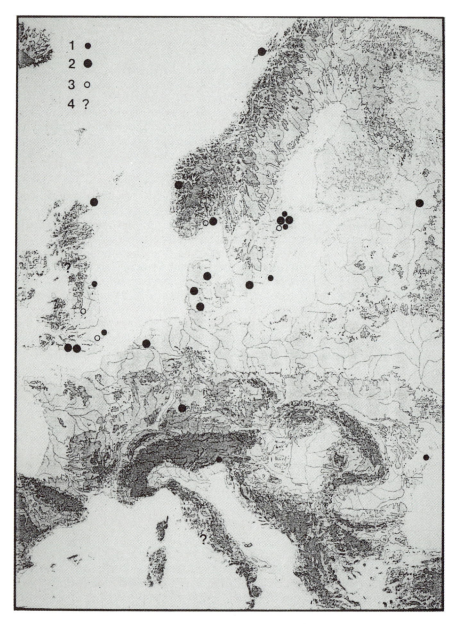

Figure 6 Distribution of 6th century glass claw beakers from Kent and East Anglia.

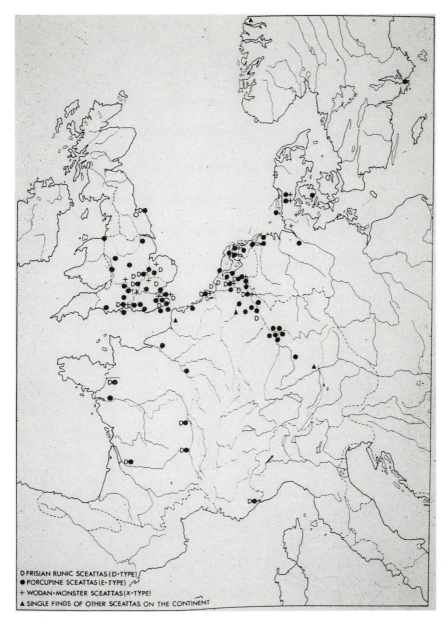

Figure 7 Distribution of 7th century coins minted in Britain.

185

Only King Cnut, to quote Brogger 'conceived the far-sighted plan of creating an extensive North Sea kingdom – a plan highly appropriate to a period so rich in maritime activity. He was the first North Sea politician' (1929, 149).

But his policies, although intermittently promoted from Norway in the middle ages, did not succeed in holding back the waters; nor have they been successfully resurrected since. The effort to unhitch the Britons from Rome in the 16th century, the creation of a world empire in the 19th or even the return to the argument about personal enterprise versus social amenity under Margaret Thatcher – which reflected so well the concerns of the 7th century – has not (or has not yet) recreated a general cultural arena for the North Sea countries.

HERITAGE AND ETHNICITY

Nowhere in Britain do the cultural currents of the North Sea meet more interestingly or more tellingly than in Scotland, where we can track back into the first millennium AD, the impact of at least five different self-defined cultures: the Britons, the Romans, the Scots, the Picts, the Anglo-Saxons, joined latterly by the Danish and the Norse. This is not the time for an attempt to chronicle the detailed sequence. Indeed, my own reason for beginning a new archaeological project on the east coast of Scotland, is that this sequence is so imperfectly known and still less understood.

My study will be dedicated to 'firthlands' in the 5–8th centuries and by collecting the evidence for pagan burial places and Christian monasteries, landing places and forts, I hope to discover the ambit of the Pictish navy and the nature of its early (pre-Viking) contacts with Scandinavia. If the south of England struggled with the conflicting attractions of Christian France and pagan Denmark, the east of Scotland was confronted with an even more complex array of ideological influences and options. But their early reactions may have been similar to those made by the builders of the Sutton Hoo burial mounds, and here in eastern Scotland too, the pre-Christian political agenda should have left its traces.

It is important to recognise that these early peoples although distinctively named are not actually distinguishable in an ethnic sense. 'Pict' ('a painty') like 'Viking' (a 'creeker') was a nickname first applied to different peoples in Scotland in the late 3rd century by Roman writers, presumably because they had the tattooing habit. The historical problem is that wherever a particular cultural characteristic is noted, an ethnic identity is the easiest and the quickest explanation to offer satisfaction, even when it is absurd. (One may take the example of 'Gothic' architecture, which owes nothing to the Goths, in Britain or elsewhere. No-one maintains that Romanesque architecture was built by Romans, but if they did it would certainly provoke hostility in someone).

Ethnic explanations of culture not only place a blight on archaeological interpretation, they also permeate that newest branch of our discipline, 'heritage management'. But although heritage management is new, the creation and construction and promotion of the heritage, or rather a particular and often imaginary heritage, is not. This can be seen in the writings of historians and indeed archaeologists, ever since the first opinions

186

were recorded. The 6th century historian Gildas thought the Picts had only just arrived in Scotland; and interestingly enough, both Gildas and Nennius seemed to think that they had come from overseas, presumably from Scandinavia (Skene, 1976, 124).

They report the Picts as first settling in the Orkneys, then conquering the lands of the east coast as far as Hadrian's Wall. Bede preferred to think that they had come from Scythia, (where tattooing was also practised) and had made a first landfall in Ireland, where they were given wives on the understanding they would always choose their ruler through the female line, even after they had settled in Scotland. More recently, archaeologists, historians and linguists have produced a number of alternatives: that the Picts are essentially Gaels like the Irish (Skene, 1876, 211), or survivals from the Bronze Age – and thus more 'original' inhabitants of Scotland (Wainwright, 1955) or – and this has the academic consensus – Celts or the p-Celtic speaking branch (Smyth, 1984) and thus disappointingly identical in demographic origin to the Britons living in the lowlands, Northumbria or the British Midlands.

The history of the early settlement of all the British island is full of supposed migrations and ethnic take-overs. The long use of the western sea-ways to bring megalithic monuments and Beaker pottery to these shores, inspired to notion of maritime migrants from the Spanish peninsula, the ancient Iberian evoked by Matthew Arnold:

> there, where down cloudy cliffs, through sheets of foam,
> Shy traffickers, the dark Iberians come.

The Beaker culture is not now thought to belong to a people at all, but to a set of beliefs – a religion in fact. Celtic invasions too are questioned by modern scholarship; Celtic art being able to cross the channel without a migrations as easily as cubism. No-one denies that the Romans invaded, but Roman Britain is currently seen as an affair more of British than of Roman execution. Bede was sure that the English of his day were compounded of immigrant peoples from north Germany; but this too is challenged in recent publications. The cultural changes which are so dramatic in the south of the island are now credited to a few aristocrats, acting in the manner of the Normans (e.g. Higham, 1992).

All these rethinkings derive essentially from a modern dislike of migration and conquest as explanations of culture change, an intellectual movement led by Gordon Childe in the 50s and in our own day by Clin Renfrew (Bahn and Renfrew, 1991, ch 12). Even a change of language itself has no necessary connection to large numbers of immigrants. The mood of the times in the archaeological community is for independent development and cultural emulation, rather than war, ideology or the immigration of refugees. These views, which of course reflect the zeitgeist of our own time, are in many cases even more difficult to substantiate than a history of invasions, but they raise interesting models and do no harm as long as they do not allow a presumption of a history determined by irredeemable regional ethnicity and localised races. For the truth is, that if there is such a thing as an ethnic group, archaeologists cannot observe it, neither with skeletal measurement, nor even with DNA.

The trend in the construction of our national heritage's has been to ignore the complexity of archaeological contacts and to insist on the variously selected elements of British culture as something ever more individual and unique, created out of nothing and maintained in a void. From an archaeological viewpoint such an attitude is unreal and distressing – as though the so-called 'English' language was available in some pure form, instead being an artefact created by a dialogue between Anglo-Saxon, Gaelic, French, Latin and Greek, as though we would seek to value unburnt clay above bricks or a house. The value of regional identities is not that they represent some precious cultural survival, but that they represent unique social constructions; not nature, but art.

THE CONSTRUCTION OF REGIONAL IDENTITIES

The use of the North Sea in ancient times is not well chronicled and its archaeology is difficult. But we can say that it could be crossed, both directly and coastwise, at any time in the last three thousand years and that natural conditions favoured westward movement from Scandinavia to Britain. The archaeological signals, however, do not report that maritime traffic was regular. The axis of exchange was generally south and west until the 5th century AD, when the North Sea became the key forum in British and arguably European history for half a millennium.

Our evidence suggests that the cultural and commercial exchanges that then took place were not determined by technology, but by politics: Saxons and Vikings created an east-west axis, Christianity pulled it south. The pagan Saxons and Vikings favoured free enterprise and free movement; Christianity canalised sea traffic into ports with customs dues. In the periods that the seas were free, coastal communities could have more in common with each other than their terrestrial neighbours, due to the relative speed of contact. Once sea-travel was inhabited by law and taxation, communities turned inward and sought the identity of a terrestrial nation.

'Regional identity' is thus composed of a demographic reality brought about by intermittent contact and interbreeding over thousands of years, overlaid with (and often concealed by) a sequence of artificial identities which are politically inspired. The long periods of contact means that any real biological differences between Britons, Scandinavians, Scots or Continental Europeans over the last millennium or so can be effectively disregarded. The regional identities that have been (and continue to be) constructed are thus mainly of historical interest, but that interest is exceptional.

Modern archaeological interpretation is aimed principally at understanding the minds of people: not only their material culture, but their assumed heritage are constructs serving the political commitment which keeps them together and at odds with their rivals. The questions we are seeking to answer are not which tribe settled where in some illusory 'original' period, but why was a particular cultural persona chosen? why that, why there and why then? In Britain, the story seems to be one of continuous vacillation between a 'French' and a 'Scandinavian' ideological allegiance, the preference of an age being reflected in its constructed heritage and its attitude to the sea.

The choice for us is whether to continue to manufacture and manipulate the heritage for our own political purposes (it remains a serviceable weapon) or to study it: to try and examine and understand the historical amalgam of a place as an asset in itself. The latter strategy is the more exciting of the two. Local differences in culture, the glory of modern Europe, are constructed from a vocabulary unique to that location, because that location is uniquely sited. To deconstruct that cultural artefact does not threaten it with extinction. To know more about a place does not blunt its impact. The study of the complex roles played through history by a region, or a single site, brings rewards for both residents and tourists. It could be argued that tourists will travel further for a mystery than they will for a cliché. And the ability of a region to perceive its identity within the global culture comes only with the strength that self-knowledge brings.

The Author

Professor Martin Carver, born Glasgow 1941, went to study early medieval Britain at Durham in 1972, following a first degree in science and a career in the army. He researched in Anglo-Saxon Art before leaving Durham to work for ten years as a free-lance field archaeologist for the British, French, Italian and Algerian Governments. His principal research projects in this period were concerned with the rebirth of towns in Dark Age England (*Underneath English Towns*, London, 1987) and Europe (*Arguments in Stone*, Dalrymple Lectures, University of Glasgow, 1993). In 1983 he was appointed Director of the Sutton Hoo Research Trust, formed to excavate the famous ship-burial site; this work is now nearing the press (*The Age of Sutton Hoo*, Woodbridge & Rochester, NY). In 1987 he was appointed Professor and Head of the Department of Archaeology at the University of York, which he has developed as a department specialising in Historical Archaeology and professional studies, particularly field archaeology, computer applications, the archaeology of buildings and archaeological heritage management. Since 1993 he has turned his attention increasingly to research of Dark Age eastern Scotland.

References

Admiralty, *Pilot North Sea* (east), 1983

Bahn, P. and Renfrew, C., *Archaeology, Theories, methods and practice* (London and NY), 1991

Binns, A., *Viking Voyagers*, 1980

Brøgger, A. W., *Ancient Emigrants: a history of the Norse settlements in Scotland* (Rhind Lectures for 1928, 1929

Carver, M. O. H., *Pre-Viking traffic in the North Sea*, in S. McGrail (ed) *Maritime Celts, Frisians and Saxons* (CBA Res Rep 71):117–125, 1990

Carver, M. O. H., *The Age of Sutton Hoo* (Boydell:Woodbridge), 1992

Carver, M. O. H., 'Ideology and allegiance in East Anglia' in R. Farrell and C. Neuman de Vegvar (eds) *Sutton Hoo – Fifty Years On* (American Early Medieval Studies 2), 1992

Carver, M. O. H., *On and off the Edda* in Olsen, O., Madsen J.S. and Rick F. (eds) *Shipshape – essays for Ole Crumlin-Pedersen* (Roskilde) 305–312, 1995

Carver, M. O. H. *Archaeological value and evaluation*, in press

Champion, T. et al, *Prehistoric Europe*, 1984

Crumlin-Pedersen, O. and Vinner, M. *Sailing into the Past* (Viking Ship Museum Roskilde), 1986

Higham, N. *Rome, Britain and the Anglo-Saxons*, 1992

Hines, J. *The Scandinavian character of Anglian England in the pre-Viking period* (BAR 124), 1984

McGrail, S. *Ancient Boats in North-West Europe*, 1987

McGrail, S. (ed) *Maritime Celts, Frisians and Saxons* (CBA Res Rep 71), 1990

Piggott, S. *Ancient Europe* (Edinburgh: UP), 1965

Skene, W. F. *Celtic Scotland* vol 1, 1976

Smyth, A. P. *Warlords and Holy men*, Edinburgh UP, 1984

Taylor, E. G. R. *The Haven-finding art*, 1956

Wainwright, F. T. (ed) *The Problem of the Picts*, Nelson) 1955

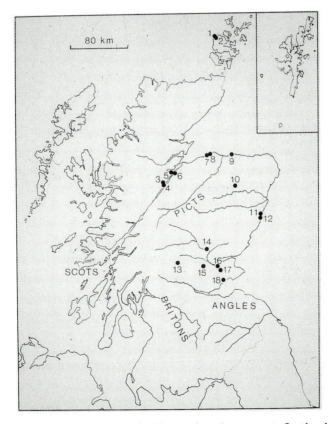

Figure 8 The five cultures found by the Norse when they came to Scotland.

18

ACCESS TO A NATION'S ASSETS
Challenges for Scottish Tourism Policy

Gordon Adams

Access is a key concept for almost all aspects of tourism policy. In this paper access is considered under three categories:

- Access to information about Scotland as a tourism destination.
- Physical access to and within Scotland.
- Access within Scotland to information about specific attractions.

An underlying assumption of the paper is that Scotland has a well-developed tourism infrastructure and no large-scale capital expenditure is necessary to provide access. We are not like, say, Canada in the second half of the nineteenth century where the tourism potential of the Rockies was recognised, but could not be realised until a railway was constructed, new hotels built, and Swiss Alpine guides brought in. Nor are we like Spain after the Second World War, where new hotels had to be built and a package industry developed dependent in turn on computer reservation systems and mass air travel. The present tourism industry in Scotland dates from early Victorian times, and indeed modern tourism in Scotland probably has a longer continuous history than tourism in almost any other country of the world. Thomas Cook started his career in the Trossachs.

The basic tourism infrastructure is already available in Scotland in terms of good hotels, good restaurants, good golf courses, good museums and so on. Some improvement still needs to be made, but a theme of this paper is that tourists still do not know enough about all that Scotland has to offer.

INFORMATION ABOUT SCOTLAND

People take holidays in Scotland for many different reasons, but they will all have acquired some information about Scotland before they come here. Some of that information (but probably a very small proportion) will have been provided by a variety of tourist agencies – in our case from the Scottish Tourist Board, or the British Tourist Authority or from an Area Tourist Board.

How then do these agencies persuade people to come to Scotland, and what image of Scotland do they present?

The recent *Which Guide to Scotland* was so complimentary about Scotland that we at STB have quoted it extensively recently, and no doubt we will do so again in future. Here is a selection of quotations from the Introduction:

> The best reason for choosing to go on holiday to Scotland is this: it is one of the last places inside the crowded and frenetic European Union where it is possible, indeed easy, to be alone in empty countryside. This is not to say that Scotland, like everywhere else, does not have its tourist traps, its crowded roads or its popular beauty spots. It is merely that it is easy to escape from them. Nor is it to imply that Scotland is a deserted wilderness – it has its great cities, its country hotels and its many festivals. But again, if you wish, it is easy to get away from them.

> In fine weather, Scotland is one of the most beautiful countries in the world. The quality of the light is not to be matched further south, while the variety of vegetation and landscape makes for constant change. At every season of the year the Scottish landscape is an extraordinary blend of subtle colours.

> Curiosity alone may lead you to Scotland. For a thinly populated mountainous country on the fringe of Europe, it has had a disproportionately large impact on the world. Scottish inventors, philosophers and scientists have been responsible for many of the ideas on which our understanding of the world is based.

> It is a mistake to think that Scotland is merely an extension of England. Indeed, no attitude is capable of causing greater offence. The Scots successfully resisted English attempts at domination for seven hundred years. Many differences between the countries remain. Scotland's history, traced in its castles, battlefields, ancient trading links with France, Flanders and Scandinavia, is distinct.

> To enjoy Scotland to the full, you must enjoy being out of doors, and not just in fine weather. For the naturalist, the angler, the walker, the golfer or the rock-climber the country is a delight. It is a delight, too, for those who are happy to track down neolithic sites, old castles, old hill roads or interesting geological outcrops across rough and sometimes boggy country.

> Edinburgh, Glasgow, Stirling, Perth or Aberdeen have enough attractions to provide solace in a rainy spell and are even better in a fine one. Both Edinburgh and Glasgow deserve better than to be tacked onto a general Scottish holiday. Both are ideal short break cities: Glasgow for its energy, its wealth of galleries and its shopping habit, Edinburgh because it is one of the most beautiful cities of Europe and has a host of sights historic and otherwise.

I think *Which?* has covered the main points succinctly and well. Key concepts are 'uncrowded, beautiful scenery, interesting history, not England'. These themes are found again and again in tourist brochures about Scotland over the last 150 years.

In tourism marketing gross over-simplifications have to be made, both for the final consumers (the tourists) or for intermediaries such as travel agents, or transport operators. A basic dichotomy is made by STB between overseas visitors and domestic (i.e. UK) visitors. For overseas visitors the image presented can be quickly traced to Sir Walter Scott and Queen Victoria. Friends of the image talk of romance and mystery; detractors talk of haggis and shortbread boxes. However, the task of summarising a country in a few minutes is very challenging, particularly perhaps if the competitors just say 'sun and sand'. Moreover, what we may call the Scott/Victoria image already had its detractors in the nineteenth century (e.g. Stevenson) and the images we associate with Scott/Victoria might well not have been accepted by Sir Walter and Her Majesty.

When Scott died in 1832 Scotland was world famous in literature, philosophy, medicine, architecture, printing, banking, technology, commerce, and soldiering. By the end of the Victorian era, however, Scotland had lost its pre-eminence in almost all these fields. Both Scott and Victoria were undoubtedly proud of Scotland's early nineteenth century achievements and it is unfair to saddle Scott and Victoria with responsibility for tartan shortbread boxes. Nevertheless in 1995 the Scottish Tourist Board ran a poster campaign on the Paris Metro with the slogan 'Ecosse: entre legende et realité', and I believe we can trace such a campaign at least to an advertising agency's image of the Scott/Victoria image. Paul Scott concluded in a paper on Sir Walter Scott at this conference last year: 'You might say that he started the tourist industry in Scotland', and his analysis is very relevant for anybody trying to promote Scotland to tourists. For domestic consumers the approach often has to be to undo some of the Scott/Victoria image. The glens may be empty, but the cities are full of life. The natural environment is balanced by modern artistic activities.

Perhaps national ambivalence about the Scottish diaspora is echoed in our tourist brochures. We are proud that Scots apparently ran the world in the nineteenth century, but we have to acknowledge that Scotland was not perfect if so many people left. In recent years Scottish tourist agencies have not mounted substantial 'roots' campaigns, and the argument that 'Canadians already know about Scotland' may soon have to be weighed against 'but ethnic links can wither'. Few Tourist Boards see themselves as guardians of national culture. Bord Fàilte has put much more effort into ethnic tourism than STB, and Ireland has had a very successful record recently in tourism. But in both Ireland and Scotland it would probably be seen as almost an admission of defeat if the slogan was merely 'Come to Ireland/Scotland because that's where your ancestors came from'.

The message about Scotland is spread by the various tourist agencies through press and TV campaigns, through international tourism promotions and exhibitions (such as the annual World Travel Market in London), and through provision of information direct to consumers and trade intermediaries. A network of Tourist Information Centres (TICs) run by local Area Tourist Boards provides information to tourists when they are in

Scotland. The Scottish Tourist Board has its own TIC in London, and uses the offices of the British Tourist Authority outside the United Kingdom.

The challenge, then, is to get complicated messages over very quickly, whether on TV, or in press advertisements, or in brochures. These messages have to fit very wide markets, and are made in competition against industries such as alcohol or tobacco or motor cars which have much higher budgets than are going to be available for tourism. A key technique must be to get economies of synergy, so that a viewer of an advertisement for, say, Scotch whisky, salmon, or knitwear, will automatically think of the joys of a holiday in Scotland.

PHYSICAL ACCESS TO AND WITHIN SCOTLAND

For more than 200 years the world has been shrinking rapidly in terms of accessibility. In 1750 it would have taken about eight to ten weeks to get a letter to Edinburgh from Milan and receive a reply, and the time taken had probably not changed much since 1500. Now an Italian travel agent expects a fax to Edinburgh to be answered the same day. Modern tourism would not be possible without this shrinking of distance, and, in the last twenty-five years the process has been accelerated by the jumbo jet. Recent forecasts that the cost of air travel will decline substantially again in the next decade must give us cause for thought. If the Milanese can go to New Zealand as easily as to Scotland, which will they choose?

Access to Scotland and access within Scotland has improved immensely in the last thirty years, so much so that it is difficult to complain simply about the availability of access facilities, although price is a very different question. The main road now being completed between Scotland and England is of normal international standard and I suspect that statement was last true in Roman times.

Electrification of the east coast railway means that journey times from England are at last faster than in the steam age. Scotland has a selection of airports now capable of handling the largest aircraft. Within Scotland crofter road schemes in the 1960s meant that travel within the Highlands was often faster than travel to the Highlands. Then oil development brought improvements to the A9 between Perth and Inverness, and now the main necessary road improvements are urban such as the Kingston bridge in Glasgow and the ongoing improvements to the Edinburgh by-pass.

One unplanned by-product of more than a century of road-building in Scotland is that road access to remote west coast villages has led to a decline in ferry services, and this phenomenon is familiar in, for example, Norway and eastern Canada. One hundred years ago it was possible to visit the west coast by steamer from Glasgow. A network of ferry services has been cut to a handful of key routes and some of the romance for tourists has gone.

The challenges facing Scottish tourism in terms of access are associated largely with price, although some of the implications of recent transport improvements have not yet arrived. We do not know the effect of the Channel Tunnel on Scottish tourism, but there seems no reason to fear a change that will make it easier for the French and Germans to visit Scotland. And we do not know the effects of likely deregulation of air travel, although my own belief is that Scotland could gain substantially – initially from the scheduled deregulation of European air travel, and eventually from deregulation of North Atlantic air travel.

For better or worse, Scotland has not developed a substantial inward package holiday industry using air travel. The reasons may be associated with the characteristics of tourists coming here, who often want to travel on their own. Or the reasons may be associated with the relative ease by which people in England can make their own travel arrangements to Scotland and so by-pass the package system. Most likely it is because the tourist flows to Scotland are simply not big enough to generate the economies of scale available for tour operators to the Mediterranean. Many would argue that this has been a blessing for Scotland. We have not suffered the excesses of rapid expansion that have blighted so much of the Mediterranean coast, and we have not suffered from the culture shock that tourism has produced in places like Cuba (formerly) and Egypt (nowadays). But we know that many potential English visitors are deterred from visiting Scotland because of perceptions of high prices. Greater package travel to Scotland could bring lower prices through economies of scale. There could well be opportunities for packaging associated with greater competition on internal air routes and more aggressive marketing by privatised railways. The railways after all had key roles in the original tourism development of, say, St Andrews or Gleneagles.

Internally, the agglomeration economies of urban Central Scotland have not been realised. In terms of distance it should be perfectly possible for the inhabitants of Bearsden to visit the new Festival Theatre in Edinburgh and return home well before midnight. Similarly, for the inhabitants of Morningside and the new Glasgow Royal Concert Hall. Rail travel between Edinburgh and Glasgow is now very good from city centre to city centre, but the suburban rail network is not very good for many outlying areas of Glasgow and is now non-existent in Edinburgh. A comprehensive Central Scotland rail network study is necessary to examine the possibilities of improving rail access in the urban area from Dunbar to Gourock and from Motherwell to Stirling. The benefits would be for general urban living rather than simply for tourism, but a recent study of the Edinburgh Festivals showed the unrealised potential of the Strathclyde market, and the relative lack of Festival go-ers from the west of Scotland seems to be associated partly with poor transport facilities.

Scotland compares badly with Norway in terms of price of access to islands by ferry, and we compare very badly with Switzerland in terms of co-ordination of our public transport system. The Scottish islands are often stunningly beautiful and are really one of the aspects of Scotland where we have a unique advantage. Barra in early summer is as beautiful as any Greek island and more beautiful than most, but for a Londoner it will often be cheaper to go to the Aegean than to the Hebrides. The tourist season in the Scottish islands is short and the weather fickle. If we are to persuade tourists to go to the islands, we will have to present lower prices. Road equivalent tariffs would certainly require subsidies, but such funding seems a pre-requisite of a serious tourism development policy.

Critics of Scottish transport systems for tourists often compare us adversely with Switzerland. That country may well have unique advantages in terms of valleys which still support large numbers of people, surrounded by large towns like Munich and Lyon and Turin which have been amongst the richest cities of Europe for more than 2000 years. For whatever reasons, however, the Swiss have managed to develop an amazingly well-co-ordinated public transport system using trains, buses, funiculars, and even ski-lifts. Moreover the system is very well publicised and apparently almost always runs to schedule. There are many lessons for Scotland, many of which would involve substantial expenditure. A train from Aviemore to the top of Cairngorm on the lines of the train from Grindelwald to the Jungfraujoch would be a marvellous tourist attraction but is probably not a realistic proposal.

As a start, however, we should provide a comprehensive public transport timetable for Scotland. In the 1970s, the Highlands and Islands Development Board showed this could be done for their part of the country. At STB, we have investigated some of the difficulties involved in the production of such a time-table for Scotland. With assistance from other agencies, however, such a timetable may still be possible. It is not nearly as easy as it should be for a tourist to find out how to travel from Melrose to Stornoway by public transport.

When the tourists get to their chosen destination in Scotland, they then need to get access to the attractions they want to visit, and care has to be taken to minimise any adverse effects of increased visitor numbers. The physical reminders of Scottish history are usually easily accessible, often because of the admirable programmes of the National Trust for Scotland and of Historic Scotland. Scotland also has a remarkably comprehensive collection of museums and art galleries operated by central and local government. However, opening hours are not always ideal, with some historical attractions closed during winter months and some local museums closed on Sundays.

The tourism industry in Scotland, as in most other countries, experiences great seasonal variations in levels of activity. In Scotland, as in most other countries, the tourism agencies are committed to reducing seasonality, for the obvious reason that the human and physical capital of the industry (employees, hotels, roads, museums, etc.) is under-utilised for most of the year. Efforts, then, to expand opening hours into shoulder months should be applauded. Nevertheless, for the attraction operator at least, the benefits from extended opening will often be less than the costs, and there is, therefore, justification for subsidy so that the private sector and the community at large,can benefit from all-year tourism attractions.

Increased access to tourism attractions in Scotland can of course have adverse as well as positive benefits. Various other contributors to this volume discuss this issue at length, so in this context it is sufficient to refer interested readers to the Tourism and Environment Initiative sponsored by the Scottish Office. A series of Tourism Management Programmes has now been started all over Scotland to show how the adverse affects of past development can be ameliorated, and to show how further development can occur without undue damage to a fragile environment.

The main challenge, then, of physical access to Scotland is to provide and publicise lower prices. Within Scotland more effort is needed to ensure that attractions are open at all times tourists want access. However, increased access must not lead to increased environmental damage.

ACCESS TO INFORMATION ABOUT ATTRACTIONS

A network of local Area Tourist Boards (ATBs) and Tourist Information Centres now exists to make sure that tourists get the information they need to move around Scotland and have enjoyable holidays. This information network is geared largely to the provision of information about accommodation, and this specialisation is probably inevitable given that the private sector funding for the network comes largely from the accommodation sector. The Scottish ATB network is extremely efficient, and may be the most efficient in Europe in terms of ensuring that a tourist is never far from the information likely to be requested. The following paragraphs, however, are concerned with the information about Scottish history and culture and landscape presented to tourists, and are not concerned with the more standard information about accommodation or transport or meals.

Complaints regularly are made that tourists come to Scotland but learn little of the country, and indeed may be provided with 'false' impressions of the country. The same complaints of course are made in other countries. Few British tourists in Crete seem concerned about Minoan civilisation. Why should tourists to Scotland be concerned with Gaelic culture, or the history of the Covenanters, or the development of ship-building on the Clyde? Certainly we must remember that holidays are meant to be enjoyable. We must not become overly concerned about stuffing academic information into people who simply want to rest and admire scenery. Nevertheless, we also have much market research information to show that many of our tourists are very keen on learning more about the country they visit. Our tourists tend to be of relatively high social class, with relatively high levels of education and with relatively high levels of income.

The main likes of tourists to Scotland are, first, the scenery, then the people, then our monuments of historic interest. So tourism agencies should ensure that information on these features is readily available.

THE SCENERY

As part of the Scottish Office Tourism and the Environment Initiative mentioned above, STB and our partners are trying to encourage tourists to enjoy the natural environment of Scotland. However, this promotion has a strong educational component, and we are trying to emphasise that damage can easily follow thoughtless use. STB and Scottish Natural Heritage have published a high quality brochure, available free, which describes and publicises some of the wilder landscapes and flora and fauna which are quite easily accessible. The Scottish landscape has suffered huge damage over the centuries. Much environmental damage associated with coal and iron extraction in the Lowlands has now been repaired, often very recently through Scottish Development Agency and Scottish Enterprise programmes. In the Highlands, repair may take longer, particularly in sub-Alpine areas like the Cairngorms, or in what Fraser Darling referred to as the 'devastated ecology of the West Highlands'. Nevertheless, in places like Knoydart, environmental repair is now taking place quite rapidly, and the vandalism of road building in mountain areas like Beinn a' Bhuird seems to have been curbed. All over Scotland, mountain footpaths are now being repaired, although a huge task remains.

The challenge is to promote access to our remote areas while ensuring that previous damage is repaired.

THE PEOPLE

We know that tourists usually consider Scots to be friendly, and we know that tourists are usually interested in our history. Inevitably, our tourist brochures have to make summaries which can make professional historians cringe. The Picts often get a mention, then Robert the Bruce, Mary Queen of Scots, Bonnie Prince Charlie and the Clearances. Museums, castles, and stately homes can fill in some of the blanks, and Jorvik has clearly influenced museum presentation throughout Scotland. David Hayes at Landmark in Carrbridge and, more recently at Inveraray Jail, deserves immense credit for presenting natural and cultural history in a responsible and serious fashion, but there are many examples of small-scale heritage centres which do us little credit. Inevitably the private sector will find it difficult to compete with Historic Scotland, and in the United States there is similar difficulties of competition between the private sector at, say, Disneyland and the endowed sector at Williamsburg. (My own bias is much in favour of Williamsburg).

Often the need in Scotland is for better social interpretation rather than new buildings. In recent years the explanations on offer at Historic Scotland sites have improved greatly, and following the Historic Scotland example STB commissioned Don Aldridge to prepare an interpretive guide, primarily for local authorities and small private sector museums and interpretation centres. I commend this guide to you.

There are many proposals now for various social interpretation or heritage centres all over Scotland. Not all of them will come to fruition, at least on the evidence from previous plans for visitor centres all over Scotland. Audiences brought up on television have sophisticated (and, therefore, expensive) tastes and competition from the New Museum of Scotland in Edinburgh will be hard to overcome. Perhaps the interpretation centre itself is even a little passé, given the world-wide growth in such attractions over the last two decades. I wonder now if there is scope in Scotland for development of the American 'living history concept'. I believe it was the Americans who popularised (at places like Williamsburg) the concepts of guides in period costume who can interpret their surroundings to visitors and the concept has been successful at Stirling. Could history and botany teachers throughout the Highlands put on guided tours to explain the cultural history and flora of the area? Some of the Scottish Universities are already offering study tours on cultural aspects of Scotland. At the end of the day, just as we provide maps so that people enjoy the hills on their own, perhaps all we need are reading lists in TICs so that people can read for themselves about the area they are visiting.

Sometimes even a few lines of poetry will be more evocative than a whole heritage centre:

What can ye shaw me here, i this land o the Scots? Breckans and maithie
yowes and virrless stots, tuim untentit crofts whaur aathing rots.

But the toun at the heid – it luiks like a place o rank? Ou ay, wi a schule,
twa hotels, three kirks, and a bank, a Masons' Lodge, and a castle let til a
Yank.

Are there nae Scots fowk think lang til their ain track? An auntran ane i the
Gorbals, Detroit, Iraq, Lagos, or Leeds. But ae day we'll aa win back.

Douglas Young, *Hielant Colloguy*, 1947

In nine lines the poet has touched on the Clearances, the difficulty of urban
development in the Highlands, over-dependence on tourism, the success of a
tourist board drive to attract Americans, and the eternal Scottish longing for a
future Jerusalem. It would take a heritage centre two or three million pounds
to cover that lot. In passing, however, we may note that Burns himself is still
a remarkably popular tourism attraction and that Burns heritage centres
continue to be successful.

In the near future STB will explore the possibility of building on the *Wild
Scotland* brochure, with, perhaps, brochures on the *Arts in Scotland*, or *Gaelic
Scotland*, or *Traditional Music*. In this way we will progress from the scenery of
Scotland to the people of Scotland.

The challenge is to provide tourists with an introduction to what is
available in terms of cultural attractions. If we can let the tourists know what
is available they may well be happy to act as their own guides.

MONUMENTS

In general the physical reminders of our history are very well presented to
tourists. Our main castles, churches, and sites of historical interest are well
maintained and displayed. Some improvements are often necessary in terms
of interpretation and foreign language provision, but these details are now
being improved.

Probably the main exception refers to Scotland's history since about 1800,
eg our military history as part of the British Empire; our ship-building
history; and our general industrial heritage. We do have a series of excellent
military museums but they are often not well publicised, and the messages
they present are often designed for ex-soldiers of a particular regiment rather
than for the public and tourists at large. The Scottish Museums Council is
now leading a Working Party which could lead to general improvements in
military museum presentation. One amazing asset which is clearly under-
utilised as a tourism attraction is Fort George near Inverness.

Sea-faring as a theme of Scottish history is well presented in the Scottish
Maritime Museum in Irvine and the Scottish Fisheries Museum in
Anstruther. Nevertheless, the story of the Clyde is not yet as well presented
as it should be. The story of oil should also be better presented.

Finally our industrial heritage presentation has improved greatly recently
but in an uncoordinated fashion. New Lanark is the flag-bearer, but even at

New Lanark the custodians had to take advantage of a series of government programmes not designed for heritage/tourism development. During 1994 a group of Scottish agencies combined to produce a strategy for industrial heritage presentation. We have now identified the main gaps in presentation that have to be filled, and a co-ordinated development and marketing programme is now being planned, for publication later in 1995.

The challenge is to show that preservation of industrial heritage can take place under the normal criteria for public sector investment.

The Author

Gordon Adams was educated at Aboyne School, Dundee High School, and the Universities of St Andrews (MA), Queen's, Ontario (MA) and McGill (PhD). Before joining the Scottish Tourist Board, where he is now Director of Planning and Development, he held posts in Ottawa with the Canadian Government (Atlantic Development Board and Department of Regional Economic Expansion), in Inverness with the Highlands and Islands Development Board, and in Glasgow with Glasgow University. He has been a visiting lecturer in Poland and India, and an adviser for the United Nations in Saudi Arabia.

References

Leslie, A. (Ed.), *The Which? Guide to Scotland*, 1994
Scott, P. H., *The Image of Scotland in Literature* in Fladmark, J. M. (Ed), *Cultural Tourism*, Donhead, 1994
Scottish Tourist Board, *Edinburgh Festivals Study 1990–1991*, 1992
Scottish Tourist Board, *Wild Scotland*, 1995
Scottish Tourist Board, *Site Interpretation: A Practical Guide*, 1993

19

ACCESS TO OUR NATURAL HERITAGE
A New Framework for Scotland

Roger Crofts

In October 1994 Scottish Natural Heritage launched its proposals for improving access to the countryside for open air recreation in the form of our report 'Enjoying the Outdoors – a Programme for Action' (Scottish Natural Heritage, 1994). This paper outlines our approach to access within the context of Scotland's cultural history, current trends and the philosophy of environmental sustainability.

HISTORICAL PERSPECTIVE

In looking at access in the last decade of the twentieth century, those involved in access issues in Scotland must never forget the very strong cultural traditions about access to the countryside which are held by many people. This is best epitomised by the widely held attitude that there is an unfettered freedom for people to visit the Scottish countryside, and particularly the open hill ground, for their own personal benefit and enjoyment (McOwan, 1994). Without going into detailed historical analysis, these views derive from an assumed freedom to use land in upland Scotland. This can be coupled with the emergence in the nineteenth century of a demand for recreational access from a mainly urban-based population (Aitken, 1975). Whatever its origin, the tradition of this 'freedom' is still cherished by those living in Scotland and is a subject which raises a great deal of passionate debate (Ramblers Association, 1984). This debate is regularly fuelled by the attitudes of some owners or their managers, who have put up uncompromising and unwelcoming signs indicating, for example, that high velocity rifles are in use, in order to dissuade or even frighten the public from entering their land. These signs and the attitudes which underline them, in turn, fuel demands for a statutory 'right to roam'.

These are not recent issues. It is more than a century ago, for instance, that James Bryce MP made three unsuccessful attempts in the House of Commons to place on the statute book a Private Member's Bill 'to secure to the public access to mountains and moorlands in Scotland' (Bryce, 1892). The Government of the day supported the principle of the Bill, but Bryce's last attempt in 1892 made no further progress. The issue of making statutory provision for access is again on the political agenda. Margaret Ewing and other MPs tabled a Freedom to Roam (Access to Countryside) Bill during 1994 (Ewing, 1994); and later in the year the Labour Party stated their intention to bring similar types of provision onto the statute book when they come to power.

The existing statutory provisions on access in Scotland are set down in legislation dating from 1967. For a wide range of reasons – particularly the perception that problems of access were not as severe in Scotland as south of the Border – there were no Scottish provisions made in the National Parks and Access to the Countryside Act 1949. It was only during the debates in the 1960s, under the banner of the 'Countryside in 1970' Conferences (Countryside Commission, 1965), that changes were agreed and formal statutory provision was made in the Countryside (Scotland) Act of 1967. Even these were not radical measures: they had disappointed the outdoor interests south of the Border in 1949, and they largely allowed Scotland to catch up with the provisions for England and Wales in the 1949 Act. There was some new thinking, in particular on powers to enable Local Authorities to play a more active role in the management of countryside recreation through, for instance, the establishment of Country Parks. A little tidying up was accomplished in the Countryside (Scotland) Act 1981, which gave Regional Parks statutory legitimacy, for example. While the provision for Access Agreements and Access Orders in the 1967 Act provided Local Authorities with a useful tool, in the event the Agreement power has been little used and the Order power never used. It was grant-aid from the then Countryside Commission for Scotland (and now Scottish Natural Heritage) which has undoubtedly been the most powerful lubricant of recreational and access provision in the countryside.

We have now come to a point in time when the situation needs to be reviewed in the light of the many changing circumstances.

CURRENT TRENDS: OPPORTUNITIES OR HINDRANCES?

There is a wide range of economic and social changes which are having a significant effect on people's desire for access to the countryside. These current trends are variously regarded as opportunities by some and hindrances by others.

The numbers seeking access to the countryside have risen enormously over recent decades. While we do not have precise figures, Aitken's useful compilation (Aitken, 1992), which shows the increase in mountain rescues, the increase in the number of climbing and walking clubs and the number of people completing the Munros, is a good illustration of the situation. Broadly speaking, this increase is something which society should welcome; but there are, of course, drawbacks.

Linked to the growth in numbers is easier 'access to access'. In many respects it is much easier to get to the countryside nowadays. Car ownership has increased considerably and is expected to increase further. The road network in Scotland has been substantially upgraded, in particular the major routes from the Central Belt into the Highlands such as the A9 and the A85

(Crofts, 1995). But for those who arrive in the countryside, access is no easier – and in some areas is more difficult – than it was. Access across private land is often seen by owners and managers of land to be detrimental to their interests, particularly in situations where, for a variety of reasons, they are struggling to achieve a reasonable financial return. Forestry planting has perhaps had the most dramatic effect, within some places dense stands of trees behind high enclosure fences cutting off access from the lower ground to the open hill.

The type of access sought by people has changed significantly. Patterns of open air recreation show a shift to more active pursuits (Scottish Natural Heritage, 1994b). More people than ever want to challenge nature, treating it as an obstacle course. With that has come a loss of the old sense of innocence, so that quiet and informal recreation in the countryside is frequently disturbed by those seeking more active pursuits. This trend is prompted in part by commercial forces exploiting the increase in disposable incomes and the use of modern technology for the production of new equipment and the promotion of new pursuits. These same market forces, responding to a thirst for information, have resulted in a rapid growth in promotional literature to encourage and guide the visitor (see, for example, Bennet, 1988; Johnstone, Brown and Bennet, 1990).

Alongside all this, the promotion of access, quite reasonably, is now being seen as an economic commodity to be marketed as part of tourism infrastructure (Scottish Tourist Board, 1994). Clearly it brings considerable benefits to the promoters and providers – especially if it encourages people to stay longer locally. However, the financial returns resulting from increased access very rarely benefit the owners of the land, and this exacerbates their feeling of frustration at a time when farm and estate management and incomes are under pressure.

As recent survey evidence shows by far the most prevalent recreational pursuit is walking (Scottish Natural Heritage, 1994c). More than two million walks are taken every week by Scottish residents alone. And this involves a large proportion of the population; around 30% take a walk in the countryside, or at the coast, every month. Most of the walks are two to five miles in length, are taken close to where people live, are on footpaths and tracks, and are in lowland countryside.

All of this material gives clear pointers to the type and location of provision which should be provided in Scotland. But has the provision of access areas kept in step with social and commercial pressures? The answer has to be a resounding 'No'. Access opportunities near where most people live, particularly in the Central Belt of Scotland, are still limited. This is in spite of the many initiatives, for example, to give new life to former railway lines, and the dedicated work which has been applied to setting up footpath networks around some settlements as part of Scottish Natural Heritage's 'Countryside around Towns' initiative. Nevertheless, many paths have been lost, some of which were merely informal routes but others which were Rights of Way. And access over farmed and other enclosed land is rarely welcoming.

As if this low level of provision were not enough, uncertainty over the law and practice of access adds to the confusion (Scottish Natural Heritage, 1994d). In general, people do not know where they are entitled to be; and there is widespread misperception about the law of trespass. Basically, anyone who is on private land without the express permission of the owner or his agent is a trespasser, and the owner is entitled to ask the person to leave the land under threat of what is called 'reasonable force' (although this is not wholly clear in law) (Rowan-Robinson, Gordon and Reid, 1993). If this situation were not intimidating enough, the erection of offensive and unwelcoming signs, on some sporting estates at least, makes the apprehensive walker feel more nervous – and the determined walker more determined: it is a recipe for confrontation and not for reconciliation.

Increased visitor numbers can, of course, have substantial impacts on wildlife (Huxley, 1994). While these are usually localised, some caution may be needed, particularly in view of legitimate concerns about the longer term implications of these impacts. Increased numbers can affect the visual amenity of landscape through creating erosion by trampling. Less obvious, but perhaps more significant, is the cumulative and incremental effect of larger numbers of people in the countryside. This can reduce the enjoyment of some visitors (Scottish Natural Heritage, 1994d). One aspect of this is that those pursuing noisier and more exuberant activities disturb those seeking peaceful enjoyment. As a result the solitude, the peace and quiet which many visit the countryside to seek, can be less easily found.

One can imagine that these activities could well have knock-on effects on the attractiveness of some locations, to the extent that they are detrimental to local economic interests. Also, as has been well documented in other countries (International Union for the Conservation of Nature, 1994), increased visitor numbers can have substantial impacts on local culture and community coherence.

We must not forget, however, that the increase in visitor numbers visiting the countryside does provide opportunities for increasing the public's appreciation and understanding of local communities and of land use and other economic systems in the countryside as well as the environment. Yet, when compared with the many other activities which relate to the land and to capturing economic benefit, very limited resources have been devoted to improving access and to moderating and mediating its impacts.

There is obviously conflict between the aspirations of visitors and local economic interests, and the need to conserve and enhance the natural heritage. That is the daily challenge facing a great many practitioners – especially Scottish Natural Heritage with its integrated remit of conservation, enhancement, enjoyment and understanding of the priceless natural heritage of Scotland (Scottish Natural Heritage, 1995).

TURNING CONFLICT TO OPPORTUNITY: A NEW FRAMEWORK

The challenge is to ensure that conflicts between visitors and the environment, between visitors and owners and managers of land, and between different economic development interests, are turned into opportunities. This cannot be done without first ensuring that the basic resource – the natural heritage – is treated in a way which sustains its future so that it is available to succeeding generations for their emotional uplift and their economic gain.

To help in meeting this challenge, Scottish Natural Heritage has developed five guidelines on sustainable development (Scottish Natural Heritage, 1993) which are as relevant to access as they are to any other uses of the land (Scottish Natural Heritage, 1994a):

(1) *Wise Use:* 'Non-renewable resources should be used wisely and sparingly, at a rate which does not restrict the options of future generations'. A major call on non-renewable resources (particularly hydrocarbons) by outdoor recreation activities is the use of the car. It is central to people's freedom and flexibility to enjoy the countryside. One of our guiding principles is that we should aim to be less dependent on the car, especially for the short and medium length journeys. The provision of better local access to the countryside, especially where this can be reached on foot or by public transport near where most people live, will benefit both the natural heritage and the wider environment.

(2) *Carrying Capacity:* 'Renewable resources should be used within the limits of their capacity for regeneration'. Some natural resources, such as upland and coastal vegetation and wildlife, are inherently vulnerable to the impact of recreational activity. Scotland lies at northerly latitudes with harsh winters and cool summers, both of which inhibit quick recovery of damage to natural vegetation especially on high ground. In this context, 'carrying capacity' refers to the physical impacts of people on the land – the so called 'treadmark' – as well as to the risk of causing undue disturbance to wildlife, and sometimes to the loss of a sense of wildness or solitude, the very qualities which attract people to remote places. The practical implication of this guideline is that there may need to be restraint on the nature and the scale of use of the most vulnerable areas.

(3) *Environmental Quality:* 'The quality of the natural heritage as a whole should be maintained and improved'. As the demand for outdoor recreation increases and recreation becomes a major land-use, its effect on the natural heritage will become more widespread. There is, therefore, a need for greater commitment to resolve problems through management, through environmental education and through strategic planning of the means of access in terms of roads, parking facilities and footpaths.

(4) *Precautionary Principle:* 'In situations of great complexity or uncertainty we should act in a precautionary manner'. Access pressures are sometimes concentrated on places which are ecologically or visually sensitive. Where there is reasonable doubt whether substantial or irreversible damage would be caused to places of special value, there needs to be a much earlier start to managing the situation; it should be tackled as soon as the problem begins to emerge. At the same time, ways should be sought of identifying the limits of acceptable change bearing in mind that the more sophisticated approaches may prove to be too complex. Meanwhile, it is only sensible to constrain and divert activities

which might prove in the future to be damaging to the health of the natural heritage.

(5) *Shared Benefits:* 'There should be an equitable distribution of the costs and benefits (material and non-material) of any development'. Everyone is a 'landuser' in one way or another. Access to the countryside confers great non-material benefits on those who participate in outdoor recreation. But there can be drawbacks for local communities and those who own and manage land used by the public. Damage now should not compromise the future, either in reducing the enjoyment of generations to come or in creating problems for present land owners and managers.

It must be borne in mind that these are not high-minded principles to be learned by rote; they are principles which should and can be brought into practice.

SUSTAINING THE NATURAL HERITAGE AND IMPROVING ACCESS

There are many things which can be done to ensure that society's aspirations for improving access to the countryside can be met without harming its general health or people's enjoyment of it, and which can at the same time bring benefits to local communities and the other economic interests involved.

First and foremost *shifts in attitudes towards access* are needed. The onus here rests both on users and on owners and managers of land. Scottish Natural Heritage has established an Access Forum to allow the many and varied interests to develop new codes of practice. Substantial progress has already been made on a 'Code of Guidance for Access to the Open Hill'. The guideline for users is that those seeking access to land or water should have consideration for its beauty, its wildlife, its operational needs and the reasonable privacy of those who live there or earn a living there. Central to this is a message of restraint and a conscious effort to cause minimal impact: it is about visitors always being thoughtful when they use other people's land – not damaging walls or fences, not leaving gates open, not taking dogs onto farmland. It is also about showing the same courtesy to people who live and work in the countryside as they in turn are expected to show to visitors. These sorts of messages have long been promoted through the Country Code (Countryside Commission). Now is the time to refresh and revise that Code in order to serve the needs of the present and the future.

Equally, those who own and manage land should respond positively to meeting society's needs for recreation and offer a more positive welcome to those seeking access over land. Helping visitors by displaying welcome signs rather than unwelcoming notices is only one obvious way forward.

Overall, there is a need, through education, to achieve a climate of mutual toleration and respect between users of land and owners and managers of land. The *consensus approach* is the preferred method for arriving at the best arrangements for access. If this is achieved, these arrangements will promote confidence in visitors about where and when they can be on land, and confidence among owners and managers of land that they will have support when they meet significant problems.

Care in the promotion of access to the countryside is also a critical factor. There are countless opportunities for increasing access and for making sure that the promotional effort reaches the target audience. This effort must be integrated with wider environmental needs, for instance, encouraging people to have a countryside experience without going to a vulnerable location. There are many ways of using technology-based techniques. The Royal Society for the Protection of Birds, for example, has shown the way successfully at Loch Garten on Speyside and other innovative ideas are in gestation such as viewing the birds on the Bass Rock from a shore location in North Berwick.

Visitor management can be improved through the redeployment of ranger services, employed by Local Authorities and private land owners and funded by Scottish Natural Heritage, and this effort should be more co-ordinated with the advice and guidance which is provided by tourism agencies, particularly via Tourist Information Centres. More information on where people can go can be provided through good maps and guides. A more integrated approach of this type should encourage visitors to stay longer and thereby give them a greater sense of place, and result in increasing their enjoyment and encouraging them to return. This approach should also benefit the providers by offering them a better return on their investment and encouraging them to invest more in facilities for visitors.

Inevitably none of this can be achieved without *increasing the level of environmental awareness* and understanding by both users and providers. Users should be expected, for example, to recognise the need for care in visiting fragile areas, and to accept that where there are problems of over-use which could destroy the resource irretrievably, or where the costs of repair are not affordable, there may be a need for restraint of access. By working with environmental interests locally, particularly Scottish Natural Heritage staff, the providers will achieve a greater but more sustainable exploitation of resources for visitors. If modern technology could be exploited by providing information through personal computers, through videos and through programmes in the media, the users would come to an area with a greater level of understanding and awareness. Once visitors arrive, these messages can be reinforced through the information given out at visitor centres, through rangers and tourist information staff, as well as on sign boards and interpretation panels.

In recognition of the rising demands for access, particularly near to where people live, *increased provision of access* is required. Scottish Natural Heritage is preparing a 'Paths for All' Initiative with the aim of 'within the next decade, communities throughout Scotland should have networks of local paths for the enjoyment of local people and visitors'. The number of networks will depend on the resources available but if the bid to the Millennium Commission is successful then 200 new networks could be in place in the next ten years. These will vary in length from a few kilometres to many tens of kilometres depending on local needs and local opportunities. It is intended to establish a Trust to administer the funds and to provide support for a 'Paths for All' project team and local access officers.

With the increasing number of visitors, whether they are tourists or just day visitors, goes the need to *increase the level and quality of management*. There needs to be a clear view of the carrying capacity of an area from the physical, ecological and perceptual viewpoints. This approach recognises that some areas are too fragile to take increased numbers of visitors – or indeed any visitors at all – and might need strict protection, while others are much more robust, especially those on lower ground and in woodlands and forests. Considerable progress has been made in Scotland as a result of the *Tourism and the Environment* Initiative (Scottish Tourist Board 1993). The appointment of a Tourism and the Environment Officer will, along with the work of the subscribing agencies, enable this to be taken forward faster. However, hard choices will have to be made about where facilities for visitors are placed. Are visitors to be channelled towards honeypots, or dispersed more widely? This is a critical question for the Scottish Tourist Board and its partners in taking forward the exciting proposals in the Strategic Plan for Scottish Tourism (Scottish Tourist Board, 1994). Scottish Natural Heritage attaches great importance to the development of facilities away from environmentally sensitive sites where increased numbers will result in, for example, irretrievable loss of habitats, reductions in the wildlife, and irreparable visual and physical damage. The preference of Scottish Natural Heritage is for development at locations which have a higher carrying capacity and which, as a result of the juxtaposition with existing infrastructure, are likely to bring economic benefits to local communities.

Visitor management, therefore, needs to be set in a *broader planning framework*. Scottish Natural Heritage would like to encourage key parties, with Local Authorities in the lead, to draw up strategic frameworks as practical tools for deciding collectively where additional facilities are most effectively placed to inform and guide visitors, to develop new access networks and at the same time to protect the natural resource.

To underpin this approach we need a *greater understanding of the effects of increased access*. Monitoring the situation, taking preventative action, finding new solutions to repair damage and identifying new ways of determining carrying capacity, are all areas for further attention.

Finally, there is an urgent need to seek *clarification of the legal situation* on trespass and on the 'removal by force'. This is a delicate area and Scottish Natural Heritage will wish to work with other interests to devise a basis for clarifying the legal position on people being trespassers and on their removal from land by force. Legal changes are also required in Rights of Way procedures (Rowan-Robinson, 1994). Simplification of the assertion of Rights of Way is required, which would allow for appeal by other parties through a simplified procedure of written objections to be reviewed by an independent reporter. With this change, Rights of Way procedures are likely to be a much more valuable asset for Local Authorities to use in their footpath plans. Without it, continued attrition of the surviving network of Rights of Way can be expected.

Scottish Natural Heritage believes that this multi-faceted approach will lead to more equitable solutions, a greater degree of clarity of rights and responsibilities, a greater welcome to the countryside for visitors, greater protection of fragile and valued areas, increased local economic advantages, a greater degree of assurance for owners and managers of land, and more provision in the right places to benefit visitors, local interests and the environment.

208

ACTION THROUGH PARTNERSHIP

This considerable agenda can only be achieved by collaboration between many parties – public, private and voluntary. Scottish Natural Heritage will continue to play its key part in providing financial support for access projects, including the maintenance of long-distance routes, and the development of footpath networks, ranger services and other necessary facilities. It will also provide advice and guidance on best practice. It will seek to facilitate working in partnership between public and private interests, and it will seek new sources of funds and new mechanisms – for instance through the Common Agriculture Policy and the Millennium Fund.

Scottish Natural Heritage considers that Local Authorities have the central role in planning and providing open-air recreation in the countryside. It is hoped that Local Authorities will invest more in this work by switching resources from built recreational facilities to countryside recreation.

Tourist boards and development agencies, including local enterprise companies, have an increasingly important role. Scottish Natural Heritage welcomes the progress being made under the *Tourism and The Environment* initiative, of which it is a contributing partner; in particular, it welcomes the involvement of local enterprise companies in investment to improve access for tourism and local use. An increased involvement and financial contribution would bring more benefits more quickly.

Scottish Natural Heritage also wishes to encourage owners of land, both public and private, to allow (in the words of the Scottish Landowners' Federation) 'Access without Acrimony'. Perhaps the major provider in this respect is Forest Enterprise. It is hoped that, under the new organisational arrangements, access for informal recreation will be maintained and enhanced throughout its managed estate. We also expect that, in disposing of land, the present customary arrangements are safeguarded and only subject to restriction on operational grounds or for the protection of natural heritage interests.

Recreation bodies and, indeed, sporting interests also have a very significant role to play in influencing the attitudes and behaviour of their members through the many valuable codes of behaviour and codes of practice. Scottish Natural Heritage encourages them to consider how they could put something back through voluntary action to help manage and care for the resources which they use.

CONCLUSION

A real opportunity now exists for improving access in Scotland through co-operative and co-ordinated effort between public agencies, owners and managers of land, and user interests. Much of this will not happen if additional resources cannot be captured. Switching of funds within public agencies, and exploration of other possibilities, such as the Millennium Fund, the National Lottery and the Common Agriculture Policy, are all essential. In taking matters forward, it must be recognised throughout that the natural heritage itself is the critical capital resource. Everyone must guard against its deterioration so that it is available for the enjoyment of future generations. At the same time, it should be made as accessible as possible for today's needs, within the constraints of caring for its future and respecting the operational needs of other land uses.

The Author

Roger Crofts has been Chief Executive of Scottish Natural Heritage since its inception in April 1992. Born in Hinckley, Leicestershire, he was educated at Hinckley Grammar School. He gained a BA in Geography at Liverpool University and a MLitt in coastal geomorphology from Aberdeen University. After training as a secondary school teacher at Leicester University, he was appointed to a research post in Geography at Aberdeen University, and later to a similar position at University College, London. He returned to Scotland in 1974 and spent 17 years working in The Scottish Office covering North Sea oil and gas developments, local government finance, sea fisheries law enforcement, the development of the Highlands and Islands, tourism, and finally nature conservation and the countryside, including leading the Natural Heritage (Scotland) Bill team and the establishment of SNH. His recreational interests are cooking, gardening, flower photography and walking.

References

Aitken, R., *Stravagers and marauders*, Scottish Mountaineering Club Journal, 351 – 357, 1975

Aitken, R., *Three indices of growth in mountain recreation*, 1992 (after Aitken, R., *Wilderness Areas in Scotland*, unpublished PhD thesis in Geography, University of Aberdeen, 1977)

Bennet, D. (ed), *The Munros*, Scottish Mountaineering Trust, 1988

Bryce, J., *Access to the Mountains (Scotland) Bill*, House of Commons, 1992

Countryside Commission, *The Country Code*, Countryside Commission

Report of Study Group 9 – *Countryside: Planning and Development in Scotland in The Countryside in 1970: Proceedings of the Second Conference'*. Royal Society of Arts, 1965

Crofts, R., *The Environment – Who Cares?*, SNH Occasional Paper 2, Scottish Natural Heritage, 1995

Ewing, M., et al, *Freedom to Roam (Access to the Countryside) Bill*, HMSO, 1994

Huxley, T., *Where the shoe hurts: the ecological imprints of tourism*, in Fladmark, J. M. (ed), *Cultural Tourism*, Donhead, 1994

International Union for the Conservation of Nature, *Parks for Life: Action for Protected Areas in Europe*, IUCN, Switzerland, 1994

Johnstone, S., Brown, H., and Bennet, D., *The Corbetts & other Scottish Hills*, Scottish Mountaineering Trust, 1990

McOwan, R., Scotland on Sunday, 1994

Ramblers Association, *Keep out: the struggle for public access to the hills and mountains of Scotland*: 1884 – 1984, The Ramblers Association, 1984

Rowan-Robinson, J., *Review of rights of way procedures*, SNH Review No.9, Scottish Natural Heritage, 1994

Rowan-Robinson, J., Gordon, W. M. and Reid, C. T., *Public access to the countryside: a guide to the land, practice and procedure in Scotland*, Scottish Natural Heritage & the Convention of Scottish Local Authorities, 1993

Scottish Natural Heritage, *Sustainable development and the natural heritage: the SNH approach*, SNH, 1993

Scottish Natural Heritage, *Enjoying the outdoors: a programme for action*, SNH, 1994

Scottish Natural Heritage, *A survey of public attitudes to walking and access issues*, SNH Research Survey & Monitoring Report 4, SNH, 1994b

Scottish Natural Heritage, *A survey of walking in the countryside*, SNH Research Survey & Monitoring Report 3, SNH, 1994c

Scottish Natural Heritage, *Enjoying the outdoors: a summary report on responses to the Consultation Paper*, SNH, 1994d

Scottish Natural Heritage, *Enjoying the outdoors: a programme of action summary*, SNH, 1994

Scottish Natural Heritage, *Scottish Natural Heritage – an introduction*, SNH, 1995

Scottish Tourist Board, *Strategic Plan for Scottish Tourism*, STB, 1994

Scottish Tourist Board, *Tourism and the Scottish Environment: A sustainable partnership*, produced on behalf of The Scottish Tourism Co-ordinating Group by STB, 1993

20

THE FREEDOM TO ROAM
A Cultural and Economic Asset

Robert Gordon Reid

This is about the few and the many. The few who own the land and the many who walk on the land. It is an issue which spans town and country, rural and urban. Above all 'the freedom to roam' is a political issue and one which will only find resolution through the democratic process, if at all. That resolution will depend on the continuing efforts of the practitioners to find technical and often pragmatic solutions. These are already occurring across Scotland and elsewhere in the world. In other words goodwill is a necessary prerequisite for any workable solution. Unfortunately, there are and always will be individuals on all sides of this debate who would rather not see goodwill engendered. That is democracy. A latter day Bryce is required, who has the vision to recognise that society in general will benefit from the civilising effect of a Freedom to Roam Bill.

In this paper I consider some of the issues surrounding the freedom to roam, but try to avoid getting hooked into a debate of the 'legal mire' which surrounds the subject (I am aware that Alan Blackshaw is working on a legal history of the freedom to roam in Scotland, and that Scottish Natural Heritage have commissioned Jeremy Rowan Robinson to examine in some depth the legal nuances of trespass and an 'implied consent to be on land'). As a planner and as a mountaineer I am certain that there are relatively straightforward solutions to many of the access issues which face us today. I explore these and also set down what I see as the cultural and economic justification for improving our current position.

> Every man, without distinction of race or colour, is entitled to nourishment, housing, covering, medical care and attention ... employment and ... the right to roam over any kind of country, moorland, mountain, farm, great garden or what not, where his presence will not be destructive of its special use, nor dangerous to himself nor seriously inconvenient to his fellow citizens.
> H. G. Wells, *War Aims: The Rights of Man'*, The Times 1939

I am not the first person to quote Wells, as a supporter of a right to roam. Marion Shoard's seminal work, 'This Land is Our Land' was where I first saw these words, and her book is one that all those interested in land management should become familiar with. It is scalpel sharp in its incisive analysis that rural landowners still have a virtual stranglehold on our countryside. With its curious land ownership system Scotland exemplifies this aphorism.

Development rights may well have been 'nationalised' through the planning system, but this has not impinged one iota upon the character of land ownership in Scotland, which still gives an exclusivity of use, and an almost feudal ability to force a fellow citizen off the land. As we go into the 21st century the landowning hegemony, save for a few liberal beacons, is clutching onto the law to prop its position against an avalanche of change in society. Moreover, the public seem ever willing to oblige those who own, almost to the point of servility.

Is it surprising that the most voluble voices ranged against any change in the present system of access in Scotland are those of the land owning and particularly the farming community? 'Hardly surprising at all', is the chorus that I often hear from 'countryside officials' whom I meet. Dogs worry sheep, people drop litter, they leave gates open and some are even vandals. At access seminars there will always be someone who shows a slide of a burnt out car abandoned in a field. Yes, that is a crime, and something which should seriously concern us all. But it is characteristic of socio-economic deprivation in society at large, and in particular in our inner cities, and in our peripheral housing estates. It is not an access problem.

All access must be responsible access, and the recommendations of the recent report of the Secretary of State's Working Group on Environmental Education are to be commended in this respect. This makes the crucial point that, whilst there is an overwhelming need for environmental education in all walks of life ... community, home, school, and workplace, it is best given and understood in the environment. Perhaps acknowledging this, Scottish Natural Heritage (SNH) entitled their first issues paper on the subject *Access to the Countryside for Enjoyment and Understanding*. This formed part of the Review of Access which has been conducted over these last four years though it was begun by the former Countryside Commission for Scotland (CCS) in 1989 following on from their Popular Mountain Areas Review.

CCS handed over a virtually completed Review of Access to the new SNH, recommending that Scotland should enjoy an access system similar to that enjoyed across Scandinavia, based on a general right of access to all land, with codified exemptions covering damage and privacy. However, the new agency's board is dominated by landowners who have difficulty countenancing such a proposal, with the notable exception of David Laird, the new Chairman of the Cairngorms Partnership. He was supportive of a move towards a right of access over open country and through woodland, but was outnumbered by others sceptical of such an approach.

The idea of a general right of access over all land was viewed with such scepticism that the advice passed on from CCS to SNH is only briefly mentioned and then written off in one damning sentence in the original consultation paper. I quote:

> There is a view, strongly held by some individuals and recreational organisations that there should be a legal right of access to open land, subject only to restrictions to protect privacy and essential land use needs.
>
> SNH Review of Access, 1993, para 17, p 6

There was no exposition of the clear benefits such a system would bring, nor of how well it works in Scandinavia and elsewhere in Europe. To compound this there was a pre-emptive paragraph in the consultation document actually presenting the arguments against such a change; '...it is not required and ...would involve a controversial encroachment on property rights'. Whose words were they?

Since then the Access Review has rumbled on with a series of papers from SNH which have gradually pulled back from their original and partial view. Wisely, the analysis of responses to the consultation paper was put out to independent consultants. The key findings are summarised below. Despite significant efforts to improve access over the last twenty years, it was quite clear that efforts were 'not keeping pace with the continuing rise in demand' (*Enjoying the outdoors; a summary report on responses to the consultation paper,* SNH 1994):

1. There is still insufficient recognition of the importance of open-air recreation to people in modern society.

2. The level of planning for access, management of access and investment in access is too low.

3. The countryside is often neither very accessible of welcoming, so that people can find it difficult to know where they are free to go.

4. Growth in recreation in the countryside affects land management operations and there are worrying indications of increasing friction.

5. People are uncertain about whether they have any legal rights to be on privately-owned land.

6. The arrangements in the Countryside (Scotland) Act 1967 for providing for formal access through footpath agreements have been little use, and new approaches are required.

Enjoying the Outdoors: A Programme for Action, SNH, 1995

SNH have now announced a programme of action to attempt to tackle some of the problems outlined above. Virtually all of this is in the form of practical help on the ground. I rather like the idea that within 10 years all of our communities will have their own footpath networks identified and in place. It is an ambitious programme, but if it is seen through, it will have done in 10 years what the rights of way system has spectacularly failed to do in 150 years. On the vexed question of rights there was a wait and see approach adopted until a supplement published by SNH in February 1995 (four months after the official review had been completed) which states; 'SNH has concluded that trying to establish in law a formal right to roam on the open hill would be extremely contentious and, most probably, counter-productive. To achieve statute which is clear and unambiguous, and which does not create even more confusion and even more uncertainty than at present, would, we believe, be difficult.'

A concordat based on the Letterewe Accord (see below) is being developed by the key players involved in the upland/open country access debate. All was going well, and a broad consensus had been reached between the principal protagonists, the Mountaineering Council of Scotland, the Ramblers Association Scotland, the Association of Deer Management Groups and the Scottish Landowners' Federation, under Magnus Magnusson's honest brokerage. Even he did not count upon the reaction to the finalised draft from the London Branch of the Scottish Landowners' Federation. Every mention of the word freedom struck out; every emphasis put on the importance of the private owner. The 'absentees' strike back.

It is perhaps time that a visionary approach to access were adopted by SNH, instead of the problem focused approach which has now been pursued for nearly six years. SNH should be setting down a vision, with the aid of all its partners, on access, to which all parties could aspire and work. A system of meaningful and secure footpath networks should be at the core of that vision, supported by a simple law of access, not trespass.

Local Authorities have for the most part ignored this issue. Worse still is an apparent inability to decide where the public interest actually lies with regard to access. Many of our peripheral housing estates in Scotland are bordered by countryside of considerable amenity. Yet in most cases that countryside is a virtual no go area and as a consequence contributes little toward the relief of the deprivation in those areas.

We nevertheless carry out field penalty studies and hear the problems of the urban fringe farmer without ever pausing to think whether the public subsidies going into those areas could not be better directed toward alternative products such as footpath networks, countryside maintenance or even green belt enhancement. Indeed, as the system presently works, many landowners in the urban fringe constructively neglect their land in order to erode its green belt value, and ease the path toward development.

The most commonly heard excuse for planning authorities ignoring the access issue tends to be a combination of lack of resources, low priority in relation to other more pressing socio-economic problems, and a fairly useless set of instruments with which to achieve anything constructive.

It is testament to the ability of certain 'enthusiasts' that a few authorities have achieved much against the odds. Perth and Kinross in particular, Strathkelvin, and West Lothian all deserve credit for their achievements to date, whilst at a regional level Strathclyde warrant praise. The latter especially for the Greening the Conurbation initiative, based on river valley and urban fringe projects. Grampian Regional Council has set down in its structure plan the key strategic footpath routes in the region; namely Deeside, Donside, Speyside and the Grampian coast. The Grampian coast is one of those undiscovered gems and would have considerable merit as a National Long Distance Route. If it linked Dundee with Inverness, via Aberdeen, it would pass through more than 60 settlements, each one an event along the way, a place which will benefit from the foot-borne tourist. The Districts within Grampian have already put in place lengthy stretches of these routes, often with assistance from SNH or the Region, on an opportunity basis. However completion of the route is fraught with difficulties as matters rest at present.

With the Southern Upland Way nine years elapsed between its conception and its completion. This is a ludicrous state of affairs when the tourism and community benefits are so clear (numerous reports, Mackay, Ash *et al* have demonstrated significant economic return from long distance routes). Local Enterprise Companies are finally seeing the economic rationale of investing in long distance routes, although the maintenance and revenue implications are still to be resolved, as well as a quicker means of designation. Were access founded upon 'a general right of access', such routes would be welcomed as the means of managing access. Instead routes are opposed and dogged by a few mean minded individuals who still pursue their exclusive rights with vigour. This often causes awkward diversions, or necessitates complex management agreements which add to the burden on the public purse. Both the Deeside Way and the Great Glen Way have met such opposition.

There is irony in comparisons with France, which is richly endowed with a network of walking paths (sentiers), from local footpaths, ancient drove roads and pilgrim routes to full-blown international long distance routes called 'GRs' which is short for 'Sentier de Grand Randonnee'. Long ago it was realised that an extensive network will lessen the impacts and spread the benefits. We still have approximately 100,000 people a year flogging the West Highland Way.

In Strathclyde, the Clyde Calders Project has taken the issue of local access further than most. Picking up upon research commissioned by CCS during its Access Review (*Footpaths and Access in the Scottish Countryside;* by P. Scott, and *Clyde Calders Access Review & Strategy* by H. Neilson & K. Kenny) the Clyde Calders Project has carried out a survey of all the paths in their area, not just the rights of way. The resulting maps resemble chopped up spaghetti. Most routes have been cut by development, or are interrupted by motorways or have been long ago forgotten and suffer from neglect. Even the most superficial analysis suggests that much is wrong with access in Clyde Calders, yet to pursue any strategy to improve matters is at present handicapped by our hopelessly arcane legislative framework.

Most of the paths which were surveyed are not rights of way. In other words while walking on them a member of the public is trespassing, ie in a place he or she has no right to be and, subject to the whim of the landowner, is exposed to the lawful use of 'reasonable force' to remove them from the land. The exact nature of 'reasonable force' is open to broad interpretation, but the present law effectively sets up the landowner as judge and juror of trespass.

To transform the present 'chopped up spaghetti' into meaningful footpath networks upon which the public has a secure right to walk is the aim of the Clyde Calders Access Strategy. This is virtually impossible without a significant recasting of the legislative framework. Magnus Magnusson has quite rightly justified the SNH focus upon rights of way in their Access Review because of the poor status of much the system. In fact that poor status is primarily a product of the present, cumbersome set of rights of way procedures. Even in Perth and Kinross, where so much has been achieved, the rights of way map still resembles 'chopped up spaghetti'.

SNH, in conjunction with Convention of Scottish Local Authorities (COSLA), published a guide to the Law, Practice and Procedure of Access in Scotland (Rowan-Robinson, J. with Gordon, W. M. & Reid, C. T., 1993) which is an excellent summary of the law of access in Scotland. It catalogues a patently unworkable system without speculating much about the implications or the potential solutions. There are no conclusions to draw upon, but a telling statement in the introduction states that 'there are, of course, problems relating to public access to the countryside that cannot be dealt with in this guide'. Some have already commented that perhaps this guide was 25 years too late, and that it should have accompanied the Countryside (Scotland) Act 1967. All those who deal with access should arm themselves with a copy of the SNH/COSLA guide, if only as evidence of the case for change. What is required, especially in enclosed land circumstances, are meaningful and secure footpath networks. To deliver this we need a new legal, administrative and financial framework which overcomes the existing problems ... and enables Clyde Calders (for e.g.) to turn their 'chopped up spaghetti', into a decent access network. I maintain that the planning system we have developed in Scotland is far and away the best means available to deliver this.

Before I examine some of the detail of those arrangements it is worth dwelling on what impetus, if any, exists for such a change. Any rationale which is couched in political terms or in terms of social justice can be dismissed in similar terms by the establishment. Age-old sympathies for the lot of the farmer are regularly used to fend off the need for more or better access to the countryside. However, the pace of change in society has accelerated to such a degree that it is difficult to maintain this stereotype. The beleaguered farmer, tilling the land is no longer a credible caricature.

In Scotland, the subsidy to farming has approached nearly £450m per annum. That is nearly £1.5m a day. An increasingly well informed public is asking 'what do we get for that' and is not satisfied with 'cheap food and rural stability' as the pat answers, because both now have a hollow ring. This is especially true from the perspective of the tax payer who has to fund both a rising Common Agricultural Policy (CAP) bill and an ever increasing social security bill. The 1992 CAP reforms carried through by Commissioner MacSharry were thought radical at the time, yet in retrospect they seem little more than tinkering. 'CAP Reform II' is on its way and the words being most often heard in this respect are non food products. I foresee access, in an ever-more-natural and better maintained countryside as one of those 'non food products' and see few problems with the tax payer in delivering this. Indeed, the increasingly affluent and mobile urban public will begin to demand this, ironically often galvanised by an alienated and non-affluent minority.

Scotland with such a small community of interest and with an influential establishment should not fear these changes. The freedom to roam is dear to the hearts of most Scots, irrespective of its curious pedigree and any attempt to rescind such a freedom would be political suicide. The Scots should be proud of this cultural icon. A society which has purged itself of the power-excesses of landownership has much to be proud of. It continues to surprise me how the foreign owner can buy large tracts of Scotland, and then think he or she can act like a feudal baron fending off the public from their newly acquired playground. In stark contrast, the traditional Scottish landowners, especially in the uplands, have generally been exemplars of fairness in this respect. Patrick Gordon-Duff-Pennington's oft quoted statement that 'the day a Scotsman cannot walk freely in the Highlands is the day he can no longer call Scotland home' is to be celebrated. I wonder as well, whether the vexed land question which still exercises much analytical thought and political consideration would be dulled were there to be a general right of access to all land. If the freedom to roam became set in, say, an outdoor recreation act, similar to that enacted in Norway in 1957, would ownership become more academic to the public. To those accustomed to travelling in the wild land of Scotland there are no boundaries manifest, and only their occasional coincidence with a significant watershed could ever be remarked upon.

However the greatest justification of all must be the economic justification. The fastest growing industry in global terms is tourism. Not so in Scotland where the last decade has seen close to a 40% decline. Scotland will always be a niche market in terms of tourism, albeit with a number of niches. The essential ingredients of sunshine, sand and manjana that go into mass tourism just do not exist here. The leisure and recreation boom, so well predicted through the 60s and 70s has however arrived, though to look at the tourism industry in Scotland you would think that it had crept up in disguise. Our wild land in Scotland is an undeniable asset in this respect, especially when coupled with the freedom to roam. Few in the tourism industry in Scotland have appreciated this so far. The biggest selling hardback guide to Scotland is in fact the Munro Guide, now approaching 100,000 copies sold. I meet people from all over Europe on the Scottish hills in summer and winter. They are the new tourists who have come to some of the most beautiful hills in the world, and for some of the best hill walking in the world.

In the Partnership areas of Loch Lomond and the Trossachs, and the Cairngorms, both reports covered access as an issue. Both come down in favour of supporting 'responsible access to open country'. However, both areas include substantial rural populations, most of whom live in small communities. These would undoubtedly benefit, as would their tourism potential, from the development of footpath networks around and between them. More fundamental is the security which could be given to a generally insecure tourist who is often reluctant to walk in the countryside for fear of being 'where he or she shouldn't be'.

In contrast, manufacturing for the leisure industry has been alert to the developments. Manufacturers and retailers in Scotland and the rest of the UK have been quick to capitalise on the changes taking place in society. Witness the exponential growth of mountain biking, which is as much a response to crowded roads as a response to changing leisure patterns. There are also growing signs that an expanding activity holiday sector, particularly in the north and west is beginning to take-off. The number of centres and guides expands year on year.

The justification for formal recognition of the freedom to roam is therefore in part about jobs, and rural development; about keeping communities viable and petrol stations open; about alternatives to the deer forest status quo which has come into disrepute for its exclusivity and its negative impacts upon the environment. It is in fact quite hard-nosed. But in Scotland that is perfectly acceptable, provided there is an administrative system, and a legal and financial framework equipped to deal with the outcome.

AN ADMINISTRATIVE AND LEGAL FRAMEWORK

The current development planning mechanism in Scotland could easily turn itself to the business of providing meaningful footpath networks. Surveys of the existing networks can be carried out with little difficulty and there are many voluntary organisations such as community councils, and rambler groups who could be relied upon to assist. There would be little difficulty for planners to subsequently design the 'meaning' into the presently disjointed networks, making circular routes, connecting communities and setting out strategic routes (e.g. along the coast or along major river valleys). Planners are presently becoming re-interested in the inter-relationship between land use and communication networks. It would be an abrogation of planning principles were footpaths not to be part of those networks because of our preoccupation with the car. Quite patently it would also not be sustainable.

The footpath network would be enshrined within the development plan at a strategic and a local level. There would be consultation, and redress through the same procedures that exist for development plans at present. A landowner could object and pursue that objection to public local inquiry in the same way as he or she can object, for instance, to a green belt designation (which is potentially a far more debilitating designation than a footpath).

Proper protection of any route within the development plan would ensue, and enforcement procedures to rectify any loss, encroachment, obstruction, etc.; would also be required.

A critical precondition for a planning administered system to be wholly successful would be a change to the law concerning trespass. The Trespass (Scotland) Act 1865 is a rogue piece of legislation which is so far past its sell-by-date it is surprising that no-one has taken it to the Court of Human Rights in the Hague. It is used far more often than many assume, and principally as a threat in circumstances where police are asked to remove someone from private land.

Although there have been numerous pieces of legislation that have superseded the 1865 Act (such as legislation concerning, *inter alia*; Travelling People, breach of the peace, protection against invasion of privacy, protection against vandalism and wilful damage, etc.) it has never been repealed. It is also reasonably well known in Scotland that the 1865 Act was enacted to prevent the dispossessed clans from reclaiming the land from which they had been cleared. Indeed references are made to specific clans in the parliamentary debates recorded in Hansard .

The government has recently passed its Criminal Justice and Public Order Act. Ostensibly this is aimed at dealing with new age travellers, raves and hunt saboteurs. When consulted by Westminster, the Scottish Office Minister concerned, Lord Fraser of Carmyllie, believed that this essentially English piece of legislation should apply to Scotland as well. This was just in case there was a displacement effect with all the newly criminalised new age travellers making a beeline for Scotland.

Those with an eye for irony will have spotted that the 130 year old Trespass (Scotland) Act which today brands us all trespassers for walking on land was enacted to deal with the 'new age travellers' of the time. Thus a narrowly focused piece of historic legislation, aimed at a specific problem, has become broad and non-specific in its present day use. Many fear that the Criminal Justice Act has made the same mistake.

Not, however, the lobbyists (NFU, SLF et al) who have hitherto adamantly opposed any civilising change in the laws of trespass. They have done a volte-face. The Act was welcomed as if the fruition of a long drawn out campaign, rather than the bolt from the blue that it actually was. The clauses on 'aggravated trespass' are particularly controversial because they criminalise trespass. As long as 'encampment' or 'the lighting of fires' is not in question, trespass was solely a civil matter. Indeed, it is the difficulty of operation of the civil element of trespass law which has contributed to a misplaced belief that a *right to roam* exists in Scotland. The legal position in England contrasts so substantially from Scotland that this bolt-on exercise, at the landowners behest, was a less than welcome turn of events at the culmination of SNH's Access Review.

Even the Law Society of Scotland had suggested that the clauses on aggravated trespass were, 'from the perspective of Scots Law unnecessary' because 'the case had not been made to legislate in this area; the provisions in respect of obstruction or disruption of lawful activity are unduly vague and could lead to innocent or lawful behaviour which obstructs or disrupts other lawful activity, being subject to the offence provisions'. What is lawful activity? It is nowhere defined.

An approach far more in-tune with today's needs would be to define in law 'a general right of access' such that any person had the right to be on any land, provided they were not causing damage, invading privacy, causing a breach of the peace, or committing any other criminal activity. This is effectively the system that has developed in Scandinavia where legislation such as Norway's Outdoor Recreation Act (1957), has provided secure access for the public to the countryside. An important part of that legislation is a codification of the obligations and responsibilities that are laid upon the walker, though there is also another deeply significant foundation for this in the shape of the distinction between *in mark* and *out mark* (effectively enclosed and unenclosed land) that exists in Norwegian Culture and is reinforced through their education system.

In Scotland there would need to be the facility to apply for exclusion (either temporal or spatial) to a 'general right of access'. This would be through the local authority, and would require thorough justification. Temporary exclusion would be by 'exclusion notice', and permanent would have to go the full route of the development plan process. The sorts of activity which would justify exclusion would be set down in statute, but would primarily be for nature conservation purposes.

An important test for assessment of exclusion would be whether the same effects could not be better achieved through land management practices. In my own view shooting, stalking and lambing would not qualify since in most instances perfectly workable and reasonable practices can integrate these uses with access, without the need for exclusion. Indeed, there is now a significant test of these issues beginning on Mar Lodge Estate recently acquired by the National Trust for Scotland where a thoroughgoing integrative approach is being adopted to prove that there can be compatibility between conservation, access and sporting use. SNH have already shown that a significant regeneration of the native forest can be achieved on Creag Meagaidh by culling deer at the correct levels. The RSPB have also achieved similar results on their Abernethy Reserve, and it is quite fitting that they have now been awarded a record conservation grant of £680,000 over 20 years by the Forestry Authority for the 700 acres concerned. Both of these successes have been achieved without ever denying a days access to the visiting public.

At Letterewe in Wester Ross, following two years of, at times, intense discussion produced the Letterewe Accord in 1994. The landowner concerned, Paul van Vlissingen, was keen to see a better understanding between the users of the estate on the one hand, and his managers on the other. The result was a groundbreaking concordat which set the pace for the rest of Scotland. However, it was criticised by the more intensively used deer forest estates, such as Atholl, because Letterewe did not let commercial stalking. This is why the demonstration project which is beginning at Mar Lodge Estate will be under such close scrutiny.

So a change in the law, such that there is effectively a 'law of access', as opposed to a 'law of trespass' would ensure that the process of administering the footpath network would be a simple one and one that all reasonable landowners would welcome. Indeed, the 'meaningful footpath network' would become the instrument for managing access within enclosed land, and farmers and landowners would be making a beeline to the planning department door for help. Adequate advice would need to be available, and besides the existing Countryside Ranger schemes, I would advocate that FWAG, having lost an 'F' for Forest, now gather an 'A' for Access, making this the Farming, Wildlife and Access Advisory Group. The various Countryside Around Towns projects would also play a key role, facilitated by both the new Unitary Authorities and SNH. To them would fall much of the physical work on the ground, predominantly in areas of high population where such provision could have maximum spread and beneficial effect. It remains one of my own admissions of failure that I have not managed to convince Aberdeen City Council of the need for such a scheme, effectively making them the only city in Scotland without one. Perhaps recognition of the immense value of their green belt by the new unitary Aberdeen will lead to such a scheme coming along soon.

FINANCIAL SUPPORT

There would need to be measures in place to ensure adequate funding for footpaths. This would not be difficult. There are already numerous sources of funding going into the countryside which could be redirected. CAP funding already mentioned above, is the most obvious, and mechanisms have recently been introduced within Environmentally Sensitive Areas to fund access strips along field margins and footpaths. The gradual and increasing inclusion of countryside maintenance within agricultural subsidy is welcome, but requires further extension. This should be seen in the light of considerable dissatisfaction with the current system of subsidy. For instance, hill livestock compensatory allowances only deliver an average income to the hill farmer of £10,000 per annum (NFU Figures, 1995), even though the average subsidy given is in the order of £25,000 per farm per annum.

There are several other areas which could provide financial support. The Transport Policy and Programme budgets of Roads Authorities should be providing more toward pedestrian, and footpath support. In conjunction with Sustrans, significant progress is already being made, and the focus

THE LETTEREWE ACCORD

Some of the finest mountain scenery in Europe is found on the Letterewe Estate in Wester Ross. It is renowned amongst hill-walkers and climbers for its wild land qualities. The Letterewe Accord is a set of principles which aim to enhance public awareness of wild land needs and to provide a guide to its use and enjoyment, both on Letterewe and perhaps elsewhere in the Scottish Highlands. The Accord has been drawn up by Letterewe Estate in co-operation with outdoor organisation representatives. It has developed from discussions initiated by the Mountaineering Council of Scotland and the Ramblers' Association with the Estate.

Fundamental to this Accord is the recognition that all who visit, or live and work on the land and water of Letterewe, must cherish and safeguard the area's wildlife and beauty. Such places are increasingly rare in a world where the natural environment is under ever growing pressure. A new approach is needed. Co-operation between individual and community interests in the sound management of wild land is one element. It reaffirms that human needs are inseparable from those of the natural world.

–The prime objective at Letterewe is to maintain, expand and enhance the area's biological diversity and natural qualities. This will ensure that these are central to the experience of all who visit the area and are recognised as an essential element in sustaining the long-term economy of Wester Ross.
–Red deer management policy is based on selective culling, aided by scientific research, with the aim of maintaining population levels appropriate to the regeneration of the natural habitat.
–All who visit the area are asked to recognise that red deer stalking is carried out across most of the estate area with the most important period being weekdays from 15 September to 15 November. Visitors are asked to contact the estate during this period for further advice.
–Visitors are encouraged to base their visit to Letterewe on the concept of 'the long walk in'. Adequate experience, training and equipment to meet the rigours of travel in this remote area are essential.
–Public use is based on the tradition of freedom of access to all land, subject to any agreed modifications for conservation or management reasons.
–There are footpaths through those areas where there are benefits for land management or for visitor access.
–Car parking, telephone and other facilities are available at Dundonnell, Kinlochewe and Poolewe.
–The estate does not favour the construction of new vehicle tracks or the use of all terrain vehicles. Ponies and boats are used for estate management.
–Mountain bikes should be used only on existing roads or vehicle tracks and not on footpaths or surrounding land.
–Minimum impact techniques should be used when camping overnight using lightweight tents. Pollution and disturbance to wildlife, especially sensitive loch shore birdlike, must be avoided.
–Visitors are encouraged to visit the area in small, rather than large groups.
–Research studies which help to further understanding of the use and protection of wild land are welcome at Letterewe.

Letterewe estate will be pleased to advise on any aspect of estate management and on ways to make any visit to letterewe as enjoyable and rewarding as possible.

THE LETTEREWE ACCORD produced by Letterewe Estate in association with John Muir Trust, Mountaineering Council of Scotland, Ramblers' Association Scotland, Scottish Wild Land Group.   December 1993 should continue to be on those more strategic routes linking communities, the spine of any meaningful network. SNH have also submitted a proposal to the Millennium Commission to seek funding for a 'Paths for All' initiative, though the final bid for this project is still in preparation.

A mechanism is required that generates funding which can be ploughed back into the infrastructure of tourism. Most of our European partners do just this. They use a system of bed-night taxes, though the trade in Scotland feels strongly that they are already being taxed enough. Hill walking brings in over £300m per annum to the Scottish Economy (Scottish Tourist Board Figures 1993), for which the treasury must be extremely grateful. It is a shame that even 1% (as opposed to 17.5% – 25% tax rates) of that figure cannot be found to help.

Finally, I believe there continues to be scope for the user to have an input to the upkeep of the footpath networks. Mechanisms are already in place where some guidebook profits are used to grant aid footpath repair, and the Scottish Mountaineering Trust deserve particular credit in this field. Voluntary bodies such as the Mountaineering Council of Scotland and Ramblers Scotland have also helped set up the British Upland Footpath Trust, to provide a fund for grant aiding footpath repair and maintenance. Other voluntaries such as the John Muir Trust, the National Trust for Scotland and the RSPB who have gone down the route of acquiring wild land are demonstrating management techniques and practices which will hopefully spread to other estates.

CONCLUSIONS

Reform of the Forestry Commission would have been far simpler had there been a general right of access to, *inter alia*, forests. Although the 'privatisation' of the Forestry Commission has been over-ruled, continuing piecemeal sell-offs are taking place. This continues in the absence of a satisfactory means of securing continued access. The access agreement route has failed, and the government continues, in effect, to privatise land which was bought with taxpayers money, afforested with taxpayers money, and hitherto enjoyed a policy of free access to the public. Of the 92,263 hectares (almost quarter of a million acres) of Forestry Commission land in Britain sold since 1981, only 13.8% still enjoys public access. 51,262 hectares of the sales have been in Scotland. Without the emotive issue of access blurring the issue the government would have been able to address the other serious issues of timber supply and sustainable forestry.

The government and its advisors have also been involved in policy reviews in several other areas where a solution on access would have given certainty and clarity to their deliberations. The new Red Deer Legislation would have been assisted. So would SNH's consideration of the whole panoply of designations and their associated management agreements which in some instances have evolved to become little more than sophisticated access agreements. However, it remains quite likely that much of this policy formulation will continue without the benefit of the access issue being satisfactorily resolved.

I am wary of the provisions of the Habitats and Species Directive. Having always supported the view that nature conservation was always the only valid justification for restrictions on access, I worry that a rather too bureaucratic approach will ensue, which coupled to the precautionary principle could lead to calls for, for instance, 'eagle sanctuaries'. With proper management I believe that the carrying capacity of much of our wild land is robust. Of course there may be other reasons for limiting numbers, such as enhancing wildness, by lessening social encounters. I maintain that subliminal approaches to this are the correct management approach, principally by managing the car, and by enhancing the long walk in.

At the start I mentioned that a new Bryce was required, for a visionary and civilising Access Bill to reach the statute books. Margaret Ewing, MP last year put forward a private members bill for a Freedom to Roam Bill. Three of the political parties going into the next election will carry manifesto pledges about access to the countryside. Perhaps Bryce's vision is about to become reality. My hope if such were to happen, is for a once and for all solution. It would be the worst of all scenarios for this to simply become a political football kicked back and forth every five, ten or fifteen years.

Many planners in local authorities reading this will be walkers or hill walkers themselves. The same will apply to other professions which deal with access such as the legal profession, and the estates professions. Yet within these professions, save for a few enthusiasts, there is virtually no evidence of a firm conviction as to where the public interest in access lies (as opposed to the establishment's). However, most who read this will be able to walk unconstrained by the introversion which is so characteristic of much of the rest of the public, simply because they are confident and knowledgeable of their rights.

I suggest they should read Rowan-Robinson's guide, but also pursue this issue further. Get to the reference libraries, approach your legal departments, whatever, in order to supplement your copy of the guide with a copy of the Trespass (Scotland) Act of 1865. It makes colourful reading.

The Author

Robert Gordon Reid is Assistant Director of Economic Development and Planning for Grampian Regional Council. He is a past President of the Mountaineering Council of Scotland (1990–1994) and had previously worked as Access and Conservation Officer for the MCofS (1986–1990). He is a member of the Scottish Mountaineering Club. He received a Winston Churchill Fellowship to look at arrangements for managing access in North American National Parks in 1991. The views contained in this paper do not necessarily represent the views of his employer.

References

Reid, R. G., *Parks People and Permits* in Mollison, D., (ed), *Wilderness With People*, John Muir Trust
Reid, R. G., *I want to solo the Exum*, in SMC Journal, 1992

Scottish Natural Heritage, *Access to the Countryside for Enjoyment and Understanding,* Review of Access, SNH, 1993

Scottish Natural Heritage, *Enjoying the outdoors; a summary report on responses to the consultation paper,* SNH, 1994

Scottish Natural Heritage, *Enjoying the Outdoors: A Programme for Action,* SNH, 1995

Wells, H. G., *War Aims: The Rights of Man',* The Times, 1939

21

NATURAL HERITAGE ZONES
A New Approach in Scotland

Roger Crofts

This chapter argues the case for a new framework to the management of the whole natural heritage in Scotland. It explores approaches to the management of protected areas and the wider countryside, and the different activities which affect the natural heritage as a whole. I argue that this framework and its implementation should reflect experience world-wide and has the potential to provide a more rational and defensible basis for developing policy and delivering action through the statutory natural heritage body: Scottish Natural Heritage. It also has the potential to align more clearly the policies and programmes of SNH's partner organisations in their contribution to the use and management of the natural heritage.

The approach described – natural heritage zonation system – draws on recent reviews by natural heritage practitioners and academic commentators. The conclusions of these reviews are now being actively put into practice in other countries, for example in the USA and in England. There are many practical lessons from experience in these countries, as well as in Scotland, to enable the basis of a new framework to be established. The relevance of this work to developing thinking in Scotland is explored.

The work reported in this chapter is currently under development. Most progress has been made on a biogeographic zonal classification. Work on natural heritage zones is still at an early stage.

THE SOCIAL AND ECONOMIC CONTEXT

The starting point for a new approach must be the recognition of the interaction between economic opportunity, social well-being and sustainable use of environmental resources. In developing a new approach in Scotland, analysis of the present situation suggests that there are some key elements which can be identified as a basis for a new approach (Crofts, 1993).

Scotland has an intensively *managed* landscape as a result of the very long interaction between people and the land. Its intrinsic interest and value and, therefore, its ability to support local populations, can not be maintained by simply leaving it alone. Any new mechanism in the future has to be a *flexible mechanism* able to be adjusted to suit the specific needs of the area.

Scotland has large areas of *high quality natural heritage* reflecting its diverse geology and climate, as well as the long interaction with man. There is a rich mosaic ranging from the relatively remote and semi-natural areas of wildland quality with high aesthetic appeal, through crofting and agricultural areas to the urban environment. We can not conserve the quality of all these areas by traditional 'protection' measures. Most of the countryside is not covered by designations but, nevertheless, contains land of high natural heritage quality. The new approach, therefore, should adopt *a wider perspective* to protection.

Scotland has essentially a *working landscape* largely created and managed by people making their living directly from the land. Natural heritage interest must be seen in this context. To achieve multiple objectives in a landscape which 'works for its living', the needs of the natural heritage will be best served through *integrated land management*. The goal of economically viable and environmentally sustainable land use can only be attained through an integrated approach. Other approaches tend simply to tinker with the edges, leaving conservation areas divorced from productive areas.

Any new approach must recognise that there are *environmental changes as a result of both natural and human factors*. The new approach must change from the vicious circle of ignoring change to the virtuous circle of *embracing inevitable change*. To cope with this inevitability of change a *strategic framework* for a wide area is necessary rather than restricting such an approach to protected areas. The framework should focus attention both on the legitimate socio-economic aspirations of local communities and the wider population as well as the protection and enhancement of the natural heritage and its enjoyment.

Scotland has a particular socio-economic history: a strong *cultural pride*, often rooted in historical association with the land. Imposed protection in any form can act against this, rather than drawing upon its strength. An essential part of any new approach to protection will be to capitalise on this sense of pride. *Local community involvement* in protecting the natural heritage is, therefore, fundamental. In other words we should design with people and not just design with nature.

The use and management of the land are profoundly influenced by the policies and actions of *diverse organisations*: local, national, international, governmental and voluntary, each pursuing their own particular remit. An essential part of a new approach in Scotland will be to work with those interests to ensure that their efforts are co-ordinated and contribute to fostering pride, rather than presenting a bewildering array of apparently contradictory activities when viewed from the perspective of any one area or zone. These organisations must be *committed to implementation* of any strategy, with adequate resources purposefully channelled.

CRITIQUE OF PRESENT APPROACHES AND MECHANISMS

In Scotland, in parallel with many other countries, there is no uniform approach to the protection and enhancement, enjoyment and understanding of the whole natural heritage of wildlife, landform and landscape. Wildlife, landforms and landscapes which are special are protected through statutory systems established since the late 1940s. The remainder of the countryside is not embraced within any systematic approach, nor is the interaction between protected areas and the larger, remaining area addressed.

In the Scottish context, this is best demonstrated by the fact that protected sites cover little of the country, and yet they consume as many of the resources of the statutory agency as the remainder. Sites protecting wildlife and landforms constitute some 10% of the land area. Areas established to protect nationally important scenery cover 13% of the land area. When taken together, and taking into account the overlap between them, some 20% of the land mass of Scotland is covered. Not only are the activities outwith these areas (80 to 90% of the land mass) likely to have some degree of impact on the sites and areas which have protected status, but much less attention or resources are devoted to these large tracts of the country. The separation between policies, programmes and actions within designated sites and areas and those for the remaining countryside is considered to be the most fundamental criticism of the site- and area-based approach to the protection of the natural heritage. This point will be developed further, as it provides the key argument for a new approach in Scotland.

In the past there has been a heavy and undue reliance on formal designation of special areas and special features to the detriment of focusing on the remainder of the countryside (Crofts, 1995). The approach of protecting special areas is valid and must continue. But experience has shown that new approaches are required to address the management needs of these areas in consultation with those who own and manage the land, local interests and other users. It is, therefore, instructive to review briefly some of the issues concerning protected sites and areas in Scotland before turning to the lessons from experience elsewhere.

The system for protecting wildlife and landform sites was set up originally under the National Parks and Access to the Countryside Act 1949 which was substantially revised and strengthened through the Wildlife and Countryside Act 1981.

The degree of protection afforded depends on the ability of the statutory nature conservation organisations (SNH in Scotland) to agree, on a voluntary basis, a management regime with owners and occupiers of those areas identified as Sites of Special Scientific Interest. These are defined as 'any area of land which is of special interest by reason of its fauna, flora or geological or physiographical features' (Wildlife and Countryside Act, 1981). The management regime will, at its minimum, safeguard the special scientific interest in respect of wildlife or landform and, where possible, will seek to enhance it. This voluntary principle provides the foundation for the protection of regionally, nationally and internationally important sites and is the mechanism by which the United Kingdom fulfils its obligations under European Community Directives on Species and Habitats and Wild Birds and under international conventions on wetlands and migratory species.

By contrast, the system for protecting areas of landscape of national and international importance in Scotland is much less well developed. There is statutory provision for landscape protection in the form of National Scenic Areas designated by the Secretary of State under the terms of Section 262C of the Town and Country Planning (Scotland) Act 1972. These are 'areas of natural scenic significance which are considered to be of unsurpassed attractiveness which must be conserved as part of our national heritage' (Countryside Commission for Scotland, 1978). The main purpose of designation is to ensure that there is consultation with the statutory landscape agency (SNH) on development within the purview of the Scottish planning system. There are also various prescriptive restrictions laid down by the Secretary of State.

There is, inevitably, some degree of geographical coincidence between sites identified for wildlife and landform protection and areas identified for landscape protection. There is, however, no single co-ordinated system. The selection criteria and selection guidelines which have been developed over time for the identification of conservation sites and areas have flaws. The guidelines for identifying nature conservation sites seek to apply a rigorous and scientific approach but the definitive volume admits that their application is subject to judgement by the operator (Nature Conservancy Council, 1989). In the circumstances these judgements are, therefore, little different from the judgements which must be made by those assessing landscape quality and character. Similarly, the spatial unit within which sites and areas are identified is arbitrary. For nature conservation sites, these are administrative units which were established in Scotland in 1974 and which will be substantially modified as a result of local government reform in 1996. Nature does not recognise such ephemeral boundaries. The spatial units used do not recognise, nor are they based on, obvious natural features such as geology, soils, landscape units or climatic and topographic factors.

Inevitably, in a country with such diversity of natural heritage as Scotland, there are very significant variations in the scale of landscape and wildlife protected areas. Sites of Special Scientific Interest or other designated sites range from as little as one hectare in size up to areas embracing tens of thousands of hectares. In the circumstances it is, therefore, extremely difficult to have any uniform approach to the strategic management of sites and areas to safeguard the conservation interest.

There is a great diversity of ownership of the land within protected sites and areas. Uniform approaches are difficult to apply as the regime on any individual's property has to be negotiated separately with that owner. This is not to advocate changes in land use; rather, it is an observation of the need for an overview of the management of a site or area which would straddle ownership boundaries.

Finally, in terms of the present system, the ability of statutory natural heritage bodies to influence, never mind determine, the management of the land and water resources in designated sites and areas is extremely limited, and outside these areas is even less so. Activities by other statutory bodies which have their own regulatory remit are of paramount importance. These bodies have, on behalf of the Government at central or local level, or increasingly on behalf of the European Community, responsibilities and associated resources to determine the use and management of land in these areas. This fact forms the second cornerstone of my argument for a new approach to designations: to ensure that the policies, programmes and actions of other statutory agencies do not have a deleterious effect on these protected sites and areas.

This brief review of the situation should not be taken as a counsel of despair; rather, it is a reflection of current thinking which seeks to break down barriers between nature conservation and landscape conservation and between protected sites and areas on the one hand and the wider countryside on the other hand. The systems which have been operating in Scotland for the last two to three decades have, to a certain extent, resulted in a reduction in the rate of damage to the natural heritage. They have not, however, been able to provide a positive framework in which economic, social and environmental interests can share a common responsibility for the natural heritage and for the well-being of the people. In terms of the six key elements set out earlier in the chapter, a broader framework is required.

A number of initiatives in Scotland are already pointing the way to a new approach which seeks to break down the barriers between the wider countryside and the special areas, which involves the community of interests both local and national and seeks to incorporate environmental and economic considerations. In the Cairngorms, for example, following the report of the Cairngorms Working Party (Cairngorms Working Party, 1993), the Secretary of State for Scotland has established a Partnership Board comprising a wide range of interests to determine the overall integrated strategy for the management of the area and to deliver particular environmental renewal projects. In the Loch Leven catchment in Kinross, the local interests have come together in a Forum to address the action necessary to reduce the input of nitrates and phosphates into the Loch and hence safeguard its economic and environmental value and its importance to the local community. And in the north west mainland of Scotland, tentative steps towards a combined natural and cultural heritage area approach are being made.

These initiatives are pointing the way towards utilising other mechanisms: agricultural and forestry incentives, and the land use planning system, as key tools for the delivery of environmental objectives alongside economic development objectives. Already there is considerable progress in widening the scope of existing schemes to take into account environmental objectives. On agri-environment, for example, there are various schemes including the designation of Environmentally Sensitive Areas and on forestry through the Woodland Grant Scheme and its specific supplements. In the context of the UK Government's Biodiversity Action Plan and its Sustainable Development Strategy, many other initiatives are being taken forward which will lead towards more integrated policies and schemes taking environmental issues into account.

LESSONS FROM OTHER COUNTRIES

Many other countries have faced the same issues concerning the lack of integration between approaches in designated areas and approaches to the remainder of the territory. There is not, nor can there be, any single international solution because of the diversity and variability of wildlife, landform and landscape, and also because of the variability of cultural, social and economic requirements. Nevertheless, there has been a great deal of international debate about the success or otherwise of protected site and area systems in different countries and their relationship in management terms to the surrounding countryside, in particular highlighting various failures and defining the new approaches required.

The protected areas approach internationally has a long history from its origins in the USA over a century ago. However, many reviews (see for example Bishop et al, in press; Lucas, 1992; Mantell, 1990; US National Parks Service, 1992) have concluded that it has not worked or is not working as well as it might or should. This is perhaps a surprising conclusion in the light of the fact that in many countries the land within protected sites and areas is publicly owned and administered by bodies responsible to the national government. There is long-standing legislative provision for the long-term protection of these sites and areas as well as their enjoyment by the public. And there has been a substantial application of resources and research-based expertise.

Public ownership of land has brought with it a number of problems. Public authorities have not necessarily proved to be the best owners. Such ownership can not set aside long-standing traditions of the use of the land formerly owned by private parties without resulting in disassociation by those parties of the new management requirements and the development of detrimental relationships between the managers and those defending traditional interests. The drive to generate resources to enable long-term management of the areas and to cope with restrictions in public expenditure has brought a refocusing of attention away from primary goals of protection and enjoyment to secondary objectives of financial leverage. Furthermore, legislative provision for these areas has not, in practice, been able to resolve growing issues about the balance between environmental protection and public enjoyment. Decisions ultimately have to be made about the choice between these goals when pressures for use reach or surpass the carrying capacity of the protected area.

Protected areas in themselves have often become islands of preservation within a sea of development. Their mere existence can result in environmental management being undertaken only within the protected areas and being ignored in the wider countryside outside. It has been increasingly recognised that the effects of the management of non-protected areas on protected areas are profound. To date there has been very little integration of policy across the boundary, despite the existence for many decades of clear scientific evidence of the need for such an approach. Indeed, it has been argued (Bishop et al, in press) that protected areas 'negate the holistic approach' to management of the countryside as a whole.

It is significant that the most recent protective vehicle being applied in Scotland as well as elsewhere within the European Community, the Habitats and Species Directive, does not focus entirely on protected areas. It has, as one of its fundamental principles, the requirement to place the new proposed Special Areas of Conservation within a properly managed wider countryside. The Directive states in Article 10 that: 'Member States shall endeavour, where they consider it necessary, in their land use planning and development policies and, in particular, with a view to improving the ecological coherence of the Natura 2000 network, to encourage the management of features of the landscape which are of major importance for wild flora and fauna' (European Council, 1992). The UK Government interprets this as 'intending to facilitate the coherence of the Natura 2000 network and encourage migration and genetic exchange. The objective is to ensure that the designated sites are not isolated but conserved in the context of a sympathetic wider countryside' (Scottish Office, 1993).

Another strand to breaking this isolationist approach is the recognition that ecosystems straddle boundaries drawn by man and that to maintain and, where possible, enhance the diversity of life demands a more broad-based approach. A biogeographic or ecosystem approach is preferred in many countries (see for example Bailey and Hogg, 1986; Elder, 1994; Mather and Gunson, 1995; US National Parks Service, 1994). It is also relevant to the linking of protected sites to each other through networks: the ECONET approach used on parts of the European mainland. And it is relevant to the work of UK statutory nature conservation and countryside agencies, like SNH, as has been demonstrated in England by the Countryside Commission's work on 'a new map of England' (Countryside Commission, 1994) and its 'Countryside Character Programme' (Countryside Commission, 1994) and by English Nature in the development of its 'Natural Areas' scheme (English Nature, 1993).

There are many examples of the recognition that areas outwith the boundaries must be taken into account. For instance, the US National Parks Service in its statement of management policies indicated that 'it is no longer sufficient to consider strategies and actions solely within the boundaries of the parks. While the National Parks Service does not support the creation of buffer zones around the parks or seek veto power over adjacent lands, it will work co-operatively with surrounding landowners and managers to help ensure action outside the park does not impoverish park resources and values' (US National Parks Service, 1988). In some countries, federal protected area authorities have been challenged in the courts because of their inability successfully to manage the protected area because they have no impact on or control over what happens outwith that area (see for example, Mantell and Metzer, 1990).

Equally significant has been the emerging concern that the community of interests in protected sites and areas has been ignored. By this, I mean local communities residing within or adjacent to protected sites and areas, as well as the wider national, social, cultural, economic and environmental interests. In some countries, for example Canada, the recognition of the need to involve such groups has resulted in substantial changes in federal legislative provision requiring full participation of the community of interests from the local through to the national level in the management plans for National Parks.

PRINCIPLES FOR A NEW APPROACH

The need for a new approach in Scotland, employing the lessons from international experience, should not and must not ignore the valuable experience already gained in Scotland. The new approach must not discard the past and the present but must identify how it can be adapted and put in a new and wider context which will enhance its success in the longer term. Neither can, nor should, the present system of designated sites and areas be discarded, particularly as many form the basis for delivery of national, European Union and international obligations. Similarly, the new approach must build on the more integrated approach and the broader based schemes already in existence.

Five principles emerge from the preceding analysis which should inform the development of the new approach advocated.

First, protected sites and areas can not be divorced from the surrounding territory. There must be recognition of environmental variation which does not stop at boundaries drawn by man. The underlying principles set out in the Biodiversity Convention recognise that the natural resources outwith protected areas and sites (given that this territory covers the vast majority of the land area) are at least as important as those within them. Equally well-founded traditional approaches of integration within water catchments which recognise the wider 'downstream' implications of activities and events should be incorporated. The first principle, therefore, is that *a new approach founded on the interaction between activity within and outwith protected sites and areas is required.*

Second, the link between landform, wildlife and landscape must be recognised as a fundamental tenet. Hence, systems which safeguard one and ignore the other are unlikely to be successful in the longer term. The second principle, therefore, is that *an integrated approach to wildlife, landform and landscape protection and management is required.*

Third, the management of the natural heritage (both wider countryside and protected sites and areas) must be seen in its wider context of the needs of society, respect for local cultures, the opportunities for economic development as well as within its environmental context. Hence the third principle is the need *actively to involve the community of interests in the management of protected areas and the wider countryside within which they are placed.*

Fourth, the management of the natural heritage can be achieved only through a variety of policy instruments embracing all sectors and activities which affect the natural heritage including agriculture, forestry, fishing and tourism. The fourth principle is, therefore, the need for *integration of environmental, economic and land use policies and schemes of assistance.*

Fifth, there is a need to ensure that the system developed is a proper balance between recognising the complexity of the environment and its interactions with human systems, and the requirement for simplicity to enable it to be usable in practice. It should be based on the range of variation in space and time and comprise a combination of environmental elements. The fifth principle is that the *new approach must be based upon rigorous but practical, simple but not simplistic subdivision of the country to recognise its diversity.*

A ZONAL APPROACH

Based on these five principles, a range of practical guidelines can be indicated for a new zonal approach.

In recognition of the geographic variability of environmental parameters, zones should be defined on the basis of a selection of variables rather than of a single attribute. Within each zone an integrated management approach is required irrespective of the designated status of parts of the area. Management frameworks, rather than specific prescriptions, are required. These should take into account environmental resource and management issues, but also cultural factors, social requirements and economic opportunities.

The notion of 'perpetual' protection should be a cornerstone of management of the total area within any zone. Allowing the natural resource base to be utilised for the benefit of the present generation and succeeding generations will require perpetual intervention as opposed to purely preservation management. However, in doing so, both the natural resource itself and the values which that resource holds for society at large must be recognised.

Within each zone, subdivision in relation to environmental quality and environmental carrying capacity as well as social and economic factors is a legitimate consideration. Application of approaches such as those explored in the European Ecological Network (ECONET) should be considered. Here connecting core areas through linking corridors, as well as separating core areas from the wider area by use of buffer areas, have successfully been put into practice through Biosphere Reserves. The use of buffers to allow development which is out of sympathy in environmental terms with stricter protection regimes in other parts of the zone will not, in the light of international experience, be successful.

The definition of zone boundaries should not be seen as an obstacle or an end in itself. The critical consideration is the identification of core areas and areas of contiguity, coincidence or separation. This process should help in the delineation of boundaries.

We intend to define strategies and programmes for the future use and management of the natural heritage for each zone. Fundamental to achieving this, given the arguments earlier in this chapter, will be to develop policies for designated areas and sites and the remainder of the zone which are mutually consistent and reinforcing. As far as SNH is concerned, this will relate to the management practices which we would like to see adopted by owners and managers of designated sites and areas. We intend to achieve this through the development of management briefs, negotiated with them and, where appropriate, the application of management agreements and associated positive management payments. We shall seek to reinforce this management by setting out our own policies and strategies for the remainder of the zone in relation to the way in which SNH would carry out its advisory role to a wide range of interests. These interests include local planning authorities, the Forestry Commission in respect of applications for grant-aid for planting and approval for felling, River Purification Authorities in respect of consents for discharge, Flood Control Authorities in respect of engineering works, as well as economic development agencies in respect of development and Roads Authorities. Overall the approach will be to provide a framework within which SNH can respond to, and hope to influence, activities within the zone on a more rational basis than it has been able to do to date.

In the light of international experience, the success of this approach will depend on involving the parties whose interests might be affected and those parties which have a key role in decision-making and advice. We need to address, therefore, the fundamental question of the type of outcome which the various communities of interest would like to see. There is a number of ways of doing this which have been tested in practice in different parts of Scotland: for example in the Tweed Catchment through the Tweed Forum, in the Loch Leven Catchment through the Loch Leven Forum, in the preliminary work in the Cairngorms and north west Scotland on a possible Natural Heritage Area, in the Forth Estuary through the Forth Estuary Forum and in various others. This approach is based not only on the need to engage the various constituent interests but also on the fact that there is no single or ultimate authority on decision-making on these issues.

The planning system holds a significant key to the implementation of any shared vision. It has to be remembered, however, that there are major issues relating to land use in the fields of agriculture and forestry which fall outwith the planning system. There are also many other issues relating to natural resource use, for instance the use of water resources, which are the responsibility of other organisations such as water and drainage authorities, River Purification Authorities and The Agriculture Department. By seeking to bring together the various parties, we would hope to facilitate a more integrated approach and thereby remove the sectoral approach which has, in the past, too often been dominant.

The approach will also enable us, over a period of time, to examine whether the designated areas and sites within each zone are fully in tune with the criteria for their designation and whether, in particular, there is under-representation of some types of features and characteristics or, indeed, over-representation of others.

In the longer term, as far as SNH is concerned, the zonal approach could serve as the framework within which audits of the state of health of the natural heritage could be undertaken. The results of such audits might in turn inform SNH's own policies and activities and those of other statutory bodies.

For each zone, it will be necessary to characterise its natural heritage attributes. This could lead to the identification of a series of sub-zones. A statement on the likely management requirements to achieve sustainable use of the resources, will lead on to an assessment of the availability or otherwise of mechanisms to address these. The outcome of these assessments will need to be in a form that can be used by the range of interests to identify and determine their contribution: in the Scottish context local authorities, local enterprise companies, local communities as well as the local representatives of national bodies such as Scottish Natural Heritage, Scottish Agricultural College, Scottish Office Agriculture and Fisheries Department, Forest Authority and Forest Enterprise will be the key players. We have to date concentrated our efforts on developing a zonation scheme which is based on objective factors applied to existing environmental data, and which will result in the subdivision of Scotland into readily recognisable and coherent zones: 'natural heritage zones'.

BIOGEOGRAPHIC ZONES

The first step in defining zones is to identify the basis for the selection of environmental parameters. There are basically two choices (Bailey and Hogg, 1986; Mather and Gunson, 1995). The *natural or functional regions* approach is best epitomised by identifying units such as river catchments or mountain massifs. Its application would result in a series of continuous zones. Alternatively, there is the *environmental variables* approach ranging from use of a single variable which would result in environmental uniformity but a fragmentation of zones through to a more complex approach involving a range of environmental variables.

The difficulty in Scotland in determining the approach to be used is its diversity of geological structure, of rock type, of soils and of topographic factors, including the all important altitudinal factor. All of these variables mean that it is very difficult to discern the spatial patterns which would result in any degree of environmental uniformity over a reasonable size of area. At a much broader scale, it is possible to recognise two major eco-systems in Scotland: the boreal coniferous zone and the temperate deciduous zone. However, it is difficult to define the boundary between them. Other boundaries which have a clear environmental basis and, indeed, affect man's activity and use can be identified, such as the major geological structural features separating the Central Valley from the Southern Uplands to the south and the Highlands to the north. However, even within these broad units there is a considerable degree of variation as a result of those natural physical factors already mentioned.

The method we have selected for identifying areas of similarity is based on species distribution (see Carey et al, 1994; Carey et al, in press). The simple but fundamental premise is that the distribution of species will reflect a wide range of environmental parameters. A preliminary trial using liverworts (on account of their sensitivity to climatic variables) proved successful. The trial was extended by using distributional data covering six taxonomic groups: breeding birds, diurnal insects, non-marine molluscs, liverworts, mosses and vascular plants. In addition, a range of climatic variables (16 in all) was added. All of the data were assembled for each ten kilometre grid square. A six-stage analytical method was employed which resulted in the definition of a biogeographical zones map for Scotland. In all, ten zones were identified (see Figure 1 with boundaries smoothed for presentational purposes).

Clearly this technique is limited by the availability of species distribution data. Nevertheless, it does produce a recognisable zonation of Scotland, albeit with a few peculiarities – for example, the coincidence of classification between the Forth Estuary area and the South West of Scotland. The characteristics of each zone are described by Carey et al (in press).

Further work to smooth the zone boundaries and also to correlate the species and climatic data to soils data has now been completed. The preliminary outcome raises four issues as far as practical use of the zonal map is concerned. First, there is little contiguity between similar zones, partly as a result of the influence of altitudinal and climatic factors. Second, the zone boundaries are regular as a result of the source material for compilation being on a grid square basis: they do not accurately reflect environmental boundaries in practice. Third, the predetermined number of zones, ten, may not be optimal for practical purposes. Fourth, species and environmental conditions vary at scales smaller than the basic grid square unit. Comparison of the output shows reasonable correlation, with most classifications of biogeographic zones in Scotland as reported in an extensive review by Mather and Gunson (1995). Although they do not fit well with recent work by Brown et al (1993), this used a single parameter – vegetation – to develop a classification for the uplands for a much narrower purpose than discussed here. However, the work by Brown et al (1993) relating to the uplands and based on upland semi-natural habitats produces a different subdivision and is based largely on vegetation and has a different and narrower purpose.

A critical issue for decision is the optimum number of zones. While this depends largely on the purpose (which in the case of Scotland is to provide a zonal classification which is soundly based on scientific data and at the same time is meaningful to a wide range of users), then eight to twelve zones would seem to be reasonable. Analysing the material available showed quite clearly that above this level some of the individual zones begin to become very fragmented, whereas below this level there is such a great degree of generalisation as to make the zonation classification less valuable. A map based on 11 zones provided the best balance between contiguity of zones maintaining a degree of homogeneity on the ground and the need to determine a reasonable number of zones. The biogeographic map with 11 zones, generated using the 100 square kilometre resolution species data, was then correlated with soils and climatic data stored at resolutions of 2.5 and 1 square kilometres. The product, as illustrated in Figure 2, is a smoothed 11 zone biogeographic map of Scotland with a boundary resolution of one km.

The proposed biogeographic zone map presented in Figure 2 has benefited from the work to overcome the issues of the first stage map. Despite its apparent complexity the zonation pattern is readily explicable in terms of three key attributes: latitude (east/west), longitude (north/south) and altitude (coastal lowlands < 200m; uplands 200–500m; montane > 500m). This is illustrated diagrammatically on Figure 3.

The resultant zones can be described simply as follows (the zone numbers refer to the numbering on Figure 2):

1. *Montane zones above 500m in altitude*: The Cairngorms (zone 4) and Western Highlands (zone 5) zones are at one end of the climatic spectrum experiencing the lowest temperatures and the highest rainfall in Scotland. Arctic alpine plants characterise both areas. The lower limit of these zones is likely to be very close to the natural tree line.

2. *Upland zones between 200–500m altitude*: The *Grampian fringe* and *Southern Uplands* (zone 2) and the *Western and Southern Highland fringe* (zone 6) zones are notable in the degree to which they span the north/south climatic gradient. Unlike other zones which are characterised by the presence of particular species, these zones are characterised by rapid change in the distribution of different species, the absence of arctic alpine species and the absence of the more oceanic species common nearer the coast.

3. *Coastal Lowland zones between sea level and 200m altitude*: Three zones span the east/west, continental/oceanic divide. The most northerly zone is the *Northern Isles* (Shetland and Orkney, zone 10) characterised by the great diversity of taxa represented (all those used in the analysis with the exception of liverworts) and having a low altitude. *Lewis and North Mainland* (zone 7), an area characterised by the presence of blanket peat and associated species, particularly mosses. The last east/west zone is *Central and Southern Lowlands* (zone 1). This is the largest single zone and is characterised

mainly by vascular plants, including common water plantain and garlic mustard.

4. *West coast zones:* There are three zones in the west coast group and are distinguished from the rest of Scotland by their degree of oceanicity: the combination of high rain fall and relatively warm winters. The *Southern Western Isles* zone (zone 9) has the highest winter temperature of the three zones, and has carbonate loving plants of the machair plus mosses. *Argyll and Inner Hebrides* zone (zone 11) is characterised by high rainfall but the winter temperatures are considerably warmer than upland zones. Representative species are mainly moisture seeking lower plants. The final zone in this group is the *Galloway Coastland* (zone 8) characterised by a low average altitude and relatively low rainfall and with the majority of the representative species at the northern edge of their range.

5. *East Coast Zones:* The only zone in this group, the *Eastern Coastal Lowlands* (zone 3), is characterised by low rainfall and good soils. Seven of the ten characteristic species for this zone are mosses.The zones can be subdivided on account of their large size and spatial discontinuity. The possibilities are: separation of the Northern Isles zones into Orkney and Shetland sub-zones, separation of the Grampian fringe and Southern Upland zones, and separation of the very large Central and Southern Lowlands. Adopting such an approach would produce 11 zones and 17 sub-zones.

The resultant map of biogeographic zones in Scotland represents a definition at only one scale order. To be of greatest value it should be capable of summary to fit into global zonation schemes. This is, in itself, difficult given the diversity of bio-geography in Scotland arising from altitudinal and related climatic factors. Equally, the system should be capable of further subdivision to be of greater value at the local scale. However, the availability of data on a 10 kilometre grid square basis does not, in itself, allow this to happen except on a very judgmental basis.

NATURAL HERITAGE ZONES

The second step in the compilation of natural heritage zones in Scotland is to describe cultural landscape parameters and relate them to the framework of biogeographic zones already devised. Unlike the availability of species distribution data used for the basic compilation, there is no comprehensive dataset on landscape in Scotland. While a number of informal approaches have been undertaken over time, it was only in 1992 that Scottish Natural Heritage began a major assessment of landscape character on a regional basis throughout Scotland. The work is currently in progress and the scale of activity is at 1:50,000. Nevertheless, the method used has been devised to allow aggregation of landscape character for the national level. It is our intention to attempt such summarisation for those parts of Scotland for which the analysis has already been completed.

We are also considering how we might seek to build land use parameters into the scheme. We have already utilised soil distribution data as one of the parameters in defining the basic biogeographical zones. While there is no agreed typology of land use in Scotland there is, as a result of extensive survey, a detailed sub-division of Scotland on a land cover basis, and this information is being related to the biogeographical zones already identified.

The definition of zones needs to be such as to allow a wide range of non-biogeographic material to give further detail to the zones so that, where appropriate for practical purposes, they can be sub-divided. At the same time they can be related to broader scale international zones. In effect, therefore, we shall have a hierarchy of zones but decide on the level which we consider most appropriate for the strategic planning and management of the natural heritage resource in Scotland.

CONCLUSION

The development of a natural heritage zonation system in Scotland is entirely in tune with approaches in other countries seeking to bring together management of environmental resources with social needs, economic opportunities and cultural inheritance. Its implementation should assist in the understanding of the natural heritage, both within SNH, partner organisations and the wider public; act as a framework for developing a natural heritage strategy; assist in the definition of SNH's own programmes and activities locally; provide a means of developing a more integrated approach by the various statutory agencies; and as a result bring about environmental as well as social and economic development.

The Author

Roger Crofts has been Chief Executive of Scottish Natural Heritage since its inception in April 1992. Born in Hinckley, Leicestershire, he was educated at Hinckley Grammar School. He gained a BA in Geography at Liverpool University and a MLitt in coastal geomorphology from Aberdeen University. After training as a secondary school teacher at Leicester University, he was appointed to a research post in Geography at Aberdeen University, and later to a similar position at University College, London. He returned to Scotland in 1974 and spent 17 years working in The Scottish Office covering North Sea oil and gas developments, local government finance, sea fisheries law enforcement, the development of the Highlands and Islands, tourism, and finally nature conservation and the countryside, including leading the Natural Heritage (Scotland) Bill team and the establishment of SNH. His recreational interests are cooking, gardening, flower photography and walking.

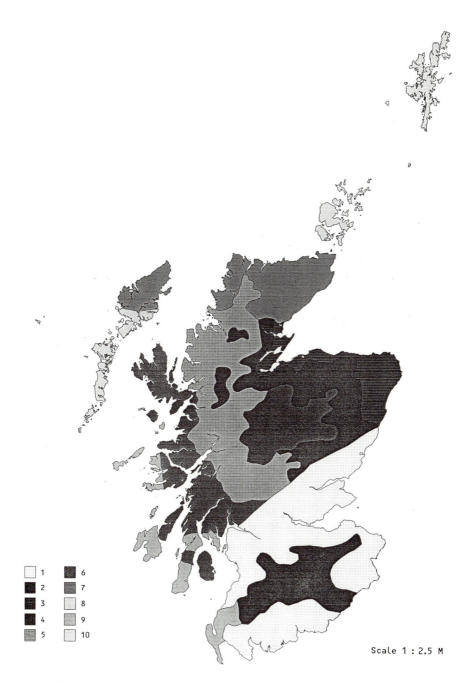

Scale 1 : 2.5 M

Figure 1 First approximation of Biogeographic Zones.

241

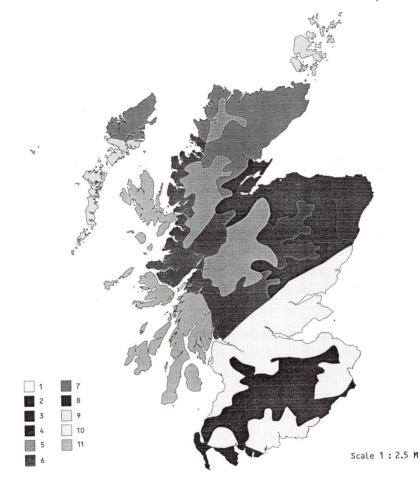

Scale 1 : 2.5 M

Figure 2 Proposed Biogeographic Zones.

1. Central and Southern Lowlands
2. Grampian fringe and Southern Uplands
3. Eastern Coastal Lowlands
4. Cairngorms
5. Western Highlands
6. Western and Southern Highland fringe
7. Lewis and North Mainland
8. Galloway Coastlands
9. Southern Western Isles
10. Northern Isles
11. Argyll and Inner Hebrides

242

References

Bailey, R. G. and Hogg, H. C., *A World Eco-Regions Map for Resource Reporting*, in Environmental Conservation 13, 1986

Bishop, K., Philips, A. and Warren, L., *Protected for Good? Factors Shaping the Future of Protected Areas Policy*, in press

Brown, A., Birks, H. J. B. and Thompson, D. B. A., *A New Biogeographical Classification of the Scottish Uplands: I – Descriptions of Vegetation Blocks and their Spatial Variation, II – Vegetation/Environment Relationships*, in Journal of Ecology 81, 1993

Cairngorms Working Party, *Common-sense and sustainability: a partnership for the Cairngorms*, The Scottish Office, 1993

Carey, P. D., Dring, J. C. M., Hill, M. O., Preston, C. D. and Wright, S. M., *Biogeographical Zones in Scotland.*, SNH Research, Survey and Monitoring Report No. 26, 1994

Carey, P. D., Preston, C. D., Hill, M. O., Usher, M. B. and Wright, S. M., *An Environmentally Defined Biogeographical Zonation of Scotland designed to reflect species distribution*, in Journal of Ecology, in press

Countryside Commission, *The New Map of England: a celebration of the south western landscape*, Countryside Commission, 1994

Countryside Commission, *Countryside Character Programme*, Countryside Commission, 1994

Countryside Commission for Scotland, *Scotland's Scenic Heritage*, CCS, 1978

Countryside Commission for Scotland, *The Mountain Areas of Scotland*, CCS, 1991

Crofts, R., *Protected Landscape and Nature Conservation in Scotland*, in *Protected Landscapes: Where Next?*, Countryside Commission, 1992

Crofts, R., *The Future of 'Protected Areas' in Scotland*, proceedings of Federation of Nature and National Parks in Europe Conference, Battleby, 1993

Crofts, R., *The Environment – Who Cares?*, Occasional Paper No 2, Scottish Natural Heritage, 1995

Elder, J., *The Big Picture: The Sierra Club's Eco-regions Programme*, in Sierra, 79(2), 1994

English Nature, *Natural Areas*, English Nature, 1993

European Council, *Directive on the Conservation of natural habitats and wild fauna and flora*, Council Directive, 92/43/EEC, Brussels, 1992

International Union for the Conservation of Nature, *Criteria for Protected Areas*, IUCN, Switzerland

Lucas, P. H. C., *Protected Landscapes, A guide for policy-makers and planners*, Chapman and Hall, 1992

Mantell, M. A. (ed), *Managing National Parks Responses*, The Conservation Foundation, Washington DC, 1990

Mantell, M. A. and Metzer, P. C., *The Organic Act and the Stewardship of Resources in Park Boundaries*, in *Managing National Park Resources*, Mantell, M. A. (ed), The Conservation Foundation, Washington DC, 1990

Mather, A. S. and Gunson, A. R., *Biogeographical Zones in Scotland, A Review.* Review No. 40, Scottish Natural Heritage, 1995

Nature Conservancy Council, *Guidelines for Selection of Biological SSSIs*, NCC, 1989

Poore, D. and Poore J., *Protected Landscapes: The UK Experience*, IUCN, Switzerland, 1987

Poore, D. and Poore J., *Protected Landscapes in the UK*, Countryside Commission, 1992

Scottish Natural Heritage, *SNH and Sites of Special Scientific Interest*, SNH, 1994

Scottish Natural Heritage, *Checklist of Designations*, SNH, 1994

Scottish Office Environment Department, *Implementation in Great Britain of the Council Directive on the Conservation of Natural Habitats and of Wild Flora and Fauna (92/43/EEC), 'The Habitats Directive'*, The Scottish Office, 1993

US National Parks Service, *Management Policies*, USNPS, Washington DC, 1988

US National Parks Service, *National Parks for the 21st Century: The Vail Agenda*, USNPS, Washington DC, 1992

US National Parks Service, *Sustainable Ecosystems Approach to reorganisation of the National Parks Service*, USNPS, Pacific North West Region, Seattle, 1994

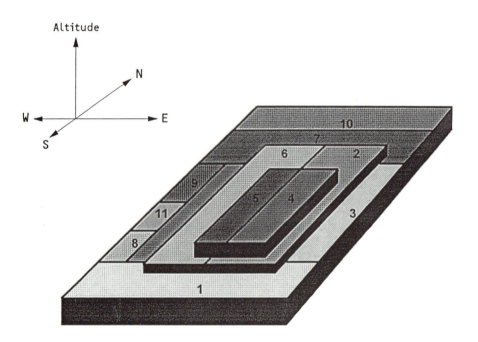

Figure 3 Three-dimentional representation of Biogeographic Zones.

1. Central and Southern Lowlands
2. Grampian fringe and Southern Uplands
3. Eastern Coastal Lowlands
4. Cairngorms
5. Western Highlands
6. Western and Southern Highland fringe
7. Lewis and North Mainland
8. Galloway Coastlands
9. Southern Western Isles
10. Northern Isles
11. Argyll and Inner Hebrides

244

22

HARNESSING HERITAGE ASSETS
The Challenge Facing Local Government

Peter Peacock

Local Government in Scotland has been in a state of flux at least since the General Election of 1992 (and some would even say since Tony Crosland, ex-Labour Government Minister, fired his broadside on Local Government expenditure in the late 1960s). The major reorganisation of 1975 established the concept of strategic authorities, but who could say the two-tier system of Region and District Councils was wholly acceptable to the broad spectrum of political opinion?

We now find ourselves in the midst of yet another major upheaval – this time the removal of the two-tier system of 20 years standing and the creation of 'all purpose' or 'most purpose' unitary authorities. For the sake of simplicity, we will forget about joint committees and agency agreements between different authorities.

While I cannot detect the excitement over reform of local government which accompanied the 1975 Reform, I can sense the acceptance by all concerned in local government that we have to make this reorganisation work if only for the sake of avoiding yet another major review five or ten years hence. The reorganisation does come at a difficult time when local government finance has been pared back and our responsibilities have been somewhat dispersed amongst a plethora of enabling mechanisms, not all immediately subject to the local democratic process.

But with change come opportunities and it is on those opportunities I would like to focus in this paper. The reorganisation gives us a chance to take stock of what local government can deliver and how it can be delivered. Perhaps this point is even more pertinent where authorities are operating in the realm of discretionary services, where they have a real choice as to where they direct resources and effort for the benefit of their communities without being told by Central Government, through statute when and how they should act.

I will concentrate on the way that local government can stimulate awareness and concern for protecting and enhancing its cultural and natural assets as part of its discretionary functions. In the Highlands of Scotland that focus is particularly apt. The influence of man on the environment is still less than in many other regions, and in many ways the environment still dominates the scale and diversity of what we can do to the landscape.

Paradoxically, the remote and often isolated communities of the Highlands have developed a rich social heritage which shows diversity in language, music, habits and pastimes which is unmatched elsewhere in the United Kingdom. More and more we, are recognising that what we have is worth keeping, worth protecting and worth nurturing – not because it adds interest for the tourist, but because for its own sake it contributes to our sense of being and our sense of place – in other words our identity.

PLACING A VALUE ON OUR CULTURAL AND NATURAL ASSETS

The Concise Oxford Dictionary defines 'assets' as advantageous possessions, wealth, property, capital. In other words, these are resources that are worth investiing in because of their intrinsic value and the benefits they will bring in future years.

We can distinguish between cultural and natural assets for the sake of definitions, but we recognise the interdependence of each in a world increasingly influenced by man. Even here in the Highlands, we recognise that the landscape we have to-day is largely a product of thousands of years of tree felling, grazing and tillage. Only the mountain tops or the deepest ravines have escaped the direct hand of man – that is until the Industrial Revolution spread its sulphiric acid bearing rain.

But what of these valued assets? Why are they of value and why should we want to protect them for our own benefit and that of future generations?

I will now use that difficult word 'heritage', which is the currency of this volume to develop my theme further. In my thinking the heritage consists of all those assets of value which contribute to the 'rootedness' of a society (Gee, 1995). Most aspects of heritage have come to us from previous generations and we want to pass them on to our children or share them with others because we have a high regard or respect for them as individual entities or because of the context in which we interact with them. Heritage can include anything that gives a community or region its special identity, landscape, language, architecture, traditional customs and occupations, clothing, flora and fauna. As I have indicated, there is often a great deal of interdependence between these different aspects of heritage with the survival of one aspect often dependent on another; characteristic crofting landscapes for example depend on a particular way of life.

These aspects of heritage are not static. They change and evolve to external and internal pressures. The modern problem we face is one of rapid change which often results in loss of heritage without adequate thought or debate. The challenge for society as a whole, and in my case, local government in particular, is to manage change in such a way that we can absorb the inherited experiences from one generation to another and appreciate their values as assets. There are various ways of placing values on heritage. I will adopt the system based upon Lipe (1984).

1. *Information/Evidence Value*: Information and evidence are the basic building blocks of awareness and understanding.

2. *Aesthetic Value:* The heritage is often valued for its visual qualities. Many examples of Highland landscapes have great aesthetic value, as do examples of art, craft, music or writing.

3. *Associative Value:* Places or objects may be associated with famous events or people in the past. They may have inspired books, paintings or songs.

4. *Symbolic Value:* Sometimes associative values are particularly strong. A place or an artefact may be a symbol of cultural, political or religious identity. Such symbols can become icons for communities and have enormous power.

5. *Economic Value:* Increasingly, the importance of heritage as part of tourism is seen to have substantial economic benefit. Good local government will ensure that those benefits are shared and managed in a sustainable way.

6. *Ecological Value:* Ecosystems fundamentally support human life, but they have value in themselves, appealing to our aesthetic sense or our sense of belonging to the web of life which uniquely, as far as we know, characterises this planet.

These value systems can be cut many ways. Museologists also talk about 'user values', 'option values', 'existence values' and 'bequest values' in a specific museums context. I propose to keep to the bigger picture which leads me to conclude that these powerful and evocative concepts need to be harnessed for the benefit of the communities we represent in local government. The well-being of our communities, whether it be our health, our ability to be economically active and self supporting or our ability to lend support to others who are less advantaged, lies at the hear of local government.

Our cultural and natural heritage affect every aspect of life and by extension every area of the work of local government. The powerful forces at work here means that it would be a fool indeed who came into a community, especially a close-knit Highland community, and stamped all over their traditions: better to respect those traditions and turn them to advantage for the community and the wider area.

The fact that we have been so cavalier with our heritage in the past has reaped a whirlwind of discontent and grievance that is all too evident in the Highlands and the world at large to-day. Communities with an understanding of the human and natural forces that have shaped their development and which have preserved their unique identity have a strong basis for confident development in the future.

This is not of course, just an exercise in nostalgia. The preservation and presentation of heritage creates wealth through tourism and leisure. Any passing reference to the Highland economy would acknowledge the crucial importance of tourism in generating wealth. MacKay (1995) estimates that despite continuing falls in domestic tourism in Scotland, the Highlands and Islands still provide a destination for 18% of tourists coming to the country from a population base of about 5% of the total for Scotland as a whole. At the individual community level this dependency on tourism is significantly increased in many of our remoter and more sparsely populated areas. The connection between remoteness, seemingly empty landscapes, discrete small rural communities and the aspirations of tourists to experience this other world from their everyday hustle and bustle in cities is well made and something we in local government in the Highlands must respect if we are to sustain our position in the tourism market.

To sum up, we place a value on our heritage for its own sake because it lends to that sense of belonging which is necessary for well balanced and self-confident communities. Respecting the importance of our heritage and recognising it has economic value in attracting tourists to come and experience it, consolidates my view that local government has to develop strong policies in partnership with others to harness the opportunities available.

McCrone et al (1995) suggests all is not well with our approach to heritage. In a tour de force of sociological concepts from manufactured authenticity to post-modernism and ethnicity his argument can be reduced to saying that because our heritage has been highjacked by powerful political forces, our ambivalence towards it is largely because we (that is the common people) have not had much of a hand in creating it. That is solid fare for me, for I believe that the worst thing that local government can do is leave behind the people it represents. We need to find new and better ways of engaging our constituents.

THE SCOPE AND RESPONSIBILITIES OF LOCAL AUTHORITIES

Cultural and natural heritage assets permeate every aspect of local government. The complexity of our environment is beyond our immediate control, but Local Agenda 21 arising from the Rio Summit of 1992, places a responsibility on local government, amongst others, to pursue sustainable development so that the resource base of our planet and its intricate web of living organisms is not irreparable damaged, and where possible is enhanced. Sustainable development rejects single minded economic gain at the expense of others. It seeks to ensure a decent quality of life for everyone, whilst preserving and enhancing what is good about our communities.

Local Agenda 21 emphasises the need for local involvement in decision making if basic resources are to be protected for future generations, and offers the opportunity for people to become pro- active about the future of their communities. Both our natural and cultural heritage articulate a collective, as well as an individual, sense of identity, so it is entirely appropriate that local government should be at the forefront of the process of representing community aspirations in this field, and facilitating their development. Within local authorities there is a need for a vision of how communities may be empowered by encouraging community action in heritage at the local level. Such developments should be welcomed and supported by the local authorities as part of their corporate strategies.

The Association of District Councils of England and Wales (1995) has offered a case for integrated cultural services to be delivered by the new unitary authorities south of the Border. They argue for a broad view of culture, both to develop a sense of identity amongst communities and to relate that to regional, national and international perspectives. Cultural Services often represent the most positive public face of local authority activity.

They encourage people to operate collectively. They bring people together in large numbers to attend events. They foster community pride and they open channels of communication. They offer opportunities to develop social skills through the management of projects and to pass skills and knowledge to others. Over a broad range of activity from health and welfare to education, environmental issues and economic development local government has 'the' crucial role in building communities which are confident, proud of their identity and balanced in their view of the world.

THE SPECIAL PLACE OF LANGUAGE IN COMMUNITY IDENTITY

I could not present this paper without making reference to the special place that language has in the identity of the Highlands. The support of Comunn na Gàidhlig for the event which led to this volume, and the policies developed by Highland Regional Council and most of the constituent District Councils show that there is a precious regard for the language of the Gael, even though I am sad to say most of the Highland population cannot speak or understand Gaelic. It faces a critical situation in its survival. It will require a monumental effort by local authorities, agencies and the voluntary sector to turn the corner by the Millennium, but that is the prospect we can hope for if the issue is tackled in an integrated way (Pedersen, 1993).

Local government has a key role to play in the further development of Gaelic medium education which at present is one of the few bright spots of growth in an otherwise declining situation (a result of an aged, Gaelic speaking generation now reducing). Likewise, the new Cultural and Leisure Services function within the Highland Council will enable a more focused approach to Gaelic development in the voluntary sector through support for the arts and heritage.

The new Council will need to develop a strong voice in encouraging and facilitating the Media to grow its Gaelic output and research diverse ways of exposing the population of the Highlands to their language heritage. The growth of bilingual road signs and bilingual town centre signs through the actions of Highland Regional Council and the Fionan project respectively, not only offer the desired exposure of the language and a valued status for it, but many authorities now recognise the economic benefit to be gained from developing Gaelic. This has effect on employment growth for Gaelic speakers (particularly Media-related), but there is also an identifiable benefit associated with cultural tourism. Visitors to the Highlands appreciate the difference in reinforcing this Gaelic identity.

The Highlands of course has a diverse range of communities. It would be remiss of me to omit a mention of the dialects of Scots language which still exist. Many visitors who have been to Avoch or Wick will realise the impenetrable nature of these local dialects. I am not suggesting that the local authority needs to develop a major strategy for protecting 'Auchy', but as part of our function to recognise and protect local identities, we must allow for local expression of ownership and action if required.

METHODS OF DELIVERY

Local government has the responsibility for meeting community aspirations through the democratic process by setting policy and agreeing the necessary resources to implement that policy. Given the problems we have in financing local government, I would not say that the process from policy to implementation is an easy path. This is one of the most frustrating aspects of trying to develop local authority services in Scotland today. We so use our ingenuity and talents to develop different funding models and different ways of achieving simple results on the ground that we wonder just what could be achieved if we had the proper resources. However, the silver lining to this cloud is that, in overcoming the funding problems, we are achieving another major objective.

Financial constraints are driving us to look at many different methods for delivery of services; forcing us into funding partnerships, finding new ways through private sector financing, to procure capital schemes, or developing trusts and limited companies through voluntary effort in our local communities. At the end of the day the processes we are adopting are achieving the objectives of increasing community awareness and ownership of different aspects of local authority services. This is particularly the case in the heritage field.

Because we have to share our objectives with so many different parties, they have to be clear and concise. Projects now need to be monitored for their effectiveness against the original objectives set. There has to be satisfaction, all round, that projects are worthwhile and they will be sustainable, both environmentally and economically. Local government, using its democratic mandate, will therefore take a key role in promoting guiding principles for heritage and use those principles as a basis for strategic planning of resources. Resources in turn will be directed at where they are most needed.

In the Highlands, because of force of circumstance or the opportunities provided in having discrete communities to deal with, we have developed new ways of engaging people at a local level. Gibson (1994) set out a model for decision making within communities which gave rise to ownership and responsibility amongst locals for such aspects of civic life as the design of houses or open spaces. We have adapted this 'Planning for Real' methodology to our own circumstances in the Highlands and carried it further into the specific subject area of heritage. By engaging local communities in developing 'Heritage Audits' and getting involved in the process of analysing what is available and accessible, and what priority for development can be placed on different sites, we are truly seeking the full involvement of local people.

The fact that such activity has major benefit for tourism dominated economies, helps the process considerably. The process also achieves a full partnership between the local authority, intent in helping the local community to develop its heritage assets, and the local community which will expect resources to be applied to achieve the agreed programme of implementation. In Ross and Cromarty, the District Council has for many years operated an enabling function in heritage (see next chapter by Graham Watson), by funding small museums based on the collecting efforts of interested local groups. In France, this enabling model would be a modification of the comuse concept.

AN INTEGRATED APPROACH

Local Government reform provides opportunities to restructure heritage services to reflect better the political and public service contexts of to-day, which are substantially different from 1975. Each new Council has the opportunity to define its own concept of heritage to meet the aspirations of its communities. There is an opportunity to avoid the departmentalism and sectoralism which has dominated public service in this country for so long.

The corporate approach, enabling individual local authorities to establish their agendas, develop strong policies and ensure appropriate resources are made available, is the goal in front of us. We will still need to develop 'critical mass' in pulling professionals together to work out policies, but the sum of the whole corporate strategy will be greater than any single department or any single committee could deliver.

Local Government will need to provide leadership on behalf of local communities in dealing with Central Government and its agencies. The 'Quango' problem will be addressed by ensuring that local government has a view, democratically derived for each area of activity in which Quasi-autonomous non-governmental organisations involve themselves. Likewise, it will offer leadership on behalf of Community Councils in developing their effectiveness.

The Association of District Councils (1995) offered three themes for developing cultural services which the Highland Council would do well to apply across the range of its heritage responsibilities. They were:

- Protecting the Past
- Enhancing the Present
- Developing the Future

As we look forward to the new Highland Council taking up its responsibilities in 1996, I suggest these themes as a fitting slogan for the heritage function within the new Highland Council.

The Author

Peter Peacock was educated at Hawick High School and holds qualifications in Youth Work and Community Studies from Jordanhill College of Education. A consultant in the field of Training, Organisation and Policy, he became Vice Convener of Highland Regional Council in 1990 and is Convener Designate of the new Highland Council. His distinguished career in Local Government has included chairing committees responsible for finance, budget and strategy, and outdoor education. He is Vice President of the Convention of Scottish Local Authorities and a member of the Scottish Valuation Advisory Council. His hobbies include golf, rugby, bird watching and politics.

The author is grateful to William McDermott for his enthusiastic support in the drafting of this paper, and appreciative thanks go to Arthur McCourt for its delivery at the Convention in Inverness.

References

Gee, K., *Wonder Web*, in *Museum Journal*, March 1995, p19

Gibson, T., *Showing What You Mean (Not Just Talking About It)*, RRA Notes Special Issue No. 21 on the Application of Participatory Inquiry in Urban Areas, 1994

Lipe, W. D., *Value and Meaning in Cultural Resources*, on Approaches to the Archaeological Heritage, (pp 1– 11), Ed. Cleere, Henry, 1984

McCrone, D. et al *Scotland the Brand: The Making of Scottish Heritage* Edinburgh University Press, 1995

Mackay, T., *Scottish Tourism Commentary*, Mackay Tourism Consultants, 1995

Pedersen, R. N., *The Dynamics of Gaelic Development*, Airadhart le Gàidhlig, Highlands and Islands Enterprise, 1993

23

MUSEUMS FROM THE GROUND UP
A Community Approach to Development

Graham Watson

Ross and Cromarty has a unique partnership between the local authority and independent museums. Many authorities give grants to independent museums, but Ross and Cromarty District Council chooses to fulfil its statutory leisure function through the independent sector. There is no local authority museum building. Instead these are seven independent museums, run by local Trusts providing a full range of displays, exhibitions and outreach programmes. There is also an active programme of service development on the Council's part. This ensures the service levels are adequate, and providing value for money. It also enables communities to be directly involved in preserving and interpreting their heritage.

This paper seeks to enable the reader to make a value for money judgement on the delivery of museum services through a community based approach. It also tries to show that museums and heritage can do more for a local authority than deliver a leisure function. It seeks to demonstrate that spending on museums and heritage can bring social, economic, and educational returns, adding value to the initial investment of time and resources.

The paper shows that, to gain these returns, the investment must be sustained, and that the approach must be rooted in the community. If it is not, there is a danger that the heritage of the Highlands will become 'plastic' and the supposed 'golden egg' that will sustain cultural tourism in the Highlands destroyed. Supporting the independent sector is not a euphemism for 'contracting out', in the sense of a money saving exercise. The cost to the Council of a heritage service is currently £4.30 per head of population. This is broadly in line with Audit Commission figures for England and Wales. The turnover is nearer £420,000. At these levels, returns become very important.

CREATING AN INDEPENDENT SERVICE

Ross and Cromarty District Council began its support for museums in 1985. It started in a traditional way, by providing itinerant curatorial support to the then four independent museums. These museums were run by local committees and volunteers. The committee structure was based on a club constitution. Members paid a fee, and elected a committee. In most cases, however, the day to day running had become reliant on one individual, or at best a small group. It was believed, rightly, that museum collections need professional care. A cheap way for an authority to provide an adequate service was for it to provide a professional collection carer who could serve a number of museums.

Unfortunately, this approach missed a couple of vital points. First of all much of the museums profession, and thereby those who receive advice from it, fall in to the trap of assuming that what it is in existence for, namely ensuring the long term survival of the material past, is more than a necessary by-product of what society wants from its museums. Society seeks a sense of a stable present through an understood past, which demonstrates a broad improvement on what has gone before. This could be the subject of numerous articles. It is sufficient here to point out that for many museum professionals the means have, quite literally, become the ends. Collection care for its own sake, because it is a 'good thing'.

The museum trusts certainly needed help with collection care, to ensure the physical survival of items in their custody. But they also needed support to improve displays, financial and administrative services, and to determine strategies and directions. In addition, assistance was needed with educational, outreach and access programmes without which preservation of objects is meaningless for anyone other than those who see themselves as having ownership. Furthermore, for all the availability of financial support, museum trusts valued their independence and were suspicious of too close a partnership with local government.

In 1987, the Council reviewed its support structure. The prevailing culture was one of enabling. This meant that the Council saw its role as, where possible, assisting communities to provide their own services, rather than direct provision from a central source. The existing museum structure fitted readily into this. The review resulted in a relaunched 'Museums Section' whose function was to provide grant support and advice, and to enable the museums to be truly independent of the Council. This meant grant levels and support increasing, and a development programme that took the museums from standard, ageing displays, to museums fully meeting the standards of museum registration, employing professional curatorial staff, having displays themed to attract a tourist market, while improving services to the local community.

The guiding principle was one of enabling museums to do for themselves, rather than doing things on the trust's behalf. The approach was assisted by registration under the aegis of the Museums and Galleries Commission in 1988. This provided a set of minimum standards, including museum trust constitutions. This allowed the Council to clearly define what was a museum, for support purposes. The Council did not see its role as full funders of community museums. First of all this would discourage true independence, and, secondly, if a diverse service spread over the district was to be achieved, it was not affordable. Tourist visitors paying entry would subsidise a local service. The Council would guarantee grants which covered roughly one-third of agreed running costs, thus covering a large part of the non-profit making activities of a museum (Lord and Lord, 1987). Grants currently vary from between £13,000 and £22,000 depending on scale, returns, and historical precedence. This approach had its consequences. It meant that the product the visitor was paying for had to be one which gave value for money. The tourist visitor looks for ways of spending leisure time constructively, a slightly different role for museum displays than that of the traditional urban museum.

In marketing themselves, museums found that a theme helped. This theme tended to reflect either the strength of the collections, or a unique aspect of the history of the community. The museums were encouraged to see themselves as the equivalent of small businesses. The consequence of this was improved services to the local community. A themed display, with gradual, developmental change, is unlikely to attract repeat visits, and small museums do not have the room for blockbuster exhibitions. Thus local services concentrated on outreach programmes. Events and activities for adults and children, lectures and talks, archaeology and history clubs, and participation in a volunteer programme has become the mainstay of the museums relevance to the local community. The need for this has underpinned the need for paid support for these museums.

This programme is very time dependent, and beyond the resources of a voluntary committee. For its grant, which is set at a level which enables the museum to appoint staff, the Council sees services targeted locally, as well as for visitors. The grant is not calculated on staff costs, but as a contribution towards each museums non income generating activities. It would be simplistic to argue that no tourist participate in educational activities, and no locals have leisure time.

To ensure that the range of services is across the board, and that standards are maintained, the Council has introduced targets. These are agreed with the each trust in advance annually, and cover three main areas. These are collection care, visitor services, and management and administration. Collection care targets build on museum registration, and seek to ensure levels of documentation, conservation and storage, as well as the environmental conditions in stores and display areas. Visitor service targets cover not only standards of displays and opening hours, but the level of educational and outreach work provided, expressed in annual participation hours. Management targets ensure that marketing, staff training, information flow and the like are of high standards. These are measured where possible, and a set of ratios are used to compare performance.

In practical terms, each museum has strengths and weaknesses. It would be fair to say that each trust agrees that the areas defined by the targets are important. However, the detailed measurement some find irksome, and the ratios are only really used by the Council. The targets have, on occasion, been used to coerce a reluctant trust, but only rarely, as the targets are not imposed, but agreed in advance of grants being set. The dialogue is an important element of the partnership, and the long term adoption of the principles contained should be normal practice. Broadly, this has happened, and the targets are now accepted as a fact of life. The reality of their working is, I believe, no more than the normal disputes between administrators and service deliverers. The administrators do not appreciate the extra work measuring imposes on already busy staff. Non-administrators do not fully recognise that those charged with bidding for resources need proof of service delivery, and at least to be seen to have facts and figures at their fingertips, even if these are not subsequently used in a sophisticated way.

In 1987, museums in Ross and Cromarty were seen as contributing primarily to the Council's economic objectives. Directly, these were job creation and underpinning Ross and Cromarty as a Tourist destination. Cromarty Courthouse, for example, gained support for its projected thirteen direct and indirect jobs, and the contribution it would make to the tourist industry. Other recent projects have been judged on the same criteria. This has allowed each to attract significant funding from other public agencies, namely the Highlands and Islands Enterprise network and Objective One European funding.

The last few years have seen a significant drop in tourist numbers to the Highlands, in the region of 20% in the last five years. Last year alone, 1994, saw a 20% drop across the board in museums in Ross and Cromarty. It is difficult to judge the success of investment in individual projects against such a backdrop. Clearly other pressures, outside of the Highlands, are affecting tourist trade. However, the agencies continue to believe that investment in heritage projects for their job creating potential is worthwhile. The local economy is underpinned at the least, if not actively stimulated.

Cromarty Courthouse has a been the focus for publicity about the quality of Highland attractions. Without detailed analysis much comment must be anecdotal. Two tearooms have opened on the route along the Black Isle to Cromarty, and the tea-rooms in Cromarty have survived the current downturn. The Courthouse figures, up to 1994, suggested that the numbers of tourists visiting remained fairly static. What did come as a surprise was the number of people from the Highlands who visited the museum, and continued to do so. Even though the Courthouse has not reached its potential yet, it is clear that Cromarty is firmly a destination for the day-trip market, which seems to be remaining steady. The local market as a base for development is perhaps undervalued by the development agencies.

Heritage is not, and cannot be, the panacea for the economic ills of the Highlands. However, it is a suitable medium for public investment, being owned by no individual. It underpins much of what the visitor market is trying to achieve. The public/private sector partnership between trusts, local authorities and development agencies has set a quality level which acts as an industry benchmark. It is interesting to see retail outlets such as that at Brodie, adopt the standards and values of the heritage sector after many years of influence being the other way round. The underpinning of the market is exampled by the planned 'Kings Route' This trail will follow the route taken by James IV on Pilgrimage to Tain. It will run the length of the Black Isle, cross the Cromarty Ferry, and run through Easter Ross to Tain. It will link a key series of attractions, but also underpin rural transport and local businesses.

In addition to the direct returns in terms of jobs, the Council sought to promote business expertise in the community. It was also thought that the promotion of small businesses in the community might promote entrepreneurial values, as outlined by Johannisson (1983, 24) and Jackson (1982)). A recent major study has suggested that the motivations of those participating in the management of these museums precludes such a result (Doughty, 1994). Trustees are motivated by a desire to help the community, to 'put something back'.

Figure 1 Market Day in Cromarty 1620 by Michael J Taylor.

Few see the link between museums and businesses. However, the existence of enterprises carrying out many of the functions of small businesses, marketing, product development, strategic planning, budget control and the like, is an opportunity for the community to pick up the values and skills of the business world. There are signs that some of the volunteers are seeking these skills, and the Curator provides a role model when speaking to schools and local groups. A readily understood example will be the role model of a female executive that some of the curators provide for their community. With joint medical practises, closure of small schools, and shared church congregations, for some children museum staff provide some of the few examples of professionals working in their own community.

The Council now has a set of published objectives which include social as well as economic returns. At a simple level it seeks to underpin the community values of fragile rural areas. The present is the result of what has happened in the past. This is true for individuals and for groups at all levels, club, community and nation. Thus a community is the result of its past. An understanding of that past can give an insight into the present. Communities under threat in the present, through economic and social factors, can gain strength and confidence through past successes. Working together for the collective good can be promoted through past examples where this has worked.

These examples gain potency when they are taken from the collective experience of the community concerned. Museums embody more than objects from the past. They are endowed with the spirit of the community they serve, storehouses of collective values and experiences; a symbol of the community itself, (for the consciousness of communities and the creations of symbols see Cohen, 1985). This may sound mere rhetoric, but may go some way to explaining why, in times of economic constraints, museums across the country remain in receipt of some level of public sector funding, and remain outside the scope of the governments privatisation programme. It may also explain why they tend to appear high on a community's development agenda. They have a fundamental role in community development.

A community is made up of individuals, and their common experiences go to form the sense of identity that a given community has. An outsider is someone who does not have a knowledge of the common experiences, and the resulting common values, that have been absorbed naturally by the local. With a large body of 'incomers' the pressure to change common values can create stress. However, by giving the community a chance to overtly express their values in a neutral environment, and by giving the incomer access to the underpinning history that has led to the development of these values, a sense of pride and belonging can be engendered.

GROAM HOUSE MUSEUM

In 1989 Groam House was the responsibility of Fortrose and Rosemarkie Community Council. It was managed, and run day-to-day, by Elizabeth Marshall. She received a small honorarium, but gave her heart and soul, and much of her time, to the museum. Groam House held a collection of Pictish stones, including the internationally important Rosemarkie stone, as well as a collection of local artefacts typical of a small burgh museum. The museum received about 3,000 visitors annually, and charged a small entrance fee. Apart from an assistant who acted as a museum attendant, local participation was small, although pride in the museum was fierce.

Museum Registration showed that the Community Council did not have powers to run a museum. The members were enthusiastic for increased local participation provided that control did not pass from local hands. It was decided to set up a Trust, made up of local people, with a separate management committee. This committee was elected from members of a society responsible for the day-to-day management of the museum. This ensured that full participation was available to anyone volunteering, but that the local trustees retained ultimate control.

Through discussion, it was agreed to a complete refurbishment of the Museum, themed on the collection of Pictish material. Groam House became a 'Pictish Centre'. The displays centred on the stones and their outstanding art. The history of the Pictish period in the area was displayed through text panels and a audio-visual area consisting of a specially commissioned twelve minute video. Over the next three years visitor numbers grew to 7,000, and membership of the trust numbered over 100. A research library was developed, and the museum was responsible for collating the first systematic collection of photographs of Pictish sculpture. This has since been copied by the Royal Commission on Ancient Monuments of Scotland. The museum also co-ordinates and publishes an annual academic lecture which brings lecturers of national standing to Rosemarkie each year.

Mindful of their responsibilities locally, and that theming was a marketing ploy, not a raison d'etre, in 1995 the Trust raised £40,000 to build a mezzanine floor to provide changing exhibition space. They also carry out a full programme of outreach activities, aimed particularly at children. Elizabeth Marshall (nee Sutherland) has now retired, and the Trust employ a full time curator. However, retirement has seen a seminal work on the Picts, (Sutherland, 1994) and she remains active on the Committee.

The local community is highly active, not just on the committee, but as volunteers. The volunteers staff the museum daily in the summer months, and over the weekends in winter. This has greatly extended opening hours and accessibility. A training programme ensure that they have a high degree of knowledge should visitors wish to find out more about the Picts. This also serves to give the volunteers confidence. Many, particularly from further afield, have an interest in the Picts and participate improve their knowledge. The training programme includes customer care and opportunities to participate in different aspects of the museums work, including marketing and fund-raising. How this impacts on the community will be explored below.

THE SEABOARD ANCESTORS PROJECT

The Seaboard villages are grouped on the coast in the Tarbat peninsula. In the 1970's they saw a massive influx of workers taken on by the Nigg fabrication yard. Since then they have seen large scale unemployment as the yard ran down. Such a large influx of visitors created problems, and a need for the public agencies to help foster community identity. One of a number of projects was carried out by the Heritage section and was built around the family history of individual children at the local school.

Each child was encouraged to talk about the experiences in their own families pasts, what there grandparents did, where the family came from, and so on. These stories were shared in a classroom project. Two points were emphasised to the children. First of all, that at sometime everyone had been an incomer to the village. In fact the villages had been creations of the nineteenth century clearances, and this was retained in the local collective memory although the significance of the point had not been taken on board. Secondly, whether a child was a recent incomer, or part of an established local family, each had an interesting story to tell.

EDUCATIONAL RETURNS

Museums and heritage projects offer both formal and informal education opportunities. They also provide a base for skills training and personal development. The museums in Ross and Cromarty do this through their individual volunteers programme, and through the appointment and training of professional curatorial staff. Recently, this policy has begun to see a pool of people training for professional qualifications in museum studies, to fill a market need for trained staff.

Museums also cater for a social need in providing opportunities for local people, particularly elderly volunteers to meet and talk to visitors. In Gairloch nearly 10% of the population, 80 out of 800 people, are involved with the museum in a voluntary capacity. An example of how their participation can have wider value is seen in the issue of speaking Gaelic. The competing concern of the decline of Gaelic as a spoken language, and antipathy towards it in Highland communities is still a real issue. Many locals who know some Gaelic are reluctant to use it because they do not feel proficient in its use.

An approach was made to the volunteers where it was stressed that even if they only knew a little of the language, the museum would welcome its use with visitors. Gaelic speakers among the volunteers were encouraged to wear badges stating that they spoke a little Gaelic. This collective action gave many the confidence to use their Gaelic in public for the first time. It also immeasurably enhanced the visitor experience. This small step is another rung in the ladder of hearing Gaelic used in everyday situations on the mainland. The same opportunity exists for gentle development in any area from communication skills to computer literacy.

HERITAGE VALUES

Heritage has certain intrinsic values in its own right. These can be described as information, associative, aesthetic, economic and symbolic values (Highlands and Islands Museums Forum, 1994, 4). An aim of the Council is to preserve and interpret heritage for the benefit of society. However, the dangers of the sole driving force of this being economic factors is apparent

(Kockel, 1994). This point was forcibly driven home at a previous Robert Gordon Heritage Convention by Phillip Hills (Fladmark, 1994, 89–100), when he accused much of the industry of creating a fake heritage. Many of the points made by Kockel and Hills are valid. However, I would argue that professionalising the approach to research and interpretation, through trained staff, is part of the answer. The second part is to let the community speak for themselves. If the community chooses to tell its own story, rather than importing a design and build company to carry out the work wholesale, then a story closer to the real past must be the result.

However, enabling the community to interpret its own past has inherent dangers. The past is always reflected through the lens of the present. Even with a professional curatorial approach, the 'history' of a community, may be overtaken by the mythical views its members have of their own past. Where the story of Sir Hector MacDonald is told in the Highlands, there is scant mention of the charges that led him to commit suicide.

Some historians have argued that the clearances have been manipulated by underplaying what would have been the results had the communities not been cleared from the land in terms of over intensive farming and the resultant disease and famine. The morality of the present must always impinge on the past in anything but a pure academic situation. No late twentieth century museum tries to survive on academic research alone. However, the survival chances of a museum telling the clearances story without discussing the moral issues would be slim. The creation of a myth can be for positive reasons.

The situation is further complicated if a required result of investment in a project is the strengthening a community. A whole series of questions come rushing to the fore, here. None of them have easy answers. Are myths not a attempts by communities to explain what happened in the past in terms relevant to the present? Could a bald presentation of what actually happened serve to undermine current community values? Indeed, are all community values intrinsically good, and does the state have the right to manipulate these for its own ends? What about bad values, racism and sexism for example; do museums and their funders have the right to attempt to change the values held by communities, and can this be morally done overtly? An attempt has been made to write this paper using non-gender specific language. Is this legitimate when it is the authors choice, when it is the editors practice, the publishers policy? When is political correctness state manipulation? As Hills pointed out (Fladmark, 1995, 93) heritage as cultural asset is a positive phenomena. As a commodity it has inherent dangers. But there is also the danger of the manipulation of cultural assets for political or social gain.

CONCLUSIONS

There are a number of areas in which a heritage funder can look for returns. These include job creation, underpinning a local economy, supporting and fostering community values, personal and group development opportunities, and the preservation of identity and culture. In some areas the Ross and Cromarty experience has provided higher returns than in others. At a museum level, the service is spread across the community, with seven museums employing the equivalent of seven professional staff. This is at a cost equivalent to that of running a single site local authority service. The community are involved at every level, with some 180 volunteers, and nearly 100 committee members and trustees. Each museum is fully registered with the Museums and Galleries Commission, and most are commended or above under various quality schemes run by the Association of Scottish Visitor Attractions and the Scottish Tourist Board. Most of the museums have won awards, Cromarty Courthouse's latest count being eleven.

There is little doubt that the successes are determined by the partnership between community and local authority, which has led to a professionalisation of approach without losing the authentic voice of 'real' culture. Through this approach it is hoped to avoid the conflict between the heritage conservation sector and the tourism industry so graphically illustrated by the Irish experience as outlined by Patrick Duffy, (1994, 84). The approach is not a cheap option, but one which does seem to provide value for money, as well as being rooted in solid museum and heritage values.

The Author

Graham Watson manages the Heritage Section of Ross and Cromarty District Council. His role is to advise the Council on heritage policy and to provide support and advice to independent trusts on museum and business matters. He sits on the board of the Scottish Museums Council, and is Vice President of the Scottish Museums Federation. He holds an MA in Archaeology and Medieval History, a Masters Degree in Entrepreneurial Studies from Stirling University, and the professional diploma of the Museums Association. Recent work includes a review of strategic planning in the not-for-profit sector in Clarke-Hill, C. and Glaister, K., (1995), *Case Studies in Strategic Management*, Pitman, London.

References

Cohen, A. P., *The Symbolic Construction of Community*, Routledge, 1985

Doughty, S., *A Training Needs Analysis for Ross and Cromarty District Council Museums Section*, Inverness, 1994

Duffy, P., *Conflicts in Heritage and Tourism*, in Kockel, U., (ed), *Cultural Tourism and Development: The Case of Ireland*, Liverpool University Press, 1994

Highlands and Islands Museums Forum, *A Heritage Strategy for the Highlands*, Highlands and Islands Museums Forum, Inverness, 1994

Hills, P., *The Cultural Potency of Scotland* in Fladmark, J. M., (ed), *Cultural Tourism*, Donhead, 1994

Jackson, G., *The Identification and Development of Entrepreneurs: Experience from New Enterprise Promotion in North Wales* in Webb, T. D., Quince, T. A., and Watkins, D. S., *Small Business Research: The Development of Entrepreneurs*, Gower, 1982

Johannisson, B., *Swedish Evidence for the Potential of Local Entrepreneurship* in European Small Business Journal, 1(2), 11–25, 1983

Kockel, U., *Culture, Tourism and Development: A View from the Periphery*, in Kockel, U., (ed), *Cultural Tourism and Development: The Case of Ireland*, Liverpool University Press, 1994

Lord, B., and Lord, G., The Cost of Collecting, HMSO, 1987

Museums and Galleries Commission, *A Scheme For Museum Registration*, Museums and Galleries Commission, 1988

Sutherland, E., *In Search of the Picts*, Constable, 1994

24

ON THE OTHER SIDE OF SORROW
Nature and People in the Scottish Highlands

James Hunter

The upper reaches of Glen Shiel, in the part of the Scottish Highlands called Kintail, are steep and rocky. A road and a river jostle here for elbow-room as they plunge through a series of narrow gorges. Especially in winter, when deep snow drives them down from the high tops, red deer are everywhere. Now and then, in places too precipitous even for deer, you glimpse long-haired, big-horned goats. But there are few other signs of life; certainly no sign of human habitation; not even when you reach the part of the glen where the mountains, as it were, draw back a little to make room for several fields and some small areas of woodland.

This spot, so larger-scale maps tell you, is Achadh nan Seileach, a Gaelic phrase denoting both the relative flatness of the place and the presence here of willow trees. In any broadly similar part of Europe – in Norway, for example – this is where you might expect to find a village. But the Scottish Highlands, though their physical structure and their climate give them something of the appearance of the region to the west and north of Oslo, have had a very different history from Rogaland, Hordaland or Nord Trøndelag. There is no settlement to be seen in the vicinity of Achadh nan Seileach. What can be seen, however, and with no great effort on your part, is a good deal of evidence that Achadh nan Seileach was not always the unpopulated locality it is today.

Leave your car by the roadside. Take a look around the grassy meadows which slope gently towards the River Shiel, its pace a lot less hectic here than further up the glen. On both sides of the river, and especially on its northern bank, you quickly come across the remains of several stone-built homes. The walls of one or two of these still stand about a metre clear of their surroundings. Others are reduced now to little more than roughly squared-off undulations in the turf.

Samuel Johnson and James Boswell, two of eighteenth century Britain's leading literary figures, came this way in the course of the trip they made from London to the Hebrides in 1773; leaving Inverness on 30 August; spending that night at Fort Augustus; staying the following night in Glen Moriston; getting to Achadh nan Seileach – with their four horses, their servant and their two guides – on the afternoon of 1 September.

Precisely how many people lived in Achadh nan Seileach in 1773 there is now no way of knowing; perhaps a hundred; perhaps half as many again; certainly 'considerable numbers', according to Johnson's description of the crowd which promptly surrounded him and his companions. But irrespective of its exact size, this, as Boswell commented, was clearly both a welcoming and a hospitable community:

> At Auchnasheal we sat down on a green turf-seat at the end of a house; they brought us out two wooden dishes of milk which we tasted. One of them was frothed like a syllabub.

Especially on a summer's afternoon as sunny as the one that brought Samuel Johnson and James Boswell to Glen Shiel, Achadh nan Seileach is still a most attractive corner. It is easy to see why Johnson and Boswell should have warmed to this spot. But it is equally easy, when sitting among the former village's ruins, to understand why Glen Shiel should have made so different an impact on one of its more recent literary visitors.

This visitor's name was Hugh MacLennan. He was one of twentieth century Canada's more eminent novelists. And he came to Kintail in the mid-1950s:

> Such sweeps of emptiness I never saw in Canada before I went to the Mackenzie River... But this Highland emptiness, only a few hundred miles above the massed population of England, is a far different thing from the emptiness of our own North West Territories. Above the sixtieth parallel in Canada you feel that nobody but God has ever been there before you, but in a deserted Highland glen you feel that everyone who ever mattered is dead and gone.

Hugh MacLennan was born in the coalmining town of Glace Bay on the eastern coast of Cape Breton Island, Nova Scotia. But his family origins were in Kintail – his grandfather having been one of the thousands of people who were forcibly expelled from Scotland as a result of Highland landlords having decided to eradicate so many communities of the sort once to be found at Achadh nan Seileach. It was inevitable, therefore, that MacLennan should have had very mixed feelings about his trip to the place where his ancestors had lived

The more casual tourist, even the visiting environmentalist, might be content to treat the Highlands as 'Europe's last wilderness'; an uncomplicatedly beautiful area; one of the few parts of our arguably overcrowded continent where it is possible to be alone. But Hugh MacLennan knew, as the more casual visitor does not always know, that the Highlands were once thickly populated. He knew that a unique and valuable human culture, together with a distinctive way of life, had been destroyed here. He thus returned to Canada with a profound sense of relief at having escaped from those places where, as he so memorably put it, you feel that everyone who ever mattered is dead and gone.

The environmental movement tends not to be very good at coping with the implications of the fact that, outside Antarctica, the world contains astonishingly little in the way of territory which has not, at one time or another, been inhabited. Since environmentalist thinking owes so much to the romantic movement of the years around 1800, and since, to the romantics, the ideal landscape was one bereft of human influence, environmentalists are all too ready, especially when contemplating some more than usually striking tract of countryside, to overlook, or even to disparage, the human aspect of the locality in question. The point can be illustrated from the writings of John Muir, the Scots-born American who, a century or so ago, did so much to develop and to popularise the modern cult of wilderness.

To venture deep into hill country, according to John Muir, was at once to be psychologically and spiritually at peace:

> Climb the mountains and get their good tidings. Nature's peace will flow into you as the sunshine into the trees. The winds will blow their freshness into you, and the storms their energy, while cares will drop off like autumn leaves.

This was a philosophy which John Muir was to expound in a long series of increasingly influential books. One of these, *My First Summer in the Sierra*, consists of extracts from the journal which Muir kept in the course of his initial foray into California's Yosemite mountains - the region with which his name is still so closely linked. The year was 1869 and with every day that passed, Muir's narrative explains, the country worked its soothing charms. Each sunrise brought another 'reviving' morning. 'Down the long mountain slopes the sunbeams pour, gilding the awakening pines, cheering every needle, filling every living thing with joy.' But every Eden has its serpent. And Yosemite's appeared to Muir some three weeks into August.

The day in question had begun promisingly enough. Muir had set out for Mono Lake by way of Bloody Canyon Pass:

> Near the summit, at the head of the pass, I found a species of dwarf willow lying perfectly flat on the ground, making a nice, soft, silky grey carpet, not a single stem or branch more than three inches high... Here, too, is the familiar robin, tripping on the flowery lawns, bravely singing the same cheery song I first heard when a boy in Wisconsin newly arrived from old Scotland. In this fine company, sauntering enchanted, taking no heed of time, I at length entered the gate of the pass and the huge rocks began to close round me in all their mysterious impressiveness.

At this point, however, it is as if a dark cloud has suddenly shut out the sun:

> Just then I was startled by a lot of queer, hairy, muffled creatures coming shuffling, shambling, wallowing towards me as if they had no bones in their bodies. Had I discovered them while they were yet a good way off, I should have tried to avoid them. What a picture they made, contrasted with the others I had just been admiring! When I came up to them, I found that they were only a band of Indians from Mono on their way to Yosemite for a load of acorns. They were wrapped in blankets made of the skins of sage-rabbits. The dirt on some of the faces seemed almost old enough to have a geological significance... How glad I was to get away from the grey grim crowd and see them vanish down the trail!

When, some three years after this encounter, Wyoming's geyser-rich Yellowstone Mountains were declared the world's first national park, the relevant legislation provided for 'the preservation... of all timber, mineral deposits, natural curiosities or wonders'. Definitely not scheduled for such preservation, however, were the park's human occupants – Wyoming's counterparts to the folk John Muir encountered in Yosemite. Several Indian bands – belonging to the Crow, the Blackfeet and Shoshone peoples – were forcibly expelled from Yellowstone in the year the park was designated. And in 1876, despite its tourist trade being already underway, Yellowstone was the scene of fighting between the US cavalry and one more of America's first nations, the Nez Perce.

Reflecting on his people's subsequent defeat and slaughter, Chief Joseph of the Nez Perce commented:

> I learned... that we were few while the white men were many, and that we could not hold our own with them. We were like deer. They were like grizzly bears. We had a small country. Their country was large. We were contented to let things remain as the Great Spirit Chief made them. They were not and would change the rivers and mountains if they did not suit them.

What the Nez Perce chieftain most disliked about our so-called western civilisation, of course, was what America's earliest environmentalists most disliked about it also. John Muir, for instance, was to spend the last years of his life defending his beloved Yosemite Valley from a planned dam which, if it had gone ahead, would have altered 'the rivers and mountains' more fundamentally than Chief Joseph could ever have thought possible. 'These temple destroyers,' Muir wrote of the Californian businessmen and politicians who were promoting the controversial dam with a view to improving San Francisco's water supplies, 'seem to have a perfect contempt for nature and, instead of lifting their eyes to the God of the mountains, lift them to the almighty dollar.' But for all that he was eventually to develop some sympathy for Indians, most notably those he met while travelling in Alaska in the 1880s and 1890s, it was never to occur to John Muir that a national park, from the perspective of the native peoples who were deprived of their lands to make its creation possible, might appear to disrupt the natural order every bit as much as the damming of a river.

Nor has such disruption been confined to North America. In the course of the 120 years since the establishment of Yellowstone National Park, some 7,000 additional areas in about 130 different countries have been subjected to legally-enforcible designations of the Yellowstone variety. No less than five per cent of the entire world's land surface is consequently affected by measures intended to safeguard the natural environment. And although the environmental case for constituting such protected areas may seem obvious enough, it is by no means clear that they have been properly integrated into the human societies on which they directly impinge. By far the most depressing feature of a remarkably high proportion of the world's national parks, for instance, is the extent to which the authorities responsible for their creation have managed to alienate and antagonise the peoples who traditionally occupied the lands from which these parks were constituted.

The outcome is well summarised in a recent American survey of the planet's protected areas:

> Many... protected areas overlap the homelands of indigenous people. Regrettably, many were also created without consultation with the communities that lived in or near them... Frequently, when protected areas were established, indigenous and local residents were moved out, often to the detriment of the land itself.

The enforced removal of Highlanders from the Highlands occurred for reasons other than those arising from a desire to safeguard this area's natural environment. But now that the conserving of the Highland environment is becoming – quite rightly – a policy priority, it is important that account is taken of the susceptibilities of those of us who believe, with Hugh MacLennan, that a deserted Highland glen is not so much a piece of wilderness as a place where you feel that everyone who ever mattered is dead and gone. Environmentalists, in other words, need to be aware of Highland attitudes to the Highlands – all the more so in view of the fact that the Gaelic-speaking people who have inhabited this part of Britain for some 1500 years traditionally held so positive a view of nature.

Western civilisation, until the eighteenth century, mostly tended to treat wild nature as something to be feared – something, ideally, to be beaten down, conquered and subdued. The Greeks, being a mountain people, had some degree of positive feeling for the hills around them. But the Romans – for all that poets like Virgil and Horace were given to sentimentalising those pastoral and farmed countrysides which had already been domesticated by Italian agriculturalists – regarded untamed territory with a deep repugnance. Typical of the products of such thinking are those Latin verses which consider it a 'serious defect' – and one which ought, by implication, to be quickly set to right – that so much of the earth is 'greedily possessed by mountains and the forests of wild beasts'.

This adversarial approach to nature was reinforced, if anything, by Christianity. The bible, as a result of its stressing humanity's God-given right of dominion over the rest of the divine creation, encourages a dim view to be taken of any components of the natural order which manage, as it were, to maintain their independence. Such was the way, at least, in which the scriptural message was initially interpreted – not just by the Romans but also by many of the Germanic peoples who were to come to prominence in Western Europe in the wake of Rome's collapse. These peoples, after all, had traditionally lived in some considerable dread of the dangers thought, by no means without reason, to lurk in still-unsettled country. That much is apparent from the Anglo-Saxon epic, *Beowulf*, where mountains and wooded places are invariably characterised as dismal, dark, wolf-haunted, weird and frightening. Wilderness, it is thus made clear, held absolutely no appeal for England's founding fathers. And in the case of woodland, in particular, most English people, over several hundred years, saw little reason to challenge the longstanding identification of unbridled nature with all that was menacing, fierce and disruptive. To cut down trees was consequently to expand civility and culture – the prevalent state of English opinion on such issues being highlighted, as late as the seventeenth century, by a poetical dictionary which suggests that woods are most appropriately described as dreadful, uncouth, melancholy or gloomy.

The sheer staying power of such ideas makes all the more remarkable the sentiments contained in thousand-year old poems like the following:

> Summer brings low the little stream, the swift herd makes for the water, the long hair of the heather spreads out, the weak white cotton-grass flourishes...
>
> ...Delightful is the season's splendour, winter's rough wind has gone; bright is every fertile wood, a joyful peace is summer.*

Such poems – composed originally in Gaelic – date from the eighth, ninth and tenth centuries. And it is easy to understand, on reading them, why Kuno Meyer, one of the earliest translators of these verses into English, should have commented in 1913:

> In nature poetry the Gaelic muse may vie with that of any other nation. Indeed, these peoms occupy a unique position in the literature of the world. To seek out and watch and love nature, in its tiniest phenomenon as in its grandest, was given to no people so early and so fully as to the Celt.

Meyer, in fact, exaggerated slightly. Eastern peoples like the Chinese and the Japanese, whose Buddhist and Shinto religions emphasise the essential unity of all living things, possess a literary tradition very similar to the Gaelic one. In the slightly more limited setting of the British Isles, or even Europe, however, Kuno Meyer was surely right to emphasise the sheer distinctiveness of the lyrics he translated. Nor is it so surprising as it might seem initially that Gaels should have been so far in advance of other Europeans in this respect.

Today, when the various dialects of Gaelic are spoken by a mere handful of people on the Atlantic fringes of Scotland and Ireland, it is easy to be unaware that the language was not always the highly marginalised tongue it has now become. Because we mostly assume Gaelic to be of no very general significance, we readily overlook the fact that Gaelic-speakers, as has been commented recently by a German historian, Michael Richter, 'developed a written culture at an earlier stage than most other European peoples'. We tend to miss the point that poems like the one quoted above, far from being the products of a primitive or unsophisticated society, were shaped in communities where there had developed modes of thought and forms of expression which, if we exclude only the overarching achievements of the Greeks and the Romans, were such as to have made these communities the originators of what was, to cite Richter again, the 'most significant European culture' of the Christian era's early centuries.

That culture – which, emanating from centres like Iona, brought both Christianity and learning to much of Britain and to much of continental Europe also – was to be steadily marginalised in the centuries following its first flowering. But something of that same culture's influence, not least its feeling for nature, is to be detected still in Highland literature. Thus Sorley MacLean, born in Raasay in 1911 and easily the most significant Gaelic poet of recent times, has stressed in interview after interview that landscape is one of the key creative influences on his work. This is apparent in the poem MacLean called *An t-Eilean*, meaning Skye, the island:

O great Island, Island of my love,
many a night of them I fancied
the great ocean itself restless,
agitated with love of you
as you lay on the sea,
great beautiful bird of Scotland,
your supremely beautiful wings bent
about many-nooked Loch Bracadale,
your beautiful wings prostrate on the sea
from the Wild Stallion to the Aird of Sleat,
your joyous wings spread
about Loch Snizort and the world.*

Here landscape is personalised, even eroticised, as it is also in Norman MacCaig's great poem, *A Man in Assynt*:

Who owns this landscape?
Has owning anything to do with love?
For it and I have a love affair so nearly human
we even have quarrels –
When I intrude too confidently
it rebuffs me with a wind like hand
or puts in my way
a quaking bog or a loch
where no loch should be. Or I turn stonily
away, refusing to notice
the rouged rocks, the mascara
under a dripping ledge, even
the tossed, the stony limbs waiting.

To read *A Man in Assynt* is immediately to be reminded of Hugh MacLennan's reaction to Kintail. For MacCaig, unlike the Gaelic poets of an earlier time, cannot treat landscape as a given fact, a simply present entity. He is ineradicably aware, as Hugh MacLennan was aware, as every Highlander has been aware since the early nineteenth century, of the extent to which community and landscape have been severed by the complex of forces, the sequence of events, we call the Highland Clearances:

Or has it come to this,
that this dying landscape belongs
to the dead, the crofters and fighters
and fishermen whose larochs
sink into the bracken
by Loch Assynt and Loch Crocach? –
to men trampled under the hoofs of sheep
and driven by deer to
the ends of the earth – to men whose loyalty
was so great it accepted their own betrayal

by their own chiefs and whose descendants now
are kept in their place
by English businessmen and the indifference
of a remote and ignorant government.

The clearances loom large, then, for Norman MacCaig. For Sorley MacLean – writing always in Gaelic and, as a result of his Raasay upbringing, rather closer to family memories of eviction – the clearances loom larger still. So intermingled are his surroundings with his locality's often tragic past, in fact, that it is difficult for MacLean to separate the one from the other:

My symbols almost automatically became the landscape of my physical environment. But, of course, that was always blended with what I knew of the history of my people.

An especially inescapable fact of that history was the clearance of the greater part of Raasay in the 1850s. It was with the implications of this clearance that Sorley MacLean was to wrestle in a poem he entitled simply *Hallaig* – the name of one of the twelve Raasay townships which the island's mid-nineteenth century owner so brutally emptied of their people. Assessing the significance of *Hallaig*, John MacInnes, perhaps the most perceptive analyst of MacLean's poetry and certainly the analyst most concious of the historical influences operating on that poetry, has commented:

Hallaig is a twentieth century poem and contains images of its time. Setting these aside, I have a feeling that it is also a poem that would have been understood a thousand years ago and more.

What would certainly have been understood by the earliest Gaels is the emphasis in MacLean's work on the link between people and locality. Community and place have always been believed by Gaelic-speakers to be integral to each other. That is one reason why the destruction of villages like Hallaig and Achadh nan Seileach had such psychologically traumatic repercussions. By no means the least powerful aspect of MacLean's *Hallaig*, therefore, is the way the poem encapsulates the terrible hurt involved in the breaking of the bond between Hallaig's human occupants and the little piece of ground to which these same folk, and so many of their ancestors, had for so long belonged.

Something of what it was that Hugh MacLennan sensed so strongly in Kintail thus resonates through *Hallaig* also; for the poem is, in a sense, a lament, a cry of heartfelt anguish for what had been so casually obliterated. As another Highland poet, Iain Crichton Smith, has observed, however, there is much more to *Hallaig* than that:

Sometimes in certain texts of literature we sense that the poet has reached levels of intuition that go beyond the intelligence and the reasoning mind, that he has made contact with his theme in a very direct way. I have myself sensed this often in Shakespeare and in some Greek poetry. We find it, I believe, very finely in *Hallaig*. In this poem it is as if MacLean felt and sensed quite clearly the desolation, the sadness, the terrible emptiness of the Highlands, its ghosts and presences, in an absolute intuitional music.

In *Hallaig*, as in a good deal of the most ancient Gaelic poetry, trees, so long regarded reverentially by Celts, are much in evidence. But MacLean's trees are clearly symbols as well as simple objects of affection. The township's former community, its 'ghosts and presences', have been transformed and transmuted into a wood. And it is this touch, perhaps, which gives to *Hallaig* its strangest, most unanticipated, quality. Iain Crichton Smith again:

> In this poem there is not only desolation, the loneliness of the Highlands, but also a deep central joy, as if there is also immortality.

This essay returns in due course to MacLean's transcendent optimism. But first to *Hallaig* itself, 'this most beautiful, mysterious and intriguing poem', as Iain Crichton Smith has called it:

The window is nailed and boarded
through which I saw the West
and my love is at the Burn of Hallaig,
a birch tree, and she has always been

between Inver and Milk Hollow,
here and there about Baile-Chuirn:
she is a birch, a hazel,
a straight, slender young rowan.

In Screapadal of my people
where Norman and Big Hector were,
their daughters and their sons are a wood
going up beside the stream.

Proud tonight the pine cocks
crowing on the top of Cnoc an Ra,
straight their backs in the moonlight
they are not the wood I love.

I will wait for the birch wood
until it comes up from the cairn,
until the whole ridge from Beinn na Lice
will be under its shade.

If it does not, I will go down to Hallaig,
to the sabbath of the dead,
where the people are frequenting,
every single generation gone.

They are still in Hallaig,
MacLeans and MacLeods,
all who were there in the time of Mac
Gille Chaluim
the dead have been seen alive.

The men lying on the green
at the end of every house that was,
the girls a wood of birches,
straight their backs, bent their heads.

Between the Leac and Fearns
the road is under mild moss
and the girls in silent bands
go to Clachan as in the beginning,

and return from Clachan
from Suisnish and the land
of the living;
each one young and high-stepping,
without the heartbreak of the tale.*

When looking on a Highland scene – on Achadh nan Seileach, perhaps, or on Hallaig itself – you find yourself imagining very often, the more so maybe if you are a Highlander, how that scene might be today if what took place in the nineteenth century had not done so. You find yourself trying to envisage the Highlands as they would be 'without the heartbreak of the tale'. You find yourself identifying with the sentiments expressed in the concluding lines of Norman MacCaig's poem, *A Man in Assynt*:

Up there, the scraping light
whittles the cloud edges till, like thin bone,
they're bright with their own opaque selves. Down here,
a skinny rosebush is an eccentric jug
of air. They make me,
somewhere between them,
a visiting eye,
an unrequited passion,
watching the tide glittering backward and making
its huge withdrawal from beaches
and kilted rocks. And the mind
behind the eye, within the passion,
remembers with certainty that the tide will return
and thinks, with hope, that that other ebb,
that sad reversal of people, may, too,
reverse itself and flood
the bays and the sheltered glens
with new generations replenishing the land
with its richest of riches and coming, at last,
into their own again.

If you want to understand the Highlands – as opposed to merely looking at them – you have, then, to begin by accepting that very little hereabouts is as many of us would like it to be. Nor is it merely that we want to repopulate our presently deserted landscapes. We want to alter these landscapes ecologically as well.

Some fifty years ago, remarking on the fate of the American south-west, the pioneer US environmentalist, Aldo Leopold, wrote:

This region, when grazed by livestock, reverted through a series of more and more worthless grasses, shrubs and weeds to a condition of unstable equilibrium. Each recession of plant types bred erosion; each increment to erosion bred a further recession of plants. The result today is a progressive and mutual deterioration, not only of plants and soils, but of the animal community subsisting thereon… So subtle has been its progress that few residents of the region are aware of it. It is quite invisible to the tourist who finds this wrecked landscape colourful and charming.

The tourist thinks a typically treeless Highland glen equally charming. The tourist probably considers such a glen to be in its natural condition. But the tourist, as was pointed out in the 1950s by one of our own pioneering environmentalists, Frank Fraser Darling, is quite wrong. The Highlands, Fraser Darling observed, had been stripped of their original vegetation every bit as comprehensively as New Mexico. And the consequences, as described by this Highland-based ecologist whose thinking was very much influenced by Aldo Leopold, were just as disastrous for the Highlands as they were for those faraway landscapes to the south of Albuquerque:

The Highlands, as a geologic and physiographic region, are unable to withstand deforestation and maintain productiveness and fertility. Their history has been one of steadily accelerating deforestation until the great mass of the forest was gone, and thereafter of forms of land usage which prevented regeneration of tree growth and reduced the land to the crude values and expressions of its solid geological composition. In short, the Highlands are a devastated countryside... Devastation has not quite reached its uttermost lengths, but it is quite certain that present trends in land use will lead to it, and the country will then be rather less productive than Baffin Land.

It is this essay's contention – a contention founded every bit as much on Frank Fraser Darling as on Hugh MacLennan, Sorley MacLean or Norman MacCaig – that the task which confronts us in the Highlands is not one of protecting or conserving what it is we see about us. No, the task we face is one of how we put right all the many things which, over several centuries, have gone so desperately wrong. And that task is all the more urgent in view of the fact that the Scottish Highlands, despite the region's longstanding demographic decline, now has one of the fastest growing populations in all Europe – with no small part of the increase occurring in the remoter areas of the West Highlands and in previously depopulating islands like Skye and Mull.

To say that the Highlands should be restored socially, culturally and ecologically is not to say that the Highlands should again be exactly as they once were. There can be no question, for instance, of attempting to replicate in new or expanded settlements – settlements of the sort which will inevitably result from our area's repopulation – the conditions of earlier ages. The families who set up home in such settlements ought certainly to be entitled to look to the land for some proportion of their livelihoods. But such families ought also to have access to the various communications and other technologies which increasingly make it possible to provide, even in relatively inaccessible locations, commercial and entrepreneurial opportunities of the sort which were previously confined to urban areas.

This essay, then, is not in the business of advocating a return to subsistence agriculture. Nor is it intended to endorse the transformation of the Highlands into some sort of cross between a national park and an open-air museum. To go down that road would simply be to evade the challenge which this magnificent piece of territory poses to anyone prepared to think seriously about its future. Central to that challenge is the need to demonstrate that the enviromental rehabilitation of the Scottish Highlands can be achieved by means which simultaneously bring about the restoration of people to some at least of the many localities where both human communities and the Gaelic culture associated with those communities were long ago destroyed.

The Highlands, if such a course were to be embarked upon, would be very different from the Highlands of today. Much of the area would be more thickly populated than has been the case in recent times. It would be more thickly wooded also – with timber and timber products being of greater economic importance, in all probability, than either sheep or deer. And since it is difficult to envisage changes of this magnitude occurring under the auspices of a landownership system which has been identified so strongly with so many of the wholly negative developments of the last two hundred years, movement in this direction will require to be accompanied, or preceded, by reforms which give Highland communities a worthwhile say in the management of land and other natural resources.

No matter what happens eventually to presently deserted spots like Achadh nan Seileach, it is worth underlining in this context, much of the Highlands will remain unpopulated. The region's higher hills, its more isolated glens and its many tiny islands will be available in the future – as they were available in the past – to those individuals who like to be able to escape occasionally from the company of other human beings. All that will have happened is that places which were once inhabited will be inhabited again. And if this can be accomplished in ways which also promote the regeneration of one of Europe's older and more distinctive human cultures, so much the better.

In the preface to his collected poetry, Sorley MacLean recalls the origin of his attempt – made more than half a century ago –to gaze far, far beyond the grim realities of what was then the present:

> It was in Mull in 1938 that I conceived the idea of writing a very long poem, 10,000 words or so, on the human condition, radiating from the history of Skye and the West Highlands to Europe and what I knew of the rest of the world.

This poem Sorley called *An Cuilithionn*, the Cuillin. It was never finished. But enough of it has now been published to allow us to grasp something of its maker's purpose. Through the poem there moves a very large cast of characters drawn from many places, many epochs; from Skye as it was at the time of the evictions; from Spain, from Poland, from Russia and all the other countries threatened, at the time of the poem's birth, by fascist takeover and conquest; from Africa, from China, from America; from many other different zones of struggle between the oppressed and their oppressors. But for all its dwelling on human suffering and on man's seemingly endless capacity to cause hurt to his fellow human beings, *An Cuilithionn*, like *Hallaig*, is ultimately redolent with hope. Here are the poem's closing lines:

> Beyond the lochs of the blood of the children of men,
> beyond the frailty of plain and the labour of the mountain,
> beyond poverty, consumption, fever, agony,
> beyond hardship, wrong, tyranny, distress,
> beyond misery, despair, hatred, treachery,
> beyond guilt and defilement; watchful,
> heroic, the Cuillin is seen
> rising on the other side of sorrow.*

In *An Cuilithionn*, then, the clearances and all the other disasters which have befallen Highlanders become – what historically, of course, they truly were – merely one small aspect of a much vaster human tragedy. And the Cuillin themselves, in all that mountain range's sharply pinnacled solidity, are transformed, by Sorley MacLean, into an emblem of salvation. Since the poem was written by a man who was, at the time of its composition anyway, a Marxist, this salvation might be construed as deriving from Marx's own vision of the classless society which is to be brought into existence by proletarian revolution. But MacLean's imagery is arguably a lot less grounded in political specifics than is suggested by this relatively limited interpretation. Not least because so much of its symbolism is drawn from the landscapes with which this essay has been concerned, *An Cuilithionn* is seen here as pointing to the part which the Highlands could play in resolving some of the dilemmas now confronting all mankind.

We have the opportunity today in the Scottish Highlands to turn around those processes which have done so much damage both to this area's people and to its natural environment. All of us with an interest in the Highlands – irrespective, incidentally, of our origins – could readily resolve to work together for the region's general benefit. We could jointly bring about the repopulation, as well as the ecological restoration, of all the numerous places where, as Hugh MacLennan commented, you feel that everyone who ever mattered is dead and gone. We could, in other words, undo some of the consequences which are, even yet, arising from the horrors of the past.

The Highlands, if were to attempt these things, would still be beautiful. The Highlands would still offer anyone who wanted it the chance to be alone in some wild corner. But the Highlands would also be a living demonstration that community, culture and nature can, in the end, be made compatible with one another. To accomplish this would be no small achievement. It would help bring all humanity a little nearer to the better-ordered world which Sorley's poem glimpses on the other side of sorrow.

The Author and Acknowledgements

Dr James Hunter is a freelance historian, writer and broadcaster who lives in the Skye crofting community of Borve. He is chairman of Skye and Lochalsh Enterprise, a member of the North West Regional Board of Scottish Natural Heritage and a member of the Forestry Commission's Advisory Panel on Native Woodland in the North of Scotland. A former member of the board of Highlands and Islands Enterprise, he was the founding Director of the Scottish Crofters Union and has had a long involvement with rural development issues. His seventh book, *On the Other Side of Sorrow: Nature and People in the Scottish Highlands,* was launched at the Heritage Convention. The author is grateful to Norman MacCaig, Sorley MacLean and Iain Crichton Smith for permission to quote from their writings.

References

Alexander, M. (ed), *Beowulf,* Penguin Edition, London, 1973
Boswell, J., *Journal of a Tour to the Hebrides,* Penguin Edition, London, 1990
Darling, F. F., *West Highland Survey: An Essay in Human Ecology,* Oxford, 1955
Hunter, J., *The Making of the Crofting Community,* Edinburgh, 1976
Hunter, J., *The Claim of Crofting: The Scottish Highlands, 1930– 1990,* Edinburgh, 1991
Hunter, J., *Scottish Highlanders: A People and their Place,* Edinburgh, 1992
Hunter, J., *A Dance Called America: The Scottish Highlands, the United States and Canada,* Edinburgh, 1994
Hunter, J., *On the Other Side of Sorrow: Nature and People in the Scottish Highlands,* Edinburgh, 1995

Jackson, K. H. (ed), *A Celtic Miscellany*, Penguin Edition, London, 1971

Johnson, S., *A Journey to the Western Islands of Scotland*, Penguin Edition, London, 1990

Kemf, E., *The Law of the Mother: Protecting Indigenous Peoples in Protected Areas*, San Francisco, 1993

Leopold, A., *A Sand County Almanac*, Ballantine Books Edition, New York, 1970

MacCaig, N., *Collected Poems: A New Edition*, London, 1993

MacLean, S., *From Wood to Ridge: Collected Poems in Gaelic and English*, Manchester, 1990

MacLennan, H., *Scotchman's Return and Other Essays*, Toronto, 1960

Meyer, K., *Ancient Irish Poetry*, Constable Edition, London, 1994

Muir, J., *My First Summer in the Sierra*, Canongate Classics Edition, Edinburgh, 1988

Muir, J., *Travels in Alaska*, Sierra Club Edition, San Francisco, 1988

Nash, R., *Wilderness and the American Mind*, Third Edition, Yale, 1982

Nicolson, M. H., *Mountain Gloom and Mountain Glory: The Development of the Aesthetics of the Infinite*, Ithaca, 1959

Richter, M., *Medieval Ireland: The Enduring Tradition*, London, 1988

Ross, R. J. and Hendry, J. (eds), *Sorley MacLean: Critical Essays*, Edinburgh, 1986

Smith, I. C., *Towards the Human: Selected Essays*, Edinburgh, 1986

Thomas, K., *Man and the Natural World: Changing Attitudes in England, 1500–1800*, Penguin Edition, London, 1984

* Indicates material which has been translated from Gaelic.

25

BEYOND THE MEMORIES
Drawing Strength from the Diaspora

John Alec MacPherson

When one lives in a country preoccupied with the politics of identity, it is tempting to become absorbed in the incendiary issues of nationalism and ethnicity or in the mythical American article of faith that communities are built through a delicate balance of ethnic, religious and other interests. On the contrary, the melting pot's assimilation of immigrant groups into a dominant English culture is an extension, not of democratic governance, but of a society founded on conquest rather than compromise, on aggression rather than adjustment. As an expatriate Gael, I carry the additional baggage of the narcissism that urges one to transform one's identity into a self-pitying sense of victimisation.

Being part of the Gaelic diaspora is sometimes sombre, sometimes exhilarating, never easy, but always interesting. There are so many creaky windmills to tilt at, both in the old world and the new. Having recently read James Hunter's excellent book, *A Dance Called America*, I have given up quixotic ventures and more or less accepted the reality of exile.

The diaspora of the Gael is not a recent phenomenon. In the fourth century AD, a Roman historian commented on 'Scotti per diversa vagantes', Scots wandering in different places. He was referring to raids by Irishmen, Picts and others on Roman territory in England and Wales, at a time when the term 'Scot' was as applicable to Ireland as to Scotland.

There are many impressions of the Gaelic footprint around the world, some strong, some tenuous and some intriguing. I occasionally pass through a small town in Manitoba called Garven, Gaelic for 'the craggy hill'. What is interesting is that Garven is in the middle of the Canadian prairie, once described by a visitor from Scotland as 'a vast expanse of bugger-all'. There is no hill, craggy or otherwise, within two hundred miles. Sentiment has little respect for topography:

Gur muladach mise 's mi seo gun duin' idir
A leughas no thuigeas no sheinneas mo dhan;
'S e durachd mo chridh' soraidh slan le na gillean
A sheol thar na linne gu Manitoba.

I am sad and alone without anyone
who can read, understand or sing my song;
my heart's desire is to bid fond farewell
to the lads who have sailed across the sea to Manitoba.

The most vivid and haunting expression of the Gael's nostalgia is to be found in emigrant songs like this that were inspired by the massive exodus from the Highlands and Islands in the 18th and 19th centuries. The extensive repertoire of this literary genre embodies the tragedy of emigration, a yearning for the old order, and the despicable chronicle of the Clearances. But the despondency is often tempered by passive acceptance of fate on the one hand or by optimism for a better life in a new land on the other.

Emigration was a major factor in the decline of the Gaelic culture. Murdo Smith, a Lewis bard of the late 19th century, observed:

Cha b'iongnadh ged a bnasaicheadh
A' chanan mhilis mhathaireil;
Cha labhair feidh nam fasaichean '
S tha 'chaora bhan gun comhradh.

It is not surprising
that the sweet mother tongue should die;
the deer in the barrens do not speak
and the white sheep has no language.

But it was a resilient, defiant and almost irrepressible culture. The expatriate Gaels cherished their heritage and endeavoured to perpetuate it in their adopted countries until societal stresses and constraints led to its inevitable erosion.

Despite the gradual decay, the diaspora created a dynamic Gaelic sub-culture which has shown a remarkable capacity to survive in language, song, music and other cultural symbols of varying significance. The Scot abroad is good at assimilating and adapting. But still the blood is strong, the heart is Highland. The metabolism, however, is not always healthy and frequently owes more to Harry Lauder than to Scottish authenticity. Bogus rituals like 'Kirking of the Tartans' are hardly representative of scenes from which Auld Scotia's grandeur springs. The Highlander abroad, who would not be seen dead in a kilt in Portree, has fewer inhibitions in Toronto, particularly on the 25th of January and the 30th of November when he relishes the opportunity of being pretentiously and conspicuously Scottish as he sheds a shameless sentimental tear for vanished glories he never witnessed. When it comes to posturing the professional Scot is as egregious as any other oaf.

The paradigm for the most genuine and sustained survival of the Gaelic language and culture outside of Scotland is Cape Breton, Nova Scotia. I believe it is also a model for what can be done to turn the tide, at least temporarily, when a culture has reached a low ebb.

Comunn Gàidhlig Cheap Breatunn – The Gaelic Society of Cape Breton grew out of a Gaelic evening class conducted at Xavier College, Sydney (now University College of Cape Breton) in the late 1960s. It was conceived as a social organisation which would establish a lasting bond between the 40 or so people of various ages and backgrounds who had found out something special about themselves during their experiences in the class. They had discovered, and in some cases, rediscovered, that the values of the Gaels who struggled for survival in the 'gloomy forest' of the daunting new world of pioneer Canada were still alive and in reasonably good health. The key to this survival was the fact that the Gaelic language had remained a strong cultural medium in Cape Breton in spite of an almost total English-speaking commercial and administrative environment.

Cape Breton had no scarcity of Scottish-oriented activity over the years. St Andrew's Day banquets, Gaelic Mods and Highland Games had all been prominent on the social calendar. But they had limited grass-roots participation. It was clear to the founders of the Gaelic Society that two disturbing trends were becoming increasingly evident. As the median age of the Gaelic community increased, Gaelic involvement in these events was decreasing. At the same time there emerged characteristics that placed these events further out of the reach of the people who still, basically, made up both the soul and the backbone of the culture. They were becoming increasingly expensive and beginning to reflect a style that is exclusive to professional people of some affluence. The folk culture was, unhappily, becoming commercialised and fast losing its validity as the language from which it emerged entered a terminal decline.

Members of the new Gaelic Society of Cape Breton frequently met the sincere and perplexing question: Why, in the midst of so many social and economic problems, are you spending so much time on something as frivolous as a dying language and a rustic folklore? The answer is so complex that it almost defies expression. But an important part of it is contained in the contemporary concern with identity and social values.

Underlying North America's search for economic parity, racial harmony and national unity has been an almost desperate struggle by individuals for self understanding on terms that would produce self-respect. This has occurred in a society that has been almost exclusively oriented to the marketplace. Music, literature, fashions and diet are designed for survival in the marketplace. And the people who are determined to dominate the marketplace have developed direct and indirect means by which they cultivate or channel our tastes for the greater glory of their products.

Culture now comes from the top down, and it does not get into the mainstream at all unless it conforms to marketing principles and the whims of the advertising industry. As a consequence, the traditional headwaters of culture, the minds and hearts of vast numbers of people, begin to dry up. No longer is there a community-based culture, or a regional culture, because what appeals only in the community or the region will not survive in the national or global marketplace. The smaller units of society are, therefore, engulfed by the mass-products provided for society at large.

It is arguable that in the long run such a ruthless process might have overall value in producing the uniform tastes and objectives that would facilitate political unity and cohesion. But several consequences which face North America have raised serious questions for individuals, ethnic groups and particularly Canadians.

Understandably, the North American marketplace is dominated by the United States. For many Canadians the prospect of cultural uniformity with the United States is unacceptable and the eventuality of political unity is unthinkable. Also there is alarming evidence that the marketplace manipulation of taste and culture has made it increasingly difficult for individuals to find their personal identities. At the same time more people, particularly the young, are asking valid questions about the values that have been fostered by North American society. Materialism is being increasingly challenged. Many are determined to attack it head on, and a few would destroy the entire political and social fabric in the process.

It was in this climate that the Gaelic Society of Cape Breton examined its role in cultural rehabilitation. In its assessment of the need for cultural development, it took the position that the old elitist compact which had nurtured the wretched rhetoric of St Andrew's Day feasts was no longer valid and that any development must emphasise language as essential to any true culture. Without its own language, a culture can rapidly evolve into a caricature, with only a loose collection of artificial trappings remaining.

It was too late to arrest the decline of Gaelic as an everyday functional language in Cape Breton, but the renewed interest in it and in other facets of cultural revival has been extraordinary. Twenty years ago, the Canadian Broadcasting Corporation produced a doleful documentary called *The Vanishing Cape Breton Fiddler*. Broadcasting organisations may be able to give reasonably accurate weather forecasts, but they are no better at cultural prognostication than the rest of us. Today the Cape Breton fiddler is alive and well, with more young players and more popular appeal than ever before. Professional performers like The Rankin Family and The Barra MacNeils have not only brought Gaelic music into every Canadian home; they have also dominated the Canadian country music scene in the past few years.

By making Gaelic more accessible and appealing to non-Gaels, just as groups like Run Rig and Capercaillie have done in Scotland, they have extended and internationalised the cultural boundaries. They have also added value by instilling greater cultural self-confidence in a younger generation subject to many other influences that are not conducive to retention of their heritage. The diaspora is no longer confined to Gaelic ghettos, whether they be in Vancouver or Melbourne or Singapore. Modern communications have helped to link them with each other and with the motherland. Although the impact may not be measurable, I personally believe that the subculture that has emanated beyond the heartland has been an inspiration to those with a mission and vision to revitalise Gaelic in its real home, Scotland.

Before I leave Nova Scotia, I must mention one other feature of the Gaelic scene there, the Gaelic College at St. Ann's in Cape Breton. Until the 1980s the college's association with Gaelic did not extend much beyond its name. It was operated by the provincial government as a tourist trap where the main attraction was Highland dancing and other peripheral recreation and paraphernalia. It was not a good advertisement for Gaelic culture, nor was it a fitting monument for the pioneering settlers of that area, who were not only part of the diaspora, but, to mix ethnic metaphors, were also Gaeldom's greatest hegira.

I refer to the Rev Norman MacLeod who, along with his faithful disciples, sailed from Assynt in Sutherland in 1817 for Pictou, Nova Scotia. Three years later the Normanites set sail for Ohio, but were forced ashore in Cape Breton by a storm. They settled at St. Ann's and stayed there for 31 years. Then, led by the 71-year-old Norman, the Presbyterian ayatollah who wished 'to withdraw the faithful from the menace of the worldly community', they sailed to Australia via South Africa in ships they had built themselves. Eventually 800 of them, including the redoubtable Norman, settled in Waipu in the North Island of New Zealand. It was one of the great adventure stories of all time, but it has not found its way into many Scottish history books. A Highland epic just could not compete with Bruce and the spider.

Today, the Gaelic College at St. Ann's is still a major tourist attraction, but with a difference. It's greater attention to the Gaelic language and to improved musical standards has enhanced its value and its allure as a heritage and cultural tourism centre. It is important not only that we make Gaelic culture accessible to non-Gaels and tourists but that, in doing so, we embrace standards that go beyond the crass commerce of kitsch, to the core values of the society being identified and portrayed. Tourism aimed merely at emptying the pockets of the mindless is an obscenity which no self-respecting community deserves.

THE FATE OF GAELIC

For the last 24 years I have been on the fringes and not at the core of Gaelic culture. I have been closer to the nucleus of the atom than to the nucleus of Gaelic. Therefore it would be presumptuous of me to pontificate on the Gaelic situation today other than to make a few observations which go beyond the memories.

When I was making a living as a Gaelic professional, I was one of a small group that considered itself influential but really looked upon Gaelic in a confined and constricted sense. More often than not, we looked through the wrong end of the telescope and saw a shrinking and shrivelled world. We were obsessed with every misdeed and misadventure that had jolted the Gael and shaken his self-confidence. We placed Gaelic in a preserving jar and isolated it from the rest of the world. Seldom did we go beyond these narrow parameters to consider both the status and the stature of Gaelic in the oontext of government policy, natural heritage, industry, education, development, social services, communications and all the other factors that comprise the infrastructure of a nation or community. The Gaelic cause was in the hands of a coterie of well-meaning but blinkered Prima Donnas who talked more than they listened and who answered the questions without questioning the answers. But times have changed. Not enough perhaps, but enough to make a difference.

If someone had told me twenty years ago that such progress as has occurred in Gaelic broadcasting and education was possible, I would have been sceptical if not completely incredulous. Having been passionately involved in these two areas, I am delighted and at the same time envious when I see the development that has taken place. When I left the BBC in 1972, we had four and a half hours a week of Gaelic on radio and half an hour a month on TV. It was quite a struggle to get even that much. A Gaelic 'soap' on television would have been a dream or, more likely, a nightmare. Only a massive hangover could have induced the idea of private producers. But these concepts are now reality.

Gaelic has benefited from a number of stimuli in recent years. Not least among them is the status afforded to the lesser languages by the European Union. Many myths surround the smaller languages. We have all heard them:

If you are going to succeed in the world, Gaelic will be more of a hindrance than a help.

Only English will earn you a livelihood.

Multilingualism gives rise to tension at best and strife or confrontation at worst.

Gaelic is so short of vocabulary that you must turn to English to express yourself fully.

If you don't use it you lose it.

What's the Gaelic for banana?

MULTILINGUALISM

I have had the good fortune to be able to visit many countries. And if I have learned anything at all from that experience, it is that having two or more languages cheek by jowl is not a burden but a benefit. Gaelic opened many doors for me, and I am not aware that it closed any. The Gaels of the diaspora have drawn comfort from multilingualism and multiculturalism and some of that solace has in turn been transferred back to the primary source.

Canada has two official languages, English and French. The government spends 700 million dollars each year on official bilingualism. Some contend that this is wanton extravagance and a pacifier for a minority of the population that threatens to break up the country if it does not get its own way. Granted, the issue involves a lot of politics and polemics. But, whatever side you are on, only the churlish would deny that bilingualism gives the country a cachet that it would lack if it were boringly monoglot.

The majority sees bilingualism as important and valuable. To the Francophones of Quebec it is crucial that their language and culture do not get smothered by the English behemoth. When the Quebecois says 'Je me souviens' he is not just saying that he remembers. He is affirming that he has not forgotten. He is expressing the thrust of the Gaelic proverb, 'Theid dualchas an aghaidh nan creag', heritage is more enduring than granite.

But Canada's mosaic is more polychromatic than the mere fact of official bilingualism suggests. Three million people, one eighth of the population, have almost 80 languages as their mother tongue. The Commissioner of Official Languages has said:

> The freedom to pursue one's cultural and linguistic ties is an unalienable right of all citizens... Bilingualism and multiculturalism are equally vital for social cohesion and cultural enrichment; no effort should be spared to bring out their importance and complementarity.

But, like the cattle-riever's boat, the language question has a black side and a white. When the Toronto Board of Education gave permission to teach languages other than English and French in schools outside normal hours, two thirds of the teachers expressed the opinion that this would be detrimental to other subjects. But the Board went ahead on the principle that fluency in one language is a help and not a hindrance when learning another. Today, Scottish and Irish Gaelic are among the heritage languages taught in Toronto.

If Canada is a model of linguistic composure it is also a metaphor for languages battling extinction. Among the indigenous peoples, the Indians and the Inuit, there are 53 languages, but it is not expected that more than three will survive beyond the next twenty years: Ojibway, Cree and Inuktitut. Among 80,000 Ojibway, only 30,000 speak the language, and no one under the age of 20 speaks it. Twenty years ago every Ojibway could speak the native language.

But the Canadian Indians are trying to keep their languages alive. In a newspaper column, an Indian woman was recalling how her grandfather used to impress upon them to be cognisant of the bond between them and the land. 'It is the land that makes us look, talk and think the way we do' he used to say. They are now returning to their language to fortify their kinship with the land. I wish them well.

LANGUAGE IS THE SOUL OF CULTURE

If language is the soul of culture, and this is particularly true of a lineage that derives its strength from oral tradition, the loss of a language is tantamount to the death of a people. My Gaelic dictionary has one word for the English word 'snow' (sneachd). How many words do the Inuit have for snow? Fourteen, I am told. A testament to the fragile and complex bond between man and nature in a part of the world we perceive as remote and intimidating.

Languages in juxtaposition are a pleasure. But they can sometimes be an irritant. Hispanic-American author Richard Rodriguez tells how he grew up in an American community alien to his Mexican background;

> It did not matter that my parents could not speak English with ease... and yet, in another way, it mattered very much... it was unsettling to hear them struggle with English. Hearing them I'd grow nervous, my trust in them weakened... but then there was Spanish. Espanol, my family's language. A mysterious private language. I'd hear strangers on the radio and in the church speaking it, but I couldn't really believe that Spanish was a public

language, like English... I was reminded of my separateness from los otros, los gringos, those in power... Spanish seemed to me the language of home. Most days it was only at home that I'd hear it. It became the language of joyful return.

An arcane, private language. That, I am sure, is how some perceive Gaelic. But it is an image that should be dispelled. I am sure the experts like Noam Chomsky have all the answers on language. Linguistics is not my field so I do not have any intellectual insights into language. But I offer the simplistic suggestion that there are two ways of looking upon a language: as something precious, distinct, discrete, and to be studied rather than spoken; or as a commodity which is vibrant, mainstream, fundamental to our lives and to contemporary society. I would prefer that Gaelic be the latter rather than the former.

THE NEED FOR POLITICAL SUSTENANCE

Whatever the future holds for Gaelic, there is no doubt that the lesser used languages require political sustenance. Governments, national and local, have an obligation to support the languages of their people. But this is not the responsibility of government alone, but also of the industrial and business and service sectors, and of all groups upon whom the language impinges. In countries where yesterday's profligacy is suffocating today's development, the largesse of government is no longer assured. In some countries I know we have become so accustomed to being propped up by government that we are today whining, like 'Chicken Little', that the sky is falling.

But there are encouraging trends towards different kinds of institutional support that supplants the traditional reliance on the public purse. At one time people in industry and business remained aloof from their environs, but they are gradually becoming more conscious of matters pertaining to their communities of interest and mote prepared to become directly involved in education, social services and recreational and cultural activities. This new interest is based on enlightened self-interest rather than on a sense of philanthropy. I think we can predict a future in which we can see government and industry and other institutions coming together in collaboration and strategic partnership to an unprecedented extent. It would be prudent to turn this emerging situation to the advantage of heritage initiatives.

BEYOND THE MEMORIES

I said above that I have been hovering on the edges of Gaelic for many years. The diaspora keeps haunting and taunting me, and I never know when to give up. The only real lesson I have learned is not to offer unsolicited advice or recommend directions that, from my limited perspective, might be enticing to me but quite inappropriate for others.

I believe Scotland can draw a measure of strength and inspiration from the diaspora, particularly if it realises that the emigrants are not all kilted caricatures at one end of the spectrum or obsessive colonial mercenaries at the other. Emigration does not change one's genetic makeup. I am sure that you will not be surprised to hear that the emigrant Gael, who emerges on the Gaelic scene in Boston or Winnipeg, is just as adept at the territorial and organisational infighting that beset Gaelic initiatives from time to time, as the best Gaelic guerrilla in Scotland. Unfortunately, cohesion and unity have not been a consistent hallmark of organisations working on behalf of Gaelic. But life would be dull without contention.

This volume is to be commended for weaving together many strands of social and cultural development in exploring issues associated with sustainable use of the earth's heritage assets. I am glad you included the Scots and Gaelic languages among these strands. All too often they are regarded as important to the past but not to the future. We should certainly look ahead. But we should look behind us also. As surely as the DNA is encrypted with our genetic past, our social structure is encoded with a historical template that transcends genealogical insignia.

We often think of language and heritage in terms of academic abstractions or constructs that require different approaches from those applied to commerce and industry. Certainly, as far as the Gaelic movement is concerned, we could well borrow from the business paradigm by doing short and long term planning, by establishing a framework of strategic direction, and by keeping our multiple stakeholders informed about where we are heading and how we are going to get there.

THE IMPERATIVE OF QUALITY

The watchword that has preoccupied the industrial world in recent times is Quality. It demands continuous and relentless improvement. It is the difference between success and failure, and it requires you to do three things: deliver what you promised; make sure your customers are satisfied; and consolidate your identity and reputation. That is what the Gaelic Society of Cape Breton set out to do as a matter of common sense long before the Harvard Business Review started touting Total Quality Management. As they say in North Carolina, 'if you're going to cackle you'd better lay an egg'. That applies to language and culture just as surely as it applies to IBM's business plan.

When I was growing up in North Uist, the crofters used to call a township meeting by hoisting what we called a 'perch'. It was simply a pole on the top of Cnoc Liath hillock, but the whole township could see it. It was the poor man's fiery cross, the catalyst that brought people together to weave consensus out of diverse and contradictory viewpoints. If the Gaelic tradition is going to flourish in Scotland or in the far outposts of the diaspora, we must raise the perch and work together.

For those of us who are isolated from our roots the hunger of memory is constantly gnawing, but it is consoling to think that heritage is stronger than granite. It takes one far beyond the memories.

The Author

John Alec MacPherson is a native of North Uist, and was educated at Portree High School and Edinburgh University. After receiving his Master of Arts degree in 1957, he trained as a teacher at Jordanhill College of Education, and spent the first five years of his career teaching. He then joined the BBC as a producer in the Gaelic Department. In 1972 he emigrated to Canada and joined Atomic Energy of Canada Limited (AECL) as a Public Affairs Officer in Cape Breton. He then became Manager of Communications at AECL's Engineering Division in Mississauga, Ontario. He was appointed Director of Public and Government Affairs in AECL's Research Division in 1990, and in 1994 he became Director of Public Affairs at HQ in Ottawa. He has recently been Chairman of an International Atomic Energy Agency Experts Group on Communications, and has given presentations at seminars in seven different countries, where he has pursued his hobby of studying manifestations of the Scottish diaspora.

References

Gaelic Society of Cape Breton, *Caidreabh '72*, GSCB, 1972
Hunter, J., *A Dance Called America*, Mainstream Publishing, 1994
MacDonell, M., *The Emigrant Experience*, University of Toronto Press, 1982
McPherson, F., *Watchman Against The World*, Breton Books, 1993
Rodriguez, R., *Hunger of Memory*, David R. Godine, 1982
Young, D., *Scotland*, Cassell, 1971

26

SCOTS GAELIC AS A TOURISM ASSET

Roy Pedersen

Tourism is the world's largest and fastest growing industry, bringing material benefits to millions. Most of us are more or less willing consumers of tourism products. The development of tourism also has a dark side characterised by a trail of human, environmental and cultural degradation. These negative characteristics pose the question – how sustainable in the long term is world tourism?

This paper describes some practical measures which are now being taken to create sustainable development in the form of a new Gaelic tourism industry. The double aim of these measures will be to exploit an underutilised resource (the Gaelic language), while at the same time enhancing the development of Gaelic culture and society. A primary goal will be to optimise economic and social benefits of tourism in the Highlands and Islands and beyond, resulting in more and better quality jobs and increased income for local populations.

The new Gaelic tourism product, which will reinforce the existing tourism industry, will be underpinned by Scotland's Gaelic resources and is expected to account for 2,000 Gaelic based jobs over the next 20 years. A key feature is community involvement in, and control of, the industry by promotion of links between Gaelic and local businesses and co-operation with existing agencies. The new industry will be closely integrated with recent developments in Gaelic arts and broadcasting, and will be an important means of raising the profile of Gaelic Scotland nationally, within the European Community and world-wide.

The terms 'Celtic tourism' and 'Gaelic tourism' both have currency. Although there is some overlap between these concepts, they are different in character. The former may be regarded as tourism which draws on the broad sweep of interest in all things Celtic from the ancient legacy of artifacts, standing stones and the like to the cultural distinctiveness of the various contemporary Celtic language communities. Specifically 'Gaelic tourism', on the other hand, enables visitors and local people to interface actively with the modern Gaelic speaking community in Scotland. Use of the Gaelic language and explanation of the culture would have a high profile, although interpretation would be provided in other languages for non-Gaelic speakers.

Gaelic tourism thus described will serve to support and enhance wider tourism objectives. It has the potential to extend the core season, broaden the range of visitors, provide reasons to visit Scotland and in particular areas of the Highlands and Islands outside the major hubs. It will bring trade to fragile remote areas and those with high unemployment, will diversify local economies, and increase the distinctiveness of the areas tourism product. With its indoor and outdoor adaptability, Gaelic tourism will enhance all-weather facilities and attractions, and special interest holidays.

A further imperative is that, within Gaeldom, itself there is an expressed need for a new more appropriate form of tourism industry, based in the Gaelic communities, under local control and which utilises cultural resources and strengths already present. This paper sets out how a start has been made in bringing this about.

THE EUROPEAN BACKGROUND

In the Europe of the 1990s and, indeed into the next millennium, tourism is destined to play an increasingly important role; it is presently regarded as the world's largest industry. Recent 'megatrends' analyses reveal that cultural tourism is one of the few sectors of the European economy where long-term growth is anticipated.

As the market becomes more competitive and sophisticated, cultural tourism is gaining in importance. This offers particular opportunities to Europe's distinctive lesser used language regions. From among the European regions, organisations in the Celtic language communities of Scotland, Ireland, Isle of Man, Wales, Brittany and Cornwall have begun to take an active interest in cultural tourism. This has led to a number of conferences which have thrown up ideas as to how to exploit viable links between language and tourism while maximising the benefits to the indigenous cultures.

As with the other Celtic countries, Scotland has maintained a distinctive Celtic language and culture through Gaelic. In fact much of what distinguishes Scotland today can be regarded as being based on or derived from Gaelic culture. There has also been some recognition in local communities that their linguistic heritage is an asset which offers potential in terms of tourism. The tourism strategy of Highlands and Islands Enterprise has also highlighted the importance of culture and environment in the area. Nevertheless, in an age of improved communications, education and travel, it is evident that the cultural assets of Gaeldom are vastly under utilised.

Indeed the linguistic and cultural assets of all Celtic cultures still remain largely untapped in terms of tourism. These surviving Celtic speech communities on the Western seaboard of Europe are the remnants of a rich, vast and ancient pan-European linguistic and cultural domain extending from Portugal and Ireland in the west to Turkey in the east, leaving myriad sites, artifacts and cultural legacies with capacity to act as a stimulus for tourism development. Emerging awareness of the immense significance of the Celts to the development of Europe, eg following an acclaimed year long exposition of Celtic artifacts in Venice, has helped to highlight the cultural tourism potential.

THE DYNAMICS OF THE GAELIC REVIVAL

The Gaelic language has been subjected to severe erosive forces over many centuries and is under threat. Recently, however, Gaelic has undergone a quite remarkable revival in terms of youth, education, the arts and media. This was driven by an intense and successfully orchestrated effort by Scotland's Gaelic development agency Comunn na Gàidhlig (CNAG). With government support, an infrastructure and the key practical measures essential for the Gaelic community's linguistic and cultural maintenance has been created.

The main tasks of the 1990s will be to bring about a major shift in the age profile, so that Gaelic will become increasingly the language of young people rather than the elderly. This will be achieved through Gaelic medium education, in developing new areas of Gaelic based employment generating economic activity, strengthening cultural self-confidence within the Gaelic community and promoting the value of Gaelic to Government, public bodies and the Gaelic community itself. By early in the new millennium it is expected that the language and culture will have been reorientated in such a way that sustained growth both in numbers of speakers and in related cultural and economic activity can ensue indefinitely thereafter.

By setting targets for development under each of these project categories, the following tentative estimates for numbers of Gaelic speakers in Scotland have been extrapolated:

	1971	1981	1991	2001	2011	2021
total number	89,000	79,000	66,000	60,000	65,000	79,000
number under age 25	18,000	17,000	14,000	16,000	22,000	42,000
% under age 25	22%	22%	20%	26%	32%	51%

One of the most important recent shifts in opinion is that the Gaelic language and culture is now seen as a powerful motor for economic development if correctly harnessed. Development agencies are increasingly geared to exploit economic opportunities which Gaelic offers. Ascribing a greater commercial worth to the language will undoubtedly raise its profile, stimulate demand for its use and justify increased education provision, particularly when wealth and jobs are created. By 1993, economic analysis revealed that 1,000 jobs had been created and the total gross output of the Gaelic economy in 1993 (with multipliers) was calculated to be £41 million

In the light of the above, for a relatively modest investment in national terms, Gaelic development represents a major opportunity for economic regeneration. Furthermore, much of Gaelic related activities will be a factor in retention of population in rural areas and the jobs created will frequently be of high income and status. A major opportunity for Gaelic based economic development is Gaelic based cultural tourism. In return Gaelic can give Scottish tourism a new quality edge.

THE MARKET

If the new Gaelic tourism sector is to have substance and credibility, it must be rooted in and have the affirmation and respect of the Gaelic community itself. For this reason internal Gaelic tourism is a small but important legitimising component of the Gaelic tourism market because it allows Gaels themselves to feel a sense of ownership of the product. Key dimensions are:

—   children attending Gaelic medium schools, and their parents, who seek Gaelic medium interpretive facilities and events throughout the Highlands & Islands and elsewhere in Scotland;

—   Gaelic speakers, including adult learners, of all ages on holiday requiring Gaelic medium tours and services while out of their own community; this can include expatriates.

The volume market will be mainly visitors from outside Scotland made up of the following categories:

—   visitors with a variety of Gaelic and Celtic related interests and affinities, eg music, history, 'culture collectors', the continental Celtic connection, archaeology, etc.;

—   minority language speakers in the European Community, especially Celtic languages, among whom there is a growing mutual interest;

—   American, Canadian, Australian etc. visitors of Gaelic decent or Scottish ancestry, some with genealogical interest;

—   the rest of the mass market who have no specific Gaelic interest but who may be introduced 'en passant' to Gaelic and Celtic culture.

The market, therefore, ranges from small scale but intense interest, through to the large scale but superficial curiosity. The product must accommodate this range while endeavouring to educate and stimulate a greater intensity of interest at the 'superficial' end of the spectrum.

THE PRODUCT

In the Scottish context, a Gaelic tourism facility should interpret, or provide an experience of, some aspect of the Gaelic dimension of Celtic culture or life. As an intrinsic part of its function, Gaelic and bi-lingual signage, written and audio-visual material, and staff should be provided.

If the market penetration and income generation are to be maximised, the product must above all be based on demonstrable quality. Switzerland and the Scandinavian countries offer models of positive tourism image, and practice based on reputations for top quality service; clean mountain, coast or lake environment, and a rich cultural and historical backdrop. Their winning formula is to display modernity and efficiency founded on antiquity and tradition. The Gaelic community has to hand these natural ingredients for a world class product given effective organisation, appropriate investment and rigorous control of quality, including cultural and linguistic integrity.

A brainstorming session by Dr John Shaw and the author in summer 1993 facilitated the development of the whole concept of Gaelic tourism, and the identification of the key product components required to create a Gaelic tourism industry as set out below.

The main hardware element proposed for Gaelic tourism is a network of interpretive centres where the history and culture of Gaeldom is explained through the medium of Gaelic but with interpretation in English and other languages. Some of these centres, especially those at main tourist gateways, would have an orientation function to lead visitors into the network, thereby to encourage multiple visits. For that reason there should be variety in style and content among these centres. Emphasis on locality and community would be generally desirable. Where appropriate, existing and proposed museums, with improved Gaelic content, should be an integral part of such a network.

The recent development of the Gaelic Arts mainly under the 'National Gaelic Arts Project' has created a major new vehicle for enhancing the appeal of Gaelic tourism. Feisean (local non-competitive music festivals), Blasad den Iar (interpretive community based tourist shows), Gaelic exhibitions, drama events etc. all have potential, with good organisation, for closer integration with the tourism product. The National Mod (the annual festival of Gaelic culture) has long been an event with important off season tourism benefits. As it evolves it may well have the potential to enhance these benefits further. The new Gaelic television industry and the mounting of high quality professional Gaelic touring 'shows' can act as ambassadors for Gaelic Scotland.

Besides the passive experience of visiting interpretive centres and events, there is a growing demand especially among young people and learners for participatory activities carried out through the medium of Gaelic, eg arts such as drama and music, and sports such as sailing and hillwalking. In addition, there is educational tourism including language courses, historical lecture tours, visiting relevant Gaelic sites, genealogy and guided tours of the Gaelic movement in Scotland.

Visual evidence of the existence of Gaelic is an important part of the process of affirming the distinctiveness of the Highlands and Islands to visitors (especially from the continent) as well as to residents. A major, and relatively inexpensive aid to creating this 'Gaelic Face' to the product is the provision of Gaelic or bi-lingual signage and written information, including street signs, shop fronts, logos etc. especially in tourist hubs such as Inverness, Oban, Portree, and Fort William. Initiatives to bring this about should be done in discussion with local authorities, chambers of commerce an possibly common good funds. A body of information in Gaelic and from a Gaelic perspective should also available to tourists in the form of booklets or brochures or videos. For tourists and local people an up to date Gaelic medium and bilingual information sheet on current Gaelic events and facilities will be an important aid to visitor penetration of the Gaelic tourism network.

There is scope to extend greatly the range and quality of Gaelic souvenirs and products including gifts, stationary, cards, kitchenware, plaques etc with Gaelic inscriptions, local Gaelic or bilingual pamphlets, guides and maps to areas of Gaelic interest. Where feasible, local manufacture by Gaelic speakers would be encouraged. Lists for tourists as to where such goods may be available throughout Scotland and beyond will require to be produced.

The provision of Gaelic accommodation, pubs and restaurants to create or to encourage a Gaelic ambience for the enjoyment of tourists and local people will not only enhance the Gaelic tourism experience but will further reinforce the development of Gaelic at community level. Accommodation ranging from hotels and B&Bs and self-catering requires to be identifed clearly in the literature and marketing material, and this can include thatched house restoration and other period buildings restorations, eg Gearranan (Lewis), Eilean Iarmain etc. Guidance material needs to be created and delivered to operators as to how to introduce good quality Gaelic traditional foods, music, customs, decor etc, employ Gaelic speaking staff and use Gaelic and bilingual menus, signs etc.

A variety of specialised Gaelic package tours are possible as contributors to and customers of Gaelic tourism. Tours may be exclusively through Gaelic, for Gaelic speakers, learners, etc, or through English or such other languages as visitors may require. Gaelic tours would generally involve more than one aspect of Gaelic culture by combining say history, entertainment, food, interpretive centres with social experiences in Gaelic communities. Lecture tours or activity related packages offer potential variants (see Gaelic Activity Tourism above). The key is to use the Gaelic dimension to enrich the tourist experience beyond what is now generally available in the Highlands.

A useful specialised market niche is inter-Celtic exchanges. These already take place to a limited extent but are capable of substantial expansion through reciprocal group package tours with Gaelic speaking couriers eg Scotland – Ireland and vice versa timed to link with feisean or other events.

The above components, which together form the Gaelic tourism product, require coherent and effective marketing as a distinct product within the overall Scottish and Highlands and Islands tourism market. Imaginatively designed campaigns and promotional material will be required. Such material, and associated on the ground facilities, could usefully give more prominence to the Gaelic 'G' symbol as a marketing device. In marketing Gaelic tourism co-operation on cultural tourism projects with other lesser used language regions should be sought together with European Union funding. Joint projects with Ireland, Wales and Brittany may be particularly beneficial. In particular joint marketing of 'Gaelic Scotland' with other Celtic countries should also be pursued possibly linking with the Welsh 'Celtica' promotion.

THE POTENTIAL SCALE OF GAELIC TOURISM

As the concept of Gaelic tourism evolved it was necessary to develop a feel for the potential scale of the new industry. The following official tourism industry statistics are revealing:

Area (population)	£ turnover	employment	£/head
UK (55,000,000)	25,200,000,000	1,600,000	460
Scotland (5,000,000)	1,500,000,000	160,000	300
H & I (360,000)	500,000,000	20,000	1,300

As a crude indicator, by drawing on the lowest of the above per capita ratios, the Gaelic community of 65,000 should be capable of generating a Gaelic tourism industry with an annual turnover of £20 million employing 2,000 people. Given proper development support and marketing there is no reason to believe that the Gaelic industry should perform less well than that of Scotland or the UK as a whole.

There are indeed a number of reasons to believe that the Gaelic tourism product, once fully in operation has a number of competitive advantages:

–   it is associated with a beautiful, dramatic and clean landscape;

–   traditional and contemporary Gaelic and Celtic arts, reinforced by Gaelic television, are perceived to be distinct from homogenised western arts, and now excite international interest;

–   interest in minority cultures and languages is growing rapidly, particularly among the 40 million EU citizens who speak a 'lesser used language';

–   Gaelic culture is increasingly understood by continental Europeans to be a survivor of a pan-European culture covering a territory whose modern population is one quarter of a billion, comparable to that of the USA.

IMPLEMENTATION

If it is to have more than marginal impact, the Gaelic Tourism product and its market must be developed in concert with existing organisations and initiatives as an enhancement of the existing Scottish tourism industry. Besides the Highlands and Islands Enterprise network, Scottish institutional support will be expected to feature Scottish Natural Heritage, Historic Scotland, Scottish Tourist Board and area tourist boards, etc. Links between these and specifically Gaelic organisations working in the fields of the Gaelic arts, broadcasting and the Gaelic learners industry will need to be forged to provide an infrastructural foundation for the creation of the new Gaelic tourism industry.

The development of Gaelic tourism product will generally be private sector led but may be supported by funding partnerships involving Higlands and Islands Enterprise and Scottish Enterprise networks, CNAG, STB and the EU. As is the case with certain other minority cultures, large scale emigration has created a wealthy and influential overseas diaspora. Its fundraising capability has already been harnessed effectively for cultural tourism projects in the Highlands and Islands in the cases, for example, of Balnain House Music

Centre and Clan Donald Lands Trust, both of which have Gaelic significance. There is believed to be further scope for encouraging such international links based on the emotional appeal of the home Gaelic culture. A few other Gaelic tourism facilities such as Hotel Eilean Iarmain in Skye, Aros in Skye and Gearranan in Lewis are already in operation. A substantial number of other projects which currently do not feature a Gaelic dimension have the potential for early enhancement in this regard, given appropriate encouragement and guidance.

As knowledge and track record evolves publicising innovations on a continuing basis will bring benefits to the industry. This can be done through media exposure to successful developments, study visits and the engagement of guest speakers to Gaelic tourism fora from successful Scottish Gaelic tourism initiatives or to describe developments in the field in Ireland, Wales, and other lesser used language regions.

A key issue is how to develop Gaelic tourism while enhancing the culture. As an early step it was felt useful to identify most effective method of raising awareness of Gaelic and marketing such aspects of Gaelic tourism as already exist. In so doing looking at parallel or related cultures eg Ireland, Wales, Brittany etc. for practical examples of language and cultural tourism was also considered desireable.

THE PILOT PROJECT

To ascertain the current position an audit of the Gaelic content and potential of existing facilities was carried out. The concept of linguistic cultural tourism was also explored at local level in a series of seminars held throughout the Highlands and Islands during 1994. Examples of good practice from Wales, Ireland and Brittany were demonstrated and useful comparisons were noted. Armed with this information, CNAG embarked on a pilot Gaelic Tourism Marketing and Training project. The project was the subject of an eventually successful ERDF application which covered the following elements:

–   a 16 page full colour Gaelic tourism brochure in four versions (Gaelic, English, French and German);

–   origination and publishing of a new Gaelic phrase book in three versions (English, French and German);

–   devising and mounting training courses for tourism operators to introduce the Gaelic dimension to tourism;

–   impact assesment study.

In parallel with the pilot study proper, CNAG, under other heads, has encouraged the spread of bi-lingual signage, extension of the 'G' symbol scheme, preparation of tourist information packs, and is aiding the design of a travelling exhibition to promote a wider understanding of the story of the Gaels.

The brochure itself, called *Fàilte – Welcome to Scotland's Gaelic Renaissance* was produced in-house with the aid of a free lance multilingual contractor and was launched in February 1995. It describes the story of the Gaels in Scotland and lists key Gaelic sites, interpretive centres, events, courses, and 270 accomodation providers. The initial print run was 60,000 of which 25,000 were mailed directly to people who had expressed an interest in Gaelic. Initial response, particularly within the Gaelic community, has been favourable.

A range of Gaelic tourism training courses to introduce the significance of Gaelic to staff in tourism establishments was designed and mounted in a number of representetive area in the Highlands and Islands. The impact assessment awaited the evolution of the 1995 season and in the meantime planning started on the next phases of Gaelic tourism development.

THE NEXT PHASES

The progress made under the pilot phase in raising awareness of the potential of Gaelic tourism was sufficiently encouraging for CNAG to start assembling the elements of a more ambitious and commercial approach. In pursuing this potentially important development opportunity, CNAG rexamined its aims and was able to restate them as follows:

- maintain and strengthen the Gaelic language and culture;
- improve the image of Gaelic among Gaels and non-Gaels;
- create sustainable jos for local people (a new industry);
- treat fragile areas as a priority;
- generate an income stream to CNAG.

CNAG's task is to translate these aims into a coherant and practical development scheme in partnership with development agencies, STB and the area tourist boards, tourist operators and most importantly the Gaelic community itself. In pursuit of integrity and quality of the Gaelic content of the product, a balance has to be struck between the opportunity to create new Gaelic businesses and the opportunity to Gaelicise, and add value to existing businesses. CNAG has already undertaken to proceed with a larger more commercial 32 page 'Fàilte' brochure for 1996. It will have a print run of at least 100,000 and will be promoted on the Internet. Both the brochure and phrase book will be produced in two further languages (Spanish and Italian).

The outcome of CNAG's deliberations on how it proposes to proceed with the longer term task of developing Gaelic tourism as a major force in Scotland will be set out in due course.

CONCLUSION

History and culture already provide strong and legitimate elements within UK's tourism attractiveness to visitors from both home and oversees. All indications are that Gaelic tourism has the potential to be an important new contributor to the Scottish economy. Its development is consistent with the strategic tourism objectives of Scottish Tourist Board and the Highlands and Islands Entreprise and Scottish Enterprise networks, and is ideally placed to form productive links with other sectors. Research and experiment will be required on how best to market the concept and develop the product.

The image of employment in the tourism industry has traditionally been poor and often unattractive to permanent indigenous residents of the Highlands and Islands. Gaelic tourism offers the desirable prospect of a greater proportion of highly skilled, high paying jobs, because of the higher than usual skill requirements of this specialised new high quality industry. Above all Gaelic tourism must be managed in such a way that the cultural resource is strengthened and not damaged by insensitive exploitation. Once the 'culture friendly' credentials of the industry become manifest, this in itself will enhance the image of the tourism industry per se.

The emergence of Gaelic tourism is timely, with active interest in cultural tourism growing both in Scotland and Europe generally. A few initiatives have already been taken forward by CNAG and by innovative entrepreneurs. The opportunity now exists for tourist organisations, development agencies, community groups and tourist operators to turn Scotland's Gaelic heritage into a major development tool.

The Author

Roy Pedersen was formerly head of Social Development with Highlands and Islands Enterprise and is now Development Director with Commun na Gàidhlig. He is Chairman of HI Arts, a director of the Gaelic publishing company Acair, and is author of *One Europe – 100 Nations* .

27

MAIR LICHT ON THE MITHER TONGUE
Scots as a National Language

Billy Kay

In the sumptuous surroundings of the court of James IV at the beginning of
the 16th century, long before gentility put down roots here, the poet Dunbar
tested his skills as a Makar in the old Scots tradition of flyting against a fellow
poet Walter Kennedy from Galloway:

Iersch brybour bard, vyle beggar with thy brattis,
Cuntbittin crawdoun Kennedy, coward of kynd,
Evill farit and dryit, as Densemen on the rattis,
Lyke as the gleddis had on thy gule snowt dynd;
Mismaid monstour, ilk mone owt of thy mind,
Renunce, rebald, thy ryming, thow bot royis,
Thy trechour tung hes tane ane heland strynd;
Ane lawland ers wald mak a bettir noyis.

[*Cuntbittin* infected; *crawdoun* craven; *as Densemen on the rattis* like deid
Danes exposed on the wheel; *gleddis* kites; *gule* yellow; *dynd* hit; *royis*
raves; *heland strynd* highland race, kind]

In its potent blend of deadly diatribe and literary posturing, it reminds me
of two very different views on our national character; the positive one
contained in the auld saw 'scartin an bitin is Scots folks wooin', and the
negative contained in the poet Norman McCaig's memorable remark: 'If any
back scratching goes on among Scottish poets, it's done wi dirks!'

Thow speiris, dastard, gif I dar with the fecht?
Ye, dagone, dowbart, thairof haif thow no dowt!
Quhair evir we meit, thairto my hand I hecht
To red thy rebald ryming with a rowt:
Throw all Bretane it salbe blawin owt
How that thow, poysonit pelor, gat thy paikis;
With ane dog leich I schepe to gar the schowt,
And nowther to the tak knyfe, swerd nor aix

299

[*dagone* villain; *dowbart* dullard; *hecht* promise; *red* clear up; *rowt* blow; *pelor* thief; *paikis* blows; *leich* leash]

When Dunbar wrote, Scots was without doubt perceived as a distinctive national language, *the langage of Scottis natioun*, as Gavin Douglas put it. The Spanish ambassador to the court Pedro de Ayala compared Scots and English to Castilian Spanish and Catalan. In his prologue to the Aeneid, Douglas states he wants the translation to be 'braid and plane, kepand na sudron bot our awyn langage'. It was also an international language, carried abroad through documents of law, diplomacy and trade, like the vernacular of any independent state. This benighted situation, the orthodoxy goes, all came to an end as the nails of the Reformation, the Union of the Crowns and the Union of the Parliaments were driven into the coffin of Scots.

For many Scottish people thirled to English language and culture today, replace nails in the coffin with stakes through the heart. For them Scots is a demotic monster whose unleashing could devour them, or at least alter their status as bona fide assimilados to English culture. They have harboured a death wish for Scots for almost three centuries, but it remains yet in the realm of the Undead. Not only that, it has sunk its ugsome wallies elsewhere. For three centuries on from Dunbar, in the very different setting of the Pennsylvania frontier at the time of the Whiskey Rebellion, there took place another poetic flyting in Scots. This is Ulster-born David Bruce on the drink at the centre of local politics in 1794:

Great Pow'r, that warms the heart an liver,
And puts the bluid aw in a fever,
If dull and heartless I am ever,
A blast o thee
Maks me as blyth, and brisk, and clever
As ony bee.

The other protagonist was Hugh Henry Brackenridge who left Campbelltown at the age of five, but was also brought up in the Ulster Scots colonies of western Pennsylvania. Both used naturally the language of their American community. They also knew the shared tradition in which they were working. In a lull from political point scoring, Brackenridge introduces a literary allusion:

Ye canna then expect a phrase
Like them ye get in poets lays;
For where's the man that nowadays
Can sing like Burns;
Whom nature taught her ain strathspeys
And now she mourns.

Brackenridge's use of Scots was not confined to prose, in his chief work 'Modern Chivalry' he introduces a Scots-speaking character with strong religious conviction called Duncan Ferguson. In an article on the two poets in *American Speech* in 1928, Claude M. Newlin, writes: 'Since Bruce was an ardent Federalist, it is not probable that his Scots verses on political topics were written in dialect for merely sentimental reasons. He no doubt considered Scots to be the most effective medium in which he could appeal to his frontier audience.' Brackenridge's son, Henry Marie Brackenridge also conveyed his native dialect in his writing, having learned a rich spoken Scots from his grandmother. 'I learned the Scottish dialect from her, and read to her The Gentle Shepherd and other poems of Ramsay and Ferguson...My father had a curious collection of the Scottish poets, from James author of the King's Quair, and Gavin Douglas, down to Burns.'

A unique feature of course of the Scottish diaspora from the Lowlands was that in general it was a literate migration. Their influence on the character of the American South and its literature was immense; names such as Ellen Glasgow, Erskine Caldwell, Jesse Stuart and William Faulkner come to mind. The Nobel Prize winner Faulkner proudly states that the place he came from was 'Scotch Mississippi, both Highland and Lowland.'

In Appallachia, the descendants of Ayrshire and Ulster Covenanters frightened their bairns with a bogeyman called Claverhouse long after the name had any historic significance. I came across Scots words like galluses, poke for a bag, redd out for clear up, and expressions like 'no worth a haet' in the everyday speech of Carolina Piedmont and Tidewater folk when I collected for a series called the Scotch South in 1994. There, in the Cape Fear district in the baking flatlands of Scotland county, I also discovered that as recently as 1907 a book titled *Lyrics from Cottonland* by John Charles McNeill was published. Descended from Kintyre folk, McNeill's poetry reflects the voices of the black, Indian and white people of the area. He is regarded as the poet laureate of North Carolina. In 'On the Cape Fear' he condenses the history of the Argyll colony in a Scots voice which rings true:

Prince Charlie an I, we war chased owre the sea
Wi naething but conscience for glory.
An here I drew sawrd, when the land wad be free,
An was whipped tae a hole as a Tory.

When the Bonny Blue Flag was flung tae the breeze,
I girded mysel tae defend it:
They warstled me doun tae my hands an my knees
An flogged my auld backbane tae bend it.

Sae the deil wan the fights, an wrang hauds the ground,
But God an mysel winna bide it.
I hae strenth in my airm yet for many a round
An purpose in plenty tae guide it.

I been banished an whipped an warstled an flogged
(I belang tae the Democrat party)
But in gaein owre quagmires I haena been bogged
An am still on my legs, hale an hearty.

I have travelled a lot, for work and pleasure. When it involves discovering pockets of Scots culture in exotic corners of the globe, work and pleasure merge and are one. Recently, my company Odyssey Productions made a radio series called 'Merchant, Pedlars, Mercenaries' about the Scottish migration to the countries of the Baltic in the 17th century. Much of the records are in Scots. Robert Porteous, of Krosno had a commercial empire which extended from Lithuania to Hungary, where he had a monopoly of the wine trade. His detailed will is 'written in the Scottish language'.

In a legal dispute between Scots in Danzig, the Consul Patrick Gordon 'avowit to caus cut the luggis out' frae Gilbert Wilson's heid. If the threat was carried out we must have appeared to the Poles as an exotic race indeed. Their country wes hoatchin wi lugless Scots. William Lithgow who described his sojourn there among 'gallant rich merchants, my countrymen', wes better kennt as Lugless Wull, his lugs cuttit aff lang syne in Lanark as punishment for fornication. 'It could hae been a lot worse', said Wull.

The Hungarian wine magnate Porteous, was a countrymen I missed when I was trawling the world's vineyards for the book *Knee Deep in Claret*. But both Robert Louis Stevenson and I were delighted to find that one of the pioneer vineyards in California's Napa Valley was planted by a man McEachran fae Greenock. '...he remembered his father putting him inside Mons Meg, and that touched me home: and we exchanged a word or two in Scots, which pleased me more than you would fancy'. McEachran's cabin can still be seen in the Scramsberg vineyard, and Stevenson's polynesian-style dwelling from his stay in the Hawaiian Royal compound can be visited in Manoa on Oahu.

Hawaii was another distant home from home, where he addressed the Honolulu Scottish Thistle Club and was feted by his countrymen. Among them was one Archibald S. Cleghorn from Auld Reekie, husband of the Hawaiian Princess Likelike. In the Bishop Museum, Honolulu there is a note written by the couple's daughter Princess Ka'iulani, inviting RLS to the palace for some '...guid Scotch kaukau' Kaukau being the Hawaiian for stovies,.and any other Scottish-Hawaiian soul food you care to mention. Stevenson was enchanted by Ka'iulani composing a lovely poem to her and declaring proudly she was 'half Edinburgh Scots like mysel'.

These are just a few examples I have come across of my mither tongue appearing in far flung places, there must be hundreds of others. Another very Scottish phenomenon is the number of people who write poetry and publish it in small volumes. The world and the commonwealth in particular must be thrang with such books. The work of some of the better know ones has come back to us, like the Border poet Will Ogilvie in Australia, or the Buchan makar Charles Murray in South Africa:

> Scotland our Mither – this from your sons abroad
> Leavin tracks on virgin veld that never kent a road
> Trekkin on wi weary feet, an faces turned fae hame,
> But lovin aye the auld wife across the seas at hame.
>
> Scotland our Mither – since first we left your side,
> From Quilimane to Cape Town we've wandered far and wide;
> Yet aye from mining camp an toun, from koppie an karoo,
> Your sons richt kindly, auld wife, send hame their love to you.

There perhaps we hear the nostalgia of the exile bordering on kailyard sentimentality. But although there is always a danger of couthy excess, exile can whiles make us see Scotland in a more focused, concentrated and detached perspective. Think of RLS himself writing Weir of Hermiston in Samoa, or Lewis Grassic Gibbon writing Sunset Song in Welwyn Garden City. It was certainly travelling when I was younger which made me realise the richness of my own Scots-speaking cultural background. The awe with which it was regarded by people my own age, in say the United States, made me angry about the erosion of the culture at home. That and the fact I was able to study the history of Scots at Edinburgh University, gave me the confidence to come home and proselitise with zeal for the language. Coming from the covenanting heartland of Ayrshire, zeal comes easy to me. I also studied French and German and realised that being bi-lingual in Scots and English was a help rather than a hindrance in learning other languages. 'Ne te fache pas' is easy when you are used to 'dinnae fash yersel', 'Meine Tochter milchte die Kuh' appears less foreign when ye hear Ayrshire fairmers say 'ma dochter milkit the coo.'

When I started work in broadcasting my mission was to uncover all the layers of culture bubbling under the stifling surface of cliches we were in danger of accepting as Scotland. Among the Odyssey programmes were a number devoted to the history of the various ethnic communities which settled here, such as the Irish, Lithuanians and Jews. Again, Scots was at the core of their experience. In David Daiches' autobiography 'Two Worlds: A Scottish Jewish Childhood he recalls vividly the mixture of Yiddish and Scots which was the lingua franca of the 'trebblers' or traivellers, the Jewish travelling salesmen who toured Scotland with their suitcases.

Daiches recalls Barmitzvahs resounding with phrases such as 'Wull ye hae a drap o the bramfen' (bramfen brandy, whisky). In a recent article in Cencrastus magazine, F.W. Freeman celebrates the Scots/Yiddish poetry of the playwright, Avrom Greenbaum whose identity with Scots comes across in the relish with which he explores his dual cultural heritage and rails against the unco froom – the unco guid.

> As for chiels wha criticise
> We'll aiblins never heed 'em
> But dance and sing and hae oor fling
> Like genuine Scots Chassidim.

In one of the programmes, I interviewed members of the small Spanish comunity imported to staff the iron works of South Ayrshire at the turn of the century. The elderly Spanish gentleman and his wife were born in Seville, but had spent most of their life in Scotland. Like me they spoke the Ayrshire dialect of Scots. I was dismayed, therefore when the tape recorder was switched on and Mr Esquierdo began to speak in stilted, broken English. It was his wife who interrupted and saved the interview, 'Here you', said she, 'Stop pittin it on, talk Scotch like the rest o us!' I spiered in Scots, because I knew I would get better material from the person if he did not feel obliged to translate himself for the microphone. Because of the overwhelming power and prestige of English language and culture in Scotland however, the response to such an obvious aesthetic decision, is not as straightforward as it ought to be.

The majority of Scots are uneducated in their own culture, therefore their reaction to fundamental aspects of it such as their native vernacular are often extreme. This passion for things Scottish is often an instinctive gut reaction to the culture being put down by the authorities, the reaction against it often the product of derived irrational prejudice. Like Pavlov's dogs many Scots are conditioned to react to any aspect of their culture with the word 'parochial' or 'tartan' or 'couthy' no matter how universal the content may be. By doing programmes which have posed questions of people's cultural identity, I have often provoked strong reactions. The ratio is in the region of seven love letters to every three hostile letters. Into the latter category came a lady from Alloway who wrote in high dudgeon, asserting that Scots did not exist and that my guests and I on Scottish Television's *Kay's Originals* television programme were all putting it on. We were a disgrace to Scotland, and what would the English think.

An example of our putting it on was our use of the place name Glesca. The lady had not, she assured me, heard it pronounced thus since she attended the Music Halls in the 1940s. In my reply, I asked her which institution she had been locked up in during the intervening years. Many Scots do not want to believe Scots exists and steik their lugs accordingly – I refuse to hear it, therefore it does not exist. Having the good fortune to travel around Scotland in my work, and unlike most, deliberately speaking Scots to the people I meet if I jalouse they are Scots speakers, I can testify to the smeddum that's still in the leid. The distinctive vocabulary may be eroded among the young, but what they speak is still recognisable as Scots. What Scots lacks most of all is recognition, and status.

Ironically, one of the main barriers to the restoration of Scots is its strength at the local level. With the decline of Scots as the national language, a sign of its fragmentation is the fact that for many Scots speakers and writers the local dialect is more important, and more clearly defined as an entity than something called Scots. This has had the beneficial effect of giving people pride in local culture and history, and encouraging writers to compose in a local form of Scots. But it has also produced the erroneous idea that the vernaculars of Buchan, Shetland or Dundee for example are unrelated, isolated in their own locality and different from all others, when in fact they are all regional dialects of the same Scots tongue.

This phenomenon is illustrated by the plethora of articles and books that have been published to satisfy local interest in the dialects, but which obscure the national dimension. In the Aberdeen Press and Journal on March 27, 1986, for example, an article on North-east speech had the following under the title 'North-east Sayings': 'aul' farrant, fair fleggit, fair forfochen, sleekit, scunnert, trauchelt'. Now every one of these is common Scots, and would be known by most Scots-speakers. I have seen the same thing in lists of Dundonese vocabulary which include words like hirple, humff, halikit, and hurdies; in the Shetland Dictionary with words such as bide, birl, and ben; in Glasgow glossaries with Glaswegian words such as neb, neeps and noak. In almost every one of these, the fact that 90% of the words are common Scots is played down, and the uniqueness of the local dialect played up.

The identity of the Doric in the North-East is particularly strong, and now has substantial backing from the North East of Scotland Heritage Trust. Doric was originally a dialect of ancient Greek, whose rustic strength contrasted with the sophistication of the literary language of Athens. In the 18th century Scots writers like Alan Ramsay justified using Scots by comparing it to the use of the Doric by Theocritus. Since then, the term has been interchangeable with Scots and has been applied to all Scots dialects. Writing to MacDiarmid in 1931 anent his bairn rhymes, William Soutar wrote '...if the Doric is to come back alive, it will come first on a cock horse'.

Older speakers all over the country will refer to their language as Scotch, or the Doric, knowing they are one and the same thing. In the North East, however, Doric has become almost an exclusive term for the Scots spoken in the area. According to the Business Plan for the Heritage Trust, the area's 'most unique feature is the Doric, the local dialect and one of Europe's neglected languages.' There is no mention of the Doric's relationship with other Scots-speaking areas or with the Scots language at all. It is simply something called Doric, and appears to have declared U.D.I. from Scots. Given the ignorance concerning Scots, this emphasis on the local at the expense of the national can only serve to diminish the case for national and international backing for the language, which is the direction we should all be heading together as one voice. Again through ignorance of the historic national language speakers of local dialects today presume that theirs and theirs only is the genuine article.

The first Aberdonian I ever met was in Munich's Hofbrauhaus at the age of 17, when I spiered 'Hou ur ye gettin oan', an he replied. 'Nae bad', I thocht tae masel – he cannae be a richt Scots speaker, awbody that kens ocht aboot Scots, says 'no bad', he must be pittin it oan. Nae dout monie fowk fae different airts hes thocht the same aboot ma Scots. Indeed, because of the controversy surrounding literary Lallans, there are those in the North-East who get things badly agley and presume that all Scots spoken south of the Dee is an ersatz kiddie on.

This intense local focus and loyalty to the dialect is also determined by social factors. People are conditioned to switch to English in formal situations, so that Scots-speaking strangers will naturally communicate, at least initially, in English. The isolation of the dialects is also heightened by lack of exposure in the media – if people became accustomed to hearing the different dialects, they would quickly realise the similarities rather than fear the differences and blow away the myth that one dialect speaker cannot communicate with another one from a different area. While all of these are signs of a language in retreat, we are not alone. Similar manifestations have occurred within every deposed language in Europe. Listen to the echoes for Scots here in Pierre – Jakez Helias's description of his native parish in Brittany in the book *Horse of Pride*.

Today most grandmothers know nothing but Breton, their children are fluent in both languages; and their grandchildren speak only French. That's why mass is celebrated in French; and too bad for the grandmothers. However, under ordinary circumstances, the parishes of Plozevet and Plonéour still speak Breton. It will take a long time to die out and will last as long as the people need it to express precisely what they are and what they want. Moreover it is such a strictly private matter that some Bretons claim that the language they speak is not the same as that spoken by the people of Plozevet or Plonéour. Indeed, you often hear them say: 'That bunch doesn't speak the same Breton that we do'. It's somewhat true and also completely false. But the difference between that 'somewhat' and that 'completely' is enough to make Breton-speaking people from two different districts speak French when they meet.'

Similarly, I have heard many Scots speakers say that they are only comfortable talking Scots to someone from the same locality. We ourselves, in other words, contribute to the decline in use of our language. With everyone conditioned to some extent by official disdain for the tongue, it takes a strong person to speak Scots in a formal situation where people may classify them according to one or other stereotype as coarse or uneducated; it is so much simpler to speak English and save yourself the hassle.

The conflict between the national and the provincial in the Scottish mentality is explored by Fionn MacColla in his book *At the Sign of the Clenched Fist*: 'Scottish education regards itself as successful, as having fulfilled its objective, in proportion as each generation is less Scottish than the last, in language, knowledge, culture, and consciousness'. Although the situation has improved dramatically, MacColla's statement still rings true to the experience of most Scots alive today.

The Portuguese colonies in Africa gave the name assimilado to the members of the native population who adopted not only the language and the culture of Portugal but also the Portuguese contempt for the native culture. To some extent Scotland is a country of assimilados, with everyone educated here inheriting this ambivalence about the Scottish/English balance within themselves and their culture. Some refer to it as the Scottish Cringe and it affects every individual and every institution.

BBC Scotland, for example, is defined within the Corporation as a 'National Region' and is constantly trying to work out whether it is 'regional' or 'national' and quite often finds it difficult to ride both horses at once. The BBC charter states that its aim is to reflect the distinctive features of Scottish culture. A sign of it having achieved that goal will be when Scots along with Scottish English and Gaelic is accepted as a natural medium of communication. When Radio Scotland encouragingly broadcast 'Amang Guid Companie' a series of six interviews by me in Scots, the reaction within the BBC was the usual mixture of approval and disapproval. One producer was heard to say: 'My mother didn't allow me to speak that way, so why are we broadcasting in it!' In response, a Gael said the level of debate reminded her of the sterility of the 'tinker Gaelic' stushie within the Gaelic media twenty years ago, when the Lewis dialect spoken by the majority of speakers, was not considered fit to be broadcast.

This is a problem confronted by all lesser used languages from Gaeldom to Galicia, the problem of 'normalising' a language for broadcast which has hitherto been deemed unsuitable. 'Artificial' is the accusation frequently thrown at me for using my mither tongue in formal, public situations where Scots speakers are expected to and conditioned to defer to English. By speaking Scots on the media, what I am doing is both totally natural – a native speaker using his mother tongue – and totally artificial – native speakers of my mother tongue have never previously had the opportunity or confidence in their ability to use their language as the medium for serious discussion. It is the scenario which is artificial, with many people so conditioned to expect English there, that anything else comes across as strange. Even generally supportive critics , who at the very least have knowledge of Scots as a literary language and should know better, are drawn into the trap and have used words like 'synthetic' and 'artificial' when discussing the programmes.

Everyone I know who shares my conviction about the need to extend the use of Scots in the public domain and has the strength of character to go against their socialisation and use their Scots in public has experienced similar stounds to their sensibilities. The poet Ellie McDonald was criticised by a family friend for demeaning herself and using 'coorse' Dundee Scots in a recent broadcast. 'How dae ye explain tae an auld bodie that ye're makin a political statement?' said Ellie. Sadly, she is correct. There should be nothing more natural in the world than using your first language in our national media, but the majority of us are so uneducated in our own culture that to use the native language of what I would still consider to be the majority of Scots, can indeed be regarded as making a political statement. For the language to break out of the cycle of ignorance, confusion and erosion that besets it, however, a lot more people are going to have to start making that same 'political statement'.

The tension between different parts of our linguistic inheritance is not, however, without its lighter moments. Joe Paterson from Dundee recalled learning English parrot fashion from the teacher when he was a child in the 1920's. The teacher declaimed the sentence, asked what it meant, then had the bairns repeat in their best accents. One phrase was indelibly etched on Joe's memory: 'The Lady forsook the child' said the teacher, and asked what it meant. Joe was good at language, so the answer came easily, 'She gied the bairn the breist, Miss!' Anecdotal evidence on the humour arising from Scots attempting to 'correct' their Scots abounds. Different sets of Scots-speaking parents told me how adverse reaction by teachers had made their young children wary of their parents tongue. So when one set of parents referred to the River Tay, and the other to a friend called Brian Tottie, the children corrected them with the 'proper' pronunciation: the River Toe and Brian Potatoe.

Attitudes to Scots are changing dramatically within education, but it will take generations of change to remove what we call the Scottish Cringe and the Catalans call the slave mentality – the 'haudin doun' mind set of peoples whose cultures have been marginalised. Many people believe that the tension can only be resolved when Scotland achieves the political autonomy she has been requesting politely since the days of Keir Hardie. Only then will Scottish culture be central to our education, our media and our life.

The political climate in Europe has never been more sympathetic to the myriad cultures it harbours. For ten years now the European Bureau of Lesser Used Languages has been working effectively at Eurpean Union level to promote and protect the language and culture of over 40 million Europeans. In the past, European Nation States regarded cultural diversity within their borders as a threat to be put down. Now the European Union accepts the concept of unity in diversity and includes in its budget a provision of 3.5 million ECU to promote regional and minority languages and cultures. In 1992 the Council of Europe adopted a Charter for Regional and Minority Languages – the first ever international legal instrument for the protection of languages like Scots and Gaelic. When the vote came to implement the Charter, it received overwhelming support. Significantly, though, the only major European States to abstain, were France and the United Kingdom, the last bastions of the centralist mentality.

With political change, languages with similar histories to Scots such as Galician and Catalan are being 'normalised' and raised in status all over Europe. One of the latest to achieve recognition is the Frankish variety of German spoken in Luxembourg, Letzebuergesh, which now enjoys equal status with French and High German. Almost every citizen speaks all three languages. Since the German Occupation during the Second World War, the desire to differentiate themselves from the Germans resulted in increased linguistic nationalism and identification with the native vernacular. In February 1984 its status as the national language was confirmed by law. Happy as I am for the Luxemburgers, I could not help but notice the stark anomalies of the Scottish and the Scots language situation, when I saw 'Merry Christmas and a Happy New Year' in Letzebuergesh up in lights above Edinburgh's George Street during the European summit there in 1992. Wee totie Luxembourg with a population of 360,000 and a newly declared national language with a sparse literary history were in at the centre of things and fully represented. Scotland, one of Europe's most ancient nations, with a population of five million and a language which has been the medium of a glittering literary tradition was not. We provided the waiters, and the demonstration. Happy New Year!

Alongside a Gaelic/English policy for the Gaidhealtachd, an active bi-lingual policy where Scots and English are fostered and encouraged is surely the only logical way forward for a civilised European nation of the 21st century. Scots will not go away, the narrow, parochial, monoglot philosophy of the Anglicisers will not prevail. For the raucle tongue is a thrawn craitur that will bide on an on, tholan ilka dunt fowk hes throwṇ at it. Even Scots who were not raised to speak it use it unwittingly in their everyday Scottish English. People care about Scots, and will continue to care about it, because they realise how central it is to our continuation as a distinctive people.

At a conference for writers in lesser used languages in Luxembourg, which I attended, someone asked provocatively, 'why do you choose to write in these languages when you are all bi-lingual and could write in the principle languages of Europe'. Pierre-Jakez Helias replied for us all when he said that it was not a matter of choice, he was enceinte, pregnant with Breton, and his creativity had to be given birth in that language. Many monoglots think you can simply translate one language into another and nothing is lost in the translation. They do not realise the nature of language, that each one is a window to the world. What is under threat is the treasure of a people's experience expressed through their native tongue, their unique way of seeing the world. A Welsh philosopher, J. R. Jones, eloquently expresses the potential loss.

> It is said of one experience that it is one of the most agonising possible…that of leaving the soil of your native country forever, of turning your back on your heritage, being torn away by the roots from your familiar land. I have not suffered that experience. But I know of an experience equally agonising, and more irreversible (for you could return to your home) and that is the experience of knowing, not that you are leaving your country, but that your country is leaving you, is ceasing to exist under your very feet, being sucked away from you as it were by a consuming, swallowing wind, into the hands and the possession of another country and civilisation.

There should be no tension between English and Scots. They are branches of the same tree and with some effort and good will are mutually intelligible and complementary to one another. Yet, they are keys to radically different world pictures. I am delighted that I am a native speaker of a national variety of English, the most powerful, prestigious and useful language in the world. But its promotion should never have been at the expense of Scots, the language of my literature, my history, my environment, my family, my town, my county – my mither tongue and that of the majority of people of my nation.

I mentioned above the ease with which German could be adapted into Scots. Further proof of that comes in the words of the great German writer, Goethe, who on his death bed is said to have cried out for 'mehr Licht'. The death wish for Scots has gone unfulfilled, both here and among the Scots communities abroad. For it to be restored fully to a central place in our national life, though, a lot mair licht has to be shone on the vigour, the rich expressiveness, and the beauty it aye hains despite the boorish attempts to eradicate it ower the years. I hope I have shed a fews rays o licht in this paper. I will end as I conclude 'Scots; the Mither Tongue', with the words of another great European writer, Hugh McDiarmid

> For we hae faith in Scotland's hidden pouers
> The present's theirs, but aw the past and future's ours.

Author

Billy Kay is a Distinguished writer and broadcaster of radio and television programmes which specialise in Scottish language, history and culture and examine their place within the context of European culture. These include *Odyssey, The Mother Tongue, Miners* and *Kay's Originals*. His books include *Odyssey: Voices from Scotland's Recent Past* and *Knee Deep in Claret*. He is a popular speaker and frequent contributor to radio and television discussion shows. He has published articles, poetry, short stories and has written plays for radio and the professional stage. Five of his radio documentaries have won international awards in Australia and the USA. He has twice won the Sloan Prize for writing in Scots.

References

Fischer, T. A., *The Scots in Eastern and Western Prussia,* Edinburgh, 1903

Kay, B., *Scots: The Mither Tongue* , Alloway Publishing, 1993

Kay, B., and Maclean, C., *Knee Deep in Claret*, Auld Alliance Publishing, 1994

Mackenzie, W. M. (ed), *The Poems of William Dunbar*, Faber and Faber, 1932

McNeill, J. C., *The Pocket John Charles McNeill*, St Andrews Press, 1990

Stevenson, R. L., *Travels in Hawaiii*, A Grove Day (ed.), University of Hawaii Press, 1973

28

TOWARDS A TRILINGUAL SCOTLAND

Magnus Fladmark

A Civilisation is locked and unlocked through its languages.

Lord Gowrie, 1995

A language, for instance, that is not in regular use may become an interesting museum-piece, may even stand as an important icon, but will not be part of a living culture.

Magnus Linklater, 1995

This paper is based on the text for an address given to the annual conference of the Scottish Association for Teaching English, in Musselburgh on 25 February 1995. The invitation to speak arose from media attention given to views expressed in my inaugural lecture in Aberdeen the previous October on the subject of 'Learning to be a Scot and Speaking Like a Scot'.

The theme for my Musselburgh lecture was to seek an answer to the question of whether the Scots language has been out of official use for so long that it is now too late to campaign for its re-instatement. I did this by looking at what happened to the English and Norwegian languages during their spells in the wilderness. Both were banned from official use, but survived as spoken tongues for several centuries and were returned by political consensus as the languages of government, education and literature.

Those who wish know more about the context of my arguments in the inaugural lecture can consult *The Wealth of a Nation: Heritage as a Cultural and Economic Asset* (Fladmark, 1994). The focus in this essay was on Scots rather than Gaelic, and the key passages from it are quoted below:

> We can blame others for the loss of our Parliament, and for the banning of highland dress, but the theft of our language can be less easily blamed on others. It is a cultural crime perpetuated through our own complicity, and redress can only be achieved by ourselves. The crime is almost unforgivable. Language lies at the heart of cultural sustainability alongside poetry, music and song. Without a living and vibrant language, a nation's culture is emasculated.

> Although in many senses now almost vestigial, Scots is not a corrupt form of English. As argued by Derrick McClure in *Why Scots Matters* (1988), it is

not a dialect, but a language in its own right, which belongs to a wider family of European Languages. These are grouped around the North Sea and include Danish, Norwegian, Swedish, Dutch and German.

How then was Scots allowed to be remaindered? The most powerful tool of territorial domination is to suppress native language. However, the dominant role of English and the perceived subservient position of Scots can not be attributed to the State alone. The Established Church has been an equal force in cultural domination for its own reasons and the word of God has been preached in English since the Authorised Version of the Bible was issued in 1611. It is perhaps ironic that the King responsible is said to have continued speaking braid Scots long after going south to become James I of England in 1603.

The shame induced in Scottish children from an early age when using their own tongue has been a decisive factor. For generations, they have been told by their elders and peers that Scots must not be heard in church, it is discouraged in school on the grounds that the path to progress is through English, and a strong Scottish accent is perceived to be a sign of ignorance. Indeed, it is only tolerated in children, so that beyond a certain age it is thought of as a childish form of speech, which is surely a sad cultural contortion of childhood.

How can Scots be pulled off the remaindered shelf? It is best done by using the pride factor. It is generally estimated that only 15% of Scottish households use standard English at home. Add to this the 2% who speak Gaelic, plus other minority languages, and that leaves about 80% of homes where children grow up with Scots. For this majority of the Scottish people, we should provide more exposure to admired literary figures of the past who wrote in their native language, as well as encouraging more new literature in Scots.

The establishment of a Scots Language Resource Centre (with help from the public purse) has been a good start, and the Scottish Language Project (The Kist) represents a great leap forward. However, it will not be possible to make real progress until Scots is given a statutory basis in law. A model is the Gaelic movement, which at the 1994 National Mod (the annual festival of Gaelic culture) received much media attention when Donald MacRitchie called for their language to be considered a human rights issue. Minority languages in Wales and Ireland enjoy full official status, and we should set the same target for Scots. There is no better way of dealing with the shame syndrome than to have affairs of state conducted in the native language of the majority.

Scottish children can follow instruction and enter examinations in all major European languages (as well as minority languages like Norwegian). Although there are now optional questions on Scots in English examination papers, human rights are certainly being ignored when over three quarters of Scottish pupils are being denied the opportunity of learning and being tested in their own tongue as a separate discipline. Confidence in our own culture should give us the courage to challenge the government to give standard Scots official status. All that is required is parliamentary time, a standard Scots Dictionary (which already exists), and an agreed standard Scots Grammar which is still to be written.

If lack of resources for such an initiative is cited as a problem, let it be a candidate for the Millennium Fund. In terms of national priority, it could be argued that reinstatement of the Scots language is more important than a Scottish assembly. It is more likely to restore the dignity and cultural potency of our nation.

The response to the inaugural lecture in October 1994, was heart-warmingly positive. Supportive messages flowed in from the most unexpected quarters, both from those who have for years been fighting for the language and from a large body of bystanders with no other axe to grind than pride in Scottish culture. There were some expressions of regret. One broadcaster said: 'my father spoke Scots but I was not allowed to do the same'.

The feedback indicated wide acceptance that Scots is not a dialect of English, and there is a strong feeling that its position as an official language should be re-asserted. However, many seriously question whether it is too late. Too much time has elapsed since King James moved to London in 1603 with an entourage of the nation's most distinguished scholars, writers and poets. Stripped of its intellectual elite, Scotland has never really recovered.

It is not too late. Indeed, the Scots language may have benefited from an extended period of organic evolution without the constraints of official status. The validity of this argument can be tested by looking at English, re-instated after 300 years, and Norwegian, re-instated after 400 years, as spoken languages.

An excellent summary of how modern English came into being was penned by George Macauly Trevelyan in a *History of England*. His new angle on history was first published in 1928 and was based on his Howell Lectures at Harvard University in 1924. His analysis goes as follows:

One outcome of the Norman Conquest was the making of the English Language. As a result of Hastings, the Anglo-Saxon tongue, the speech of Alfred and Bede, was exiled from hall and bower, from court and cloister, and was despised as a peasants' jargon, the talk of ignorant serfs. It ceased almost, though not quite, to be a written language. The learned and the pedantic lost all interest in its forms, for the clergy talked Latin and the gentry talked French. Now when a language is seldom written and is not an object of interest to scholars, it quickly adapts itself in the mouths of plain people to the needs and uses of life. This may be either good or evil, according to circumstances. If the grammar is clumsy and ungraceful, it can be altered much more easily when there are no grammarians to protest. And so it fell out it England. During the three centuries when our native language was a peasants' dialect, it lost its clumsy inflections and elaborate genders, and acquired the grace, suppleness and adaptability which are among its chief merits. At the same time it was enriched by many French words and ideas. The English vocabulary is mainly French in words relating to war, politics, justice, religion, hunting, cooking and art. Thus improved our native tongue re-entered polite and learned society as the English of Chaucer's Tales and Wycliffe's Bible, to be still further enriched into the English of Shakespeare and of Milton.

According to Trevelyan, the evolutionary stage we refer to as Middle English was a period when the grammatical shackles of Anglo-Saxon were shed and the diverse and dynamic dialects of the land provided the building blocks for a new language which was to become the Mandarin of the English speaking world. The battle of the dialects (provincial v London or rural v urban) in the struggle to find a norm for what we now know as Standard English makes a highly relevant study for those of us fighting for Scots today.

The story of Norwegian is equally interesting, and perhaps more relevant as the end of the story is closer in time, indeed still going on. The language of the Viking Kingdom of Norway was Old Norse, very close to Anglo-Saxon (as a student in Edinburgh, my school Norse enabled me to help contemporaries studying English when translating Anglo-Saxon texts). The balance of power in Scandinavia tilted in favour of the Danes at the end of the 14th Century. Following the crowning of King Eric at Kalmar in 1397, Norway fell under Danish rule and suffered the indignity of being a colonial possession for the next 400 years.

The fate of the Norwegian language during this period was almost identical to that of English. We can take Trevelyan's description above and substitute as follows:

> Norse was exiled from hall, court and cloister. It was despised as the talk of ignorant serfs, and almost ceased to be a written language. The clergy used Latin, government functionaries used Danish, and scholars went to Denmark for study. During four centuries the native language was a peasant's dialect. Freed from the grammatical strictures of Norse, it adapted to serve the needs of ordinary people. When independence eventually came, they demanded that their tongue should be the language of church, government and education.

The union with Denmark fell apart in 1814. A new Norwegian constitution was written and a parliament established. The language of the resurrected nation became that used by polite society in the capital city of Oslo (then Christiania), which was a residual form of Danish with strong Norwegian inflections (or vice versa, depending which side you supported in the subsequent struggle for linguistic ascendancy).

The cultural renaissance associated with the status of nationhood became strongly focused on folk culture and language. The folk culture had its roots in the rural community, then representing 80% of the population who spoke local dialects evolved directly from the Norse. Those who belonged to this rural culture felt that the language of polite Oslo society was an alien tongue and called it Danish. To this the Danes themselves objected, and what has evolved from the minority language of 1814 was given the name 'bookmål' (book language) as opposed to the 'folkesprog' (folk language or 'nynorsk' as it is now called).

Subsequent success in the campaign to give the folk language official status was due to early foundations laid by one person, Ivar Aasen (1813–96). A self-taught linguist of great energy, he undertook a study of all rural dialects and produced a grammar (1864) and a dictionary (1873). Rather than basing these on a single dominant dialect, he chose to develop norms based on common elements across all dialects. His approach to orthography was to adopt several parallel forms rather than a single standard form of spelling for each word. The other great protagonist at this time was Knut Knudsen (1812–95) who advocated a less radical approach.

A substantial body of literature was inspired by and written in the language promoted by Aasen et al, and the campaign was driven by a two-culture philosophy claiming equal status for the vernacular tongue of rural Norway. This required an alliance between language campaigners (many societies were formed) and politicians. At the tail end of the century and into the next, parliament yielded to pressure by enacting the following reforms:

1878 the verbal teaching medium in schools to be in the local dialect;
1885 the Folkesprog accorded equal status for use in schools and affairs of state (Samstillingsvedtaket);
1892 local education authorities given the right to choose which language to use for written work (Målparagrafen);
1907 introduction of mandatory written examinations in both languages (each local authority to choose which to adopt as main/subsidiary language), and changes to grammar and orthography to compatibilise spoken and written forms;
1917 changes to grammar and orthography of both languages;
1921 the whole Bible issued in the Folkesprog;
1930 civil servants to be literate in both languages.

We can learn many things from the English and Norwegian examples. The principal lesson from both is that it need not be a disadvantage to exist for several centuries as only a spoken language. The Norwegian case shows that a campaign for re-instatement to official status takes a long time (1814–85), success is dependent on strong key players, an alliance of scholars and politicians is essential, and a long term strategy with clearly focused objectives is imperative.

'The Scottish Language Project' of the Scottish Consultative Council on the Curriculum is a good start. They will soon publish *The Kist/A'Chiste*, an anthology of Scots and Gaelic texts for the 7–14 year old. This, together with the work of the Scottish National Dictionary Association, the Scots Language Resource Centre and academic work in the universities, are all initiatives moving us in a forward direction. They are the essential building blocks. But we need a grand strategy, as their full potential can only be realised within such a framework.

First we need to change the deeply embedded perception that we are a bilingual nation. The Scotrail welcome to Scotland at Waverly Station in Edinburgh is symbolic of our cultural half heartedness, as it uses English and Gaelic only. What about Scots? There are three Scottish languages, and our principal strategic objective should be to work towards a trilingual Scotland.

A 20 year time scale is wholly realistic, and the main priorities of the campaign strategy should be to achieve the following:

1.   A government appointed committee of interested parties to specify the parameters for a dictionary and grammar of modern

standard Scots, providing the glue to bind the many dialects together in a common framework (the same is needed for Gaelic).

2. Enactment of legislation to give standard Scots and Gaelic a statutory basis as Scotland's official languages alongside English. The new standard Scots should be a living language fit for the world of today, firmly thirled to the mither tongue.

3. Scots and Gaelic will be available in schools and universities to those who choose them as taught languages, in which they can be examined on a par with other European languages.

4. The amount of support from the public purse to promote a trilingual Scotland (in all sectors, including the media) will have regard to the level of use of each language.

Government support for Gaelic in recent years has done much to invigorate its associated culture. Those who have contributed to this achievement are to be congratulated. The critical mass of support is now such that the rules of political correctness are starting to apply, and in certain circumstances lack of active interest is equated with a lack of interest in Scotland. This is good, but is a partial achievement. Real success will come only when we have achieved the same for the Scots language.

It is now time to bring Scots out of the cupboard where it has been the preserve of mainly scholars and fellow travellers. We need to end the thinking which relegates our national language to a tradition that is regarded at best as a quaint romanticism or at worst as a sign of ignorance. An iconoclastic approach is required to bring the issue to the top of the political agenda. Of course, we will no longer speak the shiny and well preserved vowels of auld Scots so much beloved by scholars. It may be scuffed by rough handling, but it still has the strength to shatter cherished icons. Indeed, the Scots tongue alive in our dialects today, is well capable of coming into its own as English and Norwegian once did.

I consider it a mistake, as is the case at present, to confine funding from the public purse to English and Gaelic only. Those who campaign for the latter make insupportable claims of ownership that embrace Scottish culture root and branch. It should not be forgotten that modern Scotland is forged from three cultures. We are fortunate that one of the three, English, is now the lingua franca of the global village. But Scots and Gaelic are the linguistic foundations which give Scotland its unique cultural identity, and both contributed in equal measure to the world-wide diaspora. We should not allow ourselves to accept the narrow myth that the flight of our people from these shores was entirely a Gaelic phenomenon.

The diaspora applied to both cultures and, for both to survive, we must recognise our shared heritage and work together toward the shared goal of equal status. For example, let us take Roy Pedersen's excellent Gaelic tourism strategy, described in another chapter, and make it part of an overall national strategy to be built on Scotland's most unique selling point, its 'three cultures'.

The Scottish Tourist Board is at present racking its brains to come up with a suitable theme for 'Scotland the Brand'. Spoilt for choice, they are having difficulty in finding a single theme around which all concerned can unite. I recommend 'Scotland – the small nation with three big cultures'. If each language is given official status, each receiving equal attention and an equal share from the public purse, then we shall succeed in securing Scotland's diverse and vibrant cultural identity in the global village of tomorrow.

The Author

Professor Magnus Fladmark was appointed to establish a Heritage Unit for The Robert Gordon University in 1992. He holds qualifications in horticulture, architecture and town planning, and spent some time in journalism and the army. After a spell in the Scottish Office, he directed an Overseas Development Administration programme at Edinburgh University (1970–76), where he was made an Hon Fellow. As Assistant Director of the Countryside Commission for Scotland (1976–92), he established a new research division which provided the impetus for many initiatives in national heritage policy. Past Scottish Chairman of the Royal Town Planning Institute and a former Governor of Edinburgh College of Art, he is a keen student of different world cultures, and has written, contributed to, or edited eight books.

References

Aitken, A.. J. & McArthur, T. (eds), *Languages of Scotland*, Chambers, 1979

Douglas, S., *The Scots Language: European Roots and Local Destiny*, in Fladmark, J. M. (ed), *Cultural Tourism*, Donhead, 1994

Fladmark, J. M., *The Wealth of a Nation: Heritage as a Cultural and Economic Asset*, The Robert Gordon University, 1994

Kay, B., Scots: *The Mither Tongue*, Alloway, 1993

MacDonald, D. A., *The Scottish Tradition of Story Telling*, in Fladmark, J. M. (ed), *Heritage*, Donhead, 1993

McClure, J. D., *Why Scots Matters*, Saltire Society, 1988

McClure, J. D., *Varieties of Scots in Recent and Contemporary Narrative Prose*, in *English World-wide: A Journal of Varieties of English*, Vol. 14, No. 1, pp 1–22, 1993

Murison, D., *The Guid Scots Tongue*, James Thin, 1977

Robinson, M. et al (eds), *The Concise Scots Dictionary*, Aberdeen UP, 1985

Royle, T., *The Mainstream Companion to Scottish Literature*, Mainstream, 1993

Scott, P., *The Image of Scotland in Literature*, in Fladmark, J. M. (ed), *Cultural Tourism*, Donhead, 1994

Scottish Consultative Council on the Curriculum, *The Kist/A'Chiste Anthology*, SCCC & Nelson Blackie, to be published 1996

Trevelyan, G. M., *History of England*, Longmans, 1926

Figure 1 'One foot nearer and I plunge myself from the precipice.' Illustration by Andrew Cruikshank for Sir Walter Scott's *Ivanhoe*.

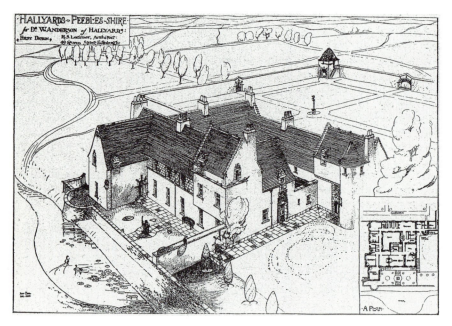

Figure 2 Robert Lorimer's unashamedly Scottish design for Hallyards in Peeblesshire.

29

GRASPING THE THISTLE
Architecture at the Edge

Frank Walker

In a recent edition of *Prospect* (No 54, 1995), the quarterly journal of the Royal Incorporation of Architects in Scotland (RIAS), contributors addressed themselves to an issue which, as the century draws to a close, seems more and more to preoccupy many north of the Border – what might be called plagiarising and adapting Nikolaus Pevsner's statement about 'the Scottishness of Scottish architecture'. Several articles appeared, both positively and negatively responsive to what *Prospect* called 'The Scottish Imperative'. Amongst those expressing misgivings or doubts about 'romantic notions of Scottish design' was one in which the writer confidently averred:

> No building of distinction in the past or the present has been created by a conscious attempt to imbue architecture with a national characteristic.
>
> G. Robertson, 1995

I feel that this is far from the case. But, in arguing such a claim, I do not intend to get hung up on the dangerous ambiguities inherent in the meanings or connotations of the word 'national', 'regional' or 'contextual' will do every bit as well. Ethnicity is an irrelevance here, and statehood a matter for another forum. Nor do I have any desire to become sidetracked by quibbling over just what might be meant by a 'building of distinction'. In fact, the criteria which we might use to form our respective judgements of quality could easily be constructed to suit our purposes. In arguing against the quasi-internationalist position taken by the writer in *Prospect*, I do not want to appear to suggest that there is any necessary correlation between, so to say, regionalist design and good architecture.

But the view that no good architecture ever emerged from a consciously national or regional programme is both a misreading of architectural history and, more alarmingly, an abdication of cultural obligation and responsibility. Given time and space it would be a relatively straightforward matter to substantiate the creative legacy of the regionalist imperative from 15th century Brunelleschi to 20th century Botta. As for the moralising reprobation, I concede – but do not apologise for – the fact that this judgemental verdict is motivated by political not aesthetic considerations.

I have chosen the theme of 'at the edge' for this paper because we are now ourselves at a historical edge. The end of the century, and indeed the millennium, draws ever nearer. We feel we are on the edge of a special moment in time. Of course, there is no reason to expect that the year 1999, 2000 or even 2001 will be any more historically significant than, say, 1918, 1945 or 1984. Yet we cannot escape the almost mystical magic of the millennial moment: we seem compelled to take stock of our place in time as we stand on this historical edge. And, as we do, we become strangely more and more conscious of that very place. In any event, we in Scotland are also at a geographical edge. We are at the periphery.

What can we say about our architecture at the edge? For our architectural identity can not but be affected by this sharpening consciousness of where we are in time and place. We are bound to locate ourselves somewhere in the context of the history of art and architecture, and somewhere in the context of what Pevsner called 'the geography of art'. There is in short, the 'spirit of the age' and the 'spirit of place', zeitgeist and genius loci, whose interplay determines cultural specificity.

As far as the 'spirit of the age' is concerned, we live in a post-modernist world. It is some time since Kenneth Frampton wrote his essay *Modern Architecture and the Critical Present*, but the situation is still largely as he described it – a fractured, pluralist spectrum of optional 'isms'. It is not that modernism has necessarily been rejected (although for some this is the case), but rather that particular aspects of the modernist ethos have achieved a kind of de facto independence under the leadership of various talented exponents.

As for the 'spirit of place', our experience as Scots is somewhat raw and peripheral. It is not any ethnic edge that cuts into our psyche, for this is blunted by the lack of any strong linguistic frontiers, but a primordial geographical edge. Beyond us is the ocean. After Scotland, the traveller falls off Europe into the abyss. Culturally speaking, we are at the existential edge which sharpens our self-awareness in a special way. As one 19th century writer, Masson, put it, the Scotsman's 'walk as a thinker, is not by the meadows and wheatfields, and the green lanes, and the ivy-clad parish churches, where all is gentle and antique and fertile, but by the bleak seashore which parts the certain from the limitless, where there is doubt in the sea-mews' shriek, and where it is well if, in the advancing tide, he can find a footing on a rock.'

Our peripheral position and perspective have honed our cultural experience in an equally unique way. The great movements in European art – the tidal surges in cultural history have taken longer to reach our shores, becoming diluted, diffused or discontinuous in their wash across the northern rocks. Yet, by virtue of our relative remoteness, we have developed a distinctive culture. For much of the time we have been intimately engaged with our neighbour, England – economically, politically and culturally. Being 'in bed with an elephant' is how Paul Scott described the Scottish experience in a Saltire Society essay some ten years ago. But often, too, to escape this single powerful relationship, we have developed or been conditioned by other European ties. An edge, after all, is a path too; and we have, as Scots, repeatedly found paths around England – some Franco-Celtic and some Norse-Baltic.

Figure 3 Grianan Building in Dundee by Nicol Russell.

Figure 4 Echoes of Mackintosh in house at Linlithgow by Alfred Cooper, 1989.

No architecture is solely national or regional. There is virtually no Scottish architecture that was not first imported from another country. 'The architecture of Scotland is chiefly of foreign origin. But the richly turreted chateau and the church of flamboyant Gothic, when transported from France to our own rugged shores and sterile moorland, adapted themselves, under the hands of our ancestors, to the necessities of their new position, and underwent a series of changes which suited better to the available materials, to the climate, and to the tastes and habits and wants (and, one might add, the expectations) of the people of Scotland,' wrote Inglis in 1868.

So this is not a polemic for an introverted, narrow-visioned Scottish architecture of updated brochs and blackhouses. However, a valid architecture, a distinct Scottish architecture, must give form to the recurrent dialectic between the history of art and architecture and the geography of art and architecture. If it is true that we can not be validly national without being in touch with the international, then we cannot be international without having something national to contribute. We can not escape history, because history is now. We can not escape geography, because geography is here. And here and now, at the edge of the century and the continent, we Scots are faced with a cultural choice.

This interaction between the more or less constant qualities imparted by the geography of art and the changing influences flooding over us in the course of the history of art is a continuing experience. It is this which impels and enriches our architectural expression.

For example, despite its international ubiquity in the 18th century, Classicism in Scotland did become distinctly Scottish. Or again, amongst its internationally indiscriminate expressions through the 19th century, historicism did put on a recognisably Scottish face. But what is interesting is that the keenness of this dialectic increased towards the turn of the centuries when identity, both historical and geographical, somehow seemed to need sharpening when culture was very much 'at the edge'. In the late 18th century, as ideas and events moved Classicism towards Romanticism, so regional identities in architecture became more attractive. And in the late 19th century as high-style historicism exhausted itself, so regional identities in architecture became more evident, more elemental and more prophetic.

Nor is this creative resolution or fusion of the national and the international effected by some impersonal agency of 'force majeure'. There is plenty of evidence to show that such design has a deliberate, self-conscious, cultural intention. Mackintosh, for instance, refers approvingly to a specifically Scottish approach to architecture 'coming to life again' and calls for 'a code of symbols accompanied by traditions which explained them.' His aims are thoroughly explicit. Or Plecnik, ultimately committed to the creation of a valid Slovenian architecture between the Germanic and Italianate edges, was already writing in 1902 that 'Like a spider, I aim to attach a thread to tradition, and beginning with that, to weave my own web.'

There is nothing disreputable and certainly no creative dead-end in the 'conscious attempt to imbue architecture with a national characteristic'. To advocate otherwise would be to commend the imposition of a deracinated, First World, cultural imperialism. But neither is there any guarantee that this will lead to good architecture. Being at the edge makes the attempt to resolve the dialectic of time and place a particularly precarious path to follow. There are pitfalls to be avoided.

At one extreme one might cite the later 20th century work of Gillespie, Kidd and Coia, of which perhaps St Peter's Seminary at Cardross might stand as an example. Do not misunderstand me, this is without question a 'building of distinction'; probably one of the most remarkable pieces of architecture built in Scotland this century. Tragically abandoned after less than a generation, its salvation is overdue. But this is an architecture obsessed with the international, wholly in thrall to 20th century developments in the history of art and architecture, to the extent that it seems without regard for indigenous tradition and climate. It is an architecture that denies the edge because it wants so much to be at the centre.

At the opposite extreme is much of Ian Begg's architecture as, for example, Glasgow's Museum of Religion. This too, in its way, is a 'building of distinction'. But it is an architecture obsessed with the national, wholly in thrall to the geography of art and architecture, to the extent that there appears to be nothing but a national tradition – and one unaffected, it seems, by two or three centuries of history. It is an architecture that wants to belong to the edge, denying the influences emanating from the centre.

If these are the pitfalls, what can we recommend? Responding to this appeal is itself a risky business, almost as precarious as actually resolving in design the conflicting claims of the national and the international. But for those of us, designers or critics, who feel the cultural compulsion to respond to what *Prospect* called 'The Scottish Imperative', there is no escaping the obligation to declare ourselves and run the risk of getting it wrong. Of those few – all too few buildings that might be regarded as valid signs of the times and of the place, I would want to mention Benson & Forsyth's extension to the Museum of Scotland, Edinburgh; Nicoll Russell's work at Scrimgeour's Corner, Crieff, and their Grianan Building, Dundee; the Students' Residences by Dixon and Jones at Garthdee, Aberdeen; a Church at Knockando in Moray by Law and Dunbar-Naismith; and, standing for many modest domestic examples, a simple cottage conversion near Glasgow by McGurn, Logan, Duncan & Opfer.

I do not pretend that any of these examples is a great piece of architecture or that they represent the only acceptable approach. However, each is a 'building of distinction' and each is imbued in some way with a national or regional character. What makes them so, and gives them this Scottish gloss, may have something to do with materials and texture, but more importantly, results from the transformation of form. There is a kind of language of national form, not only distinct and recurring formal elements, but a syntax derived from such forms. Geometry freed from its original materials and function paradoxically still acts as a symbolic mediator of regional or national culture. It is this 'geographical geometry', as one might call it, which the design of these buildings employs.

Not everyone will be convinced. I should certainly not argue that these efforts 'to imbue architecture with a national characteristic' are wholly successful. But if I retain a certain scepticism about exemplars, I still believe that a valid architecture needs to be thoroughly modern and of its time, yet being part of a living national tradition (of its place). What is wanted is an ambivalent architecture – or, rather, an ambi-valent architecture: one able to absorb these contending forces of time and place.

The Author

Professor Frank Arneil Walker is an architect turned architectural historian. His research has ranged from the national and Secession architectures of East-Central Europe to the development of urban form in Scotland. On these and other subjects he has published widely in Britain and Europe. Amongst his books are several dealing with the architecture of Glasgow and the west of Scotland. He has a strong interest in the theory and practice of critical regionalism. He is professor of architecture at the University of Strathclyde.

This text is based on a paper first delivered at the 1995 Convention of the Royal Incorporation of Architects in Scotland, and a version of it was featured in *Building Design*, 16 June 1995.

References

Frampton, K., *Raising a Challenge*, in *Prospect*, No. 54, Edinburgh, 1995, p. 9

Inglis, J., 1868, quoted in Davie, G. E., op cit., p. 323

Mackintosh, C. R., 1891, quoted in Walker, F. A., 'Scottish Baronial Architecture' in Robertson, P., (ed.), *Charles Rennie Mackintosh, the Architectural Papers*, Wendlebury Edinburgh, 1990, pp. 45–44

Masson, D., 1852 quoted in Davie, G. E., *The Democratic Intellect*, Edinburgh, 1982 (1961), p. 317

Pevsner, N., *The Englishness of English Art*, Harmondsworth, 1964 (1956), pp. 15–25 and passim

Plecnik, J., 1902, quoted in a review by Long, C., in *Journal of the Society of Architectural Historians*, Vol. 54, No. 1, Philadelphia, 1995, p. 99

Robertson, G., 'Raising a Challenge', in *Prospect*, No. 54, Edinburgh, 1995, p. 9

Scott, P. H., *In Bed with an Elephant*, Saltire Pamphlets, New Series No. 7, Edinburgh, 1985

Smith, G., 1919, quoted in introduction by Buthlay, K., to MacDiarmid, H., *A Drunk Man Looks at the Thistle*, Edinburgh, 1987, p. 23

30

SENSE OF PLACE IN TOWNS
Historic Buildings as Cultural Icons

Graeme Munro

In this paper I seek to demonstrate by examples drawn from a relatively small and arbitrarily chosen area of one city, Edinburgh, some of the many ways in which historic buildings contribute to a sense of place and are a living asset of benefit to the community and visitors alike. I deal briefly with the importance of major historic monuments for tourism but my focus is on what I believe to be the much deeper and ultimately more important significance of more modest historic buildings and streetscapes.

I should like to mention firstly the role of topography. Obviously there are some cities and towns where there are striking topographical features which form an important part of the image of that city or town. Examples might include Sugar Loaf Mountain in Rio de Janeiro, the islands of Stockholm and, nearer home, Arthur's Seat. But these cities are the exception. Even Sydney is probably better known for its Opera House and Harbour Bridge than for its spectacular natural harbour, and Rome is recognised more for the Coliseum and the Spanish Steps than for its Seven Hills.

The concept of the spirit of place, 'genius loci', is generally associated with nature, often in its wilder manifestations. The 19th Century Romantics sensed it by the English lakes and the mountains and glens of Scotland. But I would argue that it is at least as strong in urban areas and in the work of man wherever it appears in the landscape. What makes most cities, towns and villages distinct is their buildings and not their setting. Without St Paul's and Notre Dame who could tell the Thames from the Seine?

Many famous buildings stand as icons recognised around the world as symbols of the city or country where they are located. Examples of such international icons are the Eiffel Tower, the Brandenburg Gate, the Taj Mahal, the Statue of Liberty and Edinburgh Castle. Such buildings are not merely symbolic but often carry a rich patina of historic or cultural values. They are more than simply images, more than national logos or the recurrent subject of tourism posters. This is certainly true of Edinburgh Castle which is home to the Honours of Scotland, our Crown Jewels, and the Scottish National War Memorial, as well as having played a key role in some of the most exciting events in Scottish history.

It is possible to discern a hierarchy of buildings serving as icons at different levels. In addition to the international icons, there are those which fulfil this role at national level. Examples might include Reims Cathedral in France, the Reichstag in Berlin and the Palace of Holyroodhouse. Here events of importance to the nation have taken place but the monuments are not quite in the top league so far as instant recognition across the world is concerned. There are also major historic buildings or monuments which are powerful icons at a regional level. Within Scotland one thinks of the Border Abbeys, the Finnieston crane in Glasgow, Marischal College in Aberdeen, St Magnus in Orkney and the Castle in Inverness. The importance of major historic buildings as identifiers and as a focus for national, regional and local identity and pride cannot be over-emphasised.

Some of the outstanding monuments which fall into the category of icons were built as monuments and are thus fulfilling their original purpose, the Eiffel Tower and the Scott Monument being two good examples. Others were not built as monuments, but have become monuments while retaining their original function – cathedrals are perhaps the best example. Some have become monuments because they have been reduced to ruins, but ruins which are of value for their historic associations, architectural interest or aesthetic appeal, Elgin Cathedral and Urquhart Castle for example. Others again have become monuments because their original purpose has been outlived but they have become visitor attractions. Edinburgh Castle, despite a continuing army presence which provides welcome colour and continuity, is no longer primarily a fortress or Royal Palace.

Monuments can be used actively or passively. Active use implies a level of promoted public access, whether charged for or not. The monuments are marketed as part of the cultural or tourism offering of the area in which they are located. These monuments may be in private ownership, in the care of local trusts, local authorities or national organisations such as the National Trust for Scotland or Historic Scotland. An estimated five million paying visitors a year are attracted to such sites in Scotland, equivalent to one visit by every man, woman and child in Scotland. Around half that total are visitors to Historic Scotland's 60 staffed monuments with an unknown number going to the other 270 Historic Scotland open access sites.

Accordingly, there is well recognised economic activity around what has been called the heritage business. This, in turn, is a key component of the tourism industry. Tourism has been an important industry in Scotland for 150 years at least, with visitors following in the steps of Scott and Wordsworth. Nor is there anything new about selling souvenirs. I recently came across a piece of 19th century Mauchline ware depicting Stirling Castle and bearing the legend 'Bought in the Douglas Room of Stirling Castle'. Tourism is now arguably Scotland's biggest single industry and the importance of historic buildings to the economy of the country is thus crucial, with historic buildings as the second most often cited reason for foreign visitors coming to Scotland.

Provided our major monuments and historic buildings are sensitively conserved, sympathetically presented, well managed and not over-developed. I see no reason why they should not continue to play the important role which they now have in relation to tourism. That these major historic buildings are a living asset is surely beyond doubt.

Historic Scotland, as the largest operator of historic visitor attractions in Scotland, has very substantial experience of conservation, interpretation and presentation. Some of my colleagues have contributed to previous volumes in this series on some of these aspects of our work. What I should like to do now is to turn from the major historic buildings, and look instead at the very much wider canvas of historic buildings in general. Historic Scotland has 330 monuments in direct care but is also the Agency which, as part of Government, is responsible for scheduling monuments of national importance (of which there are now some 6,000) and listing buildings of special historic or architectural importance (of which there are some 40,000). We are also responsible for designating outstanding conservation areas, of which there are 204 in Scotland, including both listed and unlisted buildings.

I believe very strongly that at the local level historic buildings and other associated features such as street patterns, street names, shop fronts, street furniture and even burial grounds play a key role in sustaining civic pride and in creating a clear sense of place which is unique and which is of great economic and social value. I will develop this theme by describing the rich variety of the built heritage, in this wider sense, in an area of Edinburgh chosen more or less at random. My examples were all taken within a half-mile radius of Historic Scotland's headquarters at Longmore House in Edinburgh, where the 18th and 19th century tenements of the south side give way to the 19th century villa quarters of Grange and Newington. What follows is, I must stress, very much a personal view. It was conceived as a response to the invitation to write this paper and has evolved from a combination of two sustained weekend assaults on the area with a camera, walking around with my eyes open over a period of months and occasional recourse to the reference books.

Despite the depredations of the 1960s and 1970s and the sad loss of many fine buildings, particularly in our town centres, the core of many of our cities, towns and villages is still essentially late 18th and 19th century with some notable survivors from earlier periods.

Media reporting of built heritage issues tends to concentrate on buildings at risk from neglect or inappropriate new developments. Obviously I welcome the energies which such reporting often unleashes to find a means of saving buildings at risk. Indeed, Historic Scotland has invited the Scottish Civic Trust to maintain a register of such buildings and supports this financially. We should not, on the other hand, blind ourselves to the fact that there are many historic buildings, listed and unlisted, which continue to serve the purpose for which they were built.

Examples from the South Side of Edinburgh include:

- residential use (the largest category)
- churches (Duncan Street Baptist Church)
- schools (East Preston Street School)
- hospitals (Royal Hospital for Sick Children)
- commercial premises. (The Geographical Institute)
- industrial premises (Coach Works)

These are buildings which have stood the test of time. They may require adaptation but, provided that any alterations are sympathetically carried out, this should present no problems. They will certainly require repair from time to time, but so will modern buildings. Indeed, many would argue from personal experience that modern buildings are likely to require major repair much sooner in their cycle of use, and more expensively. Which do you think more likely to stand up to the Scottish climate – a slated, hipped roof on a Victorian Board School or a flat, felt roof on a 1960s school?

Quite apart from the aesthetic and historical arguments for retaining a high proportion of our older building stock it needs to be recognised in this more environmentally conscious age that great resources of non-renewable materials and energy have gone into their building. There is therefore a high resource cost in replacing these buildings even if they were replaced by new structures of comparable quality.

In addition to those historic buildings still serving their original function in everyday use there are many others which have been adapted to new uses in response to social, demographic and economic change. Examples from the south side of Edinburgh include:

- James Clark's School, converted into use as flats;
- South Clerk Street Church, now a concert hall
  (The Queen's Hall);
- Longmore Hospital, now Historic Scotland's headquarters;
- a mortuary, now three lock-ups;
- a fire station, now a small office;
- a police station, now an office;
- large private houses, now hotels.

The same economic arguments apply in support of the adaptation of historic buildings as apply to their retention for their original purposes. The cost of adaptation is generally much less than that of new build and it is much easier to envisage what the overall result will be when there is an existing building than looking at architect's plans and drawings. Historic Scotland recognises the arguments for imaginative and sensitive re-use and strongly supports the principle that buildings have to be economically viable if they are to have a long-term future. We operate our listing building consent procedures within the framework of that philosophy while always endeavouring to achieve the best practical, architectural and aesthetic outcome for the building. We use our historic building repair grants to assist the owners of the most outstanding of the listed buildings in Scotland to carry out approved programmes of conservation. These schemes often involve re-use. Increasingly, other organisations are becoming involved in the funding of projects – local authorities, local enterprise companies, the European Union and the National Lottery Heritage Fund.

My argument is that historic buildings are important economic assets through their direct use. They also make an indirect economic impact through their contribution to the attractiveness of the urban scene and, in turn, its power to attract tourists and inward investors. In marketing, the USP or 'unique selling proposition' of any product is of crucial importance. I would contend that the USP of many of our cities, towns and villages is their stock of historic, characterful buildings. Travellers look for variety and that we have in abundance. Inward investors are as much interested in the quality of the environment as they are in the more tangible incentives such as industrial estates and communications infrastructure. Attractive townscapes and homes of style and character contribute as much to the quality of life of the economically active and would-be inward investors as do golf courses, restaurants and theatres.

But historic buildings and townscapes have a value, are living assets, beyond the purely economic. Buildings of different periods contribute to an evolving townscape and provide a window on local history. They provide a vital link between the past and present. In the South Side of Edinburgh examples include:

- the old thoroughfare of Causewayside, of medieval or even Roman origin;
- the site of the medieval religious house of St Catherine of Siena;
- a 17th century merchant's house (Prestonfield House);
- an early 18th century Solicitor's house (Hermits and Termits);
- a mid 18th century country villa (Sylvan House);
- late 18th century tenements (Buccleuch Street);
- 19th century tenements (Causewayside);
- 19th century villas (Middlebie Street);
- a 20th century listed garage (Causewayside).

There are also a range of historical and cultural links. Many buildings and sites are marked by plaques, like those recording the foundation of the Royal Hospital for Sick Children, and the site of St Catherine's of Siena. This latter plaque has a lengthy quotation from Sir Walter Scott's *Marmion* which reminds us of the novelist's meeting, when still a boy, with Robert Burns in nearby Sciennes Hill House. A recent plaque marks this site and there is also a much older carved stone plaque in St Leonard's which records the site of Jeannie Dean's tryst in Walter Scott's *Heart of Midlothian*.

The great attraction of many of our urban areas is that they are organic and have grown up over a lengthy period. An extreme example of this is Sciennes Hill House where the original facade can still just be seen, although it is now the rear wall of a tenement. In some streets it is possible to see a wide variety of styles side by side – 18th, 19th and 20th century buildings next to each other, sometimes in pleasant harmony, sometimes not where the 20th century has inserted buildings of poor quality. There are also the contrasts of the vernacular and the exotic, like Priestfield Church described in the Buildings of Scotland as 'formidably Lombardic'. There are great houses and lodge houses. In other streets the charm derives, in contrast, from homogeneity, as in the linked single-storey villas of Middlebie Street.

In addition to the aesthetic pleasure given by many of these older buildings themselves, there is a wealth of detail to delight the eye – granite setts, iron balconies, Venetian windows, imposing doorways, pends and decorative stonework to give a few examples. There are sculptural fragments re-used from elsewhere and there are structures which were always designed to be decorative. There is a whole bestiary of carved animals.

The built environment also provides the physical evidence for many aspects of social history. The 19th century Blacket Estate with its lodges and gate piers between which chains were erected at night is an eloquent reminder that a concern for security is nothing new. The same area now has a neighbourhood watch scheme. The 'Penny Well' reminds us that the whole question of water supply and how it is paid for is not new. Another nearby well recalls the Battle of Waterloo. The watch tower and mortsafes show that body snatching was a very real concern in the city of Burke and Hare.

Other events and figures are reflected in many of the street names – Livingstone Place was no doubt erected around the time that Stanley uttered his famous words in the depths of Africa and the use of politicians' names – Lord Russell Place, Gladstone Place, Salisbury Place – could almost serve as a means of dating the streets to which they are attached.

Before summarising I should like to indicate very briefly what, in my view, does not contribute to a sense of place. False historic detailing on buildings, both inside and out, is inimical to a genuine sense of place. Public houses provide frequent examples of this. Also, proud house owners can go 'over the top' in decking out their properties in what they believe to be heritage features such as modern reproduction coach lamps, cart wheels, leaded windows, etc, and the results can be fairly disastrous. Similarly, shop fronts are sensitive and a misconceived sense of heritage can be almost as bad as an aggressively modern intrusion. Nor does reproduction street furniture out of a catalogue have a part to play. Too many good urban landscapes have been spoiled by insensitive and inappropriate paving, bollards and even 'heritage' post boxes.

Returning to the positive side of the balance sheet, what does all this add up to? It is hoped that I have demonstrated that historic buildings do contribute to a strong sense of place, indeed, are probably the key element which distinguishes one country from another, and one area from another. They play a key and well recognised economic role in relation to tourism. They also play a key economic role as usable assets whether for their own original purpose or for some new purpose. Their continuing use and re-use is highly desirable in relation to environmental sustainability and the careful use of physical as well as financial resources. Their repair, assisted by grant aid from Historic Scotland and other bodies, provides local employment throughout Scotland and helps to maintain craft skills. The need for indigenous materials to use on repairs opens up exciting opportunities to re-start local industries for the production of lime, granite setts, slate and other materials.

In addition to these direct and indirect economic benefits, there are aesthetic and social benefits. The presence of historic buildings and related features provides a sense of place for local people, with the physical evidence of the past of their community. From that arises a greater sense of community and belonging and, it is to be hoped, less alienation. I believe passionately that historic buildings should have their place in organic and evolving cities, towns and villages.

Legislation to protect historic buildings is surely right, but equally has to be applied with sensitivity. We do not want our urban areas to atrophy. In Historic Scotland we firmly believe that there is a dynamic role for historic buildings in the context of sensitively applied legislation. I invite all the various statutory bodies at national level and local level, the voluntary sector and above all the large and small private companies and the individuals, wealthy and not so wealthy, who own the buildings to work with us to protect our built heritage and to preserve and enhance our communities as attractive places in which to live, invest and sojourn.

The Author

Graeme Munro went to school in Edinburgh and studied French Language and Literature at the Universities of St Andrews and Aix-en-Provence, graduating with an Honours degree from St Andrews in 1967. He entered the Scottish Office the following year as an Assistant Principal. He has had a varied career in the Civil Service, working on such diverse areas as housing, planning, roads, health services, criminal justice, fisheries and internal management consultancy. In the course of his career he has spent six months on secondment to a local authority and taken part in exchanges with the Civil Service in both France and Germany. He was appointed Director of the Historic Buildings and Monuments Directorate in the Scottish Office in 1990 and became the first Director and Chief Executive of Historic Scotland when it was established in April 1991 as an Executive Agency. He was re-appointed in the autumn of 1993 following an open competition. He lives in an A-listed flat in an outstanding conservation area, lists local history as one of his interests, has strong Scottish roots and enjoys travel and other people's cultures.

Figure 1 Longmore House in the Southside of Edinburgh. A former hospital which has been adapted to serve as Historic Scotland's new headquarters.

Figure 1 Church of St Joseph at Manikata.

31

THE SPIRIT OF PLACE
Local Identity in Modern Architecture

Richard England

As you get to know Europe slowly ...you begin to realise that the important determinant of any culture is after all the 'Spirit of Place'.

Lawrence Durrell

Modern Architecture is not built from some branch of an old tree, but is a plant growing directly from new roots.

Walter Gropius

If Lawrence Durrell's words exalt the essence of place and cultural identity, Walter Gropius' statement emphasises modern architecture's blind commitment to a reductive rationalism devoid of any form of attachment to the past or its memory. It is because of this very dissociation and distaste for the past and its traditions that the universal took over from the particular, in the lean years of the so called International Style. In reducing architecture to a few limited universal truths the Modernists curtailed the imperative impact and interaction forthcoming from both place and past in any architectural intervention in a special time-space equation.

Modern architecture spent too much time studying joints in buildings and most of the time forgetting the most important joint of all, that of the building to its site and environment. Moreover, man belonging exclusively to an evolutionary species is able to understand only gradual change and always within a process of growth and continuity.

The object of this paper is to present an alternative belief to the philosophy of Internationalism and to accentuate an ideology of an architecture related specifically to place, and based on a 'new leaf instead of a new tree'. The buildings illustrated are a selection from three decades of my 'making' of architecture within the limited confines of the Maltese Islands. In all these buildings there is an attempt to use the cultural identity of these Islands as a spring-board towards the creation of an architecture born from their very climate, history and tradition, and which, in their final built-form, become both a symbol and celebration of their essential 'spirit of place'. Therefore, it seems appropriate, first of all, to examine the place itself, and during that process discover the essential qualities which constitute its identity.

GENIUS LOCI

The Maltese Islands measure a mere 320 square kilometres. They lie like a scorched leaf in the centre of the Mediterranean sea. The sole building material available is the natural rock of which these islands are composed. Throughout its history, this archipelago offers an interesting and valuable example of the intelligent use of this material. Through the unity of this ethnic stone, a strong sense of continuity and homogeneity is evident in the vast overlays of man's activities over many centuries in his struggle to wrest a living for survival in an environment of limited and restricted resources. The stone itself is quarried from a sedimentary rock formation of the tertiary period, and is known as globigerina limestone. It is golden in colour, easily cut, dressed and worked.

A visit to one of these quarries is a rewarding visual experience. The piling of cube upon cube of the quarried ochre blocks evokes images of the constructed complexes and it requires little imagination to crystallise these unit groupings into the cluster-forms of the buildings of tomorrow; a relationship which emphasises the strong organic link between the building material utilised and the final built form itself.

Because of their strategic position at the cross-roads between the two great traditions of Europe and the Islamic world, the built expression of Malta is a strong reflection of the meeting place of the different multi-cultural overlays which have dominated them throughout history. Here is a synthesis of not only East and West but also of North and South. The traditional closely knit cubic townscape clusters, echoes of the Island's Arab occupation, are crowned by the soft rounded curves of Baroque church domes imported through the Italian and Spanish influences of the Order of St. John of Jerusalem. The synthesis of these two cultures, provides the basis of the essence of identity which crystallises the 'Spirit of Place' of these islands. It is interesting to note a similar locational cross-cultural parallel in linguistic terms. Malta's own language is the only language of Semitic origin and sound which is written in the Roman alphabet.

This land is an architectural context of maximum utilisation of minimal resources. One is aware of a total utilisation of the limited available materials and means. The fields are built, the soil accumulated between the rubble walls and much that appears natural is, in fact, man-made. In a strange manner, this place, through its rich history-laden development has continually remodelled its rocky self in response to the specific needs of its inhabitants at different times. In Malta, perhaps more than anywhere else, the sum of the parts is actually equal to the whole. Constantly, stone is being hollowed out, cut away and built-up to suit man's requirements. What is there has always been there, it is just that some of it has been remodelled.

DESIGN METHODOLOGY

What is new and essential must of necessity be grafted to old roots.

Bela Bartok

If one is born and bred in such an environment it is only natural that one should produce an architecture which relates specifically to, not only the

Figure 2 Maltese townscape.

Figure 3 Ramla Bay.

strong visual qualities of the place, but also to its complex traditions and history. It was William Blake who said, 'We become what we see'.

Since the early period of my creative architectural life, at a time when the International Style was at the beginning of its last act, I have always believed in an expression of an architecture of Regionalism relating specifically to a process of *evolution* as opposed to *revolution*. I have never believed that one should bring in the new at the expense of the old. Earlier in this century, as referred to above, architects turned their back on the past, declaring in dogmatic terms that they were totally independent of it and that their belief was only in the development of technology. Consequently buildings were no longer to be tied to specific places, materials and history.

Architects, in attempting to wipe out the past, came frighteningly close to succeeding in creating a universal solution to what was never a universal problem. In this process of International industrialism, man ceased to be an individual and became an anonymous cipher. Today, however, as man becomes even more mobile in an ever-shrinking global-village civilisation, he is developing an increasing awareness and necessity for the values of roots. It is an essential truth that these values are recognised not only as a vital psychological need, but more so, as an essential equation to successfully relate mankind to a basic socio-cultural existence and location in a time-space framework.

The basic failure of most of the architecture of the 20th century must however be attributed, not so much to the dogmas of Modernism, but more specifically to those of Internationalism. The demands of the Modern Movement, unlike those of Internationalism, can be well adapted to a Regionalistic approach, with its crusade and search for meaning and content in specific context. Within the parameters of an expression of continuity within change, I have always attempted to graft my buildings to essential basic ethnic roots, in the process manifesting my belief that architecture must relate to and evolve from the 'Spirit of Place', be truly regional and yet be also of today.

In all my buildings I have tried to obtain an expression which is technologically progressive, yet culturally conservative, in the sense that to 'conserve' means to keep alive. Technology is part of the answer but so also is history. I have tried to evoke within contemporary design methodologies, the essential qualities of the Maltese Islands and their heritage in an architecture which reflects the formal essence and identity of place, and in the process, transfers tradition and roots from the position of a silent conscience to that of a central topic of debate. In all these works, the site, or *genius loci* has been the initiator of the whole creative process.

In any manifestation of architecture the site must be regarded as the spring-board for the whole design process, not only in terms of its *physical data* (geography, topography, climate and materials), but also its *memory data* (tradition, culture, legend and history), for it is not only what is visible that is important but more so the 'present absences' and 'absent presences' of a place, which are the inherent properties of its identity.

Architecture is about listening to and understanding this data at a specific moment in time and working on these generators in a collective, rational and intuitive manner, in such a way as to mix 'knowing' with an equal capacity to 'forget knowing'; a reminder that to acquire sophistication requires spontaneity. The element of time brings into focus the 'physical' and

Figure 4 Dolmen Hotel at Qawra.

Figure 5 Local materials, the walls of a limestone quarry.

'memory' databanks, and provides the current technologies, social movements, political and economical aspirations of the place. These 'voices of a site' provide pointers towards solutions to the particular problem. They will tell the architect whether the environment is weak and therefore requires him to be strong, or they may tell him that the environment is strong and that he is to be docile. Wherever an architect works, he needs hands that see and eyes that feel. The most essential quality for any architect attempting to produce an integrated tapestry of time and place woven into a contemporary fabric of identity remains above all an essential dose of good manners.

The Maltese Islands from the early sixties had already begun to rely on tourism as the major aspect of their economy. The housing of these travelling masses poses problems of accommodation, and consequently the majority of my buildings focus on providing solutions to this end. Tourism, very much a speculator's market, if not controlled becomes one of man's worst forms of 20th century pollution. The problem of how to accommodate masses of people without committing environmental suicide in the process, together with the preservation and development of the ethos and logos of their target areas, is the architect's prime concern and responsibility. Together with these essential factors the architect must consider the qualities of the 'Genius Loci' of the region he is building in, which in tourist buildings becomes one of the 'materialistic' functional requirements. It is this very different and particular 'Spirit of Place' which attracts the tourist in the first place. It was George Bernard Shaw who said, 'I dislike feeling at home when I am abroad'.

The pioneer path-finder in architecture's quest for an expression of Regionalism, Hassan Fathy, in Egypt, taught us that 'tradition is not necessarily synonymous with stagnation.' Later it was pioneer practitioners like Rifat Chadirji in Iraq, Aris Konstantinidis in Greece, Faraoui and De Mazieres in Morocco, and of course, Luis Barragan in Mexico, who attempted to create an expression of contemporary architecture based on historical and traditional roots which crystallised the potential of their respective regions and in the process connected buildings to both their physical and cultural backgrounds. In my own buildings, my quest has always been directed towards attaining the optimum for local culture while drawing the best from global civilisation, a form of synthesis of the best of tradition and scientific Modernism, and in the process treating the delicate fabric of this island rock with the utmost respect and humility.

The works in question attempt a conscious and intuitive blending of traditional forms, space allocations and scale requirements of the region, together with its history and symbolic past in direct quotation, allusion or metaphor, in conjunction with a modern approach and use of techniques and materials. The main object is to obtain an expression particular to its location, while evoking a strong sense of identity. Collectively this body of works attempts to demonstrate my belief that the essential act of architecture is to understand the vocation of the particular place one is building in, and in the process discovering what the place wants to become. These projects reflect my determined effort to develop a commercially viable and climatologically responsive architecture of tourism that above all enhances besides exploiting the character of a region.

338

Figure 6 The University of Malta extension.

Figure 7 The University of Malta extension.

The design and building of Manikata Church on the hill top in the centre of a small hamlet on the north west of the Island provided me with an early understanding that for architecture to have real meaning, it must function at many levels and satisfy multifarious needs. Placed on the crest like a large abstract sculpture, moulded in flowing lines and sensuous curves, the Church provides solutions, not only at a formal level, but more so at the equally important level of religious and social interactions.

Unhappy with the remoteness of the official church hierarchy of the time, my attempt was to design a sacred space modelled instead on dialogue and equality between the celebrant and the congregation. It was to be, in my mind, a place conducive, not only to communal worship, but also personal meditation. The stern autocratic image of a remote deity had to be recast into a new image permeated above all by a spirit of joy. The Church was to be read more as a house of the community than one of the deity.

In terms of architecture, society and religion, Manikata was to be above all a contemporary statement, but one which also spoke at all these levels in the vernacular language. Introducing these changes to the Baroque-ridden devotional paraphernalia attitudes of the Maltese Islands of the early sixties was no mean task. However, contemporary to the preparation of the designs for the Church, the second Vatican Council fortunately issued new directives on church art and architecture, and these liturgical reforms helped to get the project eventually approved by the local church authorities.

Twelve years in the making (inaugurated in 1974), Manikata became a symbol of a new spirit, but at the same time one which strongly evoked and recalled its origins and background. It drew its inspiration from the island's two golden ages of religious architecture, those of the Earth Goddess Megalithic Temples of pre-history, and the ornate opulent Baroque which had dominated the Island for the last five centuries. This place of gathering, carved in a contemporary Christian language also relates to and originates from lesser local traditions and building typologies, such as those of the rural toolshed dry-wall constructions known as 'girna'. These forceful images are combined together and injected with a relevance suitable to a 20th century church in order that it could act as a bridge between Malta of the past and that of the future, suspended in time and place, yet simultaneously very much of both. This *relevant* borrowing of ethnic-rooted forms produced a space of relaxed informality which pointed more towards a place for an intimate family gathering than that for solemn religious ceremonies.

Progress was slow and difficult, funds were limited, and the volunteers and small labour force available fluctuated. Although full working drawings were prepared, these proved to be virtually useless as the local village voluntary workers could not read drawings. However, what initially appeared to be a negative aspect and major stumbling block, subsequently provided me with a personal experience which radically changed my whole approach to architecture.

In order to ensure progress on site, a vital personal involvement followed in the actual building of the Church, in almost a medieval manner. The architect usually only prepares 'a means to an end', in as far as he is only concerned with the preparation of drawings and documents, and not the actual 'making' of the building itself. This involvement in the building process had a lasting effect on my future understanding of the whole architectural process. Manikata was a building fashioned by human hands as a living manifestation of the villagers' commitment, belief and creed. I count myself privileged to have worked hand-in-hand with these people, fired by a religious and parochial enthusiasm in the making of their place of prayer. Looking back on that experience, I am now strongly convinced that every architect, once in his lifetime, should make a building with his hands.

Within the Church, the ethnic limestone is utilised in the main features which exalt the fundamental elements of the Catholic faith: Consecration, Baptism and Penance. Together with the lectern where the Word of God is distributed from in complement to the Eucharist, these items are the main focus of the sanctuary area. Externally, around the main volume of the Church which spirals out of the surrounding piazza, are various vantage points and focal areas which serve as social gathering points where the villagers can gather before or after the religious services. These include the bell tower, seats, and various other sculpture-features. The whole matriarchal form of plaza, church and sacristy in respecting the spirit of place, take their pulse from their surroundings and time and the whole emerges as an architecture totally rooted to the past, yet still very much an expression of the future. This is a building that helps communication between man himself, man and his fellow beings, and more so between man and his Creator: a building built for the people by the people – a specific architecture for a specific place, in a specific time. A Church for today, yet designed on foundations of yesterday.

PLACE AND POETIC CONTENT

In the Garden for Myriam, Aquasun Lido and Ir-Razzett ta' Sandrina projects, while the concept of the 'genius loci' is again strongly maintained, either in direct quotation, allusion or metaphor, there is a strong overlay and infusion of the sense of the poetic. Perhaps the words of Tennessee Williams 'I don't want reality, I want magic' serve best to illustrate my approach in these works. In ancient days architects were probably magic practitioners involved in the making of environments concerned with the rituals and myths of man in relation to his particular relationship in space and time. These architects or master-builders were conversant in the secret knowledge of celestial bodies and proficient in the understanding of earth forms. Their cognitive learning allowed them to practice architectural enactment as a path to enlightenment.

Within today's world, tired of the superficial, the haste and consumerism which surround us, much of this magic has vanished and one can only discover such spatial realities in the literary creations of authors like Homer, Swift, Carrol, Tolkein, Borges, Verne and Calvino in their fabled territories of Ogyiga, Avalon, Lemuria, Atlantis, Wonderland, the Middle Earth and Zenobia. These places, pregnant with poetry, invite us to listen to the music of their essence in an all surrounding silence as an antidote to the overwhelming materialism of our age. In the world of reality it is only in the work of architect Luis Barragan, that great evoker of the Spirit of Place of his native Mexico, (who considered emotion the most fundamental element of architecture), that one may approach the serenity and silent magic of these imaginary locations. It was Axel Munthe who said that 'the soul needs more space than the body'. These three private arcadias, influenced by the pictorial world of Giorgio De Chirico and the writings of Italo Calvino, are an attempt to create dream-like metaphysical arrangements of fragments and memories as environments conducive to the necessary serenity for man to overcome the disruptive strategies of the dislocative tendencies prevalent in the world today.

In A Garden for Myriam, conceived as a personal silent space for meditation, the emphasis is focused on capturing the mythical poetry of a fairy-tale world: memories, real and unreal are celebrated in an intermix of time future and time past. An expression of architecture which hovers between the realms of reality and illusion: a place where the floor is the earth, the walls are the wind and the ceiling is the sky, yet always evocative and derivative from the rich cultural baggage of the Mediterranean.

In the Aquasun Lido, the evocation is again one which focuses on a traditional Mediterranean context. The visitor is invited to recollect remembered things from his childhood days. These forms borrowed from the summer of our childhood emphasise the words of Michael Ende that 'man dies when the last part of the child in him becomes an adult'. This Arcadian world allows us to walk through the threshold of 'once upon a time' into the world of make-believe and fables. The Aquasun Lido is an attempt at the recreation of a toyland fantasy involving the creation of an iconography pregnant with dreams and reveries.

In Ir-Razzett ta' Sandrina, a converted farmhouse, there is an attempt to provide a backdrop or canvas for the interweaving of image and imagery, a fade in/fade out intermix of reality and dream. This is a Magritte, De Chirico and Delveaux iconography of spaces which evokes abodes of princesses, palaces, castles and other fairy-tale fantasies. An attempt at creating a place of myth and magic, for the seduction of the soul: a choreography of images of fantasy crystallised into spatial reality. Once again, the concept is strongly related to the whole cultural identity of the region for these works juxtaposed against the clarity of sun-washed blue skies are, above all, celebrations of the Mediterranean spirit together with man's endless search for the fusion of reality and illusion.

PLACE AND HISTORICAL CONTEXT

The offices for the Central Bank of Malta are situated within the historical environment of the Counterguard bastions of Malta's capital city of Valletta. The preservation and conservation of the 16th century fortification lines were the vital element considered in the design of this project. The new building completed in 1993, is 'plugged into' the bastion walls so that in no place does it project above the fortification lines. In this manner, it is ensured that the building does not protrude externally above the ancient walls and is only visible from above.

The original bastion is retained intact and the new building, conceived as a separate almost removable entity, is carefully lowered and placed into the space defined by the old walls themselves. The separation between old and new is emphasised by a service and fire escape corridor thus enabling 'old' and 'new' to be read as entirely individual and different elements.

The project is a further expression of my belief in an eco-architecture which strikes a balance between universalism and individualism and which is situational as opposed to universal. It has long been my creed that the quality of an architect is more dependent on his faith in tradition than on the arrogance of his revolt. I still strongly maintain that architecture should vary according to place just as fruit varies according to the soil in which its seed is planted. In this Bank building there is a strong attempt to create a sense of continuity between the past and present in a synthesis of place and time.

In all my works, I have attempted to follow a philosophy where the architect, in order to design what shall be, must first of all understand and ultimately protect what has been. This is a project deeply rooted in situation, history and local culture, together with a strong sense of belonging to the cultural identity of place. The delicate 'insertion' of the new into the old could be likened to a surgeon's task of carefully grafting new tissue onto existing skin. What finally emerges is an almost singularity of concept forged by the interaction of the new built-form and pre-existent site. The old and the new are married in composition and material, and a dialogue is established by mixing the tenses of the site, illustrating my belief that architecture is a journey involving the past, present and future. In a way, this building is a manifestation of T. S. Eliot's words 'the past is altered by the present and the present is directed by the past'. In the process of respecting the sensitive historical context of the new building the architect extends his role of designer of the future into that of also being the defender of the past. This process of integration also provides an essential new breath of life to what was before a derelict and unused part of the city's outer fortification lines.

The actual building process of the Bank premises provided an interesting technical methodology of approach. Since the site had only limited access, it became necessary to first of all lift the initial machinery into place, excavate down between the defensive walls, and then utilise the excavated material to construct a ramp down to the ditch between the counterguard and the city walls themselves. This ramp was then used to provide access for, not only further construction machinery utilised, but also for the delivery of building materials. After the completion of works the ramp was removed.

The building itself consists of three polygonal floors, bounded by the pre-existent walls, at the centre of which is situated a large atrium defined by a glass curtain-wall system which provides light and ventilation to the surrounding office spaces. These three levels are linked by staircases and lifts, while the lower basement houses the Bank's strongrooms and security areas. While internally the spaces, equipped with the latest systems of technology, provide comfortable and functional contemporary solutions, externally the building pays more than respectful homage to its historical context. The amalgamation of these two approaches provides a dialectic between the universal and the particular; a synthesis of a unique enriching tradition and the comforts and utilities made available by the progress of industrial civilisation.

This building provides an exercise carved in ochre coloured ethnic stone which strongly relates today's architectural expression to the rich legacy of the tradition of the past. These forms from different eras, drawn out over the canvas of time, demonstrate that we should never open a quarrel between the past and the present, for if we do, we would only lose the future. Indeed, I firmly believe that to create the future one must of necessity build on the past. In order to look forward it becomes imperative and essential to reach backward. This project transposes the past into the present in order to preserve it for the future. With its working spaces buried deep within the invincible fortifications of the Knights the whole provides an apt metaphor for a bank building with symbolic messages of solidity, stability and permanence, while providing an interesting intermix of both contemporary images and mnemonic residues. Here is an example of architecture where the past has been utilised as a prologue. The whole is an anachronistic collage intermixed into a contextual totality of belonging: a form of threshold between the memory of the past and the imagery of the present. This exercise in 'grafting' the new onto the old reflects my philosophy that in architecture while there is a time to be bold there is more often a time to be humble.

PLACE MAKING FOR EDUCATION

The vast extension of the campus of the University of Malta was initiated in 1989 and is scheduled for completion in 1996. The original buildings designed in the early sixties by the British firm of architects, Norman & Dawburn, were a series of slit-windowed, typical of the period, masonry constructions clustered around a central Auditorium Hall which acted as a pivot for the whole layout. The total fabric of this last colonial building complex on the Island presented a not indifferent imported model, one which was well suited to regional conditions and also to the educational requirements of the time. The extension programme, necessary because of the vast increase in the number of students, consists of a series of buildings housing various large lecture halls and particular faculty buildings including that of architecture and engineering. Located on the North West part of the campus, the area in question terraces down and forms the border between the existing built-up area and the fertile valley below.

As such, the major formal considerations for the new buildings were in the direction of creating a visual link between the natural unbuilt area below and the preexisting built elements at the higher level. The new part had therefore to be designed very much in relation to the whole, following Eero Saarinen's advice 'always design a thing by considering it in its larger context: a chair in a room, a room in a house, a house in an environment, an environment in a city plan'. The concept therefore was to insert a series of new blocks which not only echoed the existing topography but also brought into play the earlier buildings themselves: Strong horizontal elements stepping up to the crest of the hill 'build the site', to borrow a phrase from Mario Botta.

The forms of this cluster focus on the creation of an animated series of processional spaces which, through the layering of space and light, give rise to an intriguing urban context and scenography. In this layout the spaces between the buildings contribute at least as much as the buildings themselves do to the overall environment. Internally evocative of the sunwashed traditional narrow street townscapes and of defensive ethnic Citadel walls externally, the whole development is conceived as an architecture based on the concept of re-codifying original archetypes and abstracting traditional forms into a valid contemporary expression. There is an attempt to produce, what Chris Abel has defined elsewhere, as a 'reciprocity between improved and traditional models and techniques each balancing and conditioning the other.'

This process of 'place-making' provides the creation of rewarding visual sequences through a variety of multi-transitional light and shade patterns which culminate in specifically focused social meeting points or nodes. The greater order of the individual buildings themselves together with the meandering lesser one of the covered porticoes attempt to bring together a sense of harmony and balance, not only between modernity and tradition in design and technology, but also between man-made settlement and nature. Once again in this project, the completed built-form becomes an icon of the collective memory of place, and in the process the totality of the complex is conceived to be in consonance with both the spirit of place and the spirit of time. Yet, the architectural language is strictly a vernacular one, which amalgamates with the previous colonial interventions in order to produce a synthesis of the indigenous and the imported, cast in a format of localisation which reflects the typical hybridisation of both past and present architecture to be found on these Islands.

CONCLUSIONS

I would like to state in conclusion that I believe that architects should spend less time analysing and talking and more on the actual design process. Most members of the profession have been too busy indulging in pseudo-intellectual masturbation to be involved in the true creative aspect of architecture. One must remember that when all is said and done there remains the building. I am for an architecture that excludes 'isms' (note how quickly they become 'wasms'), avoids pigeon-holing (uncomfortable unless you happen to be a pigeon), and focuses instead on a sense of appropriateness to not only time and place, but also to climate, tradition, memory, geography, history and context together with culture and above all to its users from both a materialistic and emotional aspect.

The recent incestuous interbreeding of Post-Modernism, where quotations from the past were rewritten as fiction, together with the hedonistic self-indulgent ego-centricity of deconstructivism are infectious diseases which our profession should take the precaution of being inoculated against. What is required is to denounce current obsessions with novelty, for novelty's sake, and to acknowledge and respond to more lasting and stable values. Architecture needs roots as much as it needs foundations.

Through architecture one should have an understanding of where one comes from and where one is going to. Architecture is about making man, not only physically, but also emotionally, comfortable. Architects must learn to give back a sense of belonging to the space which makes and surrounds their buildings. Architecture must be creation, not just industrialism, and must ultimately focus on the emotional human factor, for it is above all, in the words of Emilio Ambasz, 'an art involved in giving poetry to the pragmatic'. The notion of a contemporary architectural language must be one which does not deal with the external envelope but with the wholeness of the project in terms of spatial organisation, techniques and structure.

Architecture is about ordered space, which, besides serving the essential materialistic functional requirements, must also be capable of causing these emotive responses in man. My creed today is for a contextual architecture that is an expression of a symbiosis of past and present. It serves not only function (the architect's task starts once behavioural needs have been met), but also meaning. This meaning is a simulacrum of a hidden multiplicity of signs, moulded into a stimulating architectural language, which looks to and learns from both local culture and global civilisation. Architecture for me is the jointing of head and heart in a joyous response to life. It requires a pluralistic approach, incorporating the amalgamation of the surprising and the familiar, recalling old images and concepts from memory, and involving them with the new, in order to provide both with an enriched and extended identity. I firmly believe that the new, if it is to be valid, can only be built on the past, and that every architectural gesture should have history as its source and should have utopia as its end.

In seeking to create an architecture that is situational as opposed to universal, individual as opposed to collective, and unique as opposed to standardised, the architect of today must strive to rediscover the meaning of such words as beauty, magic, silence and enchantment These are prerequisites for creating an expression which synthesises and amalgamates both the poetic and the pragmatic. The ultimate role of architects is, I believe, to make the ordinary extraordinary in the environmental context of the place and time in which they are building.

The Author

Professor Richard England was born in Malta and graduated in Architecture at the University of Malta. He studied at the Milan Polytechnic and worked under the Italian architect and designer Gio Ponti. He is a sculptor, photographer, poet and painter. He has written several books and has had several written about his work. His buildings and designs have earned numerous international awards including the Interarch '85 and '91 Laureate Prizes, and Commonwealth Association of Architects Regional Awards in 1985 and 1987. A great crusader for sensitivity to place and setting in architecture, he is now a Visiting Professor at the University of Malta and holds appointments at a number of other universities world-wide.

References

Abel, C., *Manikata Church,* Academy Editions, 1995

Abel, C., *Transformations: Richard England 25 Years of Architecture,* Mid-Med Bank, Malta, 1987

AKAA, *Regionalism in Architecture,* Geneve, 1985

Ambasz, E., *The Architecture of Luis Barragan,* Museum of Modern Art, New York, 1976

Architectural Review, *Anatomy of Regionalism*, November 1986,

Architectural Review, *Regionalism: Searching for Identity*, May 1983

Attoe, W., *The Architecture of Ricardo Legoretta*, University of Texas, 1990

Borel, N. (Photographs), *Mediterranean Houses: Cote d'Azur and Provence*, Pascal Chossegros, Barcelona, 1991

Casals, L. & Guell, X., *Mediterranean Islands*, Gustavo Gill, Barcellona 1986

Chadirji, R., *Concepts and Influences: Towards a Regionalised International Architecture*, K.P.I. London, 1986

Doumanis, *Architecture in Greece*, No. 26, Greece, 1992

Knevitt, C., *Connections: The Architecture of Richard England*, Lund Humphries, 1984

Knevitt, C., *Manikata: The Making of a Church*, Manikata Parish Publication, Malta, 1976

Konstantinidis, A., *Projects and Buildings*, Agra Editions, Greece, 1981

Kramer, K., *Justus Dahinden: Architecture*, Verlag Stuttgart/Zurich, 1987

Los, S. (Ed), *Regionalismo dell'architettura*, Franco Muzzio Editore, Padova, 1990

Ponti, G., *In Praise of Architecture*, F.W. Dodge Corporation, New York, 1960

Portugal, S., *Barragan*, Rizzoli, New York, 1992

Thake, C., *Voices of a Site*, Demetra No. 5, Alloro, Italy, December, 1993

Zucchi, B., *Giancarlo De Carlo*, Butterworth Architecture, 1992

Figure 8 Baroque Church at Gharb in Gozo.

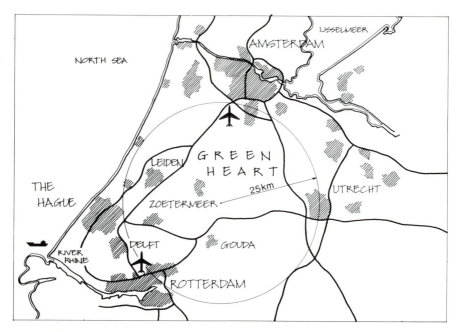

Figure 1 Randstad Holland.

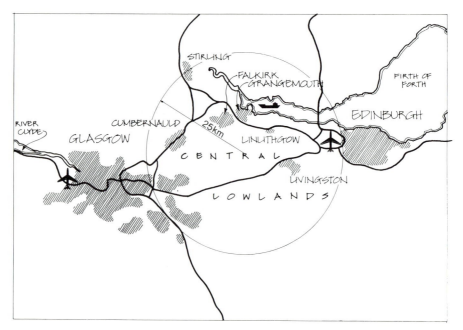

Figure 2 The Central Belt of Scotland.

32

CITY WITH A GREEN HEART
Lessons from Randstad Holland

Brian Evans

What a gift that God waud gie us, tae see oursels as ithers see us.

Robert Burns

In the past, Scotland's cities benefited from confident city fathers and the outward looking vision of architects and planners to create a unique and distinct urban legacy recognised around the world – beautiful but functional, to serve the community and the nation.

Today, the challenge of city development and expansion is greater than ever. The creation of new communities must be combined with the regeneration of those that are disadvantaged. There must be equity in our perception of achievement, disadvantage and the environment. Attention is again focused on the urban edge – the interface of city and landscape. It requires understanding and skill to balance the criteria for a new place of the highest quality with the regeneration of disadvantaged areas whilst understanding the tolerances of our environment. This balance is necessary to create a new legacy for future generations and the creative process must begin with a three dimensional examination of city form and landscape.

In another chapter of this volume, Professor Frank Walker argues that through the interaction of 'Zeitgeist – the Spirit of the Age' and 'Genius loci – the spirit of place' comes the manifestation of cultural identity in architecture. Our cultural identity affects the way we think and therefore underpins our approach, not only to architecture, but to urban design and planning. In the increasingly competitive and global community, we often learn about ourselves by studying the work of others.

It is instructive to examine how others are seeking to establish this equitable balance of urban and rural, city and landscape in an area of development pressure and limited natural resource – the provinces of Holland in the Netherlands. A measure of distance can provide clarity and help to develop the overview which is the necessary counterpoint to intimacy in the evolution of an achievable vision. First, let us examine the relevance of the comparison.

In Randstad Holland, the direct route from Rotterdam to Amsterdam is approximately 75 kilometres by road (10 kilometres longer via the Hague). This journey takes one hour by train and a little longer by car. It departs from the productive centre, principal port and petrochemical complex on the Rhine delta and, via the seat of government in the Hague and principal airport of Schipol, arrives in the cultural and financial centre on the Ijsselmeer, where the Rhine formerly met the sea. Along the way, lie the university towns of Delft and Leiden, the historic centre of Gouda and the new town of Zoetermeer. Between these towns and cities lies an open and protected area of agriculture, horticulture, recreation and small commuter settlements under pressure from development known as the 'Groene Hart' – the Green Heart.

In Central Scotland, the direct route from Glasgow to Edinburgh is also approximately 75 kilometres or just over 80 via Falkirk-Grangemouth. In a similar journey of one hour by train (again longer by car), it is possible to travel from the productive and service centre at the head of the Clyde Estuary, via the principal port and petrochemical complex of Scotland to the seat of government, culture and finance on the Forth Estuary. 'En route', the university town of Stirling, the historic centre of Linlithgow and the new towns of Cumbernauld and Livingston. The journey takes a little longer (12.5 km) to include the principal airport at Abbotsinch Glasgow regrettably not serviced by high speed trains from the other urban centres of Central Scotland unlike its counterpart in the Netherlands. The area between these towns and cities is known as the Central Lowlands and is characterised by a mix of agriculture, woodland, recreation and moorland. It is also under pressure for development.

The population of both regions is in excess of 500 inhabitants per square kilometre and both face substantial pressure to accommodate projected housing demand. The Dutch region is controlled by the two provinces of North and South Holland, the Scottish by the three regions of Strathclyde, Central and Lothian. Both have smaller municipalities or districts at the local scale. Both systems will shortly be reorganised. The Dutch system will remain two tier, but the provinces will be increased in number and reduced in size to become more responsive to local needs, not unlike the new councils in Scotland.

The wider context of these regions are very different; the Scottish example lies at the periphery of Europe, the Dutch one at its heart, and there are also fundamental differences in population, physical geography and the place the regions occupy in the respective national urban hierarchy of the Netherlands and the UK. But, the similarities of scale, function and even climate, make legitimate an inquiry to determine what, if any lessons, can be learned for Central Scotland in Holland.

Perhaps the most fundamental difference lies in the identity of the two regions. For most of this century, irrespective of administrative boundaries, the Dutch have contemplated and planned this part of the Netherlands as one urban and landscape system – the 'Randstad-Groene Hart'. The Scots are equally aware of the role of Central Scotland, the low-lying central rift valley between the Highlands and the Southern Uplands, but, with the possible exception of the 'Oceanspan' concept from the late 1960s, no real attempt has ever been made to consider Central Scotland as a whole in planning terms.

The Dutch of Rotterdam, the Hague and Amsterdam consider themselves to have an identity within Randstad and collaborate with the smaller municipalities to develop an acceptable working model where each has its place within the greater whole. The psychology of the Scots is different and the bi-polar competition of Edinburgh and Glasgow arrogantly or diffidently, depending on one's point of view, underplays the contribution of the smaller communities in central Scotland. This paper considers the evolution of Randstad, the expression of its form and the current debate about its future to determine if different perspectives can be identified to help consider the future of Central Scotland.

THE EXPRESSION OF A CONCEPT

The name Randstad is attributed to Albert Plesman, the first director of KLM who, when flying over the provinces of Holland, described the pattern of settlement he saw below him as a 'randstad', a round or rim city made up of Utrecht, Amsterdam, The Hague, Rotterdam and a number of large towns with a sparsely populated and green centre. The evocative name provided a convenient way to describe the settlement pattern in the west of Holland. However, it was Peter Hall in his book *The World Cities* who explored the dichotomy between cartographic construction and metropolis. His deliberations on 'city' and 'model' contributed greatly to the international reputation of Randstad culminating in its important contribution to the 17 International Trienalle of Milan under the theme 'World Cities and the Future of the Metropoli' (Nycolaas).

Until the Second World War, the cities of Randstad developed independently but became more closely related through road and rail connections. However, in 1958, the 'Randstad Development Plan' was prepared by the Dutch Government to guide the future urban and environmental structure of the western Netherlands and, for the first time, Randstad was defined in terms of urban planning policy. The basic components of the plan have guided the structure of Randstad until the present day: conserving the structure and identity of the individual cities; maintaining their separation by means of green buffer zones; preserving a central open area; and encouraging further urbanisation at the outer periphery.

A concern for balance between city and landscape was a key aim of the plan. Over the years, four government memoranda of 1960, 1966, 1973–83 and 1988 have been prepared to monitor progress. Each of these reappraised the basic objectives of the original plan in the light of changing circumstances and increasing development pressure. The first two memoranda sought to deal with the issues by readjusting thresholds and targets within the predefined distribution against a trend to spreading urbanisation and the development of new towns such as Spijkenisse and Zoetermeer.

However, the third memorandum recognised that pressure was too great and adopted a more radical approach through promotion of and support for the environmental and cultural potential of the old city centres. This early example of a far-sighted policy of urban regeneration also provided the opportunity for the re-examination of the identity and expression of urban form by leading Dutch architects such as Aldo van Eyck, Herman Hertzberger and Theo Bosch.

In 1988, the fourth memorandum was prepared, following municipal elections to reopen the question of the design and structure of Randstad as a whole. It underlined the importance of the Randstad to the economic future of the Netherlands and extended the concept of the 'Westwing' Randstad comprising Rotterdam, The Hague and Amsterdam and the open areas between these three cities (the Dutch horticultural centre, the university towns of Delft and Leiden, the Zeeland delta, seacoast and polder area of north Holland). This concept adopted an international perspective based on the service centre and financial markets of Amsterdam, the international airport at Schipol, the Port of Rotterdam and the governmental function of The Hague, with the specific intention of competing directly with the key northern European cities of London, Paris, Brussels, Hamburg and Frankfurt (Nycolaas).

In the Fourth Memorandum, the Dutch Government proposed a new programme or urbanisation for the Netherlands requiring the provision of over 800,000 new dwellings in the period up to 2005, the majority in Randstad. This is a very major programme of urbanisation with significant consequences for the existing form and landscape of Randstad which has already developed at an increasing rate in the 20th Century.

ARCHITECTURAL EXPRESSION

From the beginning of the century, a national and modern architecture developed in the Netherlands inspired by Gropius, Mies van der Rohe and Le Corbusier which adapted the traditional use of brick to new idioms and today expresses the character of Randstad towns and cities. The inspiration was provided by Hendrik Petrus Berlage who, after a number of 'fin de siecle' civic buildings, turned to urban design and city planning. Berlage was the inspiration for the Amsterdam School of urban building of large housing areas built in brick with three and four storey facades and skilfully sculpted corners. The style is epitomised by the work of Kramer and de Klerk at the Eigen Haard (Spaandammerplantsoen) and De Dageraad Estates from 1913 to 1923 (de Wit).

The more purist approach of the group known as 'De Stijl' influenced architects like Gerrit Rietveld and Jacobus Oud who in 1918 became city architect of Rotterdam to guide the city expansion with housing areas such as Spangen and Tuschendijken characterised by plain uncompromising brick buildings.

The approach to city expansion conceived by Berlage at the turn of the century was based on the monumental arrangement of blocks designed as a unified entity and sited along spacious squares and streets. De Klerk and Oud expanded this concept in Amsterdam and Rotterdam respectively. De Klerk tended to treat the housing block in a sculptural way whereas Oud organised the block in a consistent way with an austere and closed external facade in contrast to a softer and more open internal expression for the living apartments. The two architects typify the expressionism of the Amsterdam school and the rationalist purism of the 'Nieuwe Bouwen' school. In the era before the formal planning of Randstad, the expansion of the key cities developed in the European tradition of tenement building common in Germany, France, Belgium and Scotland each with their own expression based on a cultural interpretation of a common theme.

In the pre-war years, the picturesque disposition of green space and architecture in the form of the garden suburb was introduced from Germany and the UK. as exemplified by the plan for 'Daal en Berg' in the Hague by Moliere and Verhagen with a wide variety of street form and perspective. Interestingly, this plan was rejected in favour of the Frank Lloyd Wright inspired 'Papaverhof', a modern formal housing development laid out around a central green space (Colenbrander). This example illustrates the long-running dichotomy between Dutch expressionism and modernist rationalism evident in Dutch architecture and urban design throughout most of the 20th century.

In the 1950s, in the period of post-war reconstruction and the development of the 'Randstad Development Plan', the Dutch, like the British, embraced system building for low rise family housing and high rise apartment blocks. This period, saw the construction of many point blocks and created the debate on high and low rise buildings, a dilemma which continues in the Netherlands today but which has been laid to rest elsewhere.

This paper is concerned with examining the idea of Randstad Green Heart and its expression in terms of time and place. However it is necessary to note in passing that the Dutch are also very active at the city scale as well as the supra-city scale of Randstad or the detailed scale of individual sites. For example, Cornelius van Eesteren, a member of 'De Stijl' and former chairman of C.I.A.M, was the author of the renowned General Expansion Plan for Amsterdam which should be seen as one of a number of city components fitting within the overall Randstad theme.

In the urban regeneration of the late 1970s and early 1980s, under the third memorandum on spatial planning, Dutch housing regained the stylistic vigour which it had lost after 1945. In the opinion of Colenbrander et al, Aldo van Eyck, Herman Hertzberger and Theo Bosch evaluated and reintegrated forms from the garden city movement and the sculptural qualities of the Amsterdam School to provide a link with context through an abstract interpretation of the 'genius loci' based on scale, type and line, rather than an imitation of earlier forms. This vigour has been carried through to the implementation of the fourth memorandum with an evolutionary expression in settlements such as Kattenbroek in Amersfoord by Kuiper Compagnons – a post-modern and metaphorical interpretation of the Garden City theme.

THE LANDSCAPE CONTEXT

The Dutch landscape is the counterpoint of this evolution and expression of urban form. This cities which today make up Randstad developed on the sand bars and dunes of the delta landscape when the River Rhine and Maas meet the sea. Later expansion moved into the polders (droogmakerijen) created by the reclamation of large areas of former peat extraction which produced the internationally know Dutch polder landscape with its characteristic windmills and variable water table. For several centuries the

Figure 3 The Eigen Haard housing estate in Amsterdam, by Michel de Klerk of 'The Amsterdam School', 1917–21. Courtesy of Netherlands Architecture Institute.

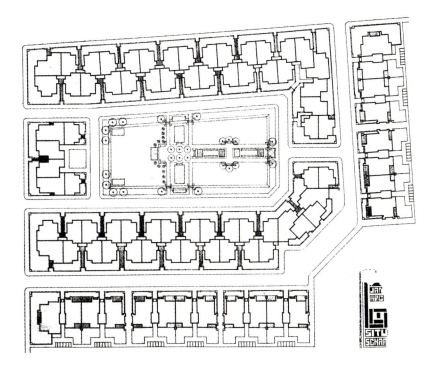

Figure 4 'Daal en Berg' garden suburb in The Hague, by J Wils, 1919-21. Courtesy of Netherlands Architecture Institute.

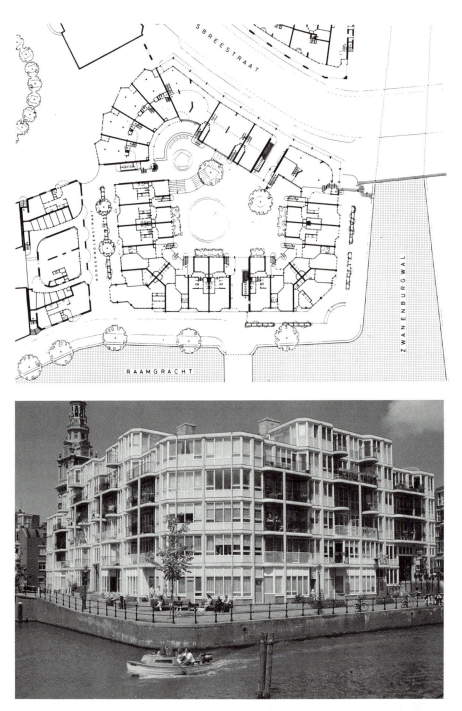

Figure 5 'Het Pentagon' housing in Amsterdam, by Theo Bosch of 'The New Amsterdam School', 1975-83.

agriculture of these polder areas was so important to the Dutch economy that it resisted pressure for urbanisation from the cities which in time created an urbanised area around the periphery of a central open area in the provinces of North and South Holland. In the period of post war reconstruction and development leading to the establishment of the Randstad Development Plan, the central area or Green Heart was given 'green belt' status to security character from urban intervention in a period of rapid growth.

The awareness of context brought about by a constant monitoring of water level and the stability of land has led to a framework based strategy for landscape design in Holland. The aim of this approach is to provide a landscape framework to help deal with the process of change in a comprehensive way. It is based on controlled development where government intervention leads the process of landscape planning and design, an approach based on the Dutch tradition of large scale integrated projects. The Dutch system of landscape planning has long been characterised by rule and order – almost a planted expression of the paintings of Piet Modrian – where beauty in landscape is associated with order, a functional and precise expression of the struggle to control the water system.

The concept of landscape frameworks are based on the premise that high quality landscapes need to be flexible yet stable to establish landscape character with ecological quality for nature reserves, forests and woodlands. The established Dutch approach is to accommodate agriculture, landscape amenity and nature conservation together. More recently, attention has been directed to separating the landscape structure from development and to formalise further the concept of a durable and stable landscape framework of interconnected zones or corridors devoted to nature conservation, forestry, outdoor recreation and water control through the expansion and connection of existing woodlands into a continuous matrix.

In a reaction to this organised system of landscape planning, an alternative perspective has evolved which views the distinction between town and county as an illusion, where reality is expressed as a collage of fragments such as business parks, bulb fields, canals, roads, nature reserves, hotels and large stores, housing areas and nature reserves. This urbanised landscape has been referred to as 'Patchwork Metropolis' (Hooftman).

It is intended that this brief review of urban form and landscape design helps to identify the unique aspects of place which in turn have informed the Dutch interpretation of European and international influences to set the context within which the debate on the implementation of the Fourth Memorandum on Spatial Planning takes place.

CREATIVITY THROUGH DESIGN COMPETITION

In the late 1970s and early 1980s a former Director of the Dutch National Spatial Planning Agency, the late Leonard Wijers, promoted the qualities of urban form and place when many designers and planners were engrossed in the administrative and legal complexities of spatial planning. In 1985, the 'Eo Wijers Foundation' was established to keep alive, promote and disseminate his ideal that design, as much as analysis, is a fundamental precept from regional spatial planning to the treatment of individual sites. One of the principal means at the disposal of the Foundation is the promotion and organisation of a series of national and international competitions staged for practising professionals and students to develop contributions on this theme. In this way the Foundation, through its influential and astute board of directors, enjoys the support of national agencies, provinces and municipalities to address important and current issues in the Netherlands in a creative and constructive way.

In 1994, the Foundation elected to stage an open international competition to consider concepts for the Randstad Green Heart Metropolis and to examine the nature and definition of the edge between the City and the Green Heart. The competition was the fourth in the series and the first of the competitions to be international. It enjoyed the support of four government ministries, six provinces and four municipalities.

The brief was demanding, calling for competitors to offer their vision or concept for Randstad Green Heart – at a regional level and in a European context; and, at the same time, to choose one of three edge locations to prepare a detailed exposition of their concept within the rigorous demands of a real site. A multidisciplinary and international jury was assembled at the invitation of the Foundation and the brief, made widely accessible by the competition language of English, was distributed to locations all over the world.

The response exceeded the organisers highest expectations with over 130 submissions and entries from Korea, Slovenia, USA, Canada and most of the European Union countries. There can be no doubt that the unique character of the landscape of the Green Heart and the special urban pattern of Randstad stimulated the imagination and provided a challenge to the creativity, expertise and insight of many to make a contribution to the development of thought about the design, planning and social issues of the area.

The entries reflect current, philosophical and professional preoccupations. There is an 'urban' viewpoint that regards the Green Heart as an area around which urban developments can be realised. Starting with the city, solutions ranged from high-rise building to suburban housing, low-rise building along the fringes of the Green Heart.

The 'landscape' approach placed the emphasis on the high value of the unique cultural-historical and landscape character of the Green Heart. Extensive urbanisation is seen as damaging to this character, to be carried out as unobtrusively as possible.

Other entries emphasise that the Green Heart is not a clear concept and that the Randstad is a fictional concept. They differentiate the half moon-shaped but monotonous 'zonal city' (bandstad) that runs to Amsterdam via Haarlem to Leiden, The Hague and Rotterdam, from the Ultrecht agglomeration. Others claim that in the Green Heart a number of parallel zones can be identified: to the east a zone of polders, reclaimed lakes used for turf dredging, and lakes that change gradually into a zone of grasslands, and, in contrast, the east-west infrastructure of rivers, roads and railways with a number of important towns and cities in the Green Heart such as Alphen, Gouda, Woerden, Boskoop and Zoetermeer.

The competition provided and excellent medium for examining design derived and process driven solutions. More than architects, it attracted the attention of planners and landscape architects preoccupied with these processes and themes. In view of the varied starting points adopted by the participants, it was not easy for the jury to arrive at a definition of prize winners but ultimately, a group of 5 entries were identified which together provide a comprehensive exploration of the issues raised in the brief.

The overall winner, submitted under the motto of 'Laddermetropolis' was the most complete, coherent and well expressed entry. The concept of developing and 'Eastwing' of Randstad is proposed to parallel the 'Westwing' with links between the cities to create a north south urban ladder in Holland from Amsterdam to Rotterdam with east west rungs picking up Zoetermeer, Gouda, Delft and the Hague. Laddermetropolis carried the concept through to examining the nature of edge locations on the city landscape interface.

Two sets of second and third prizes were awarded, the first stream were selected in recognition of the understanding of the process of design in spatial planning. Both entries recognised that market forces rather than policy intervention in part determines the location of development today. 'Chaining Waters', as its motto implies, adopted a vision of Randstad based on water resource management, whereas 'It Takes Two to Tango' addressed the same issue through a process of strategic landscape design. Both entries developed the concepts and ideas at the local scale.

The parallel stream of second and third prizes celebrated the vision of design in a elegant overview of the entire Randstad provided by a group of German students. Their entry 'XX' was a cartographic delight and conceived of a system of settlement within a woodland structure examining possible identities for different parts of the changing landscape in 'Green Heart Metropolis' by contrasting wooded polders, peat polders and river landscapes. Finally, 'Metropolder' examined the concept of a 'Transfer Park' for distribution of goods which is a key issue in the 'Edge City' of Randstad.

These five prize-winning entries provide an interesting dialogue on design and process and were complemented by commendations awarded for provocative thought: a new approach to the Dutch dilemma of high or low rise solutions to high density housing; a science fiction fable inviting the jury to look forward a few years by looking back from the distant future; and, an exploration of cultural interaction through an allegorical examination of water.

The jury concluded that the competition made a valuable contribution to the national debate about the planning concepts of the Green Heart and Randstad. Together with the competition brief, the winning and commended entries provide remarkably challenging and stimulating statements about current thought and process in design and planning and their application to the city landscape region of Randstad Green Heart. Whether as the 'model' or 'city' described by Peter Hall, the Randstad Green Heart Metropolis continues to provide the Dutch with a conceptual and cultural framework for exploring the future of the principal cities and landscape framework of the provinces of North and South Holland.

Figure 6 'Laddermetropolis' took first prize in the Inside Randstad Holland 1995 competition, by VHP Stedebouwkundigen & Landschapsarchitecten.

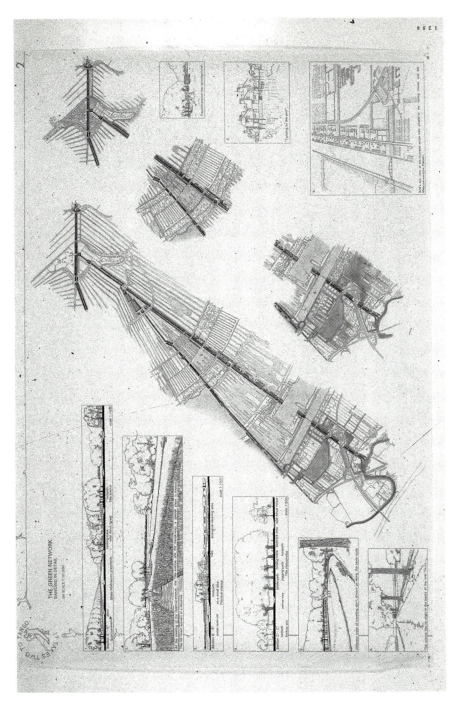

Figure 7 The Green Network of 'It takes Two to Tango' which received second equal
  prize, by Danny Eijsackers, Sander Voetberg and Corine Zwart.

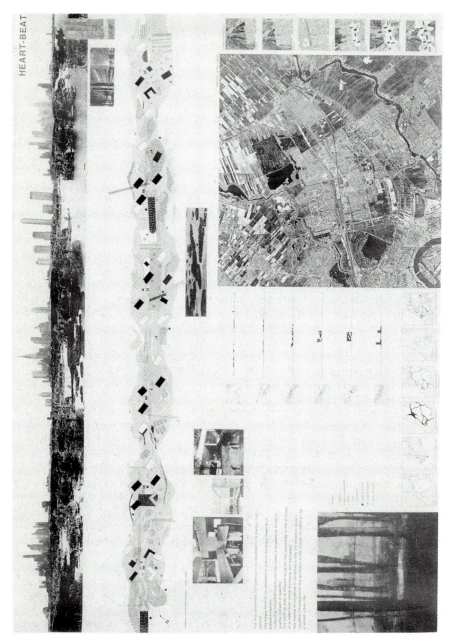

Figure 8 'Heart Beat' which received a commendation, by Erik de Jong, Leontine Lieffering and Caroline Wigleven.

To an outsider, the entire process is a remarkable statement of the vision, confidence and maturity of the Dutch for contemplating, re-examining and learning about their own circumstances. It represents a committed and outward-looking attitude and commendable maturity to be able to examine these high-profile issues when they are so prominent on the political, professional and public agendas of the Netherlands.

In recent decades, development pressure in the UK has been experienced at the outer edge of the city leaving a problem of poorly defined city centres and inner city dereliction. The increased size and decreasing density of the city has generated a legacy of problem areas which have required substantial investment for urban regeneration. With Randstad, it is clear that the converse could be true, where development pressure on the inner edge will lead to a process of concentration. As this occurs, the outer edge could become more remote and face a similar problem to that faced within the centre of UK cities. Many share the concern that this development pressure will generate a centripetal force that leads to the implosion rather than expansion of the city. At its most extreme, this continuous pressure and process could lead to the uniform development of the green heart – the so-called European Los Angeles.

The Green Heart of Randstad is very special. Leaving a Randstad city and moving inwards presents the visitor with a familiar experience of transition from city centre, through outer suburbs, to a well kept urban fringe and beyond into the countryside before the process is reversed to approach the next city. The scale is sufficiently large and the journey sufficiently long that the visitor does not seem to have passed through a city but rather to have journeyed from one city to another. Only study reveals the true nature of the journey. The process of extension on the inner edge of Randstad could push the urban edges inwards to meet and perhaps coalesce in the centre threatening the special qualities of the Green Heart where edge meets edge and eventually city meets city.

The Green Heart is a true oasis, the closest parallels in the UK are metaphorical places such as Hampstead Heath in London or Pollok Park in Glasgow where for a brief moment it is possible to lose sight of the city. It is hard for the outsider to avoid the conclusion that a mix of forestry, recreation and agriculture is the appropriate balance for the Green Heart – a National Park – a cherished landscape protected from urban development and pressure.

The competition sites were well chosen to examine these dilemmas. The Maarssen and Achtkamp locations have stimulated many thoughts about the Randstad inner edge – the heart of the debate. Maarsen in particular is a very exciting location with subtle and unique landscapes. The conservation of natural forms and development pressures place this location at the nexus of the Randstad/Green Heart debate. It was extremely well chosen and provided an excellent vehicle to challenge the skills and creativity of the participants. Its subtle appearance belies the deep understanding of the Dutch landscape and environmental processes necessary to resolve the issues.

The Dutch landscape presents a mystery to many people from elsewhere. At first flat, uniform, managed, not wild, engendering a feeling of safety. To the British it is like the Fens of East Anglian or the Norfolk Broads. Of course the complexity is much greater, the underlying hydrological framework and water management is of paramount importance. In the UK we are familiar with water, but we do not understand it. To us it is simply a miracle of life, it falls from the sky and drains to the sea. Sometimes if you build a wall across a valley you can create an artificial lake – simple as long as gravity combined with topography work in your favour. However, it seems that the water system preconditions an understanding of the Dutch landscape and cities and the process of design. Like all matters of great importance, it can become overwhelming, the foundation stone from which all premises are raised but which can limit, rather than encourage, vision. The international view has a more imprecise understanding of the complexity of the hydrology but retains an open mind and the innocence to question why it is not possible to achieve certain things. The combination of Dutch and international colleagues on the jury liberated thinking on one hand and on the other better understood the constraints and demands of the Dutch water system.

One of the most important lessons from this exercise is its relevance for thinking in the UK, and Scotland in particular. In British planning thought, cities tend to be perceived from the inside out as monocentric bodies with a protected edge or 'greenbelt', the legacy of the work of Abercrombie and others in planning exercises such as the 1946 Clyde Valley Plan. There has been a great deal of effort by many to provide a counter view of the city seen from the outside in. In this respect, the Countryside Around Towns research undertaken by Michael Dower of the Dartington Amenity Research Trust (DART) and sponsored by the Countryside Commission for Scotland at the end of the 1970s was a seminal piece of work.

This led to the establishment of the urban fringe initiatives at the periphery of Glasgow and the identification of a strategy for the improvement of the Glasgow conurbation's river valleys under the policy umbrella of the Strathclyde Structure Plan. Ultimately, the importance of the Glasgow Green Belt, the River Valleys Strategy and the urban fringe projects were combined into the one initiative entitled 'Greening the Conurbation' and promoted by a public sector partnership led by Strathclyde Regional Council and Scottish Natural Heritage. A similar initiative exists for the green belt around Edinburgh. However, these still tend, because of the nature of administrative boundaries to have a monocentric view of the city.

There are many attributes of these initiatives which serve the environmental well. But, in Central Scotland, the proximity of the major cities of Glasgow and Edinburgh, the major towns of Falkirk, Grangemouth and Stirling, the new towns of Cumbernauld and Livingston and the many smaller urban centres means that a monocentric urban policy is really inadequate. For at least two decades, development pressure has leapt the boundaries of the green belts to stimulate reactive planning in the Central Belt and create something of an urban sprawl.

The Scots are now an urban people, nearly 80% of the population live in four cities and several large towns. The Central Belt of Scotland, the low lying region embracing Edinburgh and Glasgow and the areas between, support over 60% (3 million) of the Scottish population. Our system of strategic planning means that the area between the two cities is viewed as a boundary or as a journey. The area is cared for by three Regional Councils, 19 districts and 5 Enterprise Agencies. Only one body, the Central Countryside Trust is charged with a co-ordinated programme for Central Scotland.

For over 20 years the programme of woodland planting and environmental improvement has continued within a limited financial environment and the Trust has recently produced a strategy for treating the landscape of Central Scotland. The work of the Trust is to be commended and it warrants the appropriate levels of support to continue its work. But its work is a response mechanism, not an enabling vision for Central Scotland.

In Scotland, a static population, changing economic infrastructure and declining household size results in a forecast need for 100,000 housing units in the period to 2005. The majority of these are required in the Central Belt. Many will be provided in new settlements but a non-interventionist government proposes that the Market will determine their location and scale. Plainly this is inadequate.

There is evidence that the UK and Scotland in particular has paralleled the evolution of Dutch city building from the coherent dense urban block of the early years of the 20th century, through the exploration of the garden suburb in the interwar years, the system building of post was reconstruction of the 50s and 60s, to the rediscovery of form and identity in the urban regeneration of the 1980s. Perhaps it has taken longer in this country to restate the importance of design in the process. Scottish initiatives have been at the forefront of pressing firstly for a high quality in the design of individual buildings in the landscape (Fladmark et al 1991) and later in the design of town expansion (Scottish Office Environment Dept., PAN 44). This process must be carried through to the involvement of design, the three dimensional exploration of city form and landscape framework in strategic spatial planning. This is one of the key lessons to be learned from the Dutch system examined in the case of Randstad Green Heart Metropolis. There can be no substitute for designed the three dimensional framework for the strategic planning process if we hope to create a legacy of quality for the future.

CONCLUSIONS

The family resemblance between certain cities, regions and cultures can help inform future directions, provided the results of the investigation are interpreted rather than imitated. The lessons from Randstad are clear, we must, in Central Scotland, consider design at a scale greater than the city and its immediate environs, we should take more seriously the Green Heart of Central Scotland between the cities of Edinburgh and Glasgow and pay more attention to its future. We are not alone in facing these issues but we do have our own cultural legacy of landscape and city form to draw on. We should heed Walker's words and express the spirit of the time within the spirit of our own place – on the brink the millennium and at the edge of Europe.

In April 1996, the current process of local government reorganisation will be complete with the establishment of unitary authorities for Glasgow, Edinburgh and the communities of Central Scotland. Surely this presents a unique opportunity for expansive thinking to look strategically and holistically at the planning of Central Scotland. An occasion to reflect on past achievements and plans for the future.

Perhaps the cathartic process of looking back over the successes and failures of the past four decades on one hand or the participation of international colleagues on the other will help us break away from the limitations of monocentric and monosectoral planning and the iniquities of short term opportunism to embrace the long term holistic vision that is a necessary route to a sustainable future and a shared balance of city and landscape.

The Author and Acknowledgements

Brian Evans was born in St. Andrews and educated at the Universities of Edinburgh and Strathclyde. An urban designer and planner, he is a partner of Gillespies, the multidisciplinary design practice with offices in Glasgow, Manchester and Oxford. He has worked extensively in the fields of urban design, urban regeneration and landscape planning and carried out assignments in the Netherlands, Norway and Italy. He is a Visiting Lecturer at The Robert Gordon University and joint author of *Tomorrow's Architectural Heritage* (1991) and the Design Manual for Scottish Office Planning Advice No. 44, *Fitting New Housing Development into the Landscape* (1994). In 1994–95, he was a member of the jury for 'Inside Randstad Holland' an international competition staged by the Eo Wijers Foundation to generate new visions for the transitional zones between the City and its Green Heart.

The author is indebted to the Foundation for inviting him to participate in the jury for the competition, and to his colleagues on the jury for their stimulating collaboration. He would like to thank Professor Fladmark and his editorial team for their encouragement and helpful advice.

References

AIR, *Alexanderpolder: New Urban Frontiers*, Thotts, Bussum, 1993

Barbieri, U., *Amsterdam, the Capital of the Netherlands*, in Floet, W. W. (ed) 'Randstad Holland', ACSA European Schools of Architecture Conference 1992, Publikatieburo Bouwkunde, Delft, 1992, pp 25–35

de Boer, N., *De Randstand Bestaat Neit*, NAI Publishers, Rotterdam, 1995

Boekraad, C., *Prinsenland – Kattnebroek – Niewsloten*, NAI Publishers, Rotterdam, 1995

Carter, N. et al., 'Dutch Ring Changes around Green Heart', *Planning* No 1065, 22 April 1994, pp 24–25

Central Scotland Countryside Trust, *Central Scotland Forest Strategy*, CSCT, Shotts, 1995

Cherry, G. E., *The Evolution of British Town Planning*, Leonard Hill, Leighton Buzzard, 1974

Colenbrander, B.(ed.), *Style: Standard and Signature in Dutch Architecture*, Netherlands Architecture Institute, Rotterdam, 1993

Dartington Institute , *Countryside Around Town in Scotland: A Review of Change 1976–85*, Countryside Commission for Scotland, Perth, 1987

Dower, M. et al., *The Countryside Around Towns in Scotland,* Countryside Commission for Scotland, Perth, 1976

Drijver, P., *The Hague, Green City on the Sea,* in Floet, W. W. (ed) 'Randstad Holland', ACSA European Schools of Architecture Conference 1992, Publikatieburo, Bouwkunde, Delft, 1992, pp 103–111

Elson, M. et al., *The Effectiveness of Green Belts,* DOE, Planning Research Programme, HMSO, London, 1993

Evans B. M., *'A Celebration of Enterprise: Expos and Garden Festivals',* in Fladmark, J. M. (ed) Cultural Tourism, Donhead, London, 1994

Evans B. M., Speech given on the occasion of the Prizegiving Ceremony for 'Inside Randstad-Holland', Rotterdam, 16 June 1995

Faludi, A. et al., 'Half a Million Witnesses: The Success (& Failure) of Dutch Urbanisation Strategy', *Built Environment,* Vol 17, No. 1, 1991, pp 43–52

Faludi, A. et al., 'Keeping the Netherlands in Shape', Theme issue, *Built Environment,* Vol 15, No 1, 1989

Fladmark, J. M., Mulvagh, G. Y. & Evans, B. M., The *Countryside Around Towns – A Scottish Programme of Partnership and Action,* Countryside Commission for Scotland, Battleby, 1988

Fladmark, J. M. et al., *Tomorrow's Architectural Heritage: Landscape and Buildings in the Countryside,* Mainstream, Edinburgh, 1991

Geuze, A., *In Holland Staat een huis,* Netherlands Architecture Institute, Rotterdam 1995

Hall, P., *The World Cities,* London, 1977.

Hall, P., *Urban and Regional Planning,* Third Edition, Routledge, London & New York, 1992

Harding, A., *Amsterdam and Rotterdam* in Harding, A. et al. (eds) 'European Cities Towards 2000: Profiles, Policies and Prospects', Manchester University Press, Manchester, 1994, pp 18–44

Harsema, H. (ed), *Town & Country on the Slope,* Jury Report of the Open Competition, Eo Wijers Stichting, Den Haag, 1989

Hooftman, E., 'Who's Afraid of the New Landscape', *Landscape Design,* Journal of the Landscape Institute, No 204, October 1991, pp 21–22

Ijff, J., *The Findings of the Jury,* speech by Dr J. Ijff, chairman of the Jury for 'Inside Randstad-Holland' to the Prizegiving Ceremony, Rotterdam, 16 June 1995

Lothian Regional Council, *Lothian Region Structure Plan 1994,* Finalised Written Statement, Lothian Regional Council, Edinburgh, Nov. 1994

Meyer, H., *Rotterdam, Between Europe and America,* in Floet, W. W. (ed) 'Randstad Holland', ACSA European Schools of Architecture Conference 1992, Publikatieburo Bouwkunde, Delft, 1992, pp. 71–81

Nycolaas, J., *The Randstad Exists,* in Mazza, L. (ed) 'World Cities and the Future of the Metropoles', Catalogue of the International Participations, 17th International Triennale of Milan, Electa, Milan, 1988, pp 161–171

Pasveer, E., *The Horizon of Design: Role and Contrast of Urban Design studies,* in Van Velzen, E. (ed), Design Studies, ACSA European Schools of Architecture Conference 1992, Publikatieburo Bouwkunde, Delft, 1992, pp 145–155

Pracht, L. (ed), *Europe in Figures,* Third Edition, Eurostat, Office for Official Publications of the European Communities, Brussels & Luxemburg, 1992

Scottish Office, *Scottish Abstract of Statistics 1991,* Government Statistical Service, No. 20, 1991, HMSO

Scottish Office, *The Scottish Environment – Statistics,* Government Statistical Service, No. 3, 1991, HMSO

Scottish Office Environment Department, *The Siting and Design of New Houses in the Countryside*, Planning Advice Note PAN 36, HMSO, 1991

Scottish Office Environment Department, *Fitting New Housing Development into the Landscape*, Planning Advice Note PAN 44, Scottish Office, 1994

Strathclyde Regional Council, *Strathclyde Structure Plan – the Consolidated Written Statement*, Department of Physical Planning, Strathclyde Regional Council, Glasgow, 1991

Strathclyde Regional Council & Scottish Natural Heritage, *Greening the Conurbation – a Shared Vision for the Clyde Valley*, SRC and SNH, undated.

Van Blerck, H. (ed), *Inside Randstad Holland: Designing the Inner Fringes of Green Heart Metropolis*, Jury Report of the International Open Competition, Eo Wijers Stichting, Den Haag, 1995

Van Blerck, H. (ed), *Region of Streams: Giving Shape to the Ecoregion of Breda*, Jury Report of the Open Competition, Eo Wijers Stichting, Den Haag, 1992

Van der Hoeven, E., *J.J.P Oud en Bruno Tait*, NAI Publishers, Rotterdam, 1994

Van Rossem, V., *Randstad Holland: Variaties op het thema stad*, NAI publishers, Rotterdam, 1995

Van der Valk, A., 'Randstad – Green Heart Metropolis: Invention, Reception and Impact of a National Principle of Spatial Organisation', *Built Environment*, Vol 17, No 1, 1991, pp 23–33

Walker, F. A., 'Grasping the Thistle', *Building Design*, No. 1215, 16 June 1995, pp. 12–13

Yarwood, D., *The Architecture of Europe: the 19th and 20th Centuries*, B. T. Batsford Ltd, London, 1991

de Wit, (ed), *The Amsterdam School: Dutch Expression in Architecture, 1915 – 1930*, MIT Press, Cambridge, Massachusetts, 1983

Figure 9 Kattenbroek garden suburb, Amersfoord, by Kuiper Compagnons, 1990-94.

33

THE HISTORIC BUILDINGS OF ASIA
Issues in Heritage Management

Christopher Andrew

Following studies undertaken for Historic Scotland and Scottish Enterprise, the Masonry Conservation Research Group at the Robert Gordon University, has established itself at the forefront of research into the conservation and preservation of historic buildings and monuments. The work has focused on stone conservation methods, but has also extended to the broader issues of aesthetic and perceptual aspects of built heritage management and presentation. The Group has contributed significantly to the academic and scientific understanding of masonry conservation techniques, and have provided advice for practitioners and policy makers who have direct responsibility for the management of Britain's built heritage. To this end, the Group recently published a stone cleaning guide for practitioners, as well as a series of technical advice notes for those actively involved in masonry conservation.

The knowledge base, experience and lessons learnt from many of the mistakes made with our own built heritage have application and are potentially a very useful source of information on which policy and practice beyond the shores of Britain could be based. It was for this reason that a Churchill Fellowship enabled me to travel through parts of Asia to observe at first hand the conservation and management of some of the built heritage of that region, focusing particularly on the buildings constructed during the period of direct British influence. Although I studied only a small fraction of the enormous architectural legacy of the region, it became clear that a partnership between practitioners there and those with skills and experience of heritage management in Great Britain could potentially be fruitful to both sides.

Heritage conservation is firmly established as an integral part of Western civilisation and culture. Its importance is reflected by legislation and the systems of protection, grant support and management which have been established over a number of decades to conserve and protect our cultural past. The skills, training and research base required for the conservation and restoration of our cultural heritage, ranging from small objects to urban conservation areas, are largely in place. Increasingly, attention can be turned to the broader issues of heritage management, such as reviewing the ways in which heritage is interpreted and presented.

This pool of knowledge and experience should be made available to support colleagues elsewhere who are often seriously under resourced in their work. For example, the India National Trust for Art and Cultural Heritage (INTACH), a non-governmental body promoting heritage conservation and campaigning to raise awareness and pride in India's cultural heritage, often finds itself with the fundamental task of trying to provide physical protection of cultural sites. At its most basic this can consists of attempting to prevent the fabric of historic buildings from being removed and used as construction material, almost reminiscent of what once happened in Britain where material from ancient ruins was recycled for use in new buildings.

While some of the major heritage sites in South East Asia are protected, many sites considered of lesser importance, either through lack of recognition of their cultural value, lack of financial resources or because they are regarded as having no tourism potential, are left to deteriorate. These neglected buildings range right across the historic spectrum from ancient sites to buildings constructed during the period prior to independence. In some cases the rate of deterioration of these cultural assets is quite alarming.

All too often the decay result from a lack of basic, and frequently inexpensive preventative measures. With so many other acute problem facing countries in this region of the world, its built heritage is not unsurprisingly often seen as of lesser importance that more pressing human needs. It is unfortunate that the importance of much of the built heritage of the region is often underestimated, both in terms of its intrinsic value and its potential for cultural tourism. It is not only in the area of technical conservation where the contribution and experience of the west in partnership with South East Asian countries could be made, but also in skills relating to the adaptation and presentation of cultural and historic sites.

THE BRITISH INFLUENCE IN PAKISTAN

Pakistan or 'Land of the Pure' was created when India was partitioned in 1947, to create a homeland for Indian Muslims. British involvement in the area dates much further back to 1600 and the British East India Company which started trading in the sub-continent during the rein of the Moghuls. Trade grew for the next 100 years, and with its growth came British administration and an increased military presence. By the time the Moghuls were eventually defeated, the British influence in the region was well established. During the Raj period the British set about creating an infrastructure and bureaucratic system which is still very much in evidence. When India eventually became independent, political and religious tensions within India led the British to the reluctant conclusion that the only way to try and solve the difficulties within the region was to partition the sub-continent and give the Muslims there own territory. However, political tension within the country, particularly around Karachi still remain high. In such a situation, the task of preserving the cultural heritage of the region is more difficult.

The British presence lasted nearly a century from 1849–1947. Most of the colonial buildings still remaining in Lahore are situated in or around The

Figure 1 Gradual decline of a building dating from British times in Bangalore.

Figure 2 Inappropriate porch, advertising hoardings and permanent scaffolding have left this fine Bombay facade badly damaged.

Mall (renamed Shahrah-E-Quaid-E-Azam), which runs between the old city and more recently built parts of the city. The Mall still retains its original character and atmosphere. At the western end of the road is the huge Zamzanu cannon or 'Kim's Gun', made famous by Rudyard Kipling's book *Kim*. Close inspection of the gun requires a life risking dash to the centre of the road where the gun stands on a small platform. Situated near Kim's gun at this end of The Mall is Lahore Museum. The Museum was founded in 1894 in commemoration of Queen Victoria's Golden Jubilee. The building itself is in good order, its marble frontage adding to its grandeur. The Museum is said to be the biggest and best in Pakistan, housing a large collection of artefacts from the stone age to the 20th century. Kipling's father was the first curator and today the collection housed is quite well displayed.

Near the Museum are a number of other Raj buildings, including the old campus of Punjab University, the General Post Office and the law courts. Built of brick these buildings are at present quite sound. The main concern with brick buildings of this age is rising moisture from the soil which causes physical and chemical changes to the brickwork.

Further east along the Mall are the Jinn Gardens and Zoo, laid out in 1851. Nearby is also Lawrence Gardens, site of another fine British building, the Lawrence Montgomery Hall, which now houses Lahore's Quaid-i-Azam Library. The building has recently been restored, the interior is still quite original. Within the grounds of the Library is a cricket ground with an attractive pavilion.

Other outstanding British buildings include the Cathedral built in 1927, the Town Hall and Free Masonic Lodge and Lahore's main railway station. While these public and very prominent buildings have survived relatively well, Lahore has a huge number of other interesting buildings dating from the same period which through lack of resources seems destined to slide further into decline.

Lahore also provides examples of British disregard for earlier historic monuments. Particularly during the early part of their governance, they were not always sensitive to the historic artefacts in their care. For example, during the construction of the railway line between Lahore and Multan, the British allowed the use of 4,500 year-old burnt bricks of Harappa, an ancient city of the Punjab and an important centre of the Indus Valley civilisation which prospered from 2500 to 1700 BC, as track ballast. Other ancient sites in the path of the railway were levelled to make way for its construction. One of the cities most prominent landmarks, the nine metre high city wall was dismantled and the moat filled in. Similarly, many Moghul mosques and mausoleum were either destroyed completely or indiscriminately altered.

The royal apartments at the Moghul Fort were destroyed to make way for barracks, and many other important structures were adapted for British use without thought. Even when buildings were restored they were often intensively altered. For example, when the British restored the Badshahi Mosque (after a period when it seemed they had been intent on damaging the structure) the original 80 study cells which had surrounded the great court were demolished to make way for the arcades which are now there.

However, on a more positive note, at the turn of the century Lord Curzon started a process which continued while the British remained in Pakistan, of reversing some of the destruction which had occurred during the first half of the British period. Restoration of the Fort and Shalimar Gardens was started, as was work at Jahangir's Mausoleum. A law was passed governing the preservation of old monuments, and a government department set up to oversee their welfare.

The work and efforts started by the British are still very much in evidence in conservation work presently being undertaken in Pakistan, although inevitably the resources available do not match the scale of the task. An evaluation of the impact which the British had would not be complete without some mention of the architectural style and legacy which has been left. The British architects were clearly fascinated by the Moghul architecture they found in the sub-continent and incorporated many of its features into their own architecture to create a unique style found throughout the region and probably best described as Moghul-Victorian. These buildings, where they have survived add an elegant dimension to the range and diversity of architecture found in Pakistan. The British then, like the numerous rulers before them both destroyed and added to the cultural legacy which remains in Pakistan today.

THE MOGHUL LEGACY

Pakistan has a rich legacy of built heritage from prehistoric to more recent periods in its history. One of the consequences of partition was to divide what was previously a coherent regional cultural legacy between India and Pakistan. This is particularly evident in the case of the spectacular Moghul architecture of the region. In Pakistan, Lahore is the centre of these remains. Particularly important are the Fort, the old city, Badshahi and other mosques within the city, tombs of important Moghul rulers and the gardens so beloved by the emperors. Unfortunately, the Grand Trunk road built by the Moghuls to link these sites with later Moghul buildings in India (particular of course the Taj Mahal) passes through the disputed boundary between the two countries.

From the point of view of heritage interpretation, it is unfortunate that the enormous legacy left by the Moghuls is now fragmented, with no overall management policy. Although the division between India and Pakistan does give the opportunity to observe the differing approaches of the two countries to conservation of often similar buildings, the real challenge lies in promoting cross-border collaboration in terms of both management policy and promoting cultural tourism.

As the guest of the Department of Archaeology of the Punjab, I had the opportunity to visit the Fort and other sites in Lahore to observe at first hand the conservation work taking place. Given the many problems facing the country and the limited resources available for conservation, the work is being conducted in a very commendable fashion. Restoration work is underway to replace sections of decayed sandstone pillars and screens. Care is being taken to cut the new stone to match, as near as possible, the existing stonework. Similar care had been taken with the matching and restoration of the marble floor in the Shish Mahal or 'Hall of Mirrors' some years earlier. The historic painted freezes within the Hall of Mirrors retain the evidence of their chequered history, and fortunately no attempt had been made to alter in any way their appearance.

Outside, in Shah Jahan's Royal Courtyard, the fountain has also undergone restoration. One of the most spectacular features of Moghul architecture was their use of water, both as decoration and as a means of cooling their buildings. Unfortunately, as with so many other Mogul remains, there was no water present in the fountain or any of the other numerous water channels, detracting somewhat from the visitor experience and the overall impressiveness of the architectural remains.

Another important legacy of the Moghul era were the numerous gardens created by the great rulers. Unfortunately, the only remaining one in Lahore is the Shalimar Gardens situated on the Grand Trunk Road. As with other important heritage sites in Lahore, the gardens are well preserved and maintained, although little remains of the original marble and decorative features of the buildings. As with much of the heritage of this part of the world, the subtler points of interpretation are often overlooked. The gardens and associated water channels were constructed as a series of three terraces, the original Moghul intention being to walk through the gardens from the lower to the upper terrace, the grandeur increasing with each level. Regrettably, entry to the gardens is now achieved through a door leading to the upper terrace and visitors progress through the garden in the direction opposite to that originally intended.

ISSUES FACING PAKISTAN

As elsewhere, attempts are made to alter and adorn historic artefacts with inappropriate modern additions which are misguidedly thought to appeal to visitors. Fortunately, due to the small number of tourists and the direction of the Head of Archaeology for Punjab, Dr Saifur Rahman Dar, this has not been allowed to happen in the Punjab region of Pakistan. From their cramped offices in Lahore, he and his team continue to promote the profile of the regions built heritage, as well as working on conservation and restoration measures.

The high professional standard of their work is a good example of how important it is to avoid political appointments and promote to positions of authority those with a sound knowledge and understanding of the issues involved in heritage management. If sound management can be combined with international partnerships formed for the sharing of information and experience, then both sides can learn and benefit from the exchanges. On my extensive travels in the region, examples abounded of the damage done by inappropriate and unsympathetic conservation and heritage measures. In many cases it would have been less damaging to have avoided intervention altogether. However, Pakistan has been largely spared of this type of damage.

Pakistan is in the early stages of developing a cultural tourist industry. The vast majority of the visitors to its architectural treasures are indigenous and entry tariffs are fixed to reflect local levels of income. For the western visitor, therefore, the price of entry to these buildings and monuments is a small fraction of what they might expect to pay to visit the equivalent in the West. Accordingly, revenue from visitors provides only a limited financial contribution towards the cost of management and maintenance. Site interpretation material is often non-existent or at best very limited, since available resources have clearly been focused on restoration and conservation.

Perhaps one of the greatest threats to the built heritage of Pakistan come from a lack of recognition of the immense architectural wealth which still survives today. There is some awareness of the importance of the major historic buildings and monuments and, to varying degrees, measures are in hand to protect these, but many other buildings of heritage value are simply left to decay. Although those involved in the day-to-day management are aware of the importance of the nation's built legacy and continue to campaign for its well being, the government often has more pressing concerns. It is only with an increased awareness of the nation's cultural assets that the political will for measures to protect this legacy will can be strengthened.

Some of the problems which conservationists in Pakistan face are universal. A case in point is the damage caused by air pollution. The haze from inefficient internal combustion engines in Lahore is easily visible in parts of the city. As in the rest of the world, the damage this inflicts on Pakistan's built heritage is enormous, and is probably the most pressing concern of those with the interests of its built heritage at heart. The conservation issues facing the country are the same in principle as those in Britain, although the problems are of a different degree, providing even more justification for a partnership of minds.

THE CULTURAL RICHES OF INDIA

As in Pakistan, the British have had a profound influence on the development of India since they first established a trading post at Surat in 1612. Involvement was initially restricted to the trading interests of the East India Company which had sole trading rights. From their small beginning in Surat, trading stations were established further down the west coast at Bombay, as well as in the east at Calcutta and Madras. The British were by no means the only European country with interests in India at the time. The Portuguese and French were also prolific traders, and indeed rivals for the British during this early period.

The history of India appears to the outsider as a series of conquests by consecutive invading powers, each partly destroying what previous rulers had left. As in Pakistan, the British continued the tradition of both destroying and adding to the built cultural legacy that remains today. One only has to visit the capital city to appreciate both the range and diversity of the built legacy left by at least eight towns which once stood around modern Delhi. The number of historic buildings, monuments and sites worthy of protection in Delhi alone is enormous, and these represent only a small fraction of the thousands of others throughout the rest of the country.

The scale of the task of conserving and managing this legacy is daunting, particularly in the face of so many other pressing human problems. The frequency with which one comes across the decay and destruction is therefore not surprising. Sometimes, as in the case of the once great pink city of Jaipur, it seems as if whole cities have simply been abandoned and left to decay. On other occasions, the visitor is at least heartened by the quality and state of preservation of some of the buildings of its more recent past, although even with these the visitor is left to wonder for how much longer they will remain in their present condition.

A small example of the gradual decline of part of New Delhi's more recent cultural heritage can be seen in Connaught Place, a series of concentric blocks radiating from a grand central circle. As with so much architecture in India, the buildings are covered with advertising hoardings. The fabric of the buildings themselves are altered and parts destroyed at the whim of the owners. Removing parts of the building to house large air conditioning units being a particularly common cause of damage. When parts of Connaught Place fall into disrepair, they are simply left, maintenance seemingly an expensive luxury. Some of the drains must have been broken for a least a decade. There is now a growing body of research and experience in industrialised countries on adapting and altering historic buildings for modern day use. A closer partnership between India and those in Britain who have researched and learnt from mistakes made at our own hand in this field would clearly be mutually beneficial.

A trip to the magnificent Moghul Fort in the old city raises more questions. While parts of the marble structure of the Fort are in decline, a considerable amount of money has recently been spent creating a particularly poor reconstruction of a central fountain and water enclosure. Even the floodlighting equipment for the undignified light and sound show have caused damage by its positioning.

Destruction of the Fort goes back many years, the unsightly barracks built by the British within the Fort precinct could only be constructed following demolition of original Moghul buildings. Interestingly, given the length of time these barracks have stood, there is some debate as to whether or not they are now an integral part of the history of the Fort and therefore should remain. This raises interesting philosophical questions about what to conserve.

Where attempts at conservation have been made, they have often been carried out in the absence of specialist advice. Such advice is sometimes available in India itself and, if not, usually can be sought elsewhere. Those making decisions on intervention work not only frequently lack the specialist knowledge required for informed decision making, but are simply unaware of the damage caused by their actions. What makes matters much worse is the seeming inability often to ask for the sound advice needed.

In Bombay, a particularly common form of unwelcome intervention is the practice of painting fine stonework, a recent example being the painting of Flora Fountain in the city centre. To the untrained eye, the fountain may look 'brighter'. To conservationists in the city, it is almost akin to English Heritage painting Stonehenge. In one of the city's finest hotels, the magnificent sandstone and wood central staircase has recently been 'refurbished'. When the building was constructed great care was taken to select and use fine quality matching stone. The excellent stonework has now been painted pink. The damage caused by unthinking intervention measures is often permanent. In any event, where it may be possible to reverse the measures, the costs involved will many times the original measures.

Damage not only occurs on a grand scale, there are numerous examples of small pieces of India's heritage gradually disappearing, such as the Victorian wrought iron railings beside Bombay railway station, which are gradually being removed for scrap value by some of the desperately poor people of the city. Active collaboration, particularly between the decision makers and conservationists in the east and west, could help prevent unnecessary damage. The best examples of good conservation work in India occur when there is a close link between the two groups, as in the case of those working at the Bombay Municipal Corporation building.

Conservationists in Bombay have been successful in legal moves to stop some developments which clearly threaten the cultural heritage of the city. Unfortunately, some damage is often done before the development work can be stopped. However, the Maharashtra Government has recently passed new building regulations which give official status to conservation controls and listing of important historic buildings and precincts, especially in Bombay's Fort area. This represents a first in the sub-continent, and is clearly a most welcome step.

However, decay and destruction are too common sights, particularly in the case of buildings which are privately owned and perhaps considered of lesser cultural value than the great buildings of the country. The work of INTACH in countering this remorseless decline is one of India's unsung success stories. Although inadequately resourced for the task it faces, it is welcoming to see the dedication and work of this organisation in its effort to protect the country's cultural past. A recent success has been its campaign to save the University Senate building in Madras. It seems remarkable to any visitor that the authorities could even contemplate the destruction of such a fine building. Meanwhile the Madras Ice House, another interesting building from the British period some half mile from the Senate building, is left to decline, its fate uncertain.

Almost as depressing as the buildings which are being lost, are the those by which they are being replaced, in most cases of almost no cultural merit. The unrealised potential for cultural tourism in India, particularly in areas with which it is not normally associated, is enormous and yet the very material needed for its development is being lost at an alarming rate. Even when important cultural artefacts are enclosed in museums, they are not necessarily safe from further decline. The Madras Museum contains a large number of ancient stone relics which, when under British control, were misguidedly cemented onto masonry plinths. To compound this error, the plinths were recently painted, and the overzealous decorators painted, not only the plinths, but the bases of the actual stone artefacts. Another part of the Museum contains a fine collection of bronze figures which are housed in glass display cases of an inappropriate design. Large gaps between the glass panes allow dust debris to collect on the display items inside.

Perhaps the fate of India's cultural heritage is best summed up by the current debate over the future of the Taj Mahal, one of the worlds' greatest surviving monuments. Every visitor has a high expectation of this building, and the first sight one has of it is truly one of life's greatest cultural experiences. Sadly, that first sight is through a side door and not the grand entrance which was originally intended, visitors exit through the original entrance.

Like so many other cultural sites in India, those with control over them could learn from customer care practices in countries which have had longer experience in this field. Furthermore, it has now been established that the brilliant white marble used for the Taj Mahal's construction is now being destroyed by the air pollution in Agra. The fact that this situation is allowed to continue raises questions about the value which parts of India's bureaucracy place on the protection of its cultural heritage. Whatever may be the injustices caused in India during its history, those who came to this country have left a wealth of cultural remains. The key issue is what can be done to help avoid the destruction of that heritage through negligence and lack of resources.

LESSONS FROM SRI LANKA

Sri Lanka provides an interesting contrast to India in terms of the way it has managed, and continues to manage its built cultural heritage. At one level the task facing those charged with this responsibility are at a distinct advantage. Sri Lanka's size and the smaller number of cultural sites are altogether on a much more manageable level. Not withstanding the problem with the Tamil separatists, Sri Lanka also has less pressing social problems that those apparent in India. However, an increasing pressure for development has not been without cost in terms of the preservation of its more recent cultural past. For example, the battle to save many of the buildings constructed during the British period of influence has, in some parts of the country at least, been largely lost.

Where Sri Lanka is concentrating its efforts in terms of preservation of its built cultural heritage, is in the work of its Central Cultural Fund at six world heritage sites. These are at Anuradhapura, Polonnarurwa, Sigriya, Dambulla, Nalanda and Kandy. The exemplary work carried out by the Central Cultural Fund is managed by the Director General, Dr Roland Silva. This work includes excavation, conservation and the layout of sites for both pilgrim and visitor interest. Travelling around these sites, one is struck by the care and professionalism with which these tasks are being accomplished.

Following vandalism to the site at Sigriya a number of years ago, the sites are now well protected where possible. Given the tight financial limits within which the project operates, the progress and quality of its scholarly work is an example of what can be achieved in the region. Visitors are charged realistic entry fees for access to the sites, although they sometimes lack appropriate interpretation material.

While conservationists in Sri Lanka have actively sought to benefit from knowledge and skills available in more industrialised countries, there is a strong case for continued collaboration. Indeed, through the work of its Central Cultural Fund, Sri Lanka has developed skills which could usefully benefit others working in the region.

CONCLUSIONS

Scholars and heritage practitioners interested in this part of the world cannot help but be struck by the quantity and diversity of the legacy which remains. Unlike in the West, because countries in the region have been subject to less modern economic development, much of its architectural past has not yet been irretrievably degraded and lost. A lot still remains, even if this is sometimes abused and in a poor state of preservation.

The destiny of much of this rich heritage remains in the balance, its fate seemingly resting on a number of crucial decisions. Action must be taken to campaign for a greater realisation of the immense intrinsic and economic value of this heritage. Attention should be given to the value, not only of the great buildings of the sub-continent, but also of the rich wealth of less prestigious buildings in both towns and countryside.

Legislation and policies need to be introduced which places statutory controls over buildings and monuments. Systems need to be developed and implemented, which will not only protect and conserve this legacy, but which will also put in place mechanisms to develop the wealth creating potential through cultural tourism. The best ways of ensuring the survival of these heritage assets in countries where there are so many other pressing human problems, is to demonstrate that it is in the best interests of the indigenous population that they survive intact.

Heritage management needs to be conducted within a framework of best professional practice. Where intervention takes place, it needs to be done only after sound advice and consideration. Much of this could be achieved with the collaboration and assistance of other countries who have faced similar problems and made mistakes which need not be repeated.

Cross-cultural influences have always existed between Europe and Asia, and the history of the two continents are inextricably linked. The enormous influence European countries have had an on the modern development of the Indian sub-continent have sometimes overshadowed the important influence which the east had on western cultural development in earlier times. This historic bond between the two makes the cultural assets which remain part of our shared global heritage.

It is not only incumbent on those in the Indian sub-continent to cherish that heritage, but also upon the West to take a greater interest in the issues and problems facing them, and to ask how we can help. Indeed, at times also to find out how we can learn from their experience. Such international exchange needs to be encouraged, and individuals and international agencies alike have a role to play in this process.

The role of universities is vital and, supported by national and international agencies, they could be of great help in promoting cultural developments and fostering links between the two sides. An example of this is The British Council who have been particularly successful in promoting these links. The built treasures of the Indian sub-continent are of immense importance, their loss would not only result in a diminution of local identity but of many important global assets.

Figure 3 The gradual decline of Connaught Place in Delhi.

Figure 4 Marble disfigured by poor quality repairs at Agra Fort.